THE SYSTEM

*Soviet Periodization Adapted
for the American Strength Coach*

JOHNNY PARKER
AL MILLER
ROB PANARIELLO
with Jeremy Hall

FOREWORD
DAN REEVES

ON TARGET PUBLICATIONS
APTOS, CALIFORNIA

The System—Soviet-Style Program Design

Johnny Parker, Al Miller, Rob Panariello
with Jeremy Hall

Copyright © 2018 Johnny Parker, Al Miller, Rob Panariello, Jeremy Hall

Foreword © 2018 Dan Reeves

Graphics © 2018 Jeremy Hall

Photography credits:
© 2018 Professional Physical Therapy, pages 63–65, 102–109, 112–123
© 2018 Randy E. Burke, RB Sports, pages 73–84, 211–213
© 2018 Jeremy Hall, pages 207, 341

Athlete Models: Robert Garrick, Eric Herndon, Lakamion Franklin, Ethan-Ira Mamuric

All rights reserved. Printed in the United States of America using recycled paper. No part of this book may be reproduced or transmitted in any form whatsoever without written permission from the author or publisher, with the exception of the inclusions of brief quotations in articles or reviews.

ISBN-13: 978-1-931046-44-2

On Target Publications
P O Box 1335
Aptos, California 95001 USA
otpbooks.com

Library of Congress Cataloging-in-Publication Data
Names: Parker, Johnny, 1947- author. | Miller, Al, 1947- author. | Panariello, Rob, author. | Hall, Jeremy, 1982- author.
Title: The system : Soviet-style program design / Johnny Parker, Al Miller, Rob Panariello ; with Jeremy Hall.
Description: Aptos, California : On Target Publications, [2018] | Includes index.
Identifiers: LCCN 2018008021| ISBN 9781931046442 (pbk.) | ISBN 9781931046602 (epub)
Subjects: LCSH: Physical education and training. | Muscle strength. | Physical fitness. | Exercise. | Physical education and training--Russia (Federation) | Weight lifting--Russia (Federation)
Classification: LCC GV711.5 .P37 2018 | DDC 613.7--dc23
LC record available at https://lccn.loc.gov/2018008021

CONTENTS

Dedication
Foreword
Introduction

Section One—The Foundation

Chapter One—Fundamentals of the System

The Origin of the System
Fundamentals
Hierarchy of Athletic Development
Work Capacity
Strength, Power, and Speed
The Eye of the Coach

Chapter Two—Planning Workout Programming

Exercise Selection
Fundamental Lifts
Volume
Intensity
Prilepin's Chart
Tempo Training Methods
Frequency of Training
Types of Periodization

Section Two—The System

Chapter Three—The System

Core Principles
Preparation
Fundamental Screens
The Javorek Complex
Determining Load and Volume
Running
Mach Running Drills
Jump Training Drills
Sprint Drills
Sample Four-Week Prep Phase

Chapter Four—Systematic Program Design

Training Cycle Principles
Exercise Selection
Novice Level

Chapter Four—Systematic Program Design, Continued
- Exercise Selection Principles
- Exercise Variation
- Accessory Work
- Volume
- The Break-In Cycle
- Progressing into the System
- Exercise Volume Principles
- Weekly Volume
- Sample Training Cycles
- Workout Classifications
- Training Session Volume Principles
- Intensity
- Determining Percentages
- Intensity and Volume
- Exercise Intensity Principles
- Zones of Intensity
- Selecting Training Loads
- Counting Reps
- Squat Programming
- Program Design Principles
- The Unload
- Progression
- Designing the Training Session

Chapter Five—Sprinting and Jumping
- Sprinting and Jumping Principles
- Work Capacity in Speed Training
- Strength and Speed-strength—Acceleration
- Speed
- Jumping
- Agility
- Programming Integration
- Monthly Volume
- Weekly Volume
- Sprinting and Jumping Session Design

Chapter Six—Seasonal Program Design
- Periodization
- Goals of Training
- Off-Season
  - *Goals*
  - *Volume*
  - *Progression*
  - *Running, Jumping, and Conditioning*

Chapter Six—Seasonal Program Design, Continued

    Pre-Season
        Goals
        Volume
        Progression
        Running, Jumping, and Conditioning
    In-Season
        Goals
        Volume
        Progression
        Work Performance Math
        In-Season Conditioning

Section Three—Implementing the System

Chapter Seven—Putting It All Together

    Planning Your Programs
    Designing a Program Novice Athlete Sample Four-Week Training Cycle
    Advanced Athlete Sample Four-Week Training Cycle

Chapter Eight—Football Programming

    Off-Season Eight-Week Novice Training Plan for Football
        Cycle One
        Cycle Two, Power
    Off-Season Sample Advanced Program
        Cycle One
        Cycle Two
    Preseason Sample Advanced Program
    In-Season Sample Training Program

Chapter Nine—Integrating Sprinting and Jumping

    Sprint and Jump Training Sample Program

Chapter Ten—Final Thoughts

Appendices

    Appendix A—Athlete Profiles
    Appendix B—Programming Principles
    Appendix C—Lists of Graphs, Tables, and Images
    References
    Index
    Author Biographies

DEDICATION

To Al Miller and Rob Panariello, two princes for including this pauper in our field in this project. Al and Rob have been friends—I mean true friends—for over 30 years. They, unlike acquaintances, shone the brightest when the clouds in my life were the darkest.

Speaking of friends, I have been blessed by having Ralph and Debbie Malatesta as the best friends anybody ever had. My love and deepest appreciation to Coach Bill Maloney and his wife Lisa Maloney, the most stubborn, unreasonable, bossy, caring, loving, giving, kindest folks on this planet. What makes them happy is giving to others. On the few occasions I've done something for them, I've learned to run for cover.

To Coach Bill McGuire, Coach Bill Parcells, Coach Bob Knight, and Coach Mike Nolan for teaching me how to coach. When I think of my core beliefs about coaching, I don't know from which of these great coaches I learned each of my principles. To say the least, the impact of these men on my career has been colossal.

To Mr. Jimmy Lear and Mr. Peter Jernberg, who stuck by me when there was no evidence I would ever be a good teacher or coach. They were undoubtedly the only two on earth who thought I was worth keeping around. Maybe they were impressed by my one accomplishment in my first year...I was a pretty good finish line for sprints.

I have unintentionally never given Lebaron Caruthers proper credit for all he taught me and for so freely sharing his vast knowledge with me.

To Alvin Roy, Louis Riecke, and Clyde Emrich, who were my first teachers. Their willingness to help me was never affected by their team's record. They were the same gentlemen through hundreds of annoying phone calls and a bunch of visits where I was probably in the way.

My greatest debt is to my players. For over 40 years, they made me look better than I was. My most enduring debt is to my players at Indianola Academy. In the summer, they worked on the farm from first light until dark. After those 15-hour workdays, they came to the school to lift weights and run. They will always be my heroes.

Jeremy Hall did the heavy lifting on this book. We owe him a special thank you.

Coach Johnny Parker
Former NFL Head Strength Coach
New York Giants, New England Patriots, Tampa Bay Buccaneers, San Francisco 49ers

DEDICATION

To Mom, who tried as hard as she could to help me

To my sister Rachel Newman, who was always there for me, and never turned away

To Ralph Miller, who started me lifting in the eighth grade and opened a whole new world to me

To Coach Dwight Adams, who taught me how to pay the price in athletics and to grow up

To Coach Garland Gregory, who helped give me the opportunity to play college football

To Coach Van Leigh, who was my first boss in coaching and taught me how to do it correctly and not cut corners

To Coach Paul Bear Bryant for teaching me so many details of coaching and life in general

To Coach Dan Reeves for giving me an opportunity in the NFL and making the 19 years I worked for him some of the very best years of my life—he believed in what I did

To Johnny Parker, Al Vermeil, Rob Panariello, and Don Chu for answering a million questions, and just as important, for being my friends

To my assistant coaches, who were, quite simply, the very best— thanking you seems inadequate

To the men I learned from—Alvin Roy, Mike Stone, Bob Ward, Gregori Goldstein, Charlie Francis, Ben Tabachnik, Dragomir Cioroslan, and Lorene Seagrave

A big thank you to my present wife, Fran, for making life fun again and for being my good friend.

Last, however certainly not the least, to my late wife, Janis, who for 43 years gave me all of the love and support I could ask for, plus she gave me my two best accomplishments—my son Carey Brian Miller and daughter Lisa Marie Miller Clarke. It has been a wonderful journey.

Coach Al Miller
Former NFL Head Strength Coach
Denver Broncos, Atlanta Falcons, Oakland Raiders, New York Giants

DEDICATION

To my mother Marie and father Mario who loved me and prepared me for the life ahead, I love and thank you.

To my sister Carol, I love and miss you.

To my wife Dora and my daughters, Lauren and Sara: Thank you for all of your love, support, and patience. You are the roses in my life's garden.

To the Head Coaches with whom I've been associated, Lou Carneseca, Bill Parcells, and Dick Vermeil: thank you for your leadership, wisdom, and guidance.

To Coaches Johnny Parker, Al Miller, Al Vermeil, Don Chu, Charlie Francis, and Derek Hansen: Thank you for teaching me, mentoring me, and most of all for your friendship. You have all made me a better coach and professional.

To Gregori Goldstein, thank you for teaching me this periodization system as well as for all of your advice and weightlifting instruction to enhance my abilities as a coach.

To all of the physicians, surgeons, physical therapists, athletic trainers, and strength and conditioning coaches—too many to name—who were kind enough to spend the time to teach and guide me: I thank you for all of your efforts, acceptance of me, and friendship.

To my business partners who have worked effortlessly side by side with me to build our company, Professional Physical Therapy and the Professional Athletic Performance Center: I thank you.

To all of the athletes who awoke in the early morning darkness, who worked with me well into the night regardless of their work day, personal environment, or weather conditions, and always provided me with their best efforts: You will always be my heroes.

Rob Panariello
Founding Partner, Co-Chief Executive Officer
Professional Physical Therapy
Professional Athletic Performance Center

FOREWORD

It is hard to believe, but I have been around long enough to remember the days before "strength and conditioning."

When I began my professional football career with the Dallas Cowboys in 1965, there was no single person in charge of lifting weights or running on Coach Tom Landry's staff. At the time, there were few dedicated strength coaches working in professional football, and the fears of players getting muscle-bound and slow from weight training resulted in most teams shying away from any work with weights. Each player was on his own in maintaining his fitness during the off-season, with the added challenge that most players had to work full-time jobs between seasons to support their families. Other than running drills and general conditioning during practice, there was no formal strength program to follow.

At that time, the Cowboys had not achieved the degree of success and fame now chronicled on NFL Films. Despite the guidance of Coach Landry and an immensely talented roster, we were unfortunately known as "Next Year's Champions." Our success only extended so far as the playoffs, where we would ultimately fail to achieve our championship goals.

In 1970, I became a player-coach and technically became the franchise's first unofficial strength and conditioning coach. On the recommendation of Coach Landry, I travelled to speak with Alvin Roy, who in 1963 had become the first NFL strength and conditioning coach with the San Diego Chargers. He graciously educated me on his methods of training for football, including lifting weights and running, which I took back to Dallas.

Coach Landry believed so strongly in the importance of the program I designed that we became one of the first teams to pay players to entice them to train together in Dallas during the off-season. That change not only dramatically improved the overall strength and resilience of the players, but it also created an environment of healthy competition within the team. Seeing someone else fighting and not missing a workout sent the message that if you were ever going to overcome and become a starter, you were going to have to put in the same level of work.

By the end of that first summer of training, the improved physical performance and cohesion of the team propelled us to the franchise's first Super Bowl, which we lost on a last-second field goal. Despite another missed opportunity, the confidence we gained from that first year of the program, combined with fewer injuries and buy-in from coaches and players, was no doubt a huge contributor to the change in the franchise's fortunes as well as the careers of many of our players over the next decade.

When I later became head coach of the Denver Broncos, I knew my success as a coach would be tied to maximizing the physical abilities of our athletes, and that began with instituting a comprehensive strength and conditioning program. On the recommendation of Alvin Roy, I hired Bear Bryant's strength coach at the University of Alabama, Al Miller. Not only was Al well-regarded in the field, he was a true student of the science of training for performance enhancement. He was always innovative in his approach to training and would actively seek out other successful coaches to learn and adapt his methods. He literally travelled the world to study from the best, whether they were coaching in Russian or at the Olympic training center or even within the NFL—particularly his collaboration and friendship with fellow strength coach Johnny Parker. There's no question that my success and that of my teams were directly tied to the impact of Al's constant search for the best tools and methods of performance training.

Today you will not find a single NFL team that does not employ an entire *team* of strength and conditioning professionals. You would be hard pressed to find any sports team at the professional, college, or high school level that doesn't have at least one strength coach.

This book contains the distilled knowledge and wisdom of Al Miller and Johnny Parker, who are possibly two of the most successful strength coaches in NFL history. You would need to combine the careers of about 10 people to achieve the same level of success and impact on the field and the profession as Al and Johnny.

Over more than 40 years, Al and Johnny created a system from the best training methods and strategies that consistently produced multiple championship teams. I have no doubt that in this book, you will find invaluable information to elevate the performance of your athletes. But, if there is one thing I hope you can take away, it is in recognizing there are different ways to accomplish the same goals. Principles will always remain the same, but adapting your approach to the athletes and using what the authors call the "eye of the coach" is what will have the biggest impact on your athletes' performance.

Other than getting great players, success is ultimately about making those players better. I believe that placing the athlete first and adopting an open and flexible approach to coaching are the greatest strengths of these coaches and is the true secret to their success. I can attest to the positive impact their system of training and their shared passion had on my coaching career, and I hope that you will learn and benefit from their knowledge as much as I did.

Enjoy,

Dan Reeves
NFL Head Coach
Denver Broncos, New York Giants, Atlanta Falcons

INTRODUCTION

As more coaches enter the world of strength and conditioning and face the task of developing programs for young athletes, there is no shortage of training programs to follow. The internet provides about as many exotic exercises and programs as there are gurus and coaches. Each is selling systems or methods to achieve gains in size, strength, power, or speed. It is challenging to determine which will be the best system when there is such a tremendous volume of information.

Many entering the field of strength and conditioning will choose a program they find online or one provided by a coach they respect because they trust it will help their athletes and provide a base from which to evolve. In some cases, this will generate good results; however, in other cases, it will end up as time lost to ineffective training.

Unfortunately, what is generally lacking in most coaches' repertoires is an understanding of, along with an inability to implement, fundamental principles to build their own long-term, sustainable training programs. It can be a daunting task for the novice coach and just as much of a challenge for the seasoned coach to objectively evaluate the content and outcomes of their established methods of training. We have been there and had we not put our egos aside to critically evaluate our programming and outcomes, we would not have met with the successes we did.

In this book, we lay the foundation for a scientifically based, field-tested, and tremendously effective system of training. This is not a cookie-cutter program you can install without another thought; it is a system to reinforce the fundamentals and principles with which you can design and implement programming that will make your athletes stronger, faster, and more powerful over a sustained period.

We have collectively been utilizing and refining this system for 28 years—it has propelled countless athletes from high school to the professional level, to the Olympic Games and five NFL teams to a combined eight Super Bowls. It will require organization, some basic calculations, and a discerning "eye of the coach," and then it will provide results unlike any other method we have tried or evaluated.

Our driving goal has always been to constantly improve our athletes and ourselves. With our competitive days behind us, we now want to educate the strength and conditioning community, just as we were educated almost 30 years ago.

In this book, we introduce you to the programming we call "The System."

Of those who have learned and implemented The System, it is the rare few who go back to their former methods. To master it will take time and effort. It will take a drive for excellence with a hard analysis of your previous biases and deficits in constructing training programs.

And it will all be worth it.

We have already logged the hours, the miles, and the frustration to refine our combined 80-plus years of coaching and learning into this blueprint for success. Now that we are nearing the end of our careers and the threat of young upstart coaches taking our jobs is gone, we want to pass on the methods and plans that led to our successes. Although you might think that a training system that is 28 years old is already past its prime, we promise you that its time has really just arrived.

First, a disclaimer: This is not an exhaustive review and application of our programming system. To do justice to what we were taught and learned through the years would take more than a book to capture.

Our hope is that providing a foundation of the concepts and creating a few starting points will provide even the least-experienced strength coach an opportunity to implement a more effective and systematic approach of training for sports performance.

There are endless opportunities to manipulate the training variables within our framework to account for the challenges that will inevitably arise when training athletes. There is no such thing as a one-size-fits-all approach to programming, and even the three of us had difficulty agreeing on some of the specifics we present in the book.

As you gain years in the field, you will continue to learn, reflect, and grow. We hope this book will provide either a new perspective or an opportunity to adapt your current training so you can achieve even greater success.

Johnny Parker
Al Miller
Rob Panariello

SECTION ONE
THE FOUNDATION

CHAPTER ONE
THE FOUNDATION

The origin of our system of programming comes from the former Soviet Union's National Weightlifting Team by way of Staten Island, New York. Throughout our years working with high school, collegiate, and professional athletes, we spent many weeks chasing down any coach who would spend time with us, crisscrossing the country, and then overseas to expand our knowledge.

We have always believed that if there is an opportunity to learn something that will provide a competitive edge, it would be wrong not to pursue it. As we progressed through the ranks of the profession, it became even more important to seek new information, techniques, and methods. Reaching a peak does not mean learning becomes less important. If anything, the stakes become even higher.

Beginning in the early 1980s, we individually had the opportunity to visit various Soviet republics to learn from the national coaches and sports scientists behind the Iron Curtain who at the time were developing the best Olympic athletes in the world. Each of us hoped to learn the "recipe" for their successes, with the hope of recreating it with our athletes back home.

At the time, there were estimated to be 300,000 qualified Olympic weightlifters in the U.S.S.R., compared to about 3,000 in the United States. Soviet resources were devoted to space, defense, the arts, and sport. The stakes were high for athletic dominance because the demands for Olympic medals were not commercially driven but of national significance to display the success of the Communist nation.

For that reason, the Russian approach to training generated a living laboratory of strength and conditioning, where every variable was controlled, tracked, measured, evaluated, tested, and then re-evaluated to find the most effective methods. Their only goal was to produce the world's greatest athletes to show the superiority of the Soviet Union.

Despite the obvious specter of performance-enhancing drugs, 1,200 medalists over 18 Olympic Games—including 39 gold medalists in weightlifting—speak to the Soviet proficiency in developing athletes. Despite the U.S.S.R. competing in only 18 Olympic Games, those 39 Olympic gold medals in weightlifting still stand as the most for a nation, with China second with 34, and the United States a distant third with 16.

At the Soviet Central Institute of Physical Culture and Sport Scientific Research Laboratory, Professors Yuri Verkhoshansky and Leonid Matveyev[1] were developing plyometric training progressions for power development and refining their periodization methods to ensure their athletes' progress. On one of our trips, a coach told us that theory often determines practice; however, in their view, practice should determine theory. Rather than the Russian sports scientists dictating what the coaches should do, they looked for the processes producing results and then determined why they worked.

There was a strong bond in the Soviet Union between the coaching and science professionals; however, in the long run, it seemed that the "eye of the coach" and coaching experience determined more than the scientists when it came to what was to be done. Following that model certainly helped accelerate the Russian advances of training concepts well beyond the American methods.

Some of our earliest mentors were Alvin Roy and Clyde Emrich—the first man to clean and jerk 400 pounds while weighing less than 200—and Louis Riecke, who was the last American to set a world record in Olympic weightlifting in the snatch or clean and jerk when he snatched 325 pounds at a bodyweight of 181.

Despite their collective achievements and training successes, they admitted to lacking a clear plan of progression for what came after the completion of a training program or cycle. They talked to fellow competitors and coaches, and would constantly experiment and tinker with different training systems and methods. If they saw progress using a program, they continued on it until they plateaued, and then ditched it to move on to another routine. Over time, they were able to empirically refine their approach to what worked and what did not. Still, they acknowledged it was far from the most efficient method to learn.

In contrast, those trips to the Soviet Union opened our eyes to the benefits of taking a more systematic approach to the organization of a training calendar and its sessions. It provided the concepts of training with the *whys* and *why-nots* of program design and exercise selection.

We painfully extracted the answers to our hundreds of questions from our instructors. The Russian coaches' approach was so analytical that we joked if we asked a question about progressing from "A" to "B," they would wring out and exhaust every detail, variant, and component from "A" before moving on to "B."

There was an overload of information, and any time we tried to pry the "recipes" of training from them, we were told "that depends on the eye of the coach." It became such a common refrain that it truly drove us mad.

Despite the frustration of trying to refine and implement what we learned, we progressed through the ranks of our profession, gaining confidence in our coaching skills and in the ability to maximize our athletes' performance in the NFL with the New York Giants and Denver Broncos and in running the weightroom at St. John's University in New York.

In 1988, the opportunity to truly appreciate the Soviet methods arrived in a former Russian national coach named Gregori Goldstein. Coach Goldstein, who was Jewish, had served as the weightlifting coach for the republic of Belarus. Even with his great success training Olympic athletes, he was not able to advance through the coaching ranks or travel with the national team because of his religion and his superiors' fear of his defection. With his career effectively shackled, he defected, bringing his family to the United States to settle in Staten Island, N.Y.

He was working in relative obscurity in America despite his wealth of experience and knowledge, and when we tracked him down to try to convince him to school us in the Soviet methods, we were in for a rude awakening. As Coach Goldstein's first order of business in agreeing to work with us, he asked to see copies of our current training programs so he could analyze them.

When we got the programs back from him, there was so much red ink, it looked like the pages were bleeding. He felt that everything we were doing was wrong, and we were embarrassed to realize we were not as great as we thought. Despite all the miles and hours logged between America and Russia, we failed to implement the core components of what we had seen. We had cherry picked what we wanted and discarded what we did not and ended up with a mess.

As Coach Bill Parcells said, "In a competitive atmosphere, to stay the same is to regress." We knew right then that our approach could not stay the same. We dedicated the next five years to training under Coach Goldstein's "coaching eye" of scrutiny. Coach Miller even flew in from Denver to spend time refining his approach under Coach Goldstein's critical gaze.

We had countless classroom sessions under his mentorship, filling legal pad after legal pad, absorbing his knowledge and filling the gaps to develop a true system of program design. Not only did Coach Goldstein provide us the recipes for effective strength and power training, he taught us how to build a framework for what works.

At the time, we agreed to keep the information and Coach Goldstein's input to ourselves because we recognized we had a competitive advantage over almost every other team in the league. The results of our eight Super Bowl appearances with five different organizations, and the high school, collegiate, professional, and Olympic successes of our own and our assistants through the years confirmed the superiority of the methods.

What has been most shocking is that this system of planning exists in the Soviet literature, yet almost no coaches in America effectively utilize this system of programming unless they read the training manuals translated by Bud Charniga[2] or learned it from us.

This is not the "Russian Program" or the "Belarus Program." There were no specific programs developed in each of the 13 Soviet republics. Instead, there were consistent principles and methods applied in slightly variable forms within a long-term system of training.

After our education in this system over 30 years ago, it has stood the test of time and has proven to be the most effective method for developing power and strength in athletics over extended periods of time.

This method of planning leaves no doubt as to what comes next in a progression, avoids many of the pitfalls of traditional training programs, and, until another system creates as explosive, fast, powerful, and flexible athletes as the Russian weightlifters we encountered, it should be adopted wherever possible.

FUNDAMENTALS

What we hope to convey through this book is the application of the methods and principles we learned in developing and using this system. As we discovered ourselves, it is not just about having the information, but also in applying it and being able to adapt and refine it to the specific needs of a team or group of athletes.

We should make sure we are all speaking the same language before we dive into the nuts and bolts of this type of periodization. Before any coach digs into analyzing or designing a training program, it is important to operate within a framework and to know the *whys*.

We could easily provide you with the *hows* and *whats* involved in designing an effective training system; however, the hope is that reinforcing the fundamentals will allow you to critically review both your own and other coaches' programs. If there is no established or rational *why* behind the choices you make as a coach, you are operating off biases and those rarely translate into long-term success.

During our time overseas, if we asked a Soviet weightlifter why he was performing a certain exercise or how he was selecting the weights, it would be like asking the coach himself. Being able to understand the reason behind your choices and being able to then communicate that to your athletes will help foster the same environment of the former Soviet programs. When you educate your athletes and provide them the tools to understand their training, you get their buy-in and your job becomes easier.

There could be a near-exhaustive review of the research and a healthy debate on what variables are most important to elicit physical change, what exercises are best for a particular sport, or how best to cycle and structure phases of training. However, the concepts we will cover are solely to help you understand our methods and processes of program design. We will leave further debate for the internet message boards.

If you are a seasoned strength professional, you could probably skim through this next section. It should serve as little more than a review of the basics for you. However, it never hurts to revisit the fundamentals and maintain the mindset of a beginner to "sharpen the knife."

More often than not, shining the light on old information helps illuminate a kernel of new information.

THE HIERARCHY OF ATHLETIC DEVELOPMENT

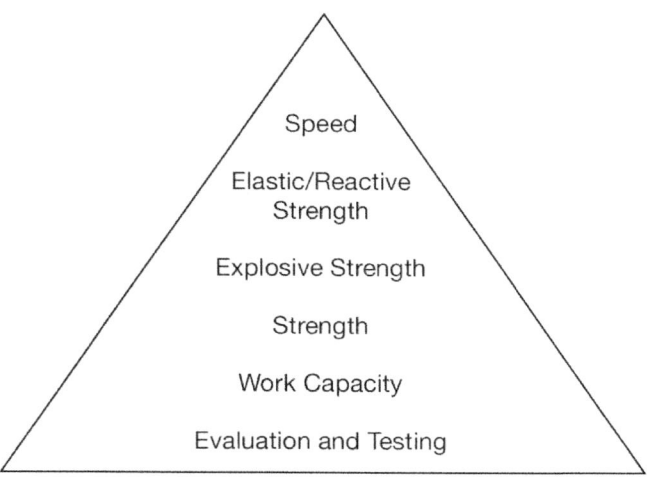

Figure 1.1 Al Vermeil's Hierarchy of Athletic Development

EVALUATION AND TESTING

Program design should always begin with an honest appraisal of the physical condition and training abilities of your athletes. It is easy to assume that high performers in a sport are physically prepared to handle high-intensity explosive training; however, that is often not the case. There will always be people who are getting by on pure athletic ability or whose past training experience is more appropriate for Gold's Gym than an athletic weightroom.

Hall of Fame strength coach Al Vermeil, M.S., C.S.C.S, whose championship resume includes time with the San Francisco 49ers and the legendary Chicago Bulls teams of the 1980s and '90s, said, "I've had few athletes who I would consider prepared to train at a high level. These deficiencies limit what we can do, so many of the athletes have to start at the bottom of the pyramid of development."

When he references the "pyramid of development," he means a model of programming he designed that builds an athlete's physical qualities through a continuum. A training program begins with the development of the physical qualities at the bottom of the pyramid. Advancement to the next ascendant quality cannot occur until the athlete displays competency in the preceding quality. We need to build the base if we want to ensure a solid foundation for progress and reduced injury risk when moving to more advanced skills.

In Coach Vermeil's and our experience, few of our *professional* athletes were prepared to train at a high level, so any strength coach working with other than the most elite athletes will benefit from taking a similar approach to program development. Most of your athletes will not be ready to dive into explosive Olympic lifting without a higher risk of injury.

Additionally, training to simultaneously improve every physical quality at once works for untrained individuals; this is suboptimal and more often counter-productive for highly conditioned athletes.

The key to the hierarchy of Figure 1.1 is the idea that proficiency of the bottom foundational qualities enhances the development of successive qualities. All training methods have their place at certain times. The key to success is in applying them at the right stage of development and in the correct amount.

This does not mean that only one quality is developed at a time. However, focusing your efforts on a more advanced component before an athlete is physically capable of a more fundamental component will lead to problems. The relative emphasis and time spent on each specific quality will ebb and flow depending on the time of year or season and each athlete's ability. Still, there should be a small thread of each quality throughout the programming.

A thorough movement and injury evaluation should occur prior to entry into any formal training program. This provides a baseline for determining mobility or movement deficiencies or prior injuries that may need to be addressed.

It also provides a baseline of an athlete's training age. Young athletes who have never participated in strength and conditioning should not immediately begin training with weights or load until they have shown proficiency in handling their bodyweight through squats, pushups, and pullups.

Taking this approach helps address many of the mobility and movement deficiencies that are present.

As we outline our principles of programming, we will differentiate between the training parameters for novice (high school or younger), advanced (collegiate), and elite (professional) athletes.

There are countless methods and systems for evaluation of where your athletes fit into this hierarchy. We recommend further reading of Coach Vermeil's work for excellent insight on his testing and evaluation tools.

WORK CAPACITY

After evaluation, work capacity is the foundational component in the hierarchy and compromises an athlete's ability to work for a prolonged period maintaining quality and intensity of work and displaying appropriate recovery from the activity. This quality can be impacted by an athlete's previous exposure to formalized training or sport participation. It requires that athletes have a base level of ideal body composition and normal joint mechanics with no active injuries. If any of these qualities are deficient, priority is given to bringing them up to at least an acceptable baseline level.

Athletes must also be able to demonstrate appropriate levels of strength endurance, core strength and stability, and aerobic capacity through bodyweight exercises or very light resistance.

Prior to entering this system of training, we also recommend that athletes demonstrate proficiency with the core lifts through complex training, which we will cover later.

STRENGTH

Strength is the base of all performance-based athletic development programs. Strength is purely the ability to exert force. Power and speed are qualities that demand that strength be applied rapidly, as is the case in most organized sports. These qualities cannot be appropriately addressed without establishing a baseline of whole-body strength.

Too many coaches spend their efforts attempting to develop power without first addressing strength. This is the wrong approach and will produce marginal benefit…if any. Strength does not just mean maximal force output; it is also the ability to stabilize or maintain a position, as well as to decelerate, such as in stopping, cutting, or changing direction.

The emphasis of all of these qualities in a controlled, technically proficient manner improves neural efficiency as well as the muscles' contractile abilities. This prepares athletes for progression into more explosive or ballistic training.

EXPLOSIVE STRENGTH AND ELASTIC/REACTIVE STRENGTH

While these two qualities can also be linked to the common strength and conditioning terms of "strength-speed" and "speed-strength," we generally approach them as two components of the larger category of "power."

For strength training to carry over to competition, athletes must have the ability to explosively produce that strength. The more rapidly the force is generated, the more power is delivered.

There is a big difference between the power requirements of pushing a loaded 300-pound wheelbarrow and pushing a 300-pound defensive tackle. The wheelbarrow is not trying to actively move in the opposite direction, and the speed at which you move the wheelbarrow probably doesn't matter. Remember that power equals force times velocity $(P=F*V)$, and particularly in contact sports, the athlete who can deliver the greatest amount of force in the shortest time is the one on the winning side of the competition.

Explosive strength is primarily focused on developing maximal force output without sacrificing the velocity of movement. Olympic lifts or other movements emphasizing rapid movement with increasing loads in the weightroom are the most often utilized tools for developing explosive maximal force.

Elastic and reactive strength is focused on improving the rate or the reactivity of force development in an athlete, trying to either increase velocity or acceleration of the movement. Elastic and reactive strength is the body's ability to quickly store and release energy and involves both the passive strength and elasticity of bones, muscles, tendons, ligaments, and the efficiency and output of the nervous system.

The body acts like a rubber band as muscles and tendons stretch and store elastic energy and then recoil and propel an athlete forward. At the same time, reflex loops between the muscle, tendons, and the spine detect and respond to stress applied to the body for rapid contraction of the muscles to withstand and redirect the forces. When those components are both developed, the body can more quickly absorb and redirect force, the period between slowing down and speeding up becomes shorter, and the movement becomes more rapid and efficient.

Developing elastic and reactive strength generally utilizes unloaded or minimally loaded movements such as jumps, hops, hurdles, or medicine ball throws. The goal is less on increasing the total amount of weight moved, and more on maximizing the speed and acceleration of the movement.

SPEED

Speed is the holy grail of sports performance and is where most coaches spend their efforts, at the expense of the foundational components. Speed is the final element of the hierarchy for a good reason: Speed is the integration and expression of all the previous qualities of strength and power—explosive strength and elastic strength. It is about maximal force output over the shortest possible time, and even though the cliché is "You cannot teach speed," you can certainly improve it.

Speed qualities include acceleration, absolute speed (the maximal velocity), speed endurance (the ability to repeat high-speed efforts), and specific speed of a sport with linear, lateral, and multi-direction speed developed through various means, including interval, sprint, agility, and quickness training.

Each quality is critical for optimal athletic development. The expectation is that as the athlete progresses in maturity and experience, the relative importance and time spent on the different qualities will begin to shift. Once the foundation is developed, you can train the higher-level qualities with more volume and a higher intensity.

As a general example, the following graph shows the increasing time spent on power and speed development as an athlete's development progresses in a sport that demands high levels of power and speed, such as football or basketball. For track athletes or in sports that require maximal speed, these values may shift to encompass an even higher percentage of the total volume, but the image in Figure 1.2 provides a general guideline for most competitive sports.

These physical attributes are all addressed throughout a training lifespan, but the demands of different sports may inherently place a greater importance on work capacity or endurance over power and speed. It is critical to remember that over-emphasizing the qualities not specific to the primary or secondary goals of training for a sport will detract from fully developing the desired traits.

Placing too much emphasis on speed or power training for a long-distance runner will detract from work capacity development, which is the most critical quality for that sport. The nervous system can only tolerate and adapt to a certain amount of stimulus; choosing the appropriate training goals and interventions is key in program design.

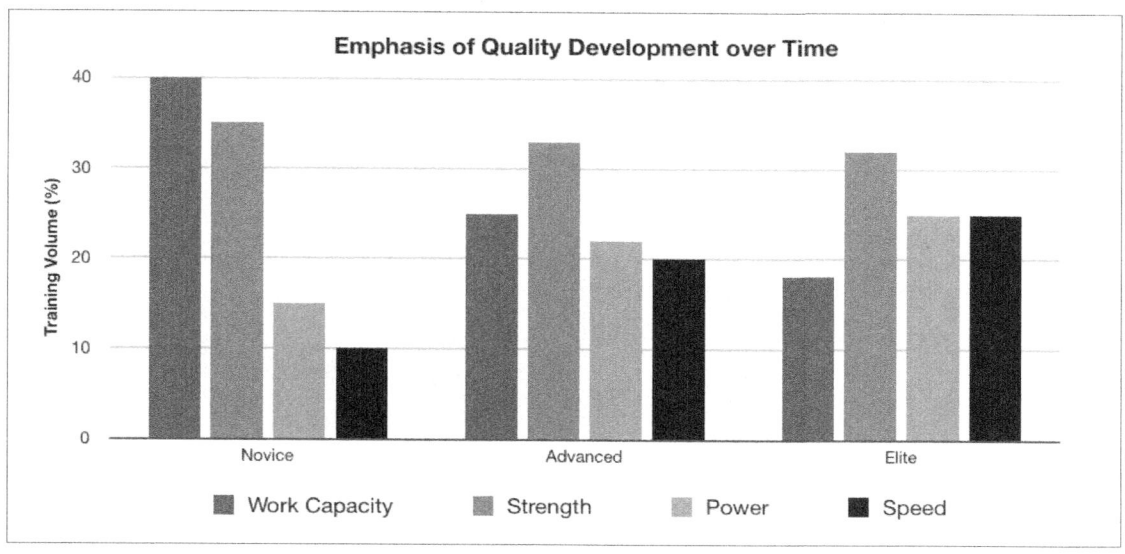

Figure 1.2 Quality Development

Although this seems like an obvious example, many training programs are often found lacking when critically appraised in this manner.

This in no way does justice to the depth and breadth of Coach Vermeil's system.[3] Every coach's career would be tremendously impacted by investigating the work of this Hall of Fame coach.

What we hope to convey is that program design and training should always follow a logical and science-based progression, and recognize that qualities sequentially build upon one another. There is no single secret to creating the ultimate training response. It is the synergistic effect of all the physical qualities that produce the strongest, fastest, and best-conditioned athletes. Recognizing when and where to emphasize one quality over another is the key to successful programming.

If your program consists of whatever you feel like training that day or something you just read on the internet, you are doing your athletes a disservice. As you gain experience in the field, intuition and creativity are valuable tools to employ, but those are skills that are refined and sharpened. That departure from the *science* of training into the *art* of training can be a treacherous one if not approached correctly.

BIG PICTURE GOALS— WHY DO WE TRAIN?

- *Enhance mobility, movement quality, and athleticism*
- *Reduce risk of injury*
- *Build foundation of work capacity— sustained output or endurance*
- *Enhance the qualities of hypertrophy and strength for physical development*

- *Enhance power, speed, and agility for carryover to sport performance*
- *Facilitate recovery from training and competition*

It is unlikely there would be much debate between coaches that the goals listed above are critical for any effective training program. These are not mutually exclusive to one another. Successfully addressing one goal can positively impact several, while neglecting one goal can negatively affect the others. The challenge is not in deciding what goal is important, but in deciding which goal takes priority during different macrocycles.

In reality, enhancing mobility, movement quality, athleticism, and reducing injury risk should be the underlying goals of *all* training for sports. These elements largely depend on the coach's abilities to assess and correct technique and build a progression of movements and exercises to enhance the quality and complexity of movement. This is the art of coaching, where the eye of the coach is constantly evaluating and modifying elements to promote an athlete's success. These goals may be more important in novice athletes with glaring deficits in physical abilities; however, even the most elite athletes will demonstrate gaps in technique or mobility that need to be addressed.

Focusing attention on the goals of enhancing the physical qualities of work capacity, hypertrophy, strength, power, speed, and agility is where clarity gets a little muddier. While our intention is to maximally develop all of the qualities for each athlete, it is impossible to train each individual quality to its peak without sacrificing another component.

Take the example of a modern decathlete. The 10 Olympic events of the decathlon demand a combination of endurance, strength, power, and speed; the athletes must train for all of those qualities to be at their highest.

However, when you compare a gold-medal decathlete's fastest sprint, longest jump, or far-

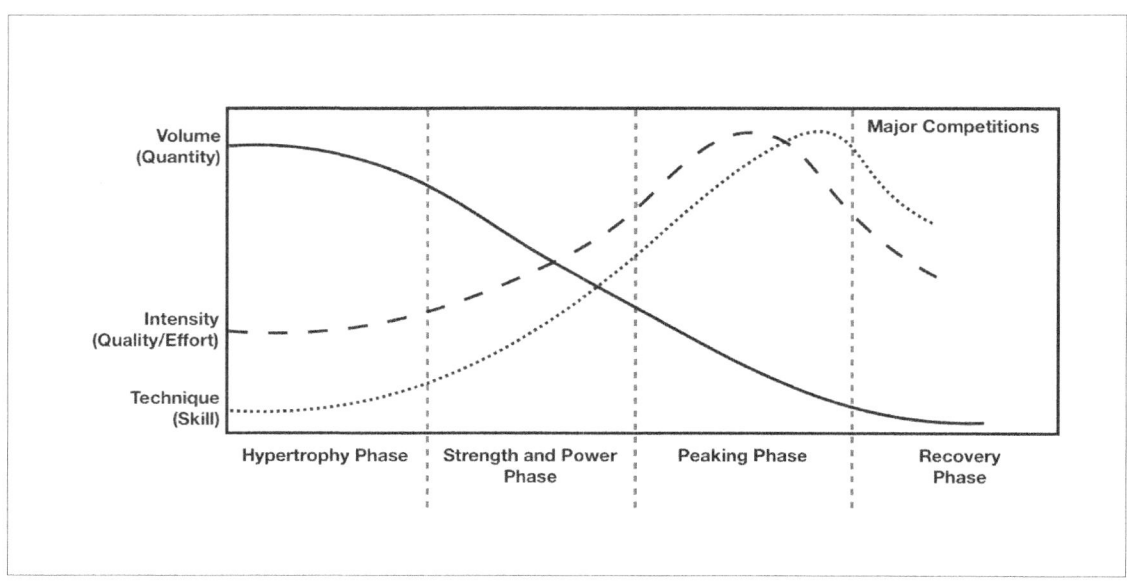

Figure 1.3 Linear Periodization Model

thest throw to an athlete's who specializes in a single event, the decathlete's best is rarely close even to a bronze-medal thrower or sprinter.

Depending on the sport, the relative importance of the various qualities may be different, but the progression of training remains the same. A coach's job is to address all the qualities in a logical progression, but with the emphasis shifting based on an athlete's needs and the timeline available for training.

Always falling back on the developmental hierarchy, the emphasis over time should move in this direction:

Work Capacity to Hypertrophy to Strength to Power to Speed and Agility

In most standard periodization models, we typically see smaller training blocks within larger blocks dedicated to developing one specific component.

The most common example is a linear off-season model starting with a hypertrophy block, followed by a strength block, followed by a power and speed block. The volume of training decreases as the intensity of the work gradually increases over the course of the off-season, with training intensity peaking just before the start of competition.

Following this model, by the time athletes are focusing on power development, they lose some of the hypertrophy they developed in prior weeks. The training stimulus shifts drastically toward higher-intensity training and the total training volume declines.

In sports with seasons that span multiple months, if the volume steadily decreases and the peak is too early, it is incredibly difficult to maintain those qualities over the course of an entire season. What may work for an athlete training toward a single event or short competitive season will be less-than-ideal for a typical team-sport athlete.

As you will see, instead of dedicating an entire cycle to a single training goal, we program the cycles based on the desired *primary* and *secondary* training effects.

We address all of the qualities, all of the time, but with one taking priority during each cycle. This way we can progress both the training volume and relative training intensity over the course of the off-season by undulating the weekly and daily volume and intensity. The primary quality of emphasis changes as the training cycles progress; however, every quality receives secondary attention to maintain gains made from cycle to cycle.

We can employ the same general strategy of periodization blocks, focusing on sequential development of the different physical qualities, but with a steady progression of both volume and intensity as the season approaches. This allows a greater work capacity to be developed once the competitive season begins, with sustained strength and power development throughout the season.

This concept and method of planning is likely foreign to most strength coaches, and we would be lying if we didn't admit that it took time and experience for us to completely buy into these Soviet methods.

The subsequent chapters will expand on the intricacies of planning that make this kind of programming possible, but keep in mind the big picture perspective of the goal of training and how your choices dictate the progression of the athletes under your care.

THE EYE OF THE COACH

"That depends on the eye of the coach."

That statement haunted our dreams. Every attempt to peel back layers of the Soviet methods of training was met with the same response from our instructors. The idea of having room for interpretation of selecting weights, reps, or frequency seemed inconsistent for a system that seemed so exacting and precise in its approach. We assumed our Soviet teachers were holding back information, not willing to give up the "secrets" of their methods. With the passing of time and our deeper education under Coach Goldstein, we learned it was just the opposite.

Time and experience would teach us that even with this "science" of program design, there is just as much importance in the "art" of coaching. The difference between a good and a great strength coach lies not just in planning and technical skills, but also in the ability to assess and correct athletes and adjust their approach in the moment. The way athletes move will tell you more about their physical capabilities than a lifetime record of their best lifts or time spent under the bar. Movement is a skill; honing the ability to rapidly analyze and correct movement is a skill as well.

Even the best-planned and executed programming cannot account for all of the outside variables that can impact an athlete's performance on any given day. A rigid system with no room for adjustment is bound to fail, either being not challenging enough for an athlete, or so challenging that it slowly grinds down recovery ability and leads to overtraining. It took us several years of implementing the Soviet style of training before we began to appreciate the nuances of this eye of the coach concept.

The idea of the "eye of the coach" represents the art of coaching. No amount of reading or theorizing about strength and conditioning will provide the skill the greatest coaches possess. There may be some people more inherently skilled in observing movement and recognizing deviations or deficits; however, this is a skill, which means you can improve with practice. Improvement comes through time spent in the weightroom diligently observing a variety of athletes to recognize what good quality movement looks like, sounds like, and feels like.

Developing that finely tuned awareness of an athlete's performance will then dictate when to progress or regress the work, just as much as what is planned for that day. There are very good coaches without this skill, yet you will not find a truly great coach who lacks a discerning eye and the confidence to trust his or her intuition.

The method of programming we recommend is a significant departure from the norm, and certainly you will have the same questions we did 30 years ago.

Whether it is when to push an athlete, what to look for in movement compensations, or when to dial back a progression, hopefully our repetition of the "eye of the coach" throughout this book will expedite your learning and help you avoid the pitfalls that for us often ended in failure or less-than-optimal results.

Despite the fact that it takes hundreds or thousands of hours of coaching to train your eye and intuition, our goal is to highlight those signs and skills of coaching we had to learn the hard way. As you continue through this book, you will find coaching cues and tips that have served us well over the years, and we hope they will serve you too.

CHAPTER TWO
PLANNING WORKOUT PROGRAMMING

EXERCISE SELECTION

Exercise selection has become a hot-button issue in recent years. Sport-specific training and exercises intended to carry over more specifically to a particular sport have grown in popularity.

As an example, we know of a well-intentioned swim coach's prescribed dry-land training that utilized about six exercises, all designed to mimic particular swimming strokes and all of them directed at the arms and shoulders. The program had no lower-body work and no total-body movements. After four of this coach's underperforming athletes went through a six-week training cycle of whole-body barbell training, they all set personal records in their respective events and one became a state champion and Division I scholarship athlete.

This is an extreme case, yet it is becoming more the norm than the exception for misguided coaches to try to simulate a sport in the weightroom with poor results in athletic performance.

The purpose of strength training is to reduce the risk of injury and to enhance performance. Sport-specific training in our world means skill training, which is the realm of the sport coach and not the strength coach. Our job is to add horsepower to the engine and improve efficiency and output in competition. We should focus the training and exercise selections on improving general strength and power while emphasizing whole-body movement. There really should not be anything happening in a weightroom that looks like a specific sports movement unless it is a squat, jump, push, pull, or throw.

A solid foundational strength program should be heavy on whole-body compound movements performed explosively. If you do nothing more as a coach than become effective at teaching and programming these core lifts, you will be more effective than many of the professionals in the field.

When it comes to developing the qualities of strength and power, there are no more effective exercises than the well-tested Olympic and fundamental barbell lifts. The universal truth in selecting exercises for the weightroom is "You have to get strong before you get exotic," and strength is what these lifts provide.

FUNDAMENTAL LIFTS

We ascribe to the 80/20 rule—attributed as Pareto's Principle, an economic principle. It states that for many events, 20 percent of the work yields 80 percent of the effects. Adapted for our purposes, 20 percent of all the exercise and movement choices yield 80 percent of the gains in strength and power development.

SQUAT VARIATIONS—
back squat, front squat, single-leg squat

EXPLOSIVE MOVEMENTS—
clean, snatch, jerk, push-press

PUSHING AND PULLING—
bench press, military press, pulls (clean and snatch), row variants

LOW BACK AND POSTERIOR CHAIN—
Romanian deadlift (RDL), hyperextension and reverse hyperextension, good morning

That very short list of fundamental lifts compromises our particular 20 percent. Although we dedicate much more than 20 percent of our programming to these basic lifts, there is no doubt that well over 80 percent of the results we have seen in our athletes can be attributed to mastering this handful of movements and lifts.

Made even simpler, placing the primary focus of your coaching on learning and refining your teaching of the fundamental lifts will yield far greater and more sustained gains in your athletes' strength and power than many more complex and "comprehensive" programs.

Any additional lifts or movements should be considered assistance or accessory work, which serve to address specific needs or deficits. Those exercises make up just a fraction of our time, as they fill gaps, rather than form the base of training—in other words, *to provide assistance*. Too many coaches try to be creative in exercise selection and end up with a collection of movements and lifts that improve nothing to any significant level.

The fundamental movements of sport are squatting, jumping, running, bending, twisting, pushing, and pulling. By building proficiency in the quality, the stability and strength, and then the speed of those movements, we provide almost all of the sport specificity we need. This is how we put first things first, and spend the greatest amount of time and repetition on refining and strengthening movements.

We encounter a similar challenge of blurred lines between the training room and the weightroom when consulting with teams and programs. While it is critically important for a strength coach to be able to recognize deficits in an athlete's mobility or to discover compensation patterns during an exercise, it is equally important to recognize that we as strength coaches are not physical therapists or athletic trainers.

Many modern coaches make the mistake of shifting emphasis and time toward "corrective" exercises or isolation work to reduce injury risk at the expense of coaching and progressing the fundamental lifts. Sometimes there is an underlying problem of mobility or control limiting performance, and sometimes the athlete just needs to be coached on how to correctly perform the movement. Time dedicated to mobilizations and corrective or prehab exercises is time not spent on preparing the athletes for the physical demands needed for competition.

The most effective organizations view the handling of injured or "dysfunctional" athletes on a continuum. An athlete doesn't spontaneously go from "injured" to "healthy" without moving through stages of healing and recovery, treatment, and training. If we think of corrective or rehab exercises versus weight-training exercises, an injured athlete who is working with the rehab staff should be spending 80 percent of the time on corrective and rehab exercises, and perhaps 20 percent of the time on modified movements in the weightroom and on maintaining or increasing work capacity.

As that athlete recovers, both the rehab and strength staff should shift the continuum of recovery in the opposite direction, where ultimately we return to having at least 80–90 percent of the work dedicated to strength and conditioning. The intensity and volume of work gradually increases to the point where the warmup and supplemental work and lifts in the programming should be adequate for addressing lingering concerns while placing the emphasis on enhancing athletic performance.

Less-than-ideal training programs are often the result of trying to maintain an even balance between the two worlds, when instead there should be a natural imbalance. Getting stronger with a progressive resistance training plan is often enough to correct many issues and concerns.

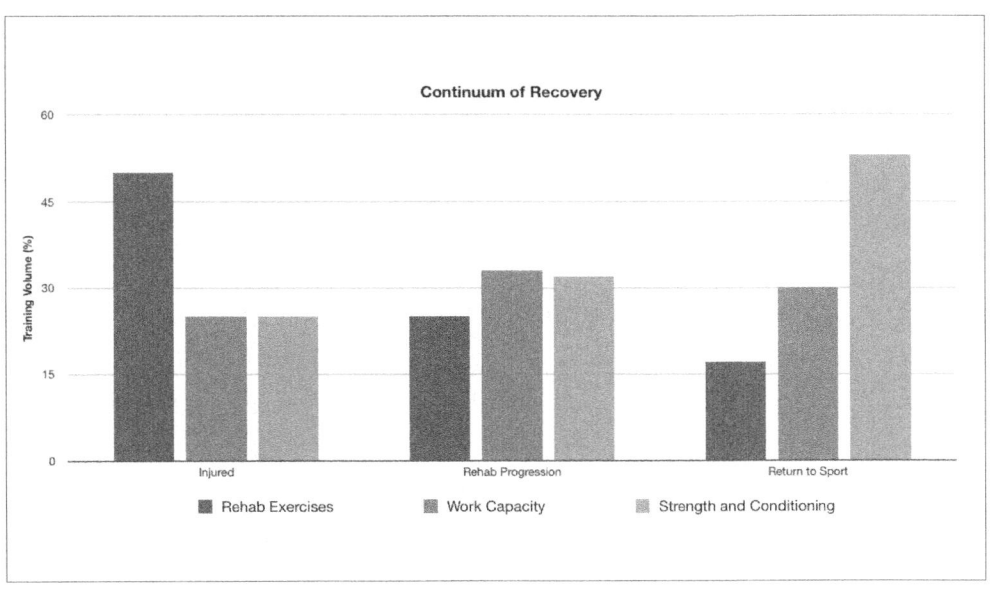

Figure 2.1 Continuum of Recovery

VOLUME

The most simplistic definition of training volume is the quantity of work performed through training in a given session or training phase. It is the sum total of sets, reps, and weight moved over the course of a session, week, month, or year. It encompasses the number of exercises, the sets and reps of each exercise, and the total weight lifted.

In the world of "more is better," training volume tends to be the first variable increased without any thought to the reason for the increase. Ask any strength coach the percentage of one-rep max (1RM) to improve an athlete's strength and you will get a correct range of intensity 90 percent of the time. Ask that same coach what training volume should be applied to that athlete's program to ensure strength gains, and you are likely to get either a set and rep scheme pulled from a bodybuilding magazine or an uncomfortable silence.

Total volume = load x reps x sets

In our view, appropriate training volume is the most important determinant of training success, and we have found it to be the least analyzed and most poorly applied of the training variables. Volume is the number one determinant of fatigue, overtraining, and injury risk… without a doubt.

As training volume increases within a session, so does the body's stress response with its increased release of cortisol. When an excessive cortisol response is triggered, the body requires more recovery time, which is generally something in short supply in athletics. The incidence of injuries from chronic repetitive strain are estimated make up about seven percent of all high school sport injuries. However, the rate of overuse injuries jumps in U.S. college sports to roughly three times the high school level.[4,5]

When it comes to strength training for sports, our goals are injury reduction and performance enhancement, in that order. Nothing we apply in the weightroom should impede athletes' performance on the field or place them at an increased injury risk over time. Although it seems like common sense, chasing performance in the weightroom should never supersede performance on the field.

The first time our NFL training programs were critically analyzed, we had to go back to the drawing board because we were so far off base. We had put a lot of attention toward exercise selection, intensity ranges, and phases of training, yet not enough toward volume.

Over the years of refining our programming, volume became the first variable we planned and then manipulated to manage fatigue and ensure continued progress throughout training cycles and into a competitive season. Volume is also somewhat tethered to the training intensity and phase of training to ensure the appropriate physiologic response with a reduced risk of overtraining.

Simultaneously increasing training volume and intensity requires a delicate balance of work and recovery to ensure an athlete's progress does not begin to slide in the wrong direction.

The total volume of training should be determined based on multiple factors:

- *The biological age of the athlete—Younger athletes may not be physically developed enough to handle high training volumes or intensities due to musculoskeletal, tendon, and ligamentous immaturity.*

- *The training age of the athlete—Training age is the duration of time the athlete has been performing some form of resistance training. The expectation is that a longer history of training will mean soft tissue and nervous system adaptations have occurred, which allow for higher volumes and higher intensity training.*

- *The medical history or history of injury—Injured athletes or those with a history of repetitive strain injuries require a lower initial training volume.*

- *Training history, especially experience with high-intensity training and Olympic lifting—Less-experienced athletes require more volume of specific exercises to improve motor control and technique.*

- *Gender—Female athletes generally respond well to a lower total training volume, and can often begin weight training earlier than male athletes because they reach physical maturity younger. They also tend to recover more quickly between training sessions.[6]*

- *Timing of the training cycle, preseason, in-season, off-season—Volume gradually decreases as the competitive season approaches and into the season to allow for adequate recovery and sport performance.*

There is no one-size-fits-all approach for determining training volume, yet there is rarely enough time spent on tracking and assessing the training volume of athletes. This will inevitably be the ticking time bomb that sabotages progress because it wears down the body's recovery ability and impacts performance in the gym and on the field.

INTENSITY

Intensity in our terms is the percentage of maximal load for performing a particular exercise. It is not to be confused with athletes' intensity of effort, or how hard they are working. Although exact values are debatable, research and experience show that particular intensity ranges will impact certain physiologic qualities more than others.[7]

Moderate intensity loads with higher training volume will generally influence muscle hypertrophy more significantly than higher-intensity loads that develop maximal strength. The variables of intensity and volume are inherently linked because the body has a finite work capacity. As the intensity of training increases, the lower the training volume should be as the nervous system fatigues.

PERCENT OF 1RM	100	95	90	85	80	75	70	65	60	55	50
MAX REPS	1	2–3	4	6	8–10	10–12	15	20–25	25	35	40–50

Figure 2.2 Maximum Repetition Percentages

MAXIMUM REPETITION PERCENTAGES

This is a bit of a simplification of the strength chart presented by Dr. Tudor Bompa in his book *Periodization Training for Sports*.[8] If you look through the research, you will see the maximum reps and percent of 1RM vary from source to source. It is difficult to standardize a chart like this because testing these values between different individuals with different backgrounds in training and different sexes will yield different maximum repetition numbers at a given intensity, and different predictive equations can also provide different estimates.

On top of that, the further we get from a maximal lift,[9] the fuzzier the values become, where we see the bigger jumps and variations in the total reps an athlete can perform as the intensity decreases. Estimating an athlete's 1RM based on more than 10 repetitions performed to the point of fatigue has demonstrated inconsistent findings when compared against a 1–10RM test for women.[10] For purposes of having a general guideline, using this rep and load chart provides a general reference point.

Our primary goal is to understand the intensity and repetition ranges in regard to the physiologic impact on the body; this will guide our selection of training loads in programming. For athletics, the goal is almost always to deliver the greatest physiologic impact on power and strength, as enhancing these two qualities is the key to improved sports performance.

In the literature, these ranges and percentages are not clearly defined and there is bleed-over of qualities between the ranges. As a general guide, these rep ranges prove valuable in determining the qualities and specifics that dictate training.

At the extremes, greater maximal strength gains will be seen with higher-intensity training above 85 percent 1RM, and greater muscular endurance will occur below 70 percent 1RM. Hypertrophy gains require a higher total volume of work, which necessitate at least some training with less-than-maximal loads.

Power development requires both strength and increased velocity of the lifts, which also is enhanced with less-than-max loads. For this reason, there are benefits to a mixed training approach to power development focusing on maximal force production (heavy load) as well as maximal velocity (light load).[11,12]

INTENSITY RANGE	POWER	STRENGTH	HYPER-TROPHY	ENDURANCE
Greater than 85 percent 1RM	High Effect	Very High Effect	Minimal or No Effect	Minimal or No Effect
75–85 percent 1RM	High Effect	High Effect	Moderate Effect	Minimal or No Effect
70–75 percent 1RM	High Effect	Moderate Effect	High Effect	High Effect
Less than 70 percent 1RM	Moderate Effect	Minimal or No Effect	Very High Effect	Very High Effect

Figure 2.3 Intensity and Repetition Ranges

One Soviet sports scientist, A.S. Medvedyev, analyzed the training logs of thousands of Soviet lifters and found that the average training intensity to develop strength and power fell within the 70–85 percent 1RM range.[13] This provided effective stimulus of the high-threshold motor units for power and strength output, while allowing enough training volume to stimulate some muscle hypertrophy and maintain technique with explosive lifting.

The optimal model of training for athletics is not the same as for bodybuilding or powerlifting. Those two realms dictate training primarily in the two extremes of the intensity range. Many programs strength coaches use in training end up as some version of one or both, to the detriment of their athletes.

The goal is always to provide the most efficient training stimulus to progress the athletes while maintaining all other qualities leading up to and through a competitive season.

The impact of overtraining from too much volume or at too high an intensity will be felt not just in stalled progress in the weightroom, but also in a higher risk of injury and poor performance.

PRILEPIN'S CHART

One Soviet weightlifting coach, A.S. Prilepin, took the relationship of intensity and volume to another level when he tried to determine the ideal training volumes and intensities to elicit gains in maximal strength and power.[14] He poured over the training logs of more than

1,000 Soviet weightlifters to find the optimal loads and volumes that allowed for steady progress in maximal force development.

The emphasis of the Soviet training methods were always on improving lifting technique and the speed of the bar while increasing the training loads. From his library of training journals, Prilepin was able to reverse engineer a programming structure that allowed his athletes to excel without placing too great or too little stress for adaptation.

Using his findings, Prilepin created a chart linking his ideals of volume and intensity for developing particular physical qualities.

PERCENT OF 1RM	REPS PER SET	OPTIMAL TOTAL REPS	TOTAL REP RANGE
90+	1–2	4	10
80–90	2–4	15	10–20
70–80	3–6	18	12–24
55–65	3–6	24	18–30

Figure 2.4 Simplified Prilepin's Chart

Figure 2.4 is a simplified version of Prilepin's chart. Prilepin was able to create an easy way to see how the training intensity, maximum repetitions, and training effect relate to one another to maximize strength and power development. He presented a range of reps per set and a rep total to account for different levels and the training history of each athlete. What made Prilepin's work unique was his recommendation of the optimal total reps per workout.

Through the analysis of his athletes' training logs, he determined there was a particular volume range within a workout that would provide the appropriate training effect without too excessive of a demand on an athlete or causing a significant decrease in the speed of the movement. A more refined version of his chart appears in Figure 2.5.

With Prilepin's focus on strength and power development for athletes competing in weightlifting, he kept the range of reps for each set fairly low to maintain technique and the speed of the bar. Despite a range of intensity of almost 20 percent—from 55 to 75 percent of the 1RM—he maintained the reps performed in each set to between three and six.

This may seem counterintuitive, since many strength coaches are inclined to have athletes train toward failure or to the point of form breaking down.

In Prilepin's model, technique and speed are never compromised, and the training effect is through the combination of intensity and volume manipulation.

The increasing intensity levels see a reduced total training volume, yet with a tight rep range within each set.

The goal is to find the optimal point between minimal and maximal training to elicit an adaptive response.

PERCENT 1RM	REPS PER SET	OPTIMAL NUMBER OF REPS	TOTAL VOLUME RANGE— NUMBER OF REPS
95 or higher	1–2	3	2–4
90	1–2	6	4–10
85	2–4	12	10–20
80	2–4	15	10–20
75	3–6	18	12–24
70	3–6	20	12–24
65	3–6	24	18–30
60	3–6	26	18–30
55	3–6	30	18–30

Figure 2.5 Refined Prilepin's Chart

To achieve the optimal training volumes at each intensity level, the rep range allows for modifications, depending on the goals of the training or an athlete's abilities that day. At 65 percent of the 1RM, we assume an athlete could perform a maximum of 20 repetitions in a set before muscle failure.

When our focus is on power development, we use a lower volume in each set to maximize the speed of movement. Based on a range of three to six reps, we might have the athlete perform four sets of six reps or six sets of four reps, or any other combination to hit the optimal 24 reps. This provides some flexibility in programming within these guidelines. The total rep ranges at the different intensities are built to account for the variables of the athlete's age, ability, training experience, and even the changes in recovery or performance noted on a given day.

There is no one-size-fits-all value for load or volume, despite many programs employing strict set, rep, and intensity levels. Recent research demonstrates that even when training volume and intensity were kept the same between two groups, the athletes performing more sets of fewer reps (8x5) showed greater gains in strength and power with comparable lean body mass gains against a control group (4x10).[15] This gives us yet more evidence that this simple chart provides opportunities for variability in the set and rep scheme to direct training toward the goal of increased strength and power.

Note that Prilepin was training Olympic weightlifters—not football, basketball, or soccer players who not only have to be strong and powerful, yet also have to be able to run, jump, twist, and turn—all in an unpredictable environment. However, strength coaches have successfully adapted his work and model of optimal training intensity and volume toward sports. His principles helped form the basis of our methods.

TEMPO TRAINING METHODS

Tempo—the speed of an exercise—is another training variable to be manipulated within the scope of intensity. When given the opportunity, most athletes will perform exercises at a self-selected speed, often without much thought of movement speed or what impact that speed may have on a body.

In reality, the tempo of an exercise can impact a body's physiologic response in the same manner as adding more weight to the bar. By manipulating the speed of the movement, additional stress can be biased toward particular muscle fibers and motor units of the nervous system, emphasizing the different qualities of power, strength, and hypertrophy depending on how fast the lift is performed.

While a bench press or military press can be performed slow and controlled, Olympic lifts and plyometrics necessitate a high rate of muscle contraction to rapidly move the bar or the body. The most effective way to get a barbell from the floor to overhead or to jump on top of a box is to accelerate the bar and body as quickly as possible. Most sports movements require rapid acceleration and speed; however, the logical application of the training stimulus to improve sports performance is often lacking.

Commonly used methods of training intensity as they relate to tempo also come from the Soviet models in what they called the "Max Effort," "Repetition," and "Dynamic Effort" methods.[16]

MAX EFFORT

Max effort is the attempt to lift a maximal load against a maximal resistance. Training with any load above 85 percent of 1RM is considered a max-effort lift, as maximum pertains to load and not speed. A max-effort lift generally does not entail as high a velocity or tempo component because the load will not allow it. The goal of max effort work is to increase maximal strength, and to produce an effort to move the bar as quickly as possible for maximal force production. However, the combination of a heavy load and gravity will ultimately dictate the speed of the lift.

This method will help develop significant strength and power; yet, because of the high intensity, there is a tremendous demand on the central nervous system. Dipping into the well too often with max-effort work will erode performance if the amount of recovery needed is not met. For sports performance, it is best utilized judiciously and with athletes who already possess a high level of technical proficiency and physical ability.

REPETITION METHOD

The repetition method, as we define it, utilizes loads that are 60–80 percent of the 1RM, and, as the name implies, the goal of this method is to emphasize repetition of a movement to failure. This method is often beneficial in improving the technique of a movement, building work capacity, and also in stimulating muscle hypertrophy over strength or power. That is the reason many bodybuilding routines draw heavily from the repetition method. As the load is relatively light, a higher volume of repetitions can be performed per set, generally in the 8–15 rep range.

Although the tempo of the lifts can be manipulated to be more rapid, extending time under tension has been shown to be effective in causing skeletal muscle breakdown, stimulating hormone release, and causing the buildup of metabolic compounds that stimulate muscle growth.[17] The longer the duration the muscle has to maintain a contraction and the more motor units that have to work, the more profound the effect. Training to the point of near muscle failure is what leads to a "pump" as the muscle swells with blood.

This often causes the muscle soreness associated with most bodybuilding routines.

Despite its primary role of hypertrophy development, there is still a place for the repetition method in sports. For young athletes and certain sports, adding muscle mass is often a goal, along with improving strength and power expression. A larger muscle has a greater capacity for output and more mass can serve as protection in physical or contact sports.

The higher repetitions in each set allow for improved technique and motor control, along with an athlete's "feel" for the lift, while improving work capacity and endurance. However, training with a lower intensity for greater than 10 will not optimally stimulate power and strength development and works best with less technical lifts.[18]

While the repetition method has a place in an overall training program, it is best in a supplementary role.

DYNAMIC EFFORT

The general definition of dynamic effort is "lifting a non-maximal load with maximal speed." That means lifting sub-max loads with the goal of maximal acceleration of the bar. The benefit of training with this method is to condition the nervous system to fire rapidly and to train explosive movement.

Power is a factor of force and velocity, so the emphasis is on training velocity under load. When utilizing this method of training, the goal is always to maintain speed of the bar in the concentric phase of the movement. The eccentric—yielding—movement is performed in a controlled manner, and the weight is then rapidly accelerated back through the concentric movement. As fatigue sets in, the bar speed will begin to slow; ideally, the load selected will stress an athlete's abilities for the desired rep range without sacrificing speed. One study showed that minimizing the eccentric component and rest at the bottom of a bench press not only produced higher power output, but also allowed more reps to be performed compared to slower eccentrics.[19]

One study presented to us during a visit with the Soviet scientists that is no longer available to reference for you related to the effects of different bar speeds on gains in explosive strength. They found that rather than performing the lifts with exclusively high or slow speeds, the most effective gains came from utilizing mixed speeds. By varying the intensity levels of the weights and always striving to move the weight as fast as possible, they saw both an increased and sustained training effect on strength and power. Lifts performed above 80 percent of the 1RM will be slower than a lift performed at 60 percent; however, the intent is always to move the load explosively. Since that time, similar approaches have been shown to develop incredibly powerful athletes.

Training for athletics should be performed with this same idea in mind. By utilizing a range of intensities and loads throughout the programming, we are able to again simultaneously train power, strength, and hypertrophy qualities, even as the training volume varies. The load dictates how quickly the bar moves. However, we should never compromise speed.

The proposed graph of power output to velocity in Figure 2.6 helps illustrate where we find the optimal training ranges, although there is some debate regarding the exact percentage ranges.

SPEED–VELOCITY CURVE

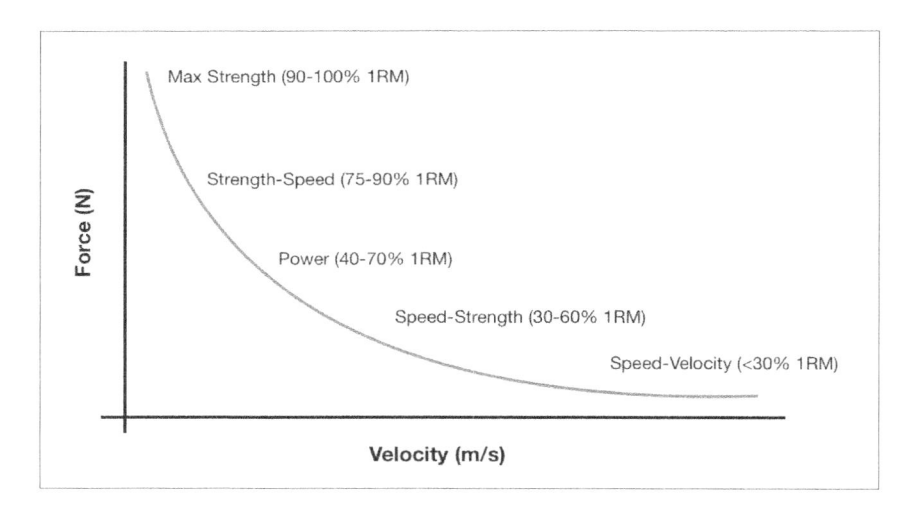

Figure 2.6 Speed–Velocity Curve

Power output in weight training forms a parabola. At the highest velocity, there is not enough load, and at the highest loads there is not enough velocity to generate maximal power. Based on the principle of Specific Adaptation to Imposed Demands (SAID), if the majority of training is dedicated to one quality, the curve will shift toward that quality at the expense of the others.

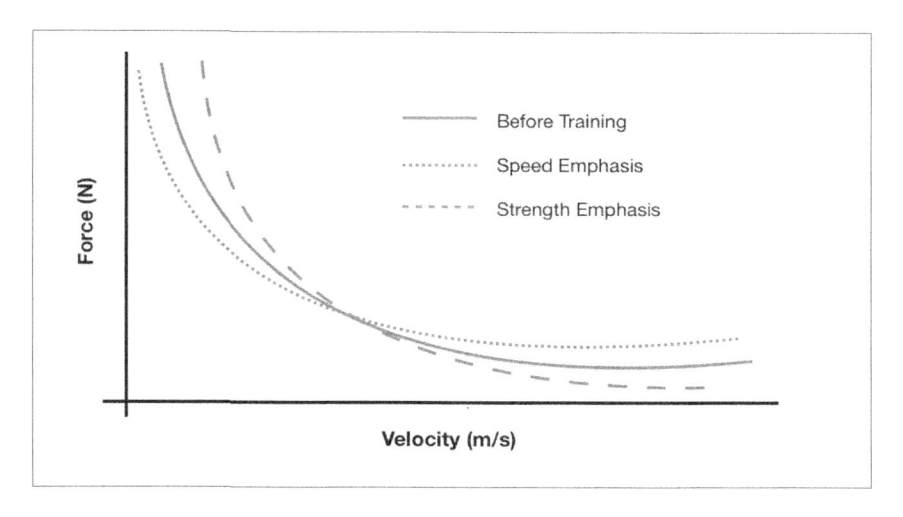

Figure 2.7 Force–Velocity Curve

Placing too great of an emphasis on training one extreme of the force-velocity curve will only enhance that end of the spectrum, and may even negatively impact the other end. If the training emphasis is only on maximal force development, the speed of muscle contraction and in turn the velocity of movement may decrease.[20] As you saw in the previous graph, there is always a cost for leaning too far to the extremes in training.

The goal of training for sports should be to shift the force-velocity curve to the right to develop greater force at higher speeds, and programs that utilize a combination of strength and power training have been repeatedly shown to improve athletic performance more than strength or speed training alone.[21, 22]

ADAPTATION TO RESISTANCE TRAINING

As we will see later, part of the secret of the Soviets' success arose from performing the bulk of their training within a narrow range of intensity. This was roughly between 70–80 percent of an athlete's max, where both strength and power could be simultaneously developed. We also found the most profound benefit from focusing on developing maximal speed with loads in the 70–85% 1RM range, but we do not neglect intensities outside that range. We look for the most efficient intensity range to focus on based on the goal of training.

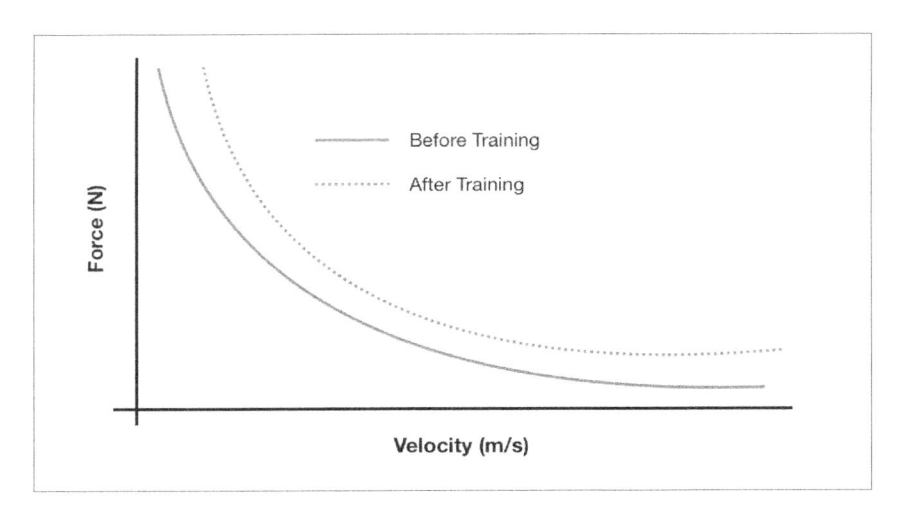

Figure 2.8 Adaptation to Resistance Training

FREQUENCY OF TRAINING

Frequency of training is an often-debated variable when it comes to optimal delivery for performance enhancement. Determining the frequency of training runs parallel with the volume of training to allow adequate time for recovery after a training session. In order to maintain a high quality of work in the weightroom without detracting from performance on the field, there needs to be a restoration period.

Just like volume, frequency has to account for an athlete's age, training history, gender, and timing of the training cycle, as well as the goals of training. Add to that the athlete's access to quality nutrition, recovery modalities, stress level, and sleep habits makes determining optimal frequency a tricky thing. Those of you working with high school athletes will have to add the drama of teenage relationships, homework, and non-sports-related activities to the equation.

Most often, training frequency is determined based on an athlete's schedule and the time of year relative to the competitive season. When all variables are ideal, three or four training sessions per week have proven to be effective in allowing for a better distribution of the training volume over the course of a cycle.

When the competitive season arrives, there will be a reduction in the training frequency to account for the additional practices and games that cut into the recovery window.

However, in our experience, less than two training sessions in a week has proven to be insufficient. Circumstances will always dictate the application, yet we have found those values to consistently work.

During the off-season or with high-level athletes, or both, it can be beneficial to split a training day into two sessions. Particularly when the training volume and intensity are high, it can be valuable to split the day's work into morning and evening sessions.

This allows for a high level of performance between training sessions, better managing fatigue. Higher-intensity work can be separated from higher volume work during the day to allow recovery time in between and to maintain the quality of the work. Outside of professional athletics, it can be a challenge to schedule and consistently carry out split routines, particularly with high school or collegiate athletes. However, increasing the training frequency this way can be beneficial if you can do it.

The greatest concern with increasing training frequency, whether through additional training days or split sessions, is over-taxing an athlete's recovery. What can begin as steady gains in strength and performance can rapidly plateau and drop off a cliff if the training volume and frequency both increase too rapidly.

Especially in the case of beginner or even lower-level advanced athletes, there should be at least one year, and ideally two years, of steady, progressive training at three days a week before advancing the volume and frequency to four days a week. You will never be wrong in keeping a high school athlete at three days per week; however, you can certainly go wrong in a hurry if you advance the training volume to the point of requiring four days too soon.

The other question that arises concerning frequency of training is how often to train the same muscle or movement in a given week.

The bulk of bodybuilding-driven programming ascribes to working a body part or region twice a week with a high volume to maximally tax the muscles and then allow for recovery from the workload to stimulate hypertrophy gains.

When muscular size is the goal, that method may work; however, training for sports is about developing good movement patterns as well as strength and power. Training a movement once per week will not provide a consistent enough stimulus to improve motor pathways and refine technique.

A growing number of studies have even begun to show that increasing the frequency of a lift, while maintaining the same total volume of the exercise, can stimulate similar and in some cases improved strength gains. When comparing performing an exercise for three sets of 10 repetitions once per week or one set of 10 repetitions three times per week, the latter method was shown to produce similar strength and lean mass gains.[23]

As we will show in subsequent chapters, training the same movement multiple times per week is a fundamental aspect of training for athletics. With planned variation in volume and intensity, we can stimulate improved strength and power gains and improved movement efficiency without the risk of overtraining.

Success comes down to building recovery into the program from the beginning.

MODELS OF PERIODIZATION

Professor Yuri Verkhoshansky defined periodization as the "long-term cyclic structuring of training and practice to maximize performance to coincide with important competitions."[24] In general terms, it is the system of program design that involves planned, systematic changes in the training variables we previously discussed—intensity, volume, frequency, exercise specificity. This is where we take all the components we can manipulate, determine the purpose of the training, and then structure a plan across a timeline to achieve that goal.

In terms of program design for athletics, the goals should always be to reduce an athlete's injury risk and maximizing athletic performance. Those are nonnegotiable. It also means your training program should not only serve to strengthen your athletes to reduce injury on the field, it should also not create injury or dysfunction from the training itself.

Too often, the programs we encounter in the weightroom are so focused on maximizing strength or work output above all else, common sense goes out the window and the athletes are consistently overtrained and breaking down before they set foot on the field. In recent years, there has been an alarming number of athletes being injured—and in some cases dying—from workouts that look more like punishment than training to improve performance.

You can build a periodized plan around a specific training objective, such as increasing vertical jumping ability or bench press strength specifically in preparation for the NFL Combine. However, more often than not, our goal is to develop the qualities of strength, power, and speed in service of a sport.

As with Coach Vermeil's Hierarchy of Athletic Development shown on page 23, there must be some level of proficiency of all components of performance, with different emphasis depending on the demands of each sport. Your program design should address all of those components to help your athletes, not hinder them.

There have been many books written on periodization for sports performance, some of which came from the coaches we spent time with in Eastern Europe and Russia. We are not looking to reinvent the wheel or retread the works of others. Today, the biggest distinctions to be made using the current concepts of periodization deal with *linear, block, and undulating periodization.*

LINEAR PERIODIZATION

Linear periodization is considered the "traditional model" of program design, where there is a progressive change in volume and intensity across multiple cycles. The basic design is that volume will steadily decrease as intensity increases over generally longer training periods. In theory, this model provides concurrent development of strength and technical abilities in a gradually advancing manner—hence, linear. The training effect will be general, and moves from more of a hypertrophy phase to a strength phase, toward a power and speed emphasis during a peaking phase, and then a recovery phase.

The greatest issue with this model of program design is that the body does not adapt and progress in a linear fashion. Linear progression will often demonstrate good results for a novice athlete, as any type of strength training produces gains in size and strength in an untrained individual.

For a more advanced lifter, there may be steady progress made over six to eight weeks, and then we either see the athlete's progress plateau or potentially even decline due to overtraining if the training intensity continues to steadily climb too long. On top of that, if you do not continue the reps per set protocols that are best for the quality you are trying to emphasize, you will lose the gains in that quality when you shift to emphasize another.

For an advanced or high-level athlete, linear periodization is particularly ineffective due in part to the much slower rate of physical adaptations in a trained individual.

It also does not fit well in the competitive model for most sports.

For track or single event sports where there is a clear point in time to achieve peak performance, planning in a more linear fashion makes sense. The problem is that most team sports have seasons that span months of competition. Where do you set the peak of training intensity and technical performance? At the beginning of the season? At the middle of the season? The risk of overtraining during the season with an extended period of linearly increasing training intensity is a very real threat for high-level athletes.

It is the simplest form of program design, yet it often leaves something to be desired for the athletic population.

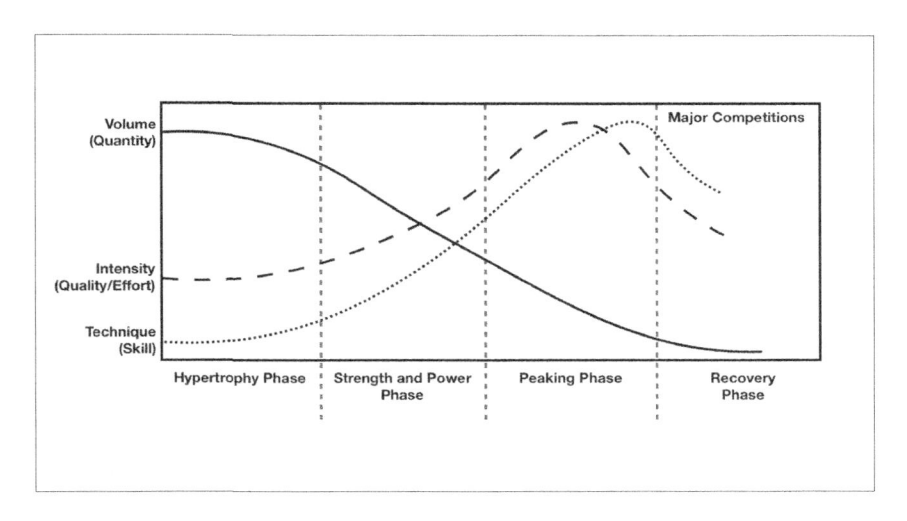

Figure 2.9 Typical Linear Periodization Model

BLOCK PERIODIZATION

Block periodization was introduced by noted sports scientist Yuri Verkhoshansky,[25] whom we had the opportunity to meet and learn from during our trips to Russia. Professor Verkhoshansky developed his conjugate sequence for Olympic athletes. In no way could our explanation of his work come close to covering the full scope of his methods, but his concepts influenced the designs we would later come to use.

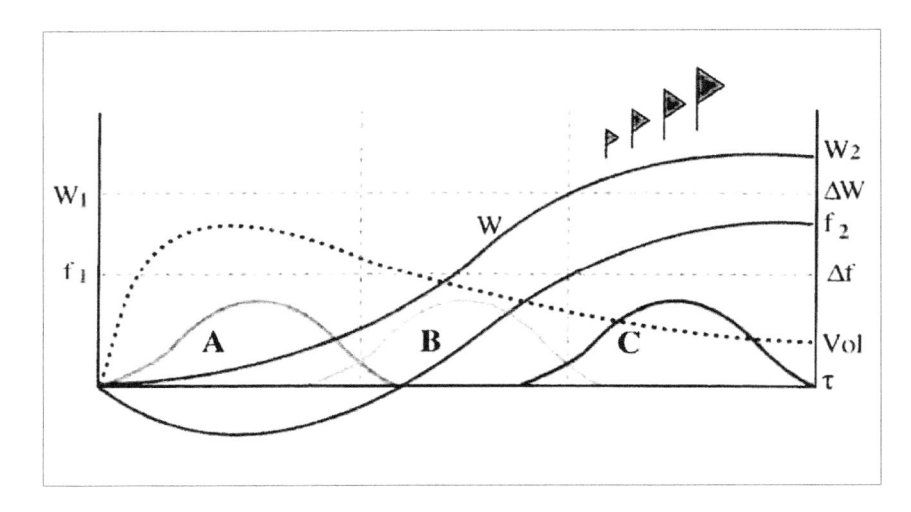

Figure 2.10 Verkhoshansky's Standard Model for the Main Adaptation Cycle Model[26]
W = Work Power   Vol = Volume   f = Maximal level of functional parameters

His method consisted of a block design of accumulation and restitution. The emphasis of the first block—Block A in the image—was on improving an athlete's motor potential and morphological and functional specialization. It was largely to build a strength base to facilitate muscular adaptation and an improved work capacity using what Verkhoshansky termed "special physical preparation (SPP) loads."

As athletes transitioned into Block B, the SPP loads would be gradually replaced by higher intensity training focused on speed and technique. Block B dedicated development to more specific work of the Olympic lifts to accustom the athletes to make full use of their increasing motor potential to execute the lifts.

Finally, Block C used competition training loads to address the maximum level of power and full motor potential of the athletes. This block would cover the most important competitions so they were performing at their peak output for competition.

The blocks would progress in the order much like Vermeil's Hierarchy: building a foundation of work capacity and strength, then advancing toward power and speed, and ultimately maximal power development.

In a general sense, the design is to overload the volume of strength and power development during an accumulation phase with higher-volume training and maintenance of the athlete's technical abilities.

Then, during a restitution phase, the training volume would be just enough to maintain and gradually progress the strength qualities while training intensity increases and the emphasis is on improved technical proficiency and speed for the sport. That is why each block appears with a gradually increasing, then decreasing line.

Multiple blocks of accumulation and restitution could then be programmed over the course of months to prepare for competition. That basic principle of a wave-like variability in training volume and intensity forms the basis for the undulating model we utilize.

UNDULATING PERIODIZATION

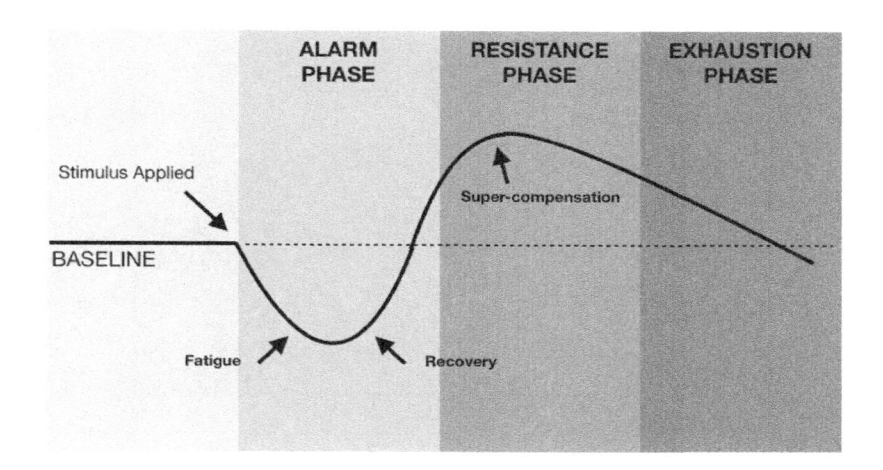

Figure 2.11 General Adaptation Syndrome

This system makes use of Verkhoshansky's periodization ideas, with the addition of a more frequent undulating periodization pattern. Within undulating periodization, the volume and intensity of work is constantly varied throughout a planned wave-like pattern.

Undulating periodization aims to maximize the body's adaptation best seen through the theory of Hans Selye's General Adaptation Syndrome (GAS).[27] His work from the 1940s and '50s explained the way the body responds to stress and works to restore itself to balance, also known as homeostasis. When a body is exposed to a stimulus, there will be an initial fatigue or strain to a physiologic process. Once the stimulus is removed, the body will recover and adapt to regain a level of balance. The body then begins the process of reinforcing, or super-compensating, to prepare to better handle the stimulus the next time it arises. If the stimulus never recurs, the body returns to the previous baseline. Given a large enough or consistent stimulus, a body will go through successive super-compensations to better handle the stresses, and that baseline level of function will gradually increase.

When a person takes up a strength training program, the body will improve the efficiency and output of the nervous system, reinforce bones and tendons, and grow new muscle fiber to withstand the repeated stress of lifting weights. Too little load, volume, or frequency, the body will not need to reinforce itself. Too much load, volume, or frequency, the body will be unable to keep pace with the strain and will begin to break down.

The body's systems will possibly reach a certain point of development at which it can tolerate the stress without an added need for adaptation. This is when most athletes hit a plateau in their progress, and the stressors need to be changed to elicit new development.

As we noted with the linear periodization example, if there is a shift in the training stress away from a hypertrophy focus, a body will gradually lose some of that hypertrophy as it adapts to the new stimulus of a higher intensity and lower volume training.

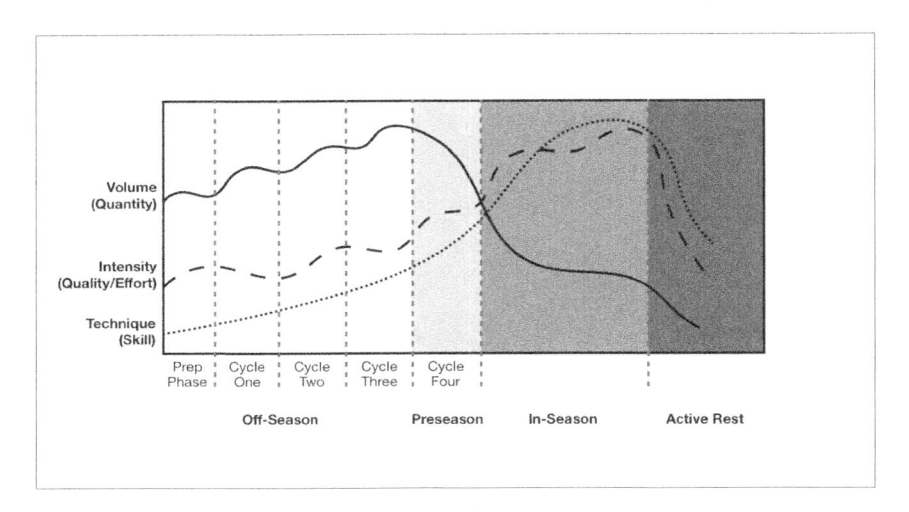

Figure 2.12 Undulating Progression

A body will adapt to the specific demands placed on it. There has been evidence that using an undulating design is superior in developing strength gains and may mitigate the risk of plateaus for well-trained athletes who are more likely to encounter training plateaus compared with less-experienced athletes.[28]

With an undulating program, the training volume and intensity are varied between each workout, week to week and month to month, making the stress to the body constantly changing.

Variability does not mean random!

There is a planned pattern of change. This method allows for simultaneous work on the primary qualities of hypertrophy, strength, and power without allowing the body to fully adapt to a single stress. As the volume is consistently waved, the risks of overtraining and hitting a prolonged plateau of progress are practically nonexistent, as recovery is built in.

Often with undulating periodization, volume and intensity will move in a reciprocal pattern to one another. When intensity increases, volume decreases, and vice versa. In our experience, an undulating model where the two variables are uncoupled is a somewhat more challenging design, yet one that has proven the most beneficial. Each variable will ebb and flow throughout the training cycle; however, both will be tightly constrained to maximize gains while minimizing the risk of overtraining.

Some coaches suggest that an undulating progression is not the best method for maximally developing a single quality. That argument has merit; however, there are not many sports that require proficiency in a single physical quality.

A football linebacker must have muscle mass to withstand impact, strength to bring down 200-pound running backs, and the power and speed to react and move rapidly to chase receivers. A basketball power forward needs speed and power to sprint and jump, strength to post up and lean on defenders, and work capacity to sustain that effort with limited breaks in the action.

Because sports require some expression of almost all of the physical qualities, any significant deficiency in one will ripple outward and negatively impact the others.

This is how we end up with a brutally strong football lineman who is too slow to get down the field to block effectively, or the lightning-quick hockey forward who is too weak to fight for position against bigger defenders.

In terms of efficiency, to train all of the physical qualities with a reduced risk of overtraining, there is no other method of program design that comes close to an undulating pattern.

USING A STRUCTURED PLAN

It is a race against the clock to physically prepare athletes in less time. Without a structured and comprehensive plan, something will fall through the cracks.

Incorporating the knowledge and experience of the hundreds of coaches we worked with throughout the years, we developed this system to provide a blueprint for success in athletic development. We are happy to share this method of programming for use with your athletes and hope it is as valuable to you as it has been for us.

SECTION TWO
THE SYSTEM

CHAPTER THREE
THE SYSTEM

The System is a collection of principles and methods of programming that sets up steady, efficient progress in strength and power for long-term athletic development. In the world of athletics, where power and strength development are critical, this system of program design has proven its worth in championships and gold medals.

It will work for any sport and any level of athlete when you apply the principles and follow the thought process we outline herein. This system of programming will refine your thinking and approach to programming to remove the guesswork and the question of "What do I do next?" In the current world of too many options, it forces you to work in a narrow framework. It demands that you be more focused and disciplined in selecting the most productive exercises, and it requires you to build your training plans around the essentials.

Once you have stripped away the excess and mastered the art and science of efficient programming, expanding your approach then becomes more systematic and less experimental. This means learning the recipe, and then getting creative once you have mastered the process.

The System is the culmination of our collective years of experience in the field and the critical analysis of our training, as well as that of our peers. Distilled to its simplest form, there are a few fundamental principles to our method.

CORE PRINCIPLES

- *Exercise selection emphasizes whole-body strength movements performed explosively, and progresses from simple to complex.*

- *There is no such thing as truly sport-specific training.*

- *Training volume is the most critical variable, with a planned range of undulating volume.*

- *Training intensity stays primarily within a narrow, undulating range for efficient training stimulus.*

- *All the physical qualities of work capacity, strength, power, and speed are addressed concurrently, yet to varying degrees.*

The core principles might not differ drastically from what most of the best strength coaches in the field define as their top priorities.

The problem for many coaches is not in having principles or a training philosophy; it is in their consistent application. With application, these five fundamentals elicit the most consistent gains in strength and power in the weightroom and on the field.

In this book, we will lay out the blueprint we utilized successfully for almost three decades. Many of the specifics are tied to the demands of football, where we spent the greatest amount of our time; however, the principles and methods can and have been applied across different sports from middle school to professional levels.

Application to other sports is about taking the same approach and refining the nuances; it will not require a complete overhaul.

Without a doubt, there will be growing pains when reframing your perspectives on the training variables and the application of these principles in your program design. This may require a complete 180-degree approach to how you train your athletes. We had to initially swallow our pride and admit we were not helping our athletes to the best of our abilities. We made more mistakes than we can count in application through the years.

It is safe to assume you will make some mistakes and find some particular challenges. However, we promise that if you come out the other side with a grasp on the foundational components of The System, you will take your athletes and your coaching to an unexpected new level.

The most valuable aspect is that it is built upon fundamentals that allow you to continue to modify and progress your training over the span of years.

The Soviet coaches in some cases programmed the subsequent four or five years of an athlete's training down to the percentages to be performed in each workout. There are even Soviet-designed programs spanning a decade.

Unfortunately, they were programming in a tightly controlled environment for Olympic weightlifters. That method will not account for all of the variables that impact the lives and training of the typical Western athlete. Still, by using their methodology with a more flexible application, it is possible to produce consistent programming to develop an athlete's potential from 13 to 30 years old. There are few other methods of program design that have made their way to the West that can make that claim.

PREPARATION

DISCLAIMER: YOUR ATHLETES ARE NOT READY

Going any further into this book without first evaluating the current status of your athletes is a purely academic exercise. There is one common thread that connects the thousands of athletes we trained, plus those trained by the coaches with whom we studied and worked through the years: Few athletes, if any, initially possess the requisite physical qualities and capabilities to dive wholesale into weight training or high-intensity running or jumping. Whether we are speaking of a 10-year-old's first time in the weightroom or the Heisman Trophy-winning first-round pick's first day of camp, you cannot base your job security on how good people tell you they are, whether that be a kid or a coach.

We have seen All-Americans who squatted with worse form than high school freshmen. We have seen high school seniors performing repetitive sprints and plyometric jumps when they could not squat or hop in place without nearly falling over.

To assume an athlete's on-the-field talent relates directly to strength or weight-training ability, or vice versa, is a dangerous bet. Your programming should be based on what you can see or measure regarding their ability and not their reputation. Your credibility is not derived from what the athletes can do in the weightroom, but on keeping them healthy and performing on the field.

In this system of strength and power development, the emphasis is on explosive, whole-body training. Early assessment of athletes is critical to success. If there is no foundation of basic mobility, balance, good movement patterns, and strength, athletes will break down or, at best, stagnate as you start adding weight to the equation.

You need to determine if your athletes can move, lift, jump, and run with a level of proficiency before you entertain the idea of adding weight to the bar or having them perform maximal effort jumps or runs.

We accomplish this through a preparation phase each athlete must complete before advancing into serious weight training.

- *It applies to all levels of athlete—novice, advanced, elite.*
- *It is non-negotiable after an extended layoff and subsequent return to training.*
- *It serves to both teach and reinforce fundamental movements and technique.*

There will be some coaches who pick up this book and say, "To heck with that, I'm not going to waste time with this easy stuff. My athletes are strong enough, and I want them to be elite. I'm going to train them like they are elite."

We have coached some of the most genetically gifted professional athletes walking the planet, and a tiny fraction of them came in fully prepared to train. An advanced or elite athlete gets that title by demonstrating the abilities required to perform at that level. These titles are earned, not given.

A coach who trains athletes based on how he or she *wants* them to perform rather than what they are physically capable of will see the wheels fall off when they break down from doing too much, too fast.

As a coach and teacher, you have to assess and develop the three components of training. Programming for lifting, running, and jumping must be intertwined, and each quality should support the others. It does not work if you emphasize one at the expense of the others or accelerate the progression of one before the other qualities are up to par. Ensuring each athlete has a foundation and has mastered the simple before moving to the complex is the only path to long-term success.

PREPARATION PHASE

Think of this preparation as a break-in phase. The preparation phase is not an option—it is a requirement, particularly for younger athletes, those with limited training experience, or those whose mobility or motor control is lacking.

Above all else, the emphasis of the training system lies in maintaining the quality of work. If an athlete does not possess a base of strength, mobility, and basic work capacity, the quality of the training will suffer. Skipping the opportunity to create a solid foundation will slow the progress your athletes manage to make, and will likely set them up for injury.

Here is a dose of reality: It takes 10 years of consistent training for athletes to reach their physical potential. There is no shortcutting this fact. It takes progressive loading and training to develop connective tissue and tendon strength, along with muscular and bone development and neurologic efficiency.

From 12–21 years old, as athletes goes through puberty, their bodies are constantly developing. The apex of speed and strength development does not occur until they are in their mid to late 20s. This means if we start 10-year-olds on some type of strength training, they will not be truly physically developed until around 20 years old, and that is under the best of conditions.

In countries that have Olympic development programs, a strength coach may have the opportunity to work with the same athletes for a decade or more. The reality for most coaches, though, is that time is not on our side. A high school coach may get three or four years of progressive training with an athlete, and collegiate and professional coaches probably less than that on average.

Recognizing that time is not on your side, your approach should be as if you are going to be in charge of your athletes for a competitive lifetime. The goal is always to maximize gains in the short term of a season, without forsaking the process of long-term athletic development. When your focus is on the success of your athletes, your job is to ensure a solid foundation so they can continue to develop no matter who handles their future training.

The primary focus of the prep phase is to increase work capacity, improve joint mobility and movement quality, develop strength, and teach or refine technique. As we train a developing athlete with weights, we first need to develop the motor pathways for movement and the lifts to enhance body position and timing.

In the instance of younger or less-experienced athletes, there also needs to be a significant frequency of training whole-body movements and of developing technical proficiency of the lifts. We train the nervous system to work efficiently and optimally by creating motor pathways to engrain the proper body position, timing, and bar position with full-body movements. Isolating particular joints or muscles with bodybuilding-type exercises or simple exercises more appropriate to a rehab setting is not nearly as efficient as repetitive, low-load training of basic barbell movements for simultaneously improving multiple physical qualities.

This prep phase will usually require one four-week cycle; however, the structure depends largely on the "eye of the coach" when determining an athlete's proficiency without compensation in the lifts. We want to condition athletes to handle progressive loading of patterns with appropriate recovery; for novice athletes, this preparation may extend over multiple four-week cycles. We have employed nothing more than a gradual advancement of the prep phase for up to a year for some of our middle school or freshman athletes resulting in significant gains.

The fundamental exercises, drills, and coaching of the prep phase will continue to have a place in the programming of even the most elite athletes. There is always room for improvement in work capacity and movement efficiency.

If athletes cannot meet the baseline benchmarks with flawless technique and explosive movement, they do not get to pass Go. "Flawless" means every rep looks alike. If they cannot handle a movement, do not put them into a program that loads that particular movement. Make sure to correct flaws or deficits early or you are setting the fuse for a breakdown as the training intensity increases.

There has to be a foundation before we build a house. Any cracks in that foundation will be weak links limiting an athlete's long-term growth.

FUNDAMENTAL SCREENS

Before starting any of the preparatory work, it is paramount to do a thorough assessment of joint mobility and flexibility in your athletes. There are many choices of and opinions about movement screens or assessments to determine appropriate postural alignment and control, so we will not cover every available option.

In our eyes, the most fundamental motion for any athlete is the squat pattern. Even in basic human development, infants learn how to squat around the same time they learn how to walk. Because it will ultimately form the backbone of our training system, it takes top billing in our initial assessment.

Despite developing the squat movement pattern around one year of age, it often takes on a different appearance in training. We can attribute this to the minimal amount of squatting adults do on a daily basis.

The squatting motion requires every joint of the lower extremities and spine to move in concert to maintain a proper center of gravity. The ability of athletes to shift their weight and appropriately load the hips and legs dictates proficiency in almost all athletic movements.

Because of that, one dysfunctional link in the chain will cause a cascade of negative effects. Loading a bad movement pattern will either limit performance or lead to injury, or likely both.

For the squat assessment, we use either the single-leg squat or the overhead squat, and often both. Each movement provides different information about an athlete's mobility and control, and also serves as a corrective exercise integrated into the program.

OVERHEAD SQUAT

We prefer using the overhead squat as an assessment because it readily exposes restrictions of the lower extremities, hips, spine, and shoulders in one movement.

Gray Cook has dedicated a good amount of time to championing the overhead squat as an assessment tool, so we do not need to retread that path.[29] In short, optimal mobility and postural control is required for an athlete to achieve the deep squat position. That is what we want to see in the weightroom.

The first assessment should always be with a dowel or some other light implement held overhead to facilitate the appropriate position. Some athletes may actually demonstrate better form with a little bit of weight overhead, but if an athlete is unable to demonstrate the appropriate form with the arms overhead, the movement pattern needs attention.

The basic benchmarks we look for are:

- *The head and neck remain in line with the spine without excessive forward tilt.*
- *The elbows remain extended and the arms fall behind the line of the ears when viewed from the side. The dowel or bar should be directly aligned above the middle of the foot.*
- *The torso and shins fall parallel to one another at the bottom position of the motion.*
- *The feet remain flat on the floor.*
- *There is no collapse of the knees inward; they should remain in line with the feet.*
- *We look for general symmetry of posture and weight-shift from all sides.*

With a deeper assessment, you may find mobility restrictions limiting the motion at the ankles, hips, thoracic spine, or shoulders resulting in weight shifting to one side or onto the toes, not achieving a parallel depth of the thighs, or the inability to maintain an upright trunk and shoulder position.

If mobility is not the limiting factor, regressing the exercise to wall squats with a ball behind the back or another supported variation can improve the quality of the motion. If motor control or stability is the limiting factor, sometimes the movement will miraculously improve when you take them off the wall to retest.

No matter the corrective method, the goal is a deep, controlled, and symmetrical motion.

Apart from mobility restrictions you may find, the priority is motor learning. You want to see as many quality repetitions as possible to hammer home the motion and to facilitate improved motor learning and kinesthetic sense.

We take a different perspective for young, inexperienced athletes.

The idea is not always about getting the fastest change, but about forcing the athletes to perform and succeed at the edge of their ability. We would rather take more time and see athletes struggle to find the appropriate position with minimal or no loading while they learn the feel of the movement.

Photo 3.1 Overhead Squat
The overhead squat will quickly expose any deficit in ankle, knee, hip, spine, or shoulder mobility or control.

One big lesson we learned about including overhead squat training as a flexibility and balance exercise came from legendary Steelers Head Coach, Chuck Knoll. One day, Coach Knoll mentioned a problem he always encountered in coaching linemen: trying to teach them to stay low in the stance.

The old saying goes "the low man wins;" a lineman standing too upright will find it challenging to maintain leverage.

As the Steelers' training program began to implement more overhead squats, they noticed the linemen were more consistently keeping their hips and center of gravity low and winning the leverage battle at the line of scrimmage. We found the same results with our athletes: Sprinkling overhead squats in our programming had significant benefits in body control.

SINGLE-LEG SQUAT

The single-leg squat is the second movement we use as an assessment and corrective exercise. In comparison with the overhead squat, the single-leg squat illuminates significant leg- or hip-strength discrepancies from side to side.

This movement starts on a box or bench, in a single-leg stance in which the athletes squat all the way down to the point of the hamstring touching the calf, and then rise back up. It is simple, yet challenges both strength and stability.

Until an athlete can correctly demonstrate the single-leg squat with the heel on the ground and the "nose behind the toes" for three sets of six reps on each leg, we do not let the person squat with significant weight.

Ideally, athletes can perform three sets of six reps on each leg, and then they get to load the bar.

That will seem extreme to some—especially to the coaches who choose an arbitrary weight and start their athletes squatting the first day in the weightroom—yet it will bear out in the end.

A failed squat pattern does not mean everything comes to a full stop. We can still train the following complexes with an athlete who fails the single-leg or overhead squat assessments, but we use modifications. We can start the squatting movements through a limited range of motion and severely restrict the load. The burden of coaching the movements with these athletes will be infinitely more challenging and more critical.

Photo 3.2 Single-Leg Squat, Top

Starting position with hands held in front to maintain balance

Photo 3.3 Single-Leg Squat, Bottom
The hamstring and calf of the supporting leg should make contact at the bottom position

Two simpler options are to remove the squatting motion altogether, and have the athlete either perform step-ups onto a box or perform the unweighted wall squat to train the motion. At the same time, including the single-leg squat as a corrective movement will mobilize restricted joints and improve body control.

When our athletes have clearly demonstrated proficiency in the squatting movements without significant limitations or compensations, we can move them into training the complexes and loading the squat pattern.

We even demanded that our long-limbed and larger athletes—whether basketball players or linemen—all reach full depth with the single-leg squat. Remember, the single-leg squat is not only an assessment, but it can serve as a corrective exercise as well.

Particularly in football, athletes will often find themselves in compromised positions at the extremes of motion. By purposefully and progressively training the body into the extremes of particular movements, we will hopefully strengthen the body's tissues to withstand the forces that arise when they get to those positions by mistake.

THE JAVOREK COMPLEX

Assuming there are no significant injuries or secondary issues to be addressed, the most effective method we have found to tackle preparatory qualities is to use training complexes—more specifically, those designed by former Romanian strength coach Istvan Javorek. Coach Javorek designed a program of simple and straightforward clusters of exercises performed in series, primarily using barbells, but also with dumbbell variations.

Stressing technical proficiency and a higher volume of the movements in succession begins to form the basis of quality movement.

Coach Javorek developed some of his complexes[30] for muscular hypertrophy and basic strength improvement, while others were intended to have a greater cardiovascular impact and improved willpower and determination. The complex below is his Complex One, which we have used with significant success in preparing athletes both physically and mentally for the demands of later stages of athletic development.

JAVOREK COMPLEX ONE	REPS
Upright Row	6
High Pull Snatch	6
Back Squat—Push-Press	6–6
Bent-Over Row	6
Romanian Deadlift (RDL)*	6
TOTAL REPETITIONS	36

Figure 3.1 Javorek Complex One

*We have replaced the good morning exercise, originally part of Complex One, with the Romanian deadlift (RDL). This is primarily because the good morning, although simple, is extremely hard to teach to young athletes. In our opinion, it is not as productive as the RDL; the deadlift is one of the staple lifts in our programming.

Each exercise is performed for six repetitions, and then the next movement is performed without releasing the bar until all five movements have been completed. With young athletes, we primarily utilize the barbell variations because it allows better coaching of the main lifts and less difficulty for the athletes in coordination and in balancing the load.

Exercise progression should go from simple and general to more complex, particularly when teaching a new movement. This is no different than learning to shoot a free throw or hit a baseball; learning a new motor pattern requires a high volume of repetition no matter what the skill. This applies to weight training too; it must be taught, practiced, and refined so it becomes engrained.

As athletes demonstrate proficiency with the barbell complexes, transitioning to dumbbells is one option to progress the complexity. Although dumbbells allow for improved carryover to sport and a greater range of motion in the joints, the physical demands and body control required are also much higher.

Make sure your athletes can perform a lift with maximal control before adding additional degrees of freedom and stability demands. You want your athletes to succeed more often than they fail.

Under ideal circumstances, the work-to-rest ratio should be 1:3—the rest interval is three times the duration of the work interval. If it took one minute to complete a complex, have the athletes rest three minutes before starting the next set. Grouping athletes of similar abilities into groups of three or four will allow for enough recovery time between sets without requiring strict timing of the rest period.

These complexes serve the dual purpose of training the neuromuscular system and conditioning the cardiovascular system. The extended time under tension while holding the bar taxes even the most conditioned athletes as the 36 reps are completed.

When performed with the right loads, the combination of resistance, sustained effort, and time under tension during these complexes develops work capacity and hypertrophy in almost every athlete. There should be heavy breathing and elevated heart rates between sets; however, we do not want so little rest between sets that the quality of the lifts deteriorates.

This phase is about teaching the movement first and developing the training effect second.

Quality comes first.

EYE OF THE COACH

If an athlete demonstrates limitations in a particular movement or difficulty with the transitions between movements, either isolate or remove movements from the complex.

Some inexperienced athletes may find it challenging to perform one portion of the complex with the prescribed load. In those cases, separate the limiting lift and perform it in isolation with a lighter weight and, as it improves, reintroduce it into the complex.

DETERMINING LOAD AND VOLUME

It is valuable to remind yourself that the purpose of the preparation phase is "training to train." The goals should first be technical proficiency, with an adequate volume of work to hammer home good patterns of movement. We are less concerned with the training effect at this point, and the load determination is based more on your qualitative assessment of an athlete's performance and the subjective reports of the athlete.

It is not just biological age that plays a role in capacity, but also the training age and experience. Younger kids who might not be the athletes their peers are may need more time "coloring inside the circles."

In the same vein, a physically mature athlete who does not have significant training experience will also need more time in the prep phase to build a base of work capacity and movement proficiency.

Ideally, the training loads should be progressed. However, if initially an athlete cannot handle the prescribed weight, you can vary the rest and recovery times to stress sustained output. Those adjustments are your main variable of manipulation.

LOADING

NOVICE	ADVANCED	ELITE
Begin with a dowel for low-functioning beginners **Progress to:** 30-percent bodyweight load for those who are able	Begin with 30 percent bodyweight **Progress to:** Smaller athlete— 50-percent bodyweight Larger athlete— 40-percent bodyweight	Begin with 30-percent bodyweight **Progress to:** Smaller athlete— 50-percent bodyweight Larger athlete— 40-percent bodyweight

Figure 3.2 Examples of Loading

Smaller athletes are less than 200 pounds. Larger athletes are greater than 250 pounds. Intermediate-weight athletes should progress to approximately 45-percent of bodyweight.

For female athletes, the novice targets will be the same as above. For advanced and elite, the targets will be 40–45 percent for smaller and 40 percent for larger athletes.

In all cases, the initial volume will be a minimum of two sets of the six-rep per movement cycle. The eventual goal will be to progress to four sets of the complex in a session. The routine should be performed three times per week, with a linear increase in load as the athletes begin to demonstrate proficiency, but with no more than a 10-percent increase from the previous session. When the target intensity is met for three sets, increase the volume, working up to four sets.

Under ideal circumstances, the prep phase would last for one four-week cycle to start the off-season training. However, that ideal was part of the "good ole' days" when we had more time to break in the athletes than is typical today.

The total timeframe for the prep phase depends on how quickly an athlete is able to progress to four sets with the target percent of bodyweight. We want to produce as much work volume as possible, but every rep should be technically sound and explosive.

Although some of the target weights for advanced and elite athletes may seem high for a preparatory phase, we have found that anything less than 40 percent of bodyweight for 275–300-pound linemen will not prepare them for the loads that come into play during the main program.

As far as intensity is concerned, choosing a set weight or using a percentage of bodyweight is a determination to make within the first week. This is where you have to use your judgment on what has previously transpired. If you err on a weight selection, always err on the side of caution. Never give your athletes something they fail with right out of the gate. Allow them to use an achievable weight; if that necessitates using a fifth week in the first cycle to reach the goal weights, so be it.

On the other hand, if an advanced or elite athlete is powering through the complexes with the prescribed loads and hits the target volume and intensity, you can shorten the prep phase to begin shifting focus toward other training qualities.

"HARDGAINER" PREP PLAN

There may be instances where an athlete cannot handle the weight for four sets. If you discover this prior to the start of the off-season, you can use an undulating pattern, which would otherwise come into play later in the off-season programming.

What has worked best for the adaptation is to introduce two series each day, Monday, Wednesday, and Friday in Week One, while maintaining the same intensity level for each session.

In Week Two, the intensity could be increased slightly, with Monday being three series, Wednesday back to two series, and Friday to either two or three series, depending on how fast the athletes are adapting—again, using the eye of the coach.

Week Three would be four series on Monday, two on Wednesday, and three or four on Friday. Then, use three series on Monday, Wednesday, and Friday of Week Four, but with a drop in reps to either three or four per series.

Clearly, for the novice or "hardgainer," it will benefit your athletes to perform successive cycles of the prep phase even if they achieve the target values.

We even encourage many strength coaches dealing with beginning athletes to focus almost exclusively on training the complexes and bodyweight exercises for at least the first year of training to simultaneously develop strength, power, hypertrophy, and work capacity. If the typical freshman high school football team performed nothing but an off-season progression of the prep phase, they would most likely be ahead of 70 percent of the competition in terms of physical development and performance.

It is important not to skip this phase, even when dealing with highly trained athletes or with a compressed training timeline. More often than not, if athletes have not previously been well coached in the Olympic lifts, there will be glaring deficits in how they perform these movements.

Similarly, the first thing to go after a layoff is work capacity. Re-establishing a baseline for sustained physical output is necessary to prevent overtraining injuries. Immediately jumping into training with loads greater than 70 percent of an athlete's 1RM combined with poor technique can spell disaster.

On top of that, the complexes always have a place as a warmup or conditioning tool for all athletes. For many training sessions, warming up with one or two sets of the complex serves to warm up and prime the muscular and nervous system for the high-intensity training that follows.

	MONDAY	WEDNESDAY	FRIDAY
WEEK ONE	2 series	2 series	2 series
WEEK TWO	3 series	2 series	2 or 3 series
WEEK THREE	4 series	3 series	3 or 4 series
WEEK FOUR	3 series— drop to 3 or 4 reps	3 series— drop to 3 or 4 reps	3 series— drop to 3 or 4 reps

Figure 3.3 Example of "Hardgainer" Preparation Plan

RUNNING AND JUMPING

As we build an athlete's baseline of strength and work capacity through the use of complexes, we should also dedicate time to refining the quality of movement in sprinting and jumping. We do not always think of running and jumping as highly technical skills, outside of world-class sprinters or jumpers.

However, sit and watch a gang of middle-schoolers stumbling down the field and you will recognize pretty quickly that it is something not always intuitively learned.

You have to teach your athletes *how* to run.

The typical inclusion of plyometrics or sprinting and jumping in a training program is usually something of an afterthought. Many coaches include ladder work, box jumps, or sprints on training days so the athletes get in some conditioning work. Other coaches will have their athletes performing "cardio" for some indeterminate timeframe, without much justification.

When programming for efficiency, you should always hold yourself to a *why* along with the specifics. An athlete's physical tolerance and recovery ability are finite, and we want to apply the optimal level of demand to facilitate gains. Extra exercises or nonspecific training "just because" is unacceptable and will only slow progress or lead to overuse injuries.

Sprinting and jumping require rapid muscular contraction and power, but both tasks also require a significant contribution from the output of the nervous system and the elastic qualities of the tendons and muscles.

The stretch reflex is a hardwired mechanism the body utilizes to rapidly deliver force with minimal effort or energy expenditure. When a muscle rapidly moves through an eccentric lengthening motion, potential energy is produced through the elastic stretch of the tendons and muscles. Within the muscle-tendon junction, muscle spindle fibers respond to the rapid stretch of the tissue with a rapid contraction of the surrounding fibers. That rapid-fire series of events bypasses the normal pathway of nerve endings that travel up to the brain and back down to the muscle and constitutes the stretch-shortening cycle (SSC).

The SSC allows a greater expression of power to be delivered from the combined stored energy in the tendons as well as the active muscle contraction. To develop maximal output, the period between the eccentric and concentric contraction of the muscle needs to happen in less than a quarter of a second. That period between the eccentric and concentric action is called the amortization phase. The efficiency of the SSC makes up the elastic, reactive strength we noted earlier in the Hierarchy of Development section.

In the Soviet Union, they used to have six-year-old kids put their toes in a small machine with their heels on the floor and push their feet up and down as fast as they could. They timed them for 10 seconds to see how quickly they could fire off repetitions, keeping their feet in sequence. They were looking for the reactivity of the feet and ankles to find the kids who innately had more reactive nervous systems. That was the difference between the kids who were selected to train at the National Sports Institute and the kids who stayed home and ended up working in mines or factories.

It is not unusual to find athletes who excel in basketball or track who can jump through the roof or sprint like the wind, yet do not have a lot of strength in the weightroom. What they have is an efficient, tuned nervous system and strong elastic and reactive abilities of the muscles and tendons. They possess the natural ability to rapidly store and release energy, and that is something you cannot coach. There are no doubt sprinters who are "stronger" than Usain Bolt; yet, his genetic potential and nervous-system efficiency clearly provide him an edge.

For the less-gifted athletes, we can improve the output of the nervous system and the muscles so when the stretch reflex kicks in, the amortization phase is a little shorter and the muscle fires with more force. Developing explosive strength and power through the legs and refining technique will improve the performance of any athlete.

During the prep phase, our greatest concern is refining technique and motor efficiency of the rhythmic nature in jumping and running, and continuing to build work capacity. Following our core principles, we begin by emphasizing simple movements—submaximal running and jumping—and progress toward more complex movements like sprinting and multiple jumps as coordination, reactivity, and strength improve.

RUNNING

Every worthwhile running program begins with warmup exercises intended to refine technique and prepare the body for the demands of running. The same progression of skipping, butt kicks, and exaggerated running movements has been recycled throughout the library of sprint training. Despite the consistency of these drills across the training literature, it is not unusual to discover their relative absence or perceived unimportance in the actual programming of many coaches.

These drills have stood the test of time. They continue to be the most effective tools for instructing proper form and reinforcing movement patterns for efficient running and sprinting. However, they demand the same degree of coaching and cueing as any other drill or exercise. The key to efficient running is in minimizing the amount of time the foot remains in contact with the ground, delivering the greatest amount of force into the ground, and maintaining forward momentum while eliminating extraneous motion.

Whether you are working with a middle-schooler or an NFL tight end, the rules remain the same, and there is always a need for improvement. If that foot is not off the ground .09 hundredths of a second after impact, the energy and power dissipates through the legs—that athlete is running slow and flat-footed. Yet, the number of coaches and athletes lazily going through the motions of most of these drills far exceeds those who stress their importance.

For the prep phase, we first dedicate our efforts to instruction of technique, and second toward advancing work capacity. Training technique is more effective if the athletes are not overly fatigued, and once they show proficiency, the workload will increase.

At this point, we are not interested in maximal speed training because the athletes are not physically prepared for that intensity of training. Even without direct sprint training, we will likely see improvements in speed because technique plays such a critical role in sport-specific speed.

MACH RUNNING DRILLS

A-SKIPS

The A-skip is a basic drill that helps develop lower-leg strength while encouraging knee lift and an efficient foot strike. The purpose of the A-skips drill is to improve running coordination, facilitate improved calf and hip extension strength, and control and train hip-flexor activation. It can be one of the most challenging running drills because of the level of coordination needed to execute it, yet it can also be one of the most beneficial drills for improving running form.

Photo 3.4 A-Skip
Notice the tall and balanced posture, and weight on the ball of the left foot. The transition between feet should be rhythmic, like a clock.

When performing an A-skip drill, the athlete will travel linearly by slightly leaning forward and then driving the lead knee up with the opposite arm in front of the body while tapping the ground with the trailing leg in an explosive "hop." The trailing leg should have a straight knee, with the calf and hip propelling the body forward off the forefoot and toes. The athlete continues moving forward in this manner—alternating legs—and striking the ground quickly with the forefoot during the mini-hops. These are like a Swiss watch—the rhythmic movement never stops between foot strikes, with a smooth, rolling motion.

The coaching emphasis should be on forward propulsion linearly rather than vertically, with the opposite arm swinging forward in tight unison with the lead leg. Here is a valuable cue to help keep the arm in a tight motion: "Pick your nose; pick your pocket."

When doing this drill for the first time, it is best to have the athlete walk through it to get the motion and coordination down, and gradually begin skipping, and then progressing the speed.

A-RUNS

An A-run is a progression from A-skips that more closely resembles the natural running motion. The A-run teaches efficient sprinting posture and arm action, training proper foot position with more rapid turnover of the feet.

It is a replacement for traditional high-knee drills, because when doing traditional high knees, often the knee goes too high and posture is poor with an almost leaned-back alignment.

Athletes have a tendency to perform them with more of a bouncing motion, where there is a lot of vertical displacement of the body. The A-run variation allows for improved feel of delivering force into the ground and forward propulsion with each stride.

Photos 3.5 a–b A-Run
Notice the difference in form between the two images.
The first image shows good posture and alignment with a strong hip drive. The second image shows how driving the knee too high can alter trunk position and impair forward momentum.

When performing A-runs, the mechanics are similar to A-skips, with the athletes starting in a slight forward lean. They drive the lead knee and opposite arm up in front of the body while driving through the forefoot of the trailing leg, maintaining a straight knee.

Instead of performing the mini-hop motion, the athlete accelerates the trailing leg up while dorsiflexing the foot, bringing the toes toward the shin. The foot should land under the hips.

The emphasis is on rapid delivery of force into the ground and a quick turnover and acceleration of the lead leg.

Lining up athletes six to eight across and pacing off about 10 yards in front of the line is an effective way to coach A-runs with a group. Have one athlete from each line start as you slowly walk backward for the distance of the drill. When the athletes complete the drill with good form, have the next row begin. This way you can efficiently watch and cue multiple athletes at once and set the pace for the lines.

BUTT KICKS

The purpose of the Butt Kick drill is to improve overall coordination and ground contact explosiveness with more emphasis on engaging the hamstrings. The most important function this drill teaches is to improve the recovery phase after the foot leaves the ground, as well as leg turnover cadence or "backside mechanics."

Photo 3.6 Butt Kicks
The athlete is pulling the heel "up" underneath the hips while maintaining a forward lean. The goal is quick turnover of the feet.

When performing these, just as with A-runs, the athlete drives the knees high with a dorsiflexed foot. The most important addition in this drill is that the athlete will rapidly bring the heel underneath the butt and hips—not behind—and make contact underneath while maintaining a high-knee lift as opposed to keeping the foot ahead of the body as in the A-runs.

Coaching the athlete to maintain the forward lean and tight arm motion will again help in maintaining the momentum forward rather than vertical. Too many coaches coach this drill with the emphasis on the heel hitting the backside rather than driving the heel underneath the body and elevating the knee.

WALL MARCHES

The wall march is another valuable drill to teach an athlete how to maintain forward body lean and quick foot turnover, but with additional support to improve movement quality.

The athlete assumes the desired running position with the feet on the floor and the hands on the wall. Make sure the heels are not on the ground and the eyes are up. The athlete will then raise the right leg and maintain the same position.

On a whistle or coach's command, the athlete switches feet as fast as possible and tries to maximize force delivered into the ground. The knee should drive up while the opposite foot drives down into the ground.

Every time the foot hits the ground counts as a repetition. This can also serve as a valuable assessment of symmetry of movement between legs by listening for a difference in the sound of impact between feet and to detect an uneven cadence.

Photos 3.7 a–b Wall March
There should be no vertical motion of the body as the feet switch.

The progression of this exercise can go from a single movement to multiple marches in a row. In our later programming, you will see a progression to three steps in sequence to further enhance control and coordination and reduce contact time with the ground.

> ### EYE OF THE COACH
>
> *The athlete needs to deliver force into the ground. You should not see the head or butt rise; any vertical motion is unacceptable. The wall march movement should be explosive and stable.*

TEMPO RUNS

All of the previous running drills are generally performed over shorts distances of 15–40 yards, with the coaching emphasis on developing good mechanics and force production through advancement of speed. We have found tempo runs to be the most effective tool for killing two birds with one stone in developing both running form and work capacity.

Tempo runs provide a higher volume of repetition to train the appropriate movement patterns developed through the drills. They allow the coach more opportunity to provide cueing and correction and more opportunity for the athletes to work on their feel for the correct movement patterns.

You should be watching for how the foot strikes the ground, looking for forefoot contact, arm carry—meaning fist and elbow coming to midline—no body lean in a tall posture, and listening for ground contact. This should be "quiet" running.

A tempo run starts as nothing more than a 100-yard run for time, followed by a 50-yard walk, which is then repeated. It is easiest to have the athlete stride the sideline on a football field, walk the end zone, and then stride the other sideline.

For an absolute novice, the expected 100-yard time should be:

- *17 seconds for linemen (maximum time limit)—offensive, defensive linemen*
- *16 seconds for mid-skill—running back, tight end, linebackers, quarterbacks*
- *15 seconds for skill—kicker, punter, wide receivers, defensive backs*

Advanced or elite-level athletes will have expected 100-yard times of:

- *16 seconds for linemen (maximum time limit)—offensive, defensive linemen*
- *15 seconds for mid-skill—running back, tight end, linebackers, quarterbacks*
- *14 seconds for skill—kicker, punter, wide receivers, defensive backs*

You can tweak the numbers to account for athletes from different sports, generally basing the values on bodyweight comparable to the football positions—less than 200 pounds, 200–250 pounds, and greater than 250 pounds. There may not seem to be a significant difference between the target times for the different levels of athletes. However, this is meant for working on form and work capacity. It is not for working maximal speed.

Using those times as benchmarks provides an effort level somewhere around 70–75 percent of an athlete's 100-yard dash time.

Soviet coaches used tempo runs heavily in their training; however, they rarely coached more than six to eight athletes at any one time. When coaching larger groups or teams, using the suggested times will allow you to assess multiple athletes at one time, at an intensity that will provide a training effect without too much demand on the recovery side.

The goal is for athletes to learn what it feels like to run with good economy, taking the form learned through the running drills and then adding repetition.

Many young athletes will do a tempo run and the heel of the foot will hit the ground first. If the heel hits first, the foot is in front of the hips, effectively hitting the brakes on the body's momentum with every stride.

We need to educate even our advanced athletes in maintaining the legs under the body and projecting the hips down the track with rapid foot recovery. We need to coach the movement, just as we would a squat or a snatch, and improve the economy of motion so it looks less like an average recreational jogger and more like an athlete. Once athletes can demonstrate acceptable technique, your goal is to add volume to hammer form and work capacity.

The 100-yard run and 50-yard recovery are performed in sets up to four or five cycles before adding a longer 100-yard recovery. The volume should start at a reasonable level of four or five runs, and can accumulate all the way up to 24 cycles; however, that is reserved for world-class athletes—think Usain Bolt. We have worked up to 18 cycles with high performers, yet that is rare. If athletes can run that volume and hit their prescribed times, they are in great condition, and will have learned and retained significantly improved form.

EXAMPLE EIGHT-CYCLE TEMPO RUN

Run (Walk)—100 (50) + 100 (50) + 100 (50) + 100 yards

Walk—100 yards

Run (Walk)—100 (50) + 100 (50) + 100 (50) + 100 yards

Walk—100 yards

JUMP TRAINING DRILLS

Jumping is the second movement utilizing elastic strength. Although jumping requires slightly less coordination than running, the balance and strength demands are higher. There is not often as much thought put into progression of jump training as there is to sprinting; however, if anything, the progression is even more important. The amount of force delivered on impact when landing from a vertical jump is at least three to four times bodyweight.[31] If we start adding jumps off boxes or resisted jumping without a solid foundation of strength, we are increasing the impact forces to the bones and the eccentric strain to muscles and tendons. Disaster awaits.

Because impact forces to the knees are significant and because it is likely novice athletes lack both the lower-extremity strength and control to perform the movement efficiently, it is best to start the progression with single-repetition linear jumping and then gradually advance the vertical jumping components. There is more room for progression with advanced and elite-level athletes, yet it never hurts to reinforce fundamentals when it comes to the prep phase. In fact, it is sometimes best to hold to the same progression.

When we think of the progression of jump training, we want to emphasize explosive power, eccentric control with landing, and foot reactivity. These are the qualities that carry over into improved performance on the field.

At the same time, programming jump training with a gradual progression of load and volume also facilitates an improved stretch-reflex response and connective tissue strengthening to the tendons and bones. Jump training also develops strength in the calves without adding excessive muscle bulk that Olympic sprint coaches believe negatively impacts foot mechanics during the swing phase of running.

STANDING LONG JUMP

The standing long jump (SLJ) is the most basic movement we use to teach an appropriate posterior weight shift and start position, explosive movement, and controlled eccentric landing. The athlete is training to "accept" the ground, not impact it.

The most appropriate progression is to first have the athlete "stick" the landing, and then repeat for repetitions, but with the primary emphasis on form. Although there is less impact compared to a vertical jump, linear jumping places compressive and shear forces on the knee to meet the demands of stopping both vertical and forward momentum.

Once an athlete can demonstrate consistent form in both the jump and landing, you can increase the distance and speed.

Photos 3.8 a–d Standing Long Jump
The landing should always be with the athlete on balance or leaning forward.

The goals for novice football athletes for SLJ distance are:

- *8 feet for linemen—offensive, defensive linemen*
- *8½ feet for mid-skill—running back, tight end, linebackers, quarterbacks*
- *9 feet for skill—kicker, punter, wide receivers, defensive backs*

Again, considerations for the application or benchmarks for athletes of different sports is tied to bodyweight. You can expect lighter athletes to achieve longer distances.

For advanced or elite football athletes, instead of focusing on single standing long jumps, which we assume are at least nine feet, the emphasis moves to long jumps in series to further enhance foot reactivity and explosive movement in succession.

These can be performed as either three successive standing long jumps or the more advanced "triple jump" form, where the athlete jumps from two feet, lands, and propels forward off first one foot and then the other to land on both feet. There should not be a significant difference between the distance covered by each jump as the athlete develops good foot and ankle reactivity and explosive lower-extremity strength.

Advanced or elite athletes should be able to cover 10 yards in three successive long jumps.

TWO-LEG HOP, ONE-LEG HOP

Photos 3.9 a–d Hops

These side to side hops are excellent for training ankle stability with reactivity.

Hopping is included in our programming primarily to improve foot reactivity and ankle strength and stability. By having an athlete maintain straight knees and a slight forward lean, the calves and dorsiflexors have to react rapidly to propel forward using only the ankles and feet. Your cueing should be for the force to be directed forward rather than up—it is multiple quick hops rather than a "bunny hop" motion.

When an athlete demonstrates proficiency with the two-leg hops, progress the drill to single-leg hops, maintaining the emphasis on rapid ankle movement rather than a "bounding" motion.

The most effective method for teaching the movement is to use the sideline and yardage hash marks. The athletes should have their arms close to their sides, focusing on jumping just far enough to maintain weight on the balls of the foot without full foot contact.

Emphasize the "hopping on hot coals" motion on or between the hash marks along the sideline to improve ankle strength and reactivity. This drill can be varied to use different directions to train ankle control in multiple planes.

GOALPOST TOUCHES

As your athletes continue to demonstrate improved control in the linear jumps, you should also be addressing vertical jumping. With goalpost touches, a vertical jump drill, athletes assume a squat stance with hands below the knees, back flat, and head up. The drill is to jump vertically and reach with both hands to try to touch the goal post crossbar.

Photos 3.10 a–c Goalpost Touch

Upon hitting the ground, the athlete should jump back up as quickly as possible. Staying on the balls of the feet and minimizing ground contact is key.

With younger athletes, you may have to hang towels over the crossbar to give them a better chance of success. Using goalpost touches can be more engaging than standard vertical jumps because of its goal-directed focus. Start with single jumps, with a reset between each repetition, and progress to where the goal is to hit the ground and rhythmically jump back up, like dribbling a basketball, minimizing contact time with the ground.

ROCKETS

Rockets are similar to goalpost touches, but are designed to train maximal force production through a larger range of motion. Rather than taking a half-squat position as in the goalpost touches, the athlete will squat down and put fingers between the feet, behind the toes—ideally touching the ground.

With the head up and back flat, the athlete jumps as high as possible, reaching with both hands. Upon landing, the athlete reassumes the deep squat stance and repeats the drill beginning from a dead stop at the bottom of the motion.

Performing the movement through this larger range of motion challenges an athlete's ability to eccentrically absorb the landing while maintaining a good posterior weight shift and quickly reversing the momentum.

BOX JUMPS

Box jumps are an incredibly effective tool for developing explosive strength and jumping and landing techniques. Assuming they are performed correctly, box jumps potentiate the nervous system for gains in strength and size. However, they are far and away the most poorly applied tool used by many coaches. Watching athletes—and even the general population in the case of many CrossFit® gyms—perform 20 or 30 box jumps in succession or seeing maximal box jumps used between high-volume lower-extremity work is painful to watch.

The key benefit of box jumps is to decrease joint stress while expressing power and practicing solid landing mechanics. With a reduced landing height compared to a vertical jump, a box jump has significantly less compressive stress and less shear stress at the knee compared to the broad jump. It is also easily scalable, allowing a gradual increase in box height and volume as an athlete's performance improves, similar to increasing intensity and volume with weight training.

Quality of these jumps is more important than quantity. Make sure your athletes maximize hip extension and land with sound technique. The height of the box should be indicated by the highest height at which an athlete can land in the same position as how the jump started.

Start your athletes with a focus on jumping up and stepping down. Once they can demonstrate good control and performance, increasing the box height, adding directional changes, load, or reactive qualities by jumping on and off will facilitate development of higher physical qualities of athletic development.

Photos 3.11 a–b Box Jump and Landing
The starting position and landing position should look almost identical on a proper box jump.

EYE OF THE COACH

Another option to challenge an athlete with jumps is to begin at the bottom position of the squat in a static hold, and then accelerate upward without a counter movement. The small dip prior to jumping primes the stretch reflex for assisting the jump.

Starting from a dead stop forces an athlete to generate a maximal muscular contraction, and lends itself well to sports that require an explosive start from a dead stop, such as sprinting, swimming, or football.

SPRINT DRILLS

In the realm of football, the 40-yard dash has taken center stage for measuring an athlete's speed. Casual fans can recite a wide receiver's 40 time—there are strength programs specifically designed to improve a player's performance at the Combine or Pro Day.

While it has become the standard for testing, it is far from the ideal test or distance when it comes to the speed demands of sports. There are few instances in organized sports where an athlete is called upon to run in a straight line, unimpeded for 40 yards. When it comes to sprinting in athletics, the battle is won and lost in the first 20 yards and because of that, the bulk of coaching and training should take place in that range.

It is through consistent training of the start and acceleration phase of sprinting that the most profound benefits will materialize on the field. The coach's eye should be directed at perfecting an athlete's form in initiating the movement and over the first 10 yards.

The two drills we prefer for training initiation and acceleration are what we call the "Hurry Go Get Em" drill and a healthy dose of 20-yard dashes.

HURRY GO GET EM

This drill also helps build competitiveness as a bonus to technique in the initiation of sprinting. Two athletes begin in a line, head-to-toe in the pushup position. On your whistle, both athletes will explode up and sprint 10 yards. The athlete in front has to make it 10 yards untouched, while the athlete behind tries to catch the other.

Photos 3.12 a–b Hurry Go Get Em
Ideally, you want to see the leg coming under the body and the body to be aligned and balanced for a strong start.

By focusing on how the athletes get off the ground, you can see restrictions in mobility at the hips or spine, and the ability to rapidly display force when pushing off the ground. You could perform this drill with a single athlete, but we have found that whenever possible, adding an element of competition inspires greater effort from athletes and helps break monotony in training.

> ## EYE OF THE COACH
>
> *As your athletes come off the ground, you should see the eyes and chest lead, and the body in the same plane as a sprinter coming off the line.*
>
> *If they cannot get off the ground correctly in a good sprinting position, you know there may be a mobility issue in the ankle, knee, or hip, or a strength deficit you can address in the lifting program. You can also modify the drill to start in a pushup position and then progress to lying flat on the ground.*

20-YARD DASH

We prefer using 20-yard dashes for coaching technique because it allows us to again focus on the first 10 yards of the sprint, with a little more opportunity to watch and refine technique. The starting position can be from whichever stance is most applicable to the particular sport or position, yet it is often most beneficial to start from the typical sprinter's start position to train the coordination and balance of an explosive push-off.

With the primary emphasis on coaching technique, the repetitions are kept low. The rest periods will be a little longer between sets, about one minute recovery for every second of sprinting.

We want to place the emphasis on the athletes learning what it feels like to deliver force through the ground and maintain form as they accelerate forward. Performing this drill to the point of significant fatigue and diminishing returns is counter-productive. Those coaches who think a good sprint workout is one that has the athletes puking or passing out at the end is misguided as to the purpose of training for speed.

KEEP YOUR PURPOSE IN MIND

These drills should ultimately form the backbone of your running and jumping program, particularly when facilitating an athlete's entry or return to training.

Remember to think through the needs of your athletes throughout the season. There should always be a purpose behind your training selections and a reasoning behind the training variables of volume, intensity, and frequency based on the goals for training.

BUILDING THE BASE OF THE PYRAMID

To revisit the Hierarchy of Athletic Development: Work capacity and movement efficiency make up the base of the pyramid. During the prep phase, you should devote the majority of the training time for that foundation; however, remember to also maintain attention to all of the levels of training.

When approached from the big picture of lifting, running, and jumping, this prep phase first builds work capacity, and also addresses strength, power, and speed on a secondary level.

This theme will repeat itself as we dive deeper into the typical programming progression.

As the athletes progress and you place more emphasis on higher-level skills and movements, there is an ebb and flow of emphasis in the primary training quality; still, you never abandon any one element.

Even when an elite-level athlete is training primarily for power and speed, all the way at the top of the pyramid, complex training or tempo runs continue to be used as a warmup or work capacity activity, just at a lesser magnitude than with a novice or advanced-level athlete.

Taking these principles into account, we can create an example of a possible prep phase, including the weightlifting and running components.

SAMPLE FOUR-WEEK PREP PHASE

WARMING UP

Any warmup before running or jumping should consist of a continuous series of movements for 30 yards, interlaced with muscle activation exercises, followed by eight-second stretches of the activated muscle group. There are countless options and routines; just make sure the athletes are moving fully through all planes of motion—sagittal, frontal, and transverse. Focus on common problem areas such as the spine, hips, hamstrings, and ankles.

Increase the intensity of the warmup by injecting 80-percent max speed runs for 30 yards. Have the athletes return via a backward run at the same speed. Remember that the goal is not just to "loosen up." This is another opportunity to train motor function, body awareness, and control, so be precise in teaching warmup activations and movements.

You can develop components of the mechanics of jumping or sprinting. We have even seen coaches use tumbling drills to good effect to challenge balance and coordination with motions that are simple for young children, but may be taxing for many high-level athletes.

Think of it this way, a 15-minute warmup performed four times a week for 12 weeks ends up being 12 hours of training time. Don't waste the opportunity to gain better movement.

WEEK ONE

DAY ONE (MONDAY)

LIFT

Box Jumps—x 5

Single-Leg Squat—2x6

Complex One—2-3x6

Step-Ups—3x5, left and right, at 20-percent bodyweight

Military Press—3x6, at 45-percent bodyweight

Abs

RUN

4x100-yard Tempo Runs, at 17–16–15-second pace, based on athlete size, as described on page 76

STRETCH

DAY TWO (TUESDAY)

Warmup

Standing Long Jump—x 6

Mach Sprint Drills—4x10 yards down and back, A-Skips, Butt Kicks, A-Runs

Double-Leg Hops—3x10 yards

Hurry Go Get Em—5x10 yards

Timed 20-yard Dash—x 5

With true sprinting, for full recovery, your athletes need to recover about one minute for each second they run. This allows full recovery of all the faculties we are training in sprinting.

Walk 20 yards, and then jog 20 yards all the way around the track. This helps bring down the heart rate and keeps the blood from pooling.

STRETCH

DAY THREE (WEDNESDAY)

LIFT

Box jumps—x5

Single-Leg Squat—2x6

Complex One—3x6

Step-Ups—3x5+5, at 20-percent bodyweight

Bench Press—3x6, at 45-percent 1RM

Abs

RUN

4x100-yard Tempo Runs, at 17–16–15-second pace, based on athlete size

STRETCH

DAY FOUR (THURSDAY)

Warmup—Change exercise and movement patterns regularly to keep athletes mentally fresh and receptive

Goal Post Touches —2x10

Mach Sprint Drills—4x10 yards

Double-Leg Hops—3x10 yards

Wall Marches—3 series of 7–10 reps, one step on the whistle

Tempo Runs—8x100 yards, at 17–16–15-second pace based on athlete size, four runs, then walk 100 yards and repeat for four runs

Walk and Jog—20-yard intervals

STRETCH

DAY FIVE (FRIDAY)

LIFT

Box Jumps—x5

Single-Leg Squat—2x6

Complex One—2x6

Step-Ups—3x5, left and right, at 20-percent bodyweight

Military Press—3x6, at 45-percent bodyweight

RUN

4x100-yard Tempo Runs, at 17–16–15-second pace, based on athlete size

STRETCH

WEEK TWO

DAY ONE (MONDAY)

LIFT

Box Jumps—x 5

Single-Leg Squat—2x6

Complex One—3x6

Step-Ups—3x5, left and right, at 25-percent bodyweight

Military Press—3x6, at 50-percent bodyweight

Abs

RUN

5x100-yard Tempo Runs, at 17–16–15-second pace, based on athlete size

STRETCH

DAY TWO (TUESDAY)

Warmup—
Continue to manipulate the movements

Standing Long Jump—x 7 reps

Mach Sprint Drills—5x10 yards

Double-Leg Hops—5x10 yards

Hurry Go Get Em—7x10 yards

Timed 20-Yard Sprints—x 6

Walk and Jog

STRETCH

DAY THREE (WEDNESDAY)

LIFT

Box Jumps—x 5

Single-Leg Squat—2x6

Complex One—2x6

Step-Ups—3x5, left and right, at 25-percent bodyweight

Bench Press—3x6, at 50-percent 1RM

Abs

RUN

4x100-yard Tempo Runs, at 16–15–14-second pace, based on athlete size

Notice the pace is now one second faster than during Week One.

STRETCH

DAY FOUR (THURSDAY)

Warmup

Goal Post Touches—3x8

*Mach Sprint Drills—
5x10 yards each*

Double-Leg Hops—4x15 yards

*Wall Marches—3 series,
8–10 reps per set*

*Tempo Runs—5x100 yards,
at 17–16–15-second pace,
100-yard recovery walk, then
5x100 yards at 17–16–15-second pace based on athlete size*

Walk and Jog

STRETCH

DAY FIVE (FRIDAY)

LIFT

Box Jumps—x 5

Single-Leg Squat—2x6

Complex One—3x6

*Step-Ups—3x5, left and right,
at 25-percent bodyweight*

*Military Press—3x6,
at 50-percent bodyweight*

Abs

RUN

*5x100-yard Tempo Runs,
at 17–16–15-second pace
based on athlete size*

Walk and Jog

STRETCH

WEEK THREE

DAY ONE (MONDAY)

LIFT

Box Jumps—x 5

Single-Leg Squat—2x6

Complex One—4x6

*Back Squat—
3x5 at 55-percent 1RM*

*Military Press—
3x6 at 55-percent bodyweight*

Abs

RUN

*5x100-yard Tempo Runs,
at 17–16–15-second pace
based on athlete size*

Walk and Jog

STRETCH

DAY TWO (TUESDAY)

*Warmup—Continue to
manipulate the movements*

Standing Long Jump—x 7 reps

Mach Sprint Drills—5x10 yards

Double-Leg Hops—5x15 yards

Hurry Go Get Em—7x10 yards

Timed 10-Yard Sprints—x 5

*Break for 6-8 minutes with walk,
jog, stretch, water*

Timed 20-yard Sprints—x 5

Walk and Jog

STRETCH

DAY THREE (WEDNESDAY)

LIFT

Box Jumps—x 5

Single-Leg Squat—2x6

Complex One—2x6

Back Squat—3x5, at 55-percent 1RM

Bench Press—3x6, at 55-percent 1RM

Abs

RUN

5x100-yard Tempo Runs, at 16–15–14-second pace based on athlete size

Walk and Jog

STRETCH

DAY FOUR (THURSDAY)

Warmup

Rockets—3x8

Mach Sprint Drills—5x15 yards

Two-Leg Hops—5x15 yards

Wall Marches—3 series, 8-10 reps

Tempo Runs—5x100 yards at 17–16–15-second pace, walk 100 yards, 5x100 yards at 17–16–15-second pace based on athlete size

Walk and Jog

STRETCH

DAY FIVE (FRIDAY)

LIFT

Box Jumps—x 5

Single-Leg Squat—2x6

Complex One—3x6

Back Squat—3x5, at 55-percent 1RM

Military Press—3x6, at 55-percent bodyweight

Abs

RUN

5x100-yard Tempo Runs, at 17–16–15-second pace based on athlete size

Walk and Jog

STRETCH

WEEK FOUR

DAY ONE (MONDAY)

LIFT

Box Jumps—x 5

Single-Leg Squat—2x6

Complex One—2x6

*Back Squat—3x5,
   at 50-percent 1RM*

*Military Press—3x6,
   at 45-percent bodyweight*

Abs

RUN

*4x100-yard Tempo Runs,
   at 16–15–14-second pace
   based on athlete size*

Walk and jog

STRETCH

DAY TWO (TUESDAY)

Warmup

Standing Long Jump—x 5

Mach Sprint Drills—4x10 yards

Single-Leg Hop—3x10 yards

Hurry Go Get Em—5x10 yards

Timed 10-Yard Sprints—x 4

Rest x 5 minutes

Timed 20-yard Sprints x 4

Walk and Jog

STRETCH

DAY THREE (WEDNESDAY)

LIFT

Box Jumps—x 5

Single-Leg Squat—2x6

Complex One— 2x6

*Back Squat—3x5,
   at 50-percent 1RM*

*Bench Press—3x6,
   at 45-percent 1RM*

Abs

RUN

*5x60-yard Tempo Runs,
   at 8–7.5-second pace
   based on athlete size,
   greater or less than 250
   pounds*

Walk and Jog

STRETCH

DAY FOUR (THURSDAY)

Warmup

Rockets—2x10

Single-Leg Hops—3x10 yards

Mach Sprint Drills—4x10 yards

Wall Marches—3 series of 6 reps, three steps on the whistle

Tempo Runs—4x100 yards at 16–15–14-second pace, walk 100 yards, 4x100 yards at 16–15–14-second pace based on athlete size

Walk and Jog

STRETCH

DAY FIVE (FRIDAY)

LIFT

Box Jumps—x 5

Single-Leg Squat—2x6

Complex One—2x6

Back Squat—3x5, at 50-percent 1RM

Military Press—3x6, at 40-percent bodyweight

Abs

RUN

4x100-yard Tempo Runs, at 16–15–14-second pace based on athlete size

Walk and Jog

STRETCH

MEETING THE BENCHMARKS

If your athletes have met the benchmark loads in the complexes at the end of this four-week cycle, they should be physically prepared to advance into the core programming

If they have not met the benchmark loads or totals, you can repeat the cycle. To reiterate, completion of this stage is non-negotiable. If it takes another week or if it takes another month, the athletes need to achieve a baseline level of performance to progress into higher-intensity training.

Young athletes who are just beginning strength training can take up to six months to achieve an adequate strength base. We have taken middle school athletes through an entire off-season with just small variations in the prep phase and seen incredible gains. If the foundation of strength and work capacity is not adequate, the risk of overtraining or injury during the off-season training will increase.

As you will see, even though this system is engineered to allow for recovery and gradual progression, the training demands will significantly tax an athlete's abilities. A weak foundation will lead to cracks in performance.

CHAPTER FOUR
SYSTEMATIC PROGRAM DESIGN

TRAINING CYCLE PRINCIPLES

Every aspect of this system exists along a continuum. We hold true to fundamental qualities and principles of programming, while manipulating the training variables across a range for lifters of all ages and experience levels. You can advance or regress the basic principles over the span of weeks, months, seasons, and years to meet the needs of any athlete in any sport at any level.

Once we establish the application of the core principles to the training variables, we can see how the shifting emphasis of the program allows optimal progression for the athletes of all training stages.

However, before we start writing a "book of training" for your athletes, we first have to learn how to write the "sentences of programming."

The most critical errors we see in applying periodization models or training systems across different groups of athletes are in failing to account for different goals based on the experience and training age or ability of each athlete, and then understanding how to effectively manipulate the variables to reach a particular goal. Too many young athletes are loaded up under a bar and thrown into a training regimen of barbell training before they are physically ready or capable of performing the required lifts—the Olympic lifts in particular.

There are no plug-and-play programs that allow for sustained gains or have built-in progressions of both training intensity and volume over a longer span than eight or twelve weeks. However, by using the Soviet methods and principles, you can take athletes all the way from introductory bodyweight training up through college and the professional ranks without a need to completely overhaul the training program.

The System utilizes sequential four-week training cycles that follow an undulating wave pattern of volume and intensity manipulation. The undulating pattern offers constant variation in the training stimulus that results in continuous gains and built-in recovery. Rather than a linear model or block periodization, where there is a constant tug-of-war for adaptation to particular stresses in the weightroom, undulating waves of volume and intensity introduce a simultaneous stimulus to the multiple physical qualities required of a high-performing athlete.

The best way to describe our approach is that it is a system of checks and balances for programming that facilitates the development of strength, power, and speed, while addressing the recovery demands of high-intensity training. When each four-week cycle is designed to build upon the previous month's work, athletes are capable of extending the training window into and through the competitive season, without the risk of breakdown or overtraining often seen in other methods.

From a bird's eye view, our system looks a little different from most models of periodization, with a progressive increase in training volume and intensity over the course of an off-season, rather than the inverse relationship seen in most programs.

This approach allows the athletes to progressively build work capacity and training intensity throughout the off-season and then continue to progress training intensity throughout the extended competitive season.

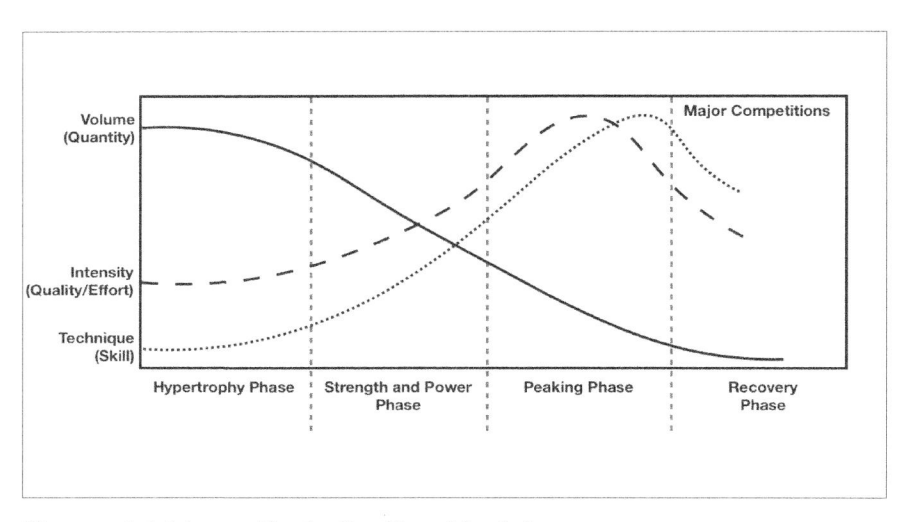

Figure 4.1 Linear Periodization Model

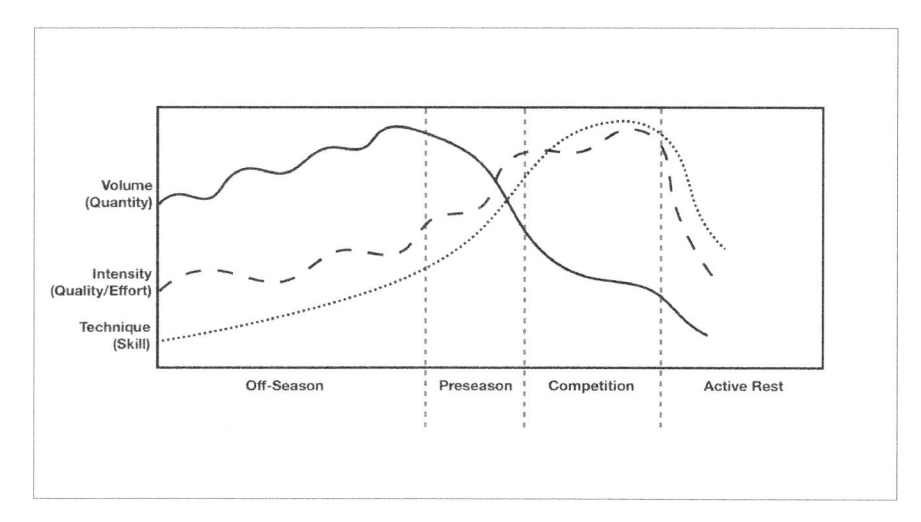

Figure 4.2 The System's Undulating Periodization Model

The off-season ideally consists of three four-week training cycles. The preseason is a single cycle. Over the course of a single four-week training cycle, the volume of work undulates weekly and from session to session, and the training intensity also undulates over the course of the month.

The ultimate goal is to provide progressive overload into higher training volumes and intensities as the athlete develops, with built-in periods of unloading where both intensity and volume fall to allow recovery periods within each cycle.

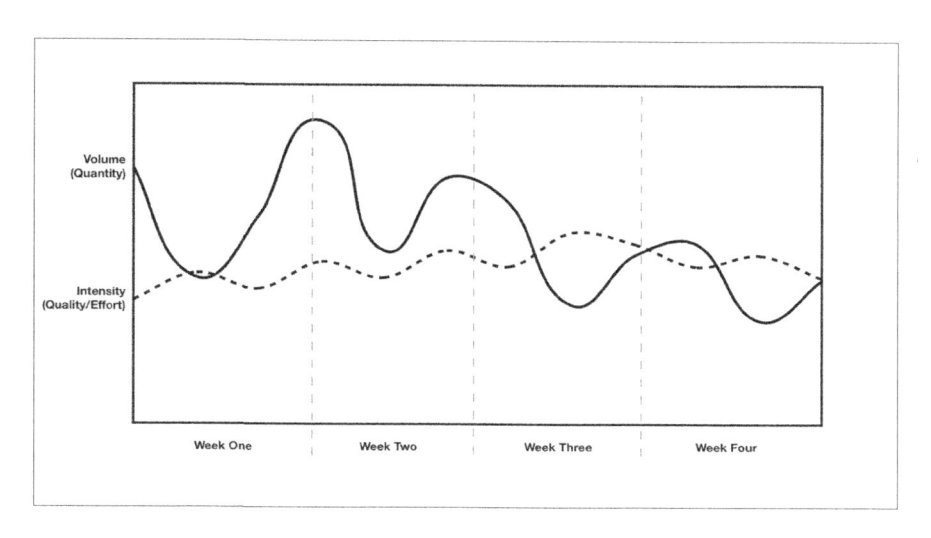

Figure 4.3 Example of Four-Week Program

Over the larger span of the training seasons—off-season, preseason, in-season—we address each of the physical qualities of work capacity, strength, power, and speed. Depending on the time of the season and the emphasis for the sport or athlete, there are varying levels of emphasis on the different qualities at different times.

Just as under Vermeil's Hierarchy shown on page 23, we address all the necessary qualities to some degree, yet we tweak the volume or time spent on each. During each particular cycle, there should be one quality that takes precedent and is the primary focus of a training cycle, while secondarily addressing the other qualities.

The question becomes how to allocate the time for each athlete. Think of it as having 100 "points" to allocate within each training cycle. You need to distribute those points across the qualities of work capacity, strength, power, and speed—and not just with lifting, but with running and jumping as well. It will be your decision where the time is spent and what is most important at that particular point in the year.

Early in the season for a novice athlete, you may allot 40 points toward work capacity, 35 to strength work, 15 to power, and 10 on speed work. As the season moves on, some of those work capacity points may move into the strength, power, or speed columns.

You still have to work within a limited total, yet the program adapts with the athlete.

A lot of those choices and decisions are developed through the eye of the coach and we will dive deeper into that end of the pool later.

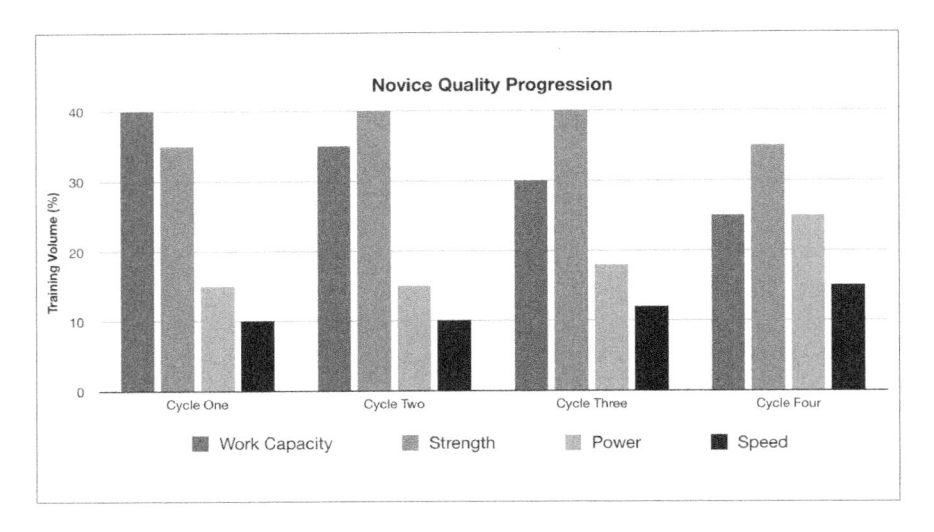

Figure 4.4 Novice Progression

Throughout the process, is important to keep in mind that what we do as strength coaches is a combination of science and art. The science demands that we know why something works. That is imperative for the selection process, and if you know how something works, you will know how to progress it.

If you do not know why something works and you choose to use it, maybe you get lucky… and maybe you do not. When you think, "This is great! My athletes are getting better," you need to ask yourself, "Where do I go from here?" If you do not know why something is working, you will not know how to progress or adapt it for continued gains. That is the importance of the science.

The art of coaching is saying to yourself, "We need to squat; we know that is important." The question now is, "Should we front squat, back squat, or split-squat? What weight should we start with? How many sets and reps? How can I best teach this movement?"

These questions rarely come with clear, definitive answers, and your path will have to take into account the variables. This is the art of coaching. If you asked these questions of 50 coaches, you might get 50 different answers, and not all of them would be in your best interest to follow.

In the field of strength and conditioning, this is the aspect that takes the most time and commitment to develop and refine. Ultimately, cultivating balance between the art and science of coaching is what separates the elite from the average.

At first glance, this approach can seem like an overwhelming method of programming, as most coaches are unfamiliar with undulating intensity and volume. It feels safer to go with dedicated sets and reps or defined periods for strength, hypertrophy, or speed.

That is understandable, and while taking a standard approach can certainly yield positive results, it will inevitably lead to less clear decisions and progressions down the road. You may be taking a safer route in the short term, just to pull your hair out in the future.

We will peel back the layers and look at each training variable discussed in The Foundation section beginning on page 19. Once you appreciate the basics in application of the core principles to designing a periodized strength and power program, you will see that this system will continue to grow, develop, and produce the further you take it.

EXERCISE SELECTION

Exercise selection emphasizes whole-body strength movements performed explosively.

In our decades in the weightroom, we have seen about 1,000 different exercises and variations on top of variations meant to target different muscles, improve postural imbalances, enhance body control, or influence any number of other issues.

The strongest, most prolific strength athletes of the past and present reached their physical peaks through a steady diet of the same basic weightlifting movements. They squatted; they pressed; they pulled, and they performed variations of the Olympic lifts.

These exercises are simple; they are effective, and they have stood the test of time.

The problem is that many training programs sacrifice fundamentals for more exotic options and are devoid of a significant portion of this very short list. To top it off, sadly, more and more weightrooms have only a handful of athletes correctly performing these fundamental movements.

The simple collection of foundational training movements employed consists of:

SQUATS—
back squat, front squat, and others

POWER MOVEMENTS—
clean, snatch, jerks

PRESSING MOVEMENTS—
bench press, military press, push-press

PULLING MOVEMENTS—
clean pulls, snatch pulls

POSTERIOR CHAIN MOVEMENTS—
RDL, hyperextension and reverse hyperextension, good mornings, trap bar deadlifts, and others

That simplicity can feel like a severely restricted menu of options—anxiety may be setting in. Learning how to design effective programming for your athletes is no different than learning how to read. You start with letters, then you learn words; eventually you learn sentences, and you take off from there. Our goal is to keep it simple.

Think of these categories and movements as the "essential few." There will be room for the addition of other supplemental exercises, like rowing, pullups or abdominal work; however, these will be a small percentage of the total program. Restricting your coaching and the training to a narrow range will improve movement quality and your coach's eye. That does not mean sacrificing variety within these movements, yet the goal should always be to first get strong with the simple before you get strong with the complex.

We are using the principles of weightlifting to enhance athleticism and make better athletes; we are not trying to make weightlifters out of our athletes. However, using the barbell and Olympic lifts and explosive full-body training creates the strongest and most powerful athletes.

One of the most important lessons we learned from our time studying with Coach Goldstein was on the relative importance of a movement in carryover of power and performance in sports. When he asked us what exercises we felt were most important for generating functional strength and power for sports, we all agreed. There was—and is—no doubt that squats and cleans should take priority as two of the most important exercises for developing strength and explosive power through the lower body and trunk.

Picture these: If you are a boxer, sit down on the ground and see how much force you can generate in your punches. If you are a shot putter, sit on the ground and see how far you can throw the shot. If you are a baseball pitcher, see how fast you can throw the ball without your legs involved. Any athletic motion on dry land is predicated on transferring force from the body into the ground. When an athlete lacks lower-body strength or the ability to deliver force into the ground, performance will suffer.

Coach Goldstein suggested that if squats and cleans were so important to an athlete's performance, a clear majority of our training volume should be dedicated to those two movements. We were again all in agreement. Obviously, we should spend the bulk of our training on the movements that have the greatest net effect on performance.

Unfortunately, the first time he analyzed our programs, we were doing upward of 40 percent of our total volume in presses and significantly less in cleans and squats. That teaching moment was a clear demonstration of our personal detachment from reality, and an opportunity for reflection toward applying what should have been common sense.

Taking the lesson to heart, in terms of relative importance to developing full-body strength and power, the training movements should be in this order of priority:

Squat—Clean—Press—Pulls
Snatch—Jerk—Posterior Chain

This again is based on relative importance in carryover to sport. As we will see in our program design, different levels of athletes and different times of the year may see a change in the importance or priority of each movement. We want the primary emphasis to always be on squats and cleans to develop full-body strength and explosive qualities, while pressing, pulling, deadlifting, and the Olympic lifts will take a secondary position.

Now, before you begin to debate that a different movement or lift is more important than our recommendation, recognize that the order we suggest is based on our collective experience. There will certainly be some exceptions to this general hierarchy, particularly with novice-level athletes.

The novice must initially establish confidence and basic strength in the strength movements of the squat, press, and posterior chain. By first building full-body strength and stability, athletes are more physically prepared for the higher-intensity Olympic lifting to follow.

Priority goes to fortifying squatting, pressing, and hinging because if an athlete cannot effectively control the more simple movements, the more technical and complex movements will break down almost immediately, especially under load.

You can still train cleans, pulls, and the snatch to address explosive qualities, power development, and technique. However, in many cases, the jerk will be excluded from programming for the novice. The jerk, when performed appropriately, is a technical lift demanding a high degree of full-body acceleration, coordination, and stability, particularly with a significant load.

With an emphasis on simpler overhead lifts like strict military pressing or the push-press, strength and coordination in the overhead position can be properly developed with minimal risk. That is why you will see such an emphasis on use of the complexes with light loads early in the prep phase to train both technique and full-body strength in the most critical movements.

THE OLYMPIC LIFTING CONTROVERSY

In recent years with the increasing emphasis on safety in strength training and what is termed "sport specific" training, the Olympic lifts have fallen out of favor with many strength coaches. The argument is that if you are not competing in Olympic lifting, there are better options for training explosive strength that translate more readily to sports performance, without the risks and strain inherent in rapidly moving heavy weights.

Variations of medicine ball throws or more creative exercises have taken the place of cleans, snatches, and jerks in the strength programming of many teams as coaches try to reduce those risks. In our opinion, the pendulum has swung too far away from using the movements that have consistently produced the strongest and most explosive athletes in the world.

The main goal of the Olympic lifts is to generate maximal power and explosive strength in the entire body through large ranges of motion, particularly for the lower extremities.

The differences you will most often find between the training regimen of an Olympic weightlifter and of athletes performing more "sport specific" training are that weightlifters consistently take the lower extremities through high-speed, large range-of-motion exercises. Many of the substituted movements and exercises used by a well-intentioned strength coach do not come close to demanding and developing the flexibility, coordination, and force output demanded by the weightlifting exercises.

Photo 4.1 Using Olympic Lifts
Using large amplitude Olympic lifts develops explosive strength and stability at the extremes of the joint positions—positions the body is likely to encounter on the field of play.

It is true that subjecting an athlete to a full snatch or jerk with a substantial amount of weight without the proper instruction or progression will often result in injury. However, that holds true for any exercise. It is not the fault of the exercise, but rather the coach's fault for failing to prepare the athlete to succeed.

Dynamic sports like football or basketball require suppleness and strength expressed through large ranges of motion; the Olympic lifts are more effective at facilitating those qualities than a medicine ball toss. If you assess an athlete to be physically capable of performing the movements safely and if the lifts are programmed and coached effectively and progressed in both weight and complexity, many concerns diminish.

You will discover that when implemented effectively and appropriately, the benefits of the Olympic lifts far outweigh the drawbacks.

POWER DEVELOPMENT

A significantly high volume of Olympic lifting is best left to the athletes with at least a few years of training under their belts. For developing athletes such as these, the power and explosive qualities can be addressed through jumping or plyometric training as the Olympic lifts are coached and refined over time.

After mastering technical efficiency and form, no matter what the movement, speed should always be the priority. Although strength and muscle hypertrophy are important in the world of sports, the rapid expression of that strength is what separates athletes on the field of play.

In the sport of powerlifting, the speed of the movement is not critical. The goal is to lift the maximum weight, however long it takes. On the football field, the strongest linemen will rarely succeed if they cannot rapidly translate that strength to control an oncoming defender. A shot putter who can military press hundreds of pounds will not take home a medal without the ability to explosively accelerate the entire body to throw the shot.

Power and speed are the qualities at the top of the pyramid for athletic success; use every opportunity to coach speed and acceleration.

Training an athlete to move the bar as fast as possible through the concentric portion of the lift with a controlled eccentric phase trains the muscles and nervous system to recruit the largest and most powerful muscle fibers and motor neurons.

The largest motor units will not engage unless the load or the speed of the lift calls for at least 50 percent of the maximum force of muscle contraction. The high-force, high-velocity performance of these core exercises creates the potential to produce large power outputs across a variety of load ranges.

Power output during the snatch and the clean has commonly been found to be greatest at loads equivalent to 70–85% of 1RM, which the Russian coaches intuitively learned decades earlier. Stimulating those large motor units provides the rapid force generating properties an athlete needs to excel in a sport.

At the Olympic Training Center in Colorado Springs, it was incredible to watch the athletes from the Soviet Union who defected to the United States before the Berlin Wall came down. The speed and technique they displayed in the lifts made it look like the bar jumped off the floor and over their heads. There was no wasted effort or movement as they accelerated the bar.

Watching the power and fluidity they displayed during other activities clearly demonstrated the transfer of their training to athletic performance. It became a point of emphasis for us from then on to always demand the athletes move the bar with the fastest speed they could handle.

If we train our athletes slow, they will be slow—train fast, and they will be fast.

THE STRENGTH MOVEMENTS

SQUAT VARIATIONS— BACK, FRONT, AND SINGLE-LEG

There is little debate about the importance of the squat as a critical fundamental human movement pattern. In strength and conditioning, no training movement has a greater effect on the entire body in not only strength and stability, but also in its hormonal and hypertrophic effects.

The value of the squat is analogous to throwing a rock into a pond. There is a splash where it hits, and then a cascade of ripples extends outward touching every part of the water's surface.

Similarly, the squat builds strength in the legs and hips, yet the entire trunk and even the arms get involved in stabilizing the load. In the 1970s, the always-controversial Arthur Jones claimed that his clients' arm size and strength could improve simply as a secondary effect from heavy squatting.

Photo 4.2 The Back Squat
Differences in body dimensions may necessitate different foot positions. The width of the squat stance should be adjusted to allow for maximal depth and postural alignment. There is no one-size-fits-all position for squatting.

In addition to muscular strength and stability, nearly every team sport is a lower-body game. Chuck Knoll, former head coach of the Pittsburgh Steelers, used to categorize his athletes as "upper-body" players and "lower-body" players. The best were almost always "lower-body" players.

Add to that the fact that squatting under load improves stability between the trunk, pelvis, and hips, and you can see why squats should always be the cornerstone of any athletic training program.

We addressed the importance of single-leg squats and overhead squats as screens during the prep phase. After the screening, these movements continue to be part of our programming both in the warmup and as training movements.

However, the question inevitably arises as to which squat is "best." We have choices between back squats, front squats, split squats, and every "Russian" or "Bulgarian" variation under the sun. Each has its supporters and detractors, benefits and deficits, and a place in a well-rounded training program.

In reality, the "best" exercise is the exercise an athlete is capable of performing and that most efficiently addresses our needs. All of the variables and qualities used to determine an athlete's level of training have to be considered when choosing specific exercises, as well as the coach's teaching comfort and ability.

In terms of developing all of the qualities mentioned, in our minds the back squat is second to none. The back squat is superior in developing strength and hypertrophy gains, mostly because of the higher loads that can be used with the weight on the back and both feet on the ground. When beginning with the basics, the back squat is always our default.

First, before the bar goes on an athlete's back, we need to consider if the person can perform this movement well and if there a medical reason to use another lift.

The back squat places significant compression on the lumbar spine, as well as shear forces on the discs in cases of poor form or mobility deficits. If an athlete has a history of low back issues from disc herniations, starting with back squats may run counter to our goal of developing strong, pain-free athletes. In that case, front squats or split squats that maintain a more upright trunk might be a better option, although the argument could be that if we strengthen the back and coach the movement, back squatting should still be a viable option for almost every athlete.

Our focus is always on developing strength and building confidence in our athletes. Nothing builds confidence in a developing athlete faster than a steady addition of plates on the bar.

Photo 4.3 The Front Squat
The front squat demands a more upright torso at the bottom position compared to a back squat. This can reduce shear forces to the lumbar spine in particular.

The front squat is the second most-utilized squat variation we employ because it pairs nicely with the Olympic lifts and also provides an increased training effect for the quadriceps. Although this may be a better option to spare the lumbar spine, a high degree of shoulder and spinal mobility are required for good front squat form.

If an athlete has a history of patellofemoral pain or patellar tendonitis, the front squat will place more demand on the quads and compression at the knee, potentially causing irritation to the joint or tendons. That athlete may benefit from back squatting with a more vertical shin position.

Single-leg work has become increasingly popular in the strength and conditioning world over the past decade, particularly in "sport-specific" training. Because single-leg work also spares the compressive force to the low back, allows for correction of strength imbalances from side to side, and challenges the athlete's balance and coordination, some strength programs have abandoned standard barbell squats altogether.

While there is certainly a place for single-leg work in a long-term development program, it is not without its drawbacks. Sacroiliac joint issues will generally not respond well to split-stance or single-leg work because of the increased shear forces from a rotated pelvis.

On top of that, the coordination and balance demands may be so high for an athlete that any meaningful loading of the movement may not be possible for an extended period of time. Fixating on a particular exercise variation over all others while failing to account for the medical history or an athlete's ability is the epitome of hammering a round peg into a square hole.

The main point in training a squat variation is to achieve the lowest possible squatting position athletes can handle while maintaining optimal mechanics. As long as there are no prohibitory factors of having them go deep, they need to go deep.

The old evidence showing significant increases in knee ligament stress with deep squats[32] created a huge over-reaction to squatting deep, and in some cases to even squatting at all. Unfortunately, this fear has continued as evidence mounts against the dangers of deep squats.

Photos 4.4 a–d The Split Squat
Taking a 360-degree view while coaching the lifts ensures that you do not miss movement compensations such as a rotated pelvis or excessive weight shift.

Research out of the University of Alberta showed greater muscle EMG activity and relative muscular effort (RME) for the calves and ankle musculature as the load increases, and for the glutes with increased squat depth and load.[33]

For the quads, the increased RME was more depth-dependent than load-dependent, and we have seen less significant joint stress with squatting compared to knee extension exercise equipment when performed with good technique. Why would we avoid the most beneficial muscular activity of an exercise if the athlete can physically handle it? We continue to gain new evidence that the risk of squatting to full depth is no more harmful to an athlete's body than a parallel depth squat, assuming the athlete is capable of performing the lift with good form.[34]

The challenge in choosing the correct exercise and dosage is less science and more the art of coaching. You will not find a cookbook with specific recipes of what to give a particular athlete. Should we have our athletes squat deep on day one if they are terrible squatters? No. Should we even give them a bar if their form is less than ideal? Maybe not.

No matter an athlete's stage of training, a coach's job is to teach proper movement from simple to complex, to ensure progress, and to constantly challenge the abilities of the athletes.

Too many coaches are eager to load a bar and get athletes training, but if they cannot master the basics, they will never master the advanced movements.

Following a simple progression like that listed in Figure 4.5 allows athletes to build a foundation of movements with the squat from which they can expand outward.

BACK SQUAT	FRONT SQUAT	SINGLE-LEG VARIATIONS
Wall Squat with a Ball ↓ Overhead Squat with a Stick—Supported ↓ Overhead Squat with a Stick—Unsupported ↓ Overhead Squat with a Bar ↓ Back Squat	Goblet Squat ↓ Front Squat	Single-Leg Squat to a Bench ↓ Single-Leg Squat off a Bench ↓ Split Squat ↓ Split Squat with Rear-Foot Elevated ↓ Step-Up ↓ Lunge Variations ↓ Walking Lunge

Figure 4.5 Squat Teaching Progression

EYE OF THE COACH

One of the biggest challenges of coaching the squat is in teaching body mechanics and keeping the trunk erect, especially in the front squat. Popularized by Coach Dan John, a goblet squat with a dumbbell or kettlebell is a great, scalable way to train athletes to feel how to use their legs to lift the weight while maintaining an upright trunk. When they can show solid goblet squat form with 45 pounds, replace the 'bell with a bar. They should now have the feel of the movement.

PRESS—OVERHEAD, BENCH, INCLINE, PUSH-PRESS

The goal of each of the fundamental movements is in training the body to deliver force through the ground and moving explosively. The press is another of our foundational strength movements.

Photos 4.5 a–f The Overhead Press

Thoracic and shoulder mobility and stability are critical in avoiding excessive lean-back while pressing and achieving a strong finish position with the bar and arms in line with the ears and torso. Too many overhead presses turn into a standing incline press as athletes strain and arch under the load.

When most coaches think of a press, they think of the bench press. We can blame the NFL Combine and traditional bodybuilding routines for that, as there is certainly no shortage of time and effort dedicated to benching in gyms and weightrooms around the world.

Although the bench has its place in developing pressing strength, when it comes to sports performance and developing full-body strength, overhead pressing carries a much higher value. It is therefore a staple of our programming.

Overhead pressing demands anterior and posterior stability to the shoulders, trunk, and hips to maintain a neutral posture and efficient movement. An athlete with a strong and technically sound military press is an athlete who is probably total-body strong.

Particularly for novice-level athletes, a high percentage of the training volume should be dedicated to pressing overhead to develop strength, and also to prepare the body and shoulder girdle for the more dynamic Olympic lifts.

As proficiency with a strict military press improves and weights begin to move up, progressing into the push-press will support the transition toward power training.

Photos 4.6 a–d The Push Press
Utilizing leg drive in a push-press facilitates heavier loading in the progression of power development.

The push-press is nothing more than a cheated press, with a little assistance from the lower body to get the bar moving. It is a means to use more weight; however, an athlete first needs a solid foundation with the military press because adding load and speed to a weak motion is a recipe for disaster. An athlete should be able to perfect an overhead position where the arms are directly in line with the ears and the trunk is engaged and vertical.

Whenever possible, program your pressing movements in a standing posture to generate the connection between the lower and upper body in force production. In instances where you want to change the stress on the body or train for greater strength and hypertrophy, the incline and bench press are other options. The bench press can serve a valuable role in a program because, just like the back squat, it allows heavier loads for more upper-body strength and hypertrophy, but it is far from an ideal movement for most athletes.

An NFL scout told us in the early days of the Combine that the purpose of the bench press in testing was that it showed teams who the "workers" were. The expectation was that if an NFL hopeful demonstrated a strong performance in the bench press, he had dedicated a significant amount of effort into developing that strength. By that logic, he could be expected to put that same dedication toward the next level of competition. However, over time, the bench took on an identity of its own, where too much training time is dedicated to boosting bench totals at the expense of more productive exercises.

When programming incline or flat bench pressing, as soon as your athletes are on their backs, you have taken them out of an athletic position. Unless the sport somehow involves lying down and pushing something off the chest, the carryover to total-body strength and sport performance is limited. This is why, even though we utilize the bench and incline press in our programming, we remind you the goal is to develop explosive strength and power, not to wow the scouts at the Combine with the number of reps performed in succession.

EYE OF THE COACH

Watch for excessive spinal extension or lean-back in any of the overhead movements. The most common reason you will see this is limited shoulder or spinal mobility, preventing an athlete from extending the arms straight overhead.

You want to see the arms in line with the ears. When you do not see that, you need to spend some time addressing the mobility deficits. In the case of weakness limiting a press overhead, cue the athlete to bring the chin down toward the chest as the bar approaches eye level. This slight flexion of the head will often help limit excessive extension compensation. The chin does not have to touch the chest; it is just a small tuck. With a chin tuck, the bar has to go directly up.

OVERHEAD PRESS	BENCH PRESS	INCLINE PRESS
Strict Military Press ↓ Dumbbell Military Press—can add alternating arm motion ↓ Push-Press ↓ Dumbbell Push-Press—can add alternating arm motion ↓ Jerk	Push-Up ↓ Barbell Bench Press ↓ Dumbbell Bench Press	Decline Push-Up ↓ Incline Barbell Press ↓ Dumbbell Incline Press ↓ Landmine Press

Figure 4.6 Press Teaching Progression

Figure 4.6 represents a general progression of the pressing movements from simple to complex to help guide teaching and progressing the movements.

POSTERIOR CHAIN

The posterior chain has garnered attention over the past decade for its importance in injury prevention, postural control, and performance. This attention is certainly earned, as the glutes, hamstrings, and low back are critical for propulsion and dynamic control of the trunk, pelvis, and legs.

We train the posterior chain, but at a lower total volume than the other movements. This is mostly because we are training the muscles of the posterior chain with the majority of our other foundational movements, and adding more training volume on top of that can lead to overuse injuries.

Novice-level athletes are the exception to this rule, as they have a higher percentage of work dedicated to the posterior chain to build strength in the spinal musculature and hips. The novice—or really, any athlete who will be performing explosive Olympic lifting—should be able to reach the benchmark of three sets of 12 repetitions of hyperextensions while holding 45 pounds.

If an athlete cannot hit that mark, you should train hyperextensions two times a week with 12–20 reps per set. The low back musculature is generally tonic in nature, with a higher density of slow-twitch endurance muscle fibers. You want to see some noticeable hypertrophy of the spinal erectors with a heavy dose of posterior chain work before you start significantly loading the more explosive movements.

Photos 4.7 a–b The Romanian Deadlift
Romanian deadlifts should be a staple of almost every training program for developing strength and stability in the low back and pelvis.

Advanced and elite-level athletes will not dedicate as much time to the posterior chain, and there is a reason for that. The deadlift in particular is demanding on the central nervous system, especially when handling significant loads. Considering recovery, training the deadlift heavy and often requires more recovery time than we usually have at our disposal. With the additional volume dedicated to cleans and the Olympic movements, the hip-hinging motion will get a fair amount of overall attention.

One shift we made in recent years is in utilizing the trap bar deadlift more than the standard barbell deadlift. Research has shown the trap bar deadlift to be more effective for power development than the standard deadlift,[35] and the positioning of the line of pull with the trap bar takes some stress off the low back.

Photo 4.8 The Trap Bar Deadlift
The trap bar deadlift allows for the line of pull to be more vertical, reducing stress at the low back.

The bulk of the work to the hamstrings and low back consists of a heavy dose of RDLs, glute-ham raises, and hyperextensions and reverse hyperextensions. The glute-ham is particularly effective at emphasizing eccentric strength of the hamstrings with combined knee flexion with hip extension, which is vital for preventing hamstring strains.

[CHAPTER FOUR—SYSTEMATIC PROGRAM DESIGN]

Photos 4.9 a–c The Glute-Ham Hyperextension

Glute-ham hyperextensions are excellent for developing eccentric strength of the entire posterior chain.

TRAP BAR DEADLIFT	RDL AND GOOD MORNING	GLUTE-HAM RAISE	HYPEREXTENSION AND REVERSE HYPEREXTENSION
Kettlebell Deadlift ↓ Deadlift from Blocks ↓ Deadlift from the Floor	Hip-Hinge with a Stick ↓ RDL with Bar to the Knees ↓ RDL below the Knees ↓ Good Morning	Eccentric Heel Slide ↓ Glute-Ham Raise on the Floor— Slow Eccentric for Hypertrophy ↓ Hyperextension into Glute-Ham Raise	Performed from the Floor ↓ Increase ROM on a Roman Chair or Table ↓ Add Load

Figure 4.7 Posterior Chain Teaching Progression

THE POWER MOVEMENTS

PULLS— CLEAN PULL, SNATCH PULL

Our definition of pulls as they pertain to this fundamental movement is slightly different than that used by many coaches. "Pulls" in this case denotes variations on the pulling movements of the clean and snatch, not rowing or back work. Rowing motions or lat work has an important place in accessory movements, yet not as our primary training emphasis on strength and power development.

Clean or snatch pulls could be categorized as either strength or power movements; however, because the emphasis is on rapid acceleration of the bar, we consider them primarily power movements.

Pulls are effectively simplified versions of the primary Olympic lifts of the clean and snatch through an abbreviated range of motion. They are still performed explosively and with the emphasis on the speed of the bar and delivering force into the ground, yet they serve to develop a strength base for the more complex Olympic lifts.

The smaller range of motion and lack of a catch of the bar at the top of the movement means pull variations can often employ heavier weights than the pure Olympic movements, with less stress on the joints and nervous system.

Photos 4.10 a–c The Clean Pull
The clean pull from the mid-thigh position helps train force delivery into the ground and sets the stage for transitioning into the power clean.

Photos 4.11 a–c The Snatch Pull

Like the clean pull, beginning a teaching progression with the snatch pull will reinforce good technique when initiating the movement of the full snatch.

Novice athletes need to hit our benchmark for low-back strength described on page 111 before adding much volume to pulls in the program. Every repetition of extension-based movements places an increased demand on the spinal extensors. We want to ensure the strength and endurance of the spinal erectors and glutes are adequate to handle the repetition and load.

The goal of using pulls is to develop the same explosive movement and the ability to generate force through the ground without the technical demands of the Olympic lifts. We can fine-tune the initiation of the clean and snatch, which in turn improves the Olympic lifts as well as an athlete's ability to rapidly initiate coordinated movement.

There is research showing mid-thigh pulls produce more force into the ground than actually doing the Olympic lifts.[36] This is probably because we can use more weight, and also because these pulls are not as technically challenging since we do not have to make the bar travel as far to make a catch.

In many cases, when training the pulls, we do not need to extend below the knee joint because the greatest speed occurs as the bar comes above the knee. The higher the bar starts, the less time it takes to complete the lift and therefore, the more explosive our athletes have to be.

For the initial introduction of the clean and snatch pulls—and full cleans and snatches as well—it is best to teach the movement from the top down, or from a mid-thigh position to the floor.

If you start an athlete in the standing position with the bar just above the knees, the decreased range of motion makes it easier to learn. Starting from the hang position or with the bar supported on blocks or a rack allows an athlete to learn the set-up for the lifts with less complexity than lifting from the floor.

Photos 4.12 a–d Pull Start Positions

Starting the pull from a higher position will generally be less technically demanding than a lower position, but will require more rapid output due to the shorter distance the bar has to travel.

> ## EYE OF THE COACH
>
> *Younger athletes or people who have never done pulls tend to pull the bar with their arms. If you demonstrate what something should feel like, people are more apt to get it than if you just show them the movement.*
>
> *Here is a great trick we learned at the Olympic Training Center in Colorado: Take a broomstick or dowel, put it in back of the athlete's knee in a clean or snatch grip, depending on which movement you are training. At first, use a bent knee position with the hips back, assuming the position of performing the lift. Now say, "Very slowly, stand up." The athlete will know what you want, and that dowel will go up the back of the legs, up to the bottom of the butt.*
>
> *Then say, "Now do it faster and faster." With the arms extended behind the midline of the body, arms are eliminated from the equation. When athletes start to go fast, they feel it as "all legs" and that there is no arm involvement. Then tell them, "Now hold the bar in front of you; the movement should feel the same, even though your arms are now part of the process."*
>
> *You can build from there, but with this technique you have engrained the pattern of using the legs to generate force into the ground without pulling with the arms.*

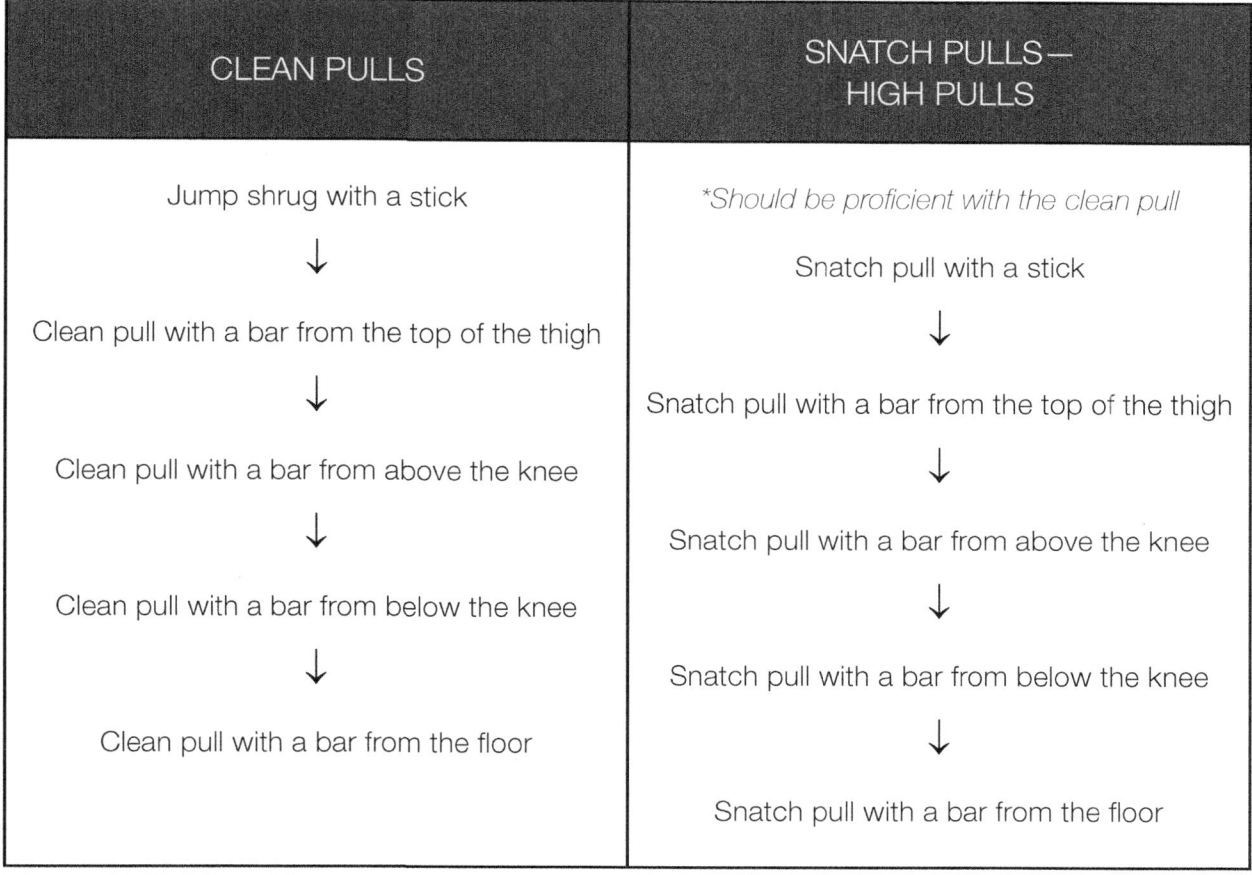

CLEAN PULLS	SNATCH PULLS— HIGH PULLS
Jump shrug with a stick ↓ Clean pull with a bar from the top of the thigh ↓ Clean pull with a bar from above the knee ↓ Clean pull with a bar from below the knee ↓ Clean pull with a bar from the floor	*Should be proficient with the clean pull Snatch pull with a stick ↓ Snatch pull with a bar from the top of the thigh ↓ Snatch pull with a bar from above the knee ↓ Snatch pull with a bar from below the knee ↓ Snatch pull with a bar from the floor

Figure 4.8 Pull Teaching Progression
*Once you have trained the snatch pull, it can be transitioned into a full clean or snatch.

The goal could be to ultimately progress an athlete to initiating the movement from the floor; however, that is where mobility, technique, and coordination need to be optimal to produce an acceptable lift. Even more-experienced athletes struggle with consistent performance of the pulls from the floor, and spend years perfecting the perfect pull and transition from the floor. For athletic development in most sports, we could argue that lifting from the floor may even be unnecessary. Starting from the hang position or blocks, then gradually moving toward the floor will set athletes up to succeed.

Combining the pulls with the snatch or clean in the same workout and beginning the pull movement from just below the Olympic movement position is a great programming tool. For example, if you program cleans from the mid-thigh position, you could follow them with clean pulls from just below the knee. This facilitates technique carryover with the progression of the snatch or clean to the next lowest position toward the ground.

There are few drawbacks to including pulls in strength programming. If you are proficient at teaching the pull, progressing your athletes to the full Olympic lifts should be seamless.

CLEAN

If the squat is exercise priority number one, the clean is "one-b." The clean is our other top-priority movement because performing a technically proficient clean requires high-speed sequencing of about 70 percent of the muscles in the body. The explosive triple extension motion of the ankle, knee, and hip during the clean is the underlying motion of jumping and acceleration of most sport movements. Developing that ballistic movement and control is the key to rapid force development on an athletic field.

The clean is also the foundational component of the more complex snatch movement, and therefore has to be solid in both technique and strength to successfully advance in Olympic lifting.

There is no single movement that carries over more readily to on-the-field explosiveness than the clean. Whether we are talking about linemen rising off the ground and into one another, a high jumper preparing to leave the ground, or a swimmer diving off the starting blocks, the clean trains the explosive hip hinge and triple extension of the ankles, knees, and hips needed for acceleration.

Not only should the clean be in every athlete's training program, it is vital to success. Really, there should be no debate.

Photos 4.13 a–d The Clean
Power clean performed from the hang position

Another benefit of training the clean is in training the body to absorb force. Just as with pulls, it is generally easiest to teach an athlete this through an abbreviated range of motion. By starting with a power clean where an athlete starts and ends the movement at the thighs, we are adding a component of eccentric strengthening to the low back and hips when absorbing the weight of the bar on the descent.

Eccentric strength and control of the lower body is critical in developing agility and braking ability for changes of direction in sports. Poor eccentric strength of the hamstrings is often suspected to be the primary cause of strained hamstrings that arise when an athlete tries to rapidly decelerate and change direction on the playing field.[37]

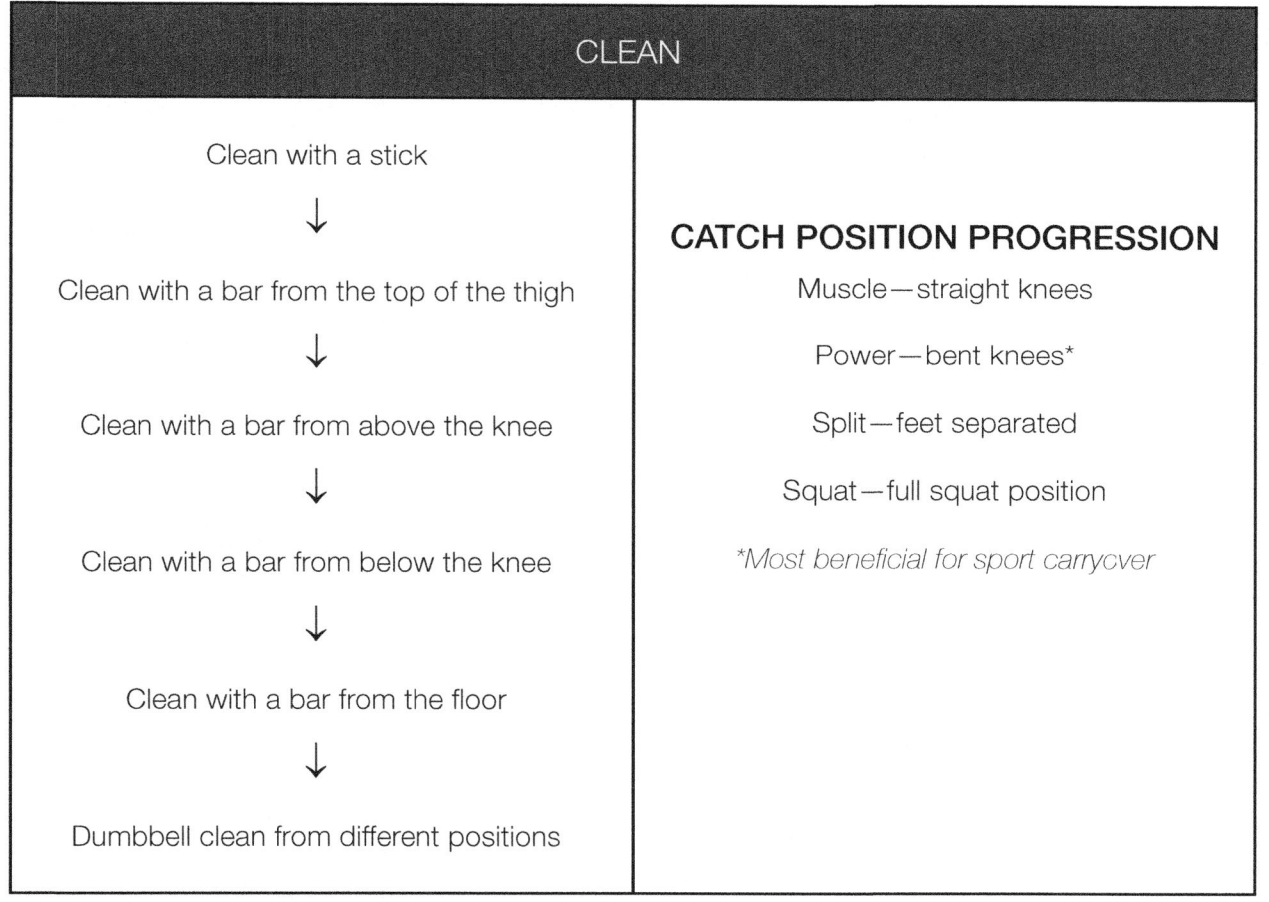

CLEAN	
Clean with a stick ↓ Clean with a bar from the top of the thigh ↓ Clean with a bar from above the knee ↓ Clean with a bar from below the knee ↓ Clean with a bar from the floor ↓ Dumbbell clean from different positions	**CATCH POSITION PROGRESSION** Muscle—straight knees Power—bent knees* Split—feet separated Squat—full squat position *Most beneficial for sport carryover*

Figure 4.9 The Clean Teaching Progression

Starting the movement with the barbell on blocks or in the power rack allows an easier set-up to find the right positions, but also demands a much higher force output because it eliminates the benefit of the stretch-reflex when holding the weight. This is especially beneficial for lineman or sprinters who have to generate maximal power from a dead start.

EYE OF THE COACH

Performing the clean with the bar starting on the floor can be challenging for even experienced athletes, and can be challenging for the less-experienced strength coach to teach.

The same study that showed higher force development from hang pulls also showed higher output from cleans starting the above the knee position compared with the floor.[38]

While a clean from the floor can enhance coordination and strength development through a larger range of motion, you can emphasize cleans from the hang position to maximally develop force into the ground and power development.

SNATCH

Of all our training movements, none are as technically and physically demanding or require as much explosive power as the overhead snatch. Just as the clean requires a high degree of rapid, coordinated muscle activation, the snatch takes that demand to another level to deliver the bar overhead. It would be easier to list the muscles *not* involved in performing an efficient snatch than to acknowledge the number that are involved. No movement is as effective at developing total-body strength, power, and stability than the snatch.

The reasons the snatch is such a valuable exercise are also some of the same reasons it is such a challenge to teach and effectively program. It not only demands a high degree of coordination and balance, it also demands that almost every joint is able to move through a full range of motion, while stabilizing the weight at the extremes of the joint positions—particularly the shoulder girdle. That is the reason it is a critical component of the prep phase and why you should only advance the weight when an athlete can demonstrate near-flawless technique.

Many strength coaches dismiss the snatch as too risky for their athletes or feel its place is strictly for those competing in Olympic weightlifting. We have not found that to be the case. We would argue that if an athlete is physically capable of performing the lift and achieving the required positions, the snatch is an invaluable exercise for athletes.

There are not many options in the exercise library that can simultaneously improve full-body power output, dynamic coordination, body control, and stability. An athlete needs to demonstrate full shoulder mobility and good scapular control so the shoulder girdle is stable in the overhead position.

If appropriately programmed and progressed, the snatch has no greater risk of injury than any other training movement.

In most cases, exercises are not bad; they are just inappropriately programmed or coached, which can place athletes at an increased risk of injury. There are many coaches who are not comfortable with either of those factors concerning the snatch.

We will illuminate the programming aspect, yet it is critical to learn firsthand how to coach the Olympic lifts. Without them, your athletes may never fully develop their physical potential.

Photos 4.14 a–d The Power Snatch
Power snatch from the hang above the knees

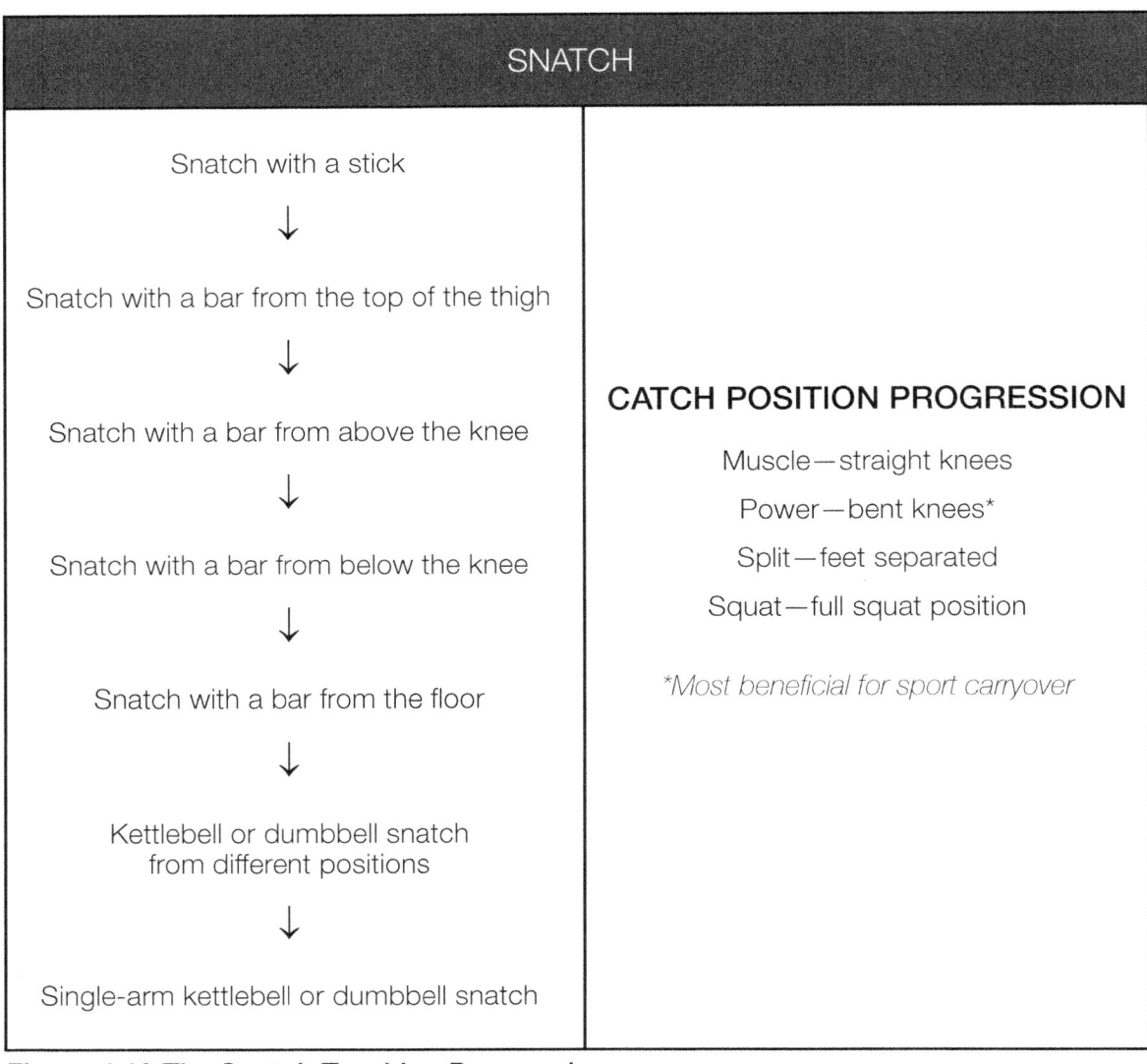

SNATCH	
Snatch with a stick ↓ Snatch with a bar from the top of the thigh ↓ Snatch with a bar from above the knee ↓ Snatch with a bar from below the knee ↓ Snatch with a bar from the floor ↓ Kettlebell or dumbbell snatch from different positions ↓ Single-arm kettlebell or dumbbell snatch	**CATCH POSITION PROGRESSION** Muscle—straight knees Power—bent knees* Split—feet separated Squat—full squat position *Most beneficial for sport carryover*

Figure 4.10 The Snatch Teaching Progression

Similar to the clean, the snatch movement can be started from blocks or the power rack at the different positions.

JERK

The jerk is the third of the Olympic training movements. It is basically the progression of the pressing movements to develop power. The version most familiar to coaches is the split jerk, where the lifter finishes in a staggered stance with the bar overhead.

Just as with the snatch, the jerk demands a high degree of force production and coordination to drive the bar overhead and then stabilize the body underneath.

[CHAPTER FOUR—SYSTEMATIC PROGRAM DESIGN]

Photos 4.15 a–g The Jerk

To give you an idea of how explosive a properly performed and loaded jerk can be, our camera barely captured a single frame of Robert transitioning between driving through the floor and finishing with the bar overhead. That is a true expression of power.

Developing strength and stability in a single-leg position is where the jerk can be of particular benefit. Once the bar moves overhead, the athlete has to rapidly drive the feet apart and down, with the lead leg striking the ground and accepting the weight of the athlete with the weight overhead.

At the same time, the hips, trunk, and shoulder girdle have to maintain a high degree of stiffness to maintain balance and control in the wide staggered stance. Any weak link from the shoulders down will lead to poor movement quality and limited progress.

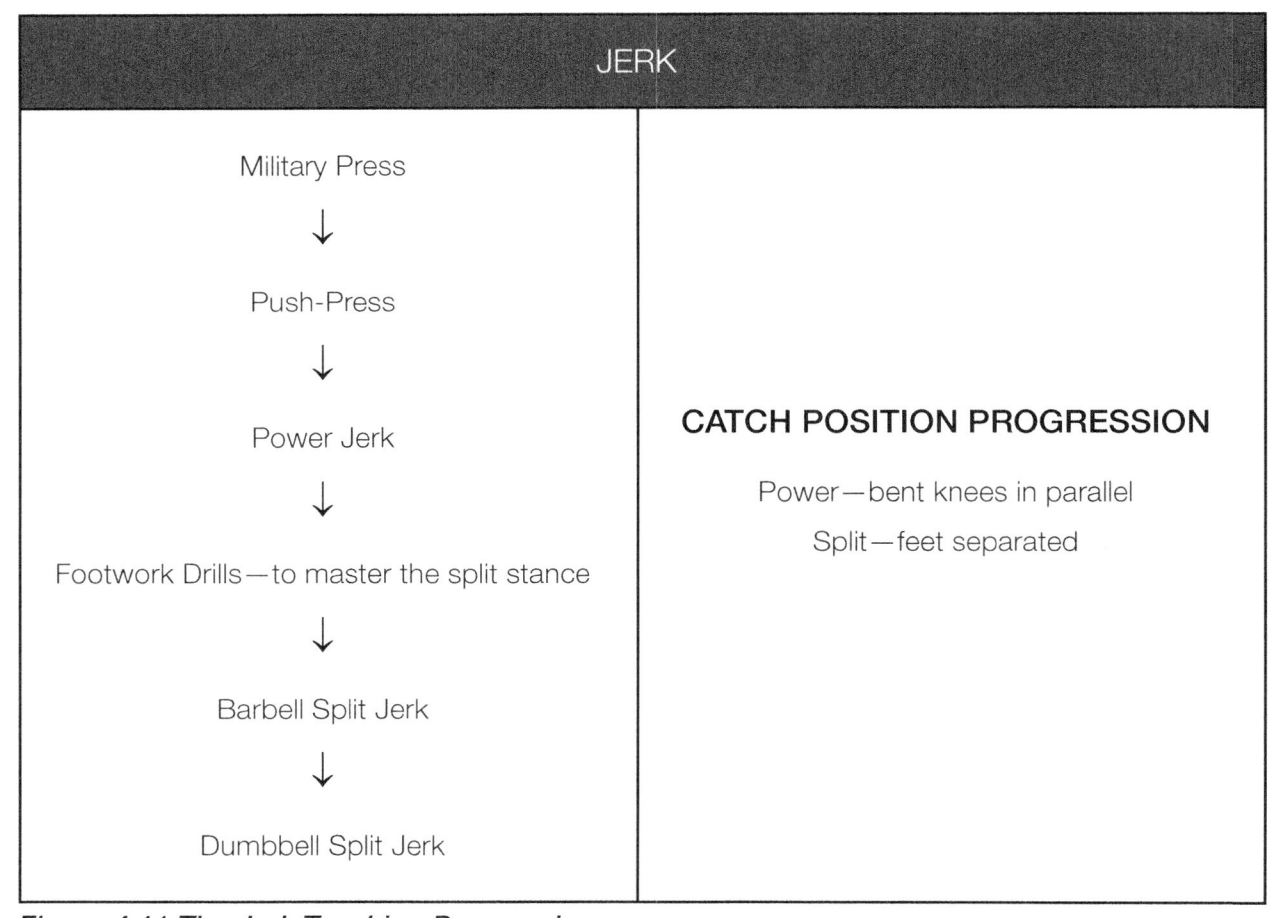

JERK	
Military Press ↓ Push-Press ↓ Power Jerk ↓ Footwork Drills—to master the split stance ↓ Barbell Split Jerk ↓ Dumbbell Split Jerk	**CATCH POSITION PROGRESSION** Power—bent knees in parallel Split—feet separated

Figure 4.11 The Jerk Teaching Progression

The caveat in programming the jerk, which we will cover later, is to reserve it for more experienced lifters. The jerk will not be a foundational lift for typical novice lifters. The majority of their overhead work will be dedicated to building strength through overhead pressing, push-pressing, and lighter loads with the snatch. The required trunk and hip stability and shoulder strength for handling the higher loads of the jerk are not normally developed until athletes have spent at least a year of dedicated training in the other fundamental lifts.

EXERCISE SELECTION PRINCIPLES

- *Progress exercises from simple to complex*
- *Exercises change every four-week cycle*
- *Exercise percentages change every four-week cycle*

PROGRESSING FROM SIMPLE TO COMPLEX

No matter what an athlete's experience, you are teaching movement. Movement is a skill similar to learning to speak a second language—it is just that most of that learning takes place unconsciously.

We did not critically break down the components of jumping as children, yet we probably did when we learned how to hit or kick a ball. In the same manner, we start the progression of a training program from simple to complex exercises to first master the basics.

The goal of focusing on the fundamental movements is to use an exercise selection that gives the biggest return and that also works best with a group. It is hard to create individual programs for 53 athletes on a football team.

Whatever sport you coach, you can categorize by position or size or some other variable; however, the focus should be on starting simple with both your programming and movement choices. Then you can advance both as you and your athletes grow more comfortable with the program.

Our definition of "simple" is a movement that is stabilized, symmetrical, or performed with an even load.

"Complex" means multi-joint, multi-movement, unilateral, or explosive movements. The bench press is a relatively simple movement, while the split jerk and snatch are complex. The more complex or compound the movement, the more demand on the nervous system.

Once a simple movement can be performed well, you can advance your athletes to a more complex movement. You can achieve that simply by taking a simple exercise and performing it through a larger range of motion, unilaterally, removing support, or combining it with another movement. The change does not need to be a completely different movement.

In the continuum shown in Figure 4.12, you can see a natural progression of cleans and presses from the simplest form to more complex variations.

SIMPLE				COMPLEX
Clean Pull	Snatch Pull	Power Clean from the Thigh	Power Clean from the Floor	Squat Clean from the Floor
Military Press	Push-Press	Dumbbell Push-Press	Squat Jerk	Split Jerk

Figure 4.12 Progression from Simple to Complex Variations

Although dumbbell training can be valuable in correcting strength imbalances and progression to dumbbells can allow for improved carryover to sport and improved range of motion for the joints, intensity should be very gradually progressed. Performing a lift with a barbell will be inherently more stable than with two dumbbells, even if the total load with the dumbbells is lower. The muscular stability demands on the shoulder girdle and abdominal musculature with dumbbell training are incredibly high if the lifts are performed explosively or with significant weight.

You should lay the groundwork for the foundational movements and the athletes should demonstrate increasing competency in the lifts before advancing to dumbbells for the complex movements such as the clean or snatch.

If the movements are appropriately loaded and progressed with barbell training, there is reduced risk in advancing to dumbbells and you can focus on fine-tuning technique rather than coaching the movements.

Pulls in relation to cleans and snatches are another example of moving from simple to complex. Pulls are considered more simple than cleans or snatches because they are only performed through part of the range of motion without a catch of the bar. If performing cleans and snatches with the bar at mid-thigh, the clean and snatch pulls would be performed at the knees. If starting the cleans and snatches from the knees, the pulls start from the mid-shin.

Progressively making the pulls more complex by taking them deeper into the range of motion prepares athletes for the progression to the Olympic lifts and conditioning the nervous system and body for the more complex Olympic lifts from the floor.

> **EYE OF THE COACH**
>
> *You need to demand perfect technique with every lift. If you have a novice athlete who is untrained or de-trained and is having difficulty mastering the movements, dedicate one workout to working strictly on a single foundational movement and then gradually loading it.*
>
> *The next workout could focus on another specific foundational movement. You can build in more accessory work, but for an athlete struggling with the lifts, focusing on multiple movements during the same session can stall progress.*

EXERCISE VARIATION

The focus of an athlete and coach should always be toward refining technique and efficiency of movement in the weightroom. We want the same general movement, repeatedly performed with precision to learn the motion and hardwire the motor pathway. The body is an incredibly efficient machine, and for a young, healthy athlete, it can rapidly adapt to a repetitive stress.

The concept of muscle confusion—the need to constantly change exercises from session to session or week to week—has been debated and contested. These changes create plenty of stress to the body, as it cannot adapt to a consistent stimulus; however, it also does not do much to improve movement quality or maximal power training.

The most effective exercises are movements that require some level of technique, and those qualities are only developed through practice and repetition. Every time the training shifts to even a variant of a known exercise, the initial intensity drops slightly to allow for learning and refining the new movement pattern.

By constantly varying intensity and volume, which we will expand on shortly, we change the stimulus from session to session without using completely different movements. This allows more time to perfect technique and efficiency before the need to change exercises. It provides more simplistic programming and removes a lot of the guesswork and indecision about which exercise to use next. At the end of each four-week cycle, we do not need a wholesale change to the routine. To quote Coach Charles Poliquin,[39] "Change the emphasis; do not change the exercise."

We can change a hang clean to a clean from the floor, add an overhead press to the motion, or perform it with dumbbells instead of a barbell. Similarly, we can perform a split jerk with the bar in the front rack position or from behind the neck. We are not overhauling the routine or the movement. We are just changing the stimulus of those fundamental movement patterns to allow for continued adaptation.

We recommend programming full-body training for each session. You will train the same primary movement at least twice and sometimes three times in the same week. By planning different variations of a movement in the same week, we continue to train the same motor pattern, yet with slightly different loads or positions to reduce the repetitive strain on the muscles.

For example, if you want to train the squat movement three times in the same week, two sessions could be a back squat, while one session might be step-ups or lunges.

When using the clean three times, twice could be from the hang position and once off racks or boxes. The fundamental movement remains largely the same, yet we can train different ranges, positions, or qualities of the movement.

Once a cycle is complete, we change the movements to elicit a new training effect while still building on the foundation. There is no right or wrong progression, as long as you hold to the principle that an athlete must master the simple version of a movement before moving to something more complex.

CYCLE ONE	CYCLE TWO
Back Squat—Step-Ups—Back Squat	Back Squat—Reverse Lunge—Front Squat
Hang Power Clean—Clean from the Rack or Blocks—Hang Power Clean *all performed just above the knee*	Hang Power Clean—Clean from the Rack or Blocks—Hang Power Clean *all performed just below the knee*
Bench Press—Military Press—Incline Press	Bench Press—Push-Press—Incline Dumbbell Press

Figure 4.13 Example Movement Progression

ACCESSORY WORK

There is no such thing as sport-specific training.

Trying to mimic a particular sport's demands or movements in the weightroom is where the debate often arises regarding sport-specific training. In our view, the weightroom is where we enhance force production. We squat; we press; we Olympic lift; we do everything with the intention of increasing the rate and intensity of the body's output. That approach is generally non-specific.

If we improve the strength and power of the legs and hips in a basketball player, we can increase the vertical jump. The same approach with a baseball player can increase bat speed and throwing velocity. By focusing on full-body power training, we address specific sports qualities with the bleed-over of general strength and power gains to performance.

When it comes to sport-specific training, it is often thought that by mimicking a particular motion or specific action of a sport, we might see a more profound carryover into the sport.

The truth is, we only have one nervous system. We do not have a nervous system for soccer and separate nervous system for football or basketball.

The purpose of weight training is to improve the output and efficiency of the nervous and musculoskeletal systems. The carryover to sport is through practice of the sport itself. Shooting a basketball is a skill. Hitting a 90-mph fastball is a skill. In the weightroom, we enhance athleticism. We do nothing for skill. Skills are sport-specific. Through the practice of the skill, we hope to transfer the improvement of the physical qualities that have evolved in our training to the sport.

Two examples from the literature demonstrate the carryover of "non-specific" training for strength and power and the carryover to performance. A 2006 study in the *Journal of Strength and Conditioning Research*,[40] demonstrated that maximal leg strength in the squat relative to bodyweight was highly correlated to acceleration, max sprint speed, agility in the cone T-test drill, and vertical and linear jumping. It seems difficult to connect the mechanics of a squat to an agility drill, but it demonstrates that the more efficient athletes become at maximal force production, the more effective they will be at expressing that quality in more "sport-specific" ways.

Another study in the *Journal of Athletic Training* compared a "sport-specific" combination of strength and power training for the trunk and abdominals to a general abdominal endurance protocol using static holds.[41] The "sport-specific" approach demonstrated superior results in improving throwing velocity for baseball athletes compared to a static hold group.

This may seem to run counter to our argument against specificity. However, the "sport-specific" routine the authors of the article utilized consisted of loaded rotational and stability exercises using a rep-per-set range in line with our recommendations of between one and eight reps for the movements. Nothing in the study looked like swinging a bat or throwing a ball, unless you consider twisting the hips and torso to be uniquely sport specific.

There is nothing wrong with addressing particular demands of a sport in the training program; the problem is in the emphasis. There is certainly a place for correcting strength imbalances and working in different planes of motion such as in rotation or lateral movements.

However, that should always come secondary to developing generalized strength and power in the fundamental movements. Jumping, sprinting, variations of medicine ball throws, or agility work all facilitate transfer of physical training to sports, but in reality they are first and foremost natural human movements.

What we call exercises of "local effect" encompass the accessory work of a program. The problem occurs when coaches spend the majority of their programming doing accessory work rather than training the fundamental movements.

Accessory work involves movements or exercises that either help improve performance in the fundamental lifts, or address a particular requirement of a specific sport or position. This is about as sport-specific as you will get, and it makes up a very small percentage of the total work in the weightroom.

For example, an MMA fighter may require a significant amount of biceps and chest work to effectively hold an opponent and deliver powerful punches. Exercises that specifically address those muscles or movements can and should be included; however, they will make up less than 10 percent of the total training volume. Rowing motions or lateral and rotational strengthening also fall under the umbrella of accessory work. They are in the program, but are not the top priority.

Our primary experience has been with American football, and there is no debate that the essential accessory work for success on the football field is dedicated abdominal, grip, and neck work.

For abdominal work, the volume should be 12–20 reps per set, focusing on rotational and bracing, anti-rotational exercises. The higher volume per set is due to the muscles being more tonic in nature and able to handle a higher total volume of stimulus.

Once a foundation of strength is established, the natural progression will be to utilize an approach similar to the previously mentioned research, performing fewer reps per set and focusing on strength and power development in the trunk.

Grip training should be done with sustained holds and repetitive movement, generally in the five-to-eight rep range to develop greater strength.

In neck work, we utilize both higher and lower rep ranges, working concentric and eccentric strength in all planes, primarily with partner-assisted manual resistance work.

This allows for more even distribution of force throughout the movement and a closer eye on correct form.

Although direct strength training to the neck has somewhat fallen out of favor, the sport of football in particular demands that the stability of the head and neck is enough to absorb the high impacts of the game. Add to that the increased attention on head injuries and concussions, and the importance of the ability to stabilize the head and neck becomes all the more important.

There are some other qualities we alter in the accessory work, depending on the demands of a particular position. Linemen have more emphasis on strength in the four-to-six rep range and slightly higher for hypertrophy, as well as dedicated triceps and lat work to improve the punching and pulling required in the trenches.

Skill players have more emphasis on explosive strength development in the one-to-three rep range, with dedicated work on chin-ups, pullups, and posterior chain development to improve pulling ability when fighting for position.

These same principles are applied to other sports; again, any specific movement or muscle work is secondary to the larger program. Putting $2,000 tires on a $1,000 car will not make a lot of difference in how it performs. Spend your time adding horsepower to an athlete's engine, and then focus on the smaller elements.

VOLUME

Training volume is the most critical variable to monitor in long-term athletic development.

No variable is more critical to success and continued progress as training volume. As the Russians found, varying the training volume from session to session, week to week, and month to month ensures athletes are exposed to a consistent training effect that allows for adequate recovery and steady progress of strength and performance gains.

Particularly for athletes with significant training experience, when the general approach is progressive overload, the gains in strength seen over the first three or four weeks will begin to slow at six to seven weeks.[42] Those gains will steadily plateau and in some cases regress if you try to continually increase training volume or intensity.

Even novice athletes will ultimately hit a training plateau—albeit much later—if the training variables are not regularly altered. Although few studies span greater than 10 to 12 weeks, the findings suggest that novelty or training variety are important for stimulating further strength development.[43]

Through the diligence of the Russian method, certain principles of the application of training volume were developed that are both exercise-specific and athlete-specific. The emphasis is always to elicit an effective training stimulus while mitigating the effects of overstimulation.

Using an undulating pattern of volume and intensity works best. The Russian texts as well as our thousands of personal hours of training time have proven these values effective.

MONTHLY VOLUME PRINCIPLES

In each four-week training cycle, there will be a prescribed total training volume. Determination of this monthly total depends largely on the variables previously discussed on page 37, such as the athlete's age, training experience, and time of year.

The absolute floor of volume for a novice athlete is 750 total exercise repetitions per month, and the ceiling for the elite athlete is 1,600 total reps. During our time in the former Soviet Republics, we witnessed athletes performing even higher monthly training volumes. However, as we found later, that was often with the benefit of performance-enhancing substances that allowed for more rapid recovery.

The goal is always to balance the training effect with recovery time to minimize overtraining and reduced performance on the field.

TOTAL TRAINING VOLUME RANGES PER FOUR-WEEK CYCLE		
NOVICE	ADVANCED	ELITE
750–1,000 reps	1,000–1,200 reps	Up to 1,600 reps

Figure 4.14 Example of Volume Ranges

In a single cycle, the total number of repetitions pertains to all exercises performed in the key movements. This means 750 total repetitions are spread between the different exercises among the range of training intensities we want to emphasize.

On the surface, these can seem like small numbers when we consider they may be spread out over 12 to 16 training sessions. That 750-rep total is really more like the basement rather than the floor of total volume—any less than 750 will not budge the needle on gains. That does not mean advanced or elite-level athletes will not have cycles that dip below 1,000 reps. These ranges should be more prescriptive of the ceiling of higher volumes to avoid exceeding. Pushing monthly volume beyond these ranges erodes recovery more rapidly than any other factor.

An elite-level athlete can use a month with a total volume of under 1,000 reps, as will often be the case when returning to training. However, a novice athlete can rarely exceed the 1,000-rep ceiling without risking an injury or a significant overtraining effect.

Many coaches worry their athletes will not do enough work to promote gains in strength and power. They do not want to "waste" a month by aiming too low on total volume and leaving some gains in the tank. That is a natural feeling when adopting this method, and each of us went through the same mental struggle.

Strength coaches in America are not hard-wired to accept less than maximum. However, trust us when we say that without fail, these ranges have proven to be the most effective in generating progress with almost no risk of overtraining.

Fine-tuning where your athletes fall in a volume range takes skill, experience, and consideration of their medical and training history, biological and training age, and gender.

The bloody trail of our mistakes can save you a lot of added stress: When in doubt, it is always better to err on the side of less volume than too much.

The total volume number does not include accessory work or exercises of "local effect." Those exercises are more targeted muscle strengthening or exercises to support the main movements.

We are mainly concerned about the most physically taxing exercises that demand more of an athlete's attention to technique—hence, the volume restrictions.

Although the accessory work is not included in the volume calculations, you still cannot go wild, adding as much as you want. Always remember this: efficiency first.

THE BREAK-IN CYCLE

For the novice, advanced, or elite athlete returning from an extended post-season layoff, we recommend a break-in cycle to establish a good baseline or to re-prime the system. This is the one instance in which we generally will not use an undulating volume pattern. The initial return cycle can take a more linear design because we anticipate a strong nervous system response to the added workload of training, and there is less need to significantly vary load or volume. There is almost no fear of overtraining from this early adaptation to the training.

In the next chart, Figure 4.15 on page 134, you can see the increasing training volume over the first three weeks of the first cycle.

NOVICE ATHLETE BREAK-IN OR RETURN TO TRAINING	ADVANCED OR ELITE ATHLETE RETURN TO TRAINING
750–1,000 reps	Greater than 1,000 reps
Week One—22 percent total reps	*Week One*—22 percent total reps
Week Two—28 percent total reps	*Week Two*—27 percent total reps
Week Three—35 percent total reps	*Week Three*—32 percent total reps
Week Four—15 percent total reps	*Week Four*—19 percent total reps

Figure 4.15 Return-to-Training Break-in Cycle

For the break-in cycle, the training of the complexes from the prep phase is critical to re-establish work capacity and technique in the primary lifts. For the novice, it can take up to two months to build adequate work capacity, while the advanced or elite athlete may take as little as two or three weeks of training the complexes to return to baseline levels.

For example, if a football team fails to make the playoffs or a bowl game, after returning from the Christmas break and two or three weeks off, there should be anywhere from two to four weeks using the break-in cycle before diving back into higher-intensity training.

As you can see, each week of the month is broken into a percentage of the total monthly volume. The volume increases in a step-wise pattern each week until unloading in the last week of the cycle.

The unloading week is critical for each four-week cycle because it allows continued training while the nervous system and musculoskeletal recover from the previous weeks. This pattern holds true throughout The System.

The drop in volume is less severe for the advanced or elite-level athletes. Experienced athletes possess better recovery ability than a newer lifter and can tolerate more volume and intensity during the unloading week.

For the novice athlete, we also significantly limit the training intensity on top of less volume during the fourth week. It is difficult for many coaches to feel comfortable with their athletes leaving the weightroom not particularly tired, not particularly sweaty, and without spending a lot of time under the bar.

You have to convince yourself that it is for their long-term benefit and that you are not going soft. It takes some self control, yet that week serves as an active recovery most athletes do not often get, and will ultimately allow for more rapid accumulation of the gains made over the first three weeks.

[CHAPTER FOUR—SYSTEMATIC PROGRAM DESIGN]

Advanced or elite athletes also may not see a reduction in training intensity during that fourth week, with continued higher-intensity work but with a "recovery" due to lower volume.

As an example, if we compared a novice-level football player—think of a freshman in high school—who was starting out at 800 total repetitions for the month, and an advanced-level senior on varsity starting at 1,000 reps, the breakdown for the training weeks would look like the table shown in Figure 4.16.

FRESHMAN FOOTBALL NOVICE BREAK-IN CYCLE	SENIOR FOOTBALL ADVANCED BREAK-IN CYCLE
800 reps	1,000 reps
Week One—176 total reps—22 percent	*Week One*—220 total reps—22 percent
Week Two—224 total reps—28 percent	*Week Two*—270 total reps—27 percent
Week Three—280 total reps—35 percent	*Week Three*—320 total reps—32 percent
Week Four—120 total reps—15 percent	*Week Four*—190 total reps—19 percent

Figure 4.16 Football Break-in Cycle

Those weekly repetitions are further broken down among the training sessions during the week. If the athletes are demonstrating steady gains without signs of overtraining such as fatigue, irritability, or listlessness, they can advance into the full program.

You can increase the following month's volume, but generally by no more than 10 percent of the previous month's total volume.

PROGRESSING INTO THE SYSTEM

After the initial month of training, athletes should be physically prepared to progress into to the full program of The System. The significant change in the design going forward is that rather than following a linear progression, the volume will undulate, with the first two weeks' volume effectively flipped.

The total repetitions decrease twice during the month, with the heaviest volume week always preceding the unloading week.

This allows for a super-compensation effect, where the athlete is over-reaching during the third week, and then recovering during the fourth week due to the drop in volume.

Later, we will see how the relative training intensity in most cases also follows an undulating pattern, but the chart in Figure 4.17 shows how we flip the first and second week volumes.

NOVICE OR ADVANCED ATHLETE MONTHLY VOLUME	ADVANCED OR ELITE ATHLETE MONTHLY VOLUME
750–1,000 reps	Greater than 1,000 reps
Week One—28 percent total reps	*Week One*—27 percent total reps
Week Two—22 percent total reps	*Week Two*—22 percent total reps
Week Three—35 percent total reps	*Week Three*—32 percent total reps
Week Four—15 percent total reps	*Week Four*—19 percent total reps

Figure 4.17 Weekly and Monthly Volumes

Considering the freshman football player who began the break-in cycle at 800 repetitions, the planned progression could look something like this:

NOVICE-LEVEL BREAK-IN FIRST OFF-SEASON CYCLE	NOVICE-LEVEL SECOND OFF-SEASON CYCLE
800 reps	850 reps
Week One—176 total reps—22 percent	*Week One*—238 total reps—28 percent
Week Two—224 total reps—28 percent	*Week Two*—187 total reps—22 percent
Week Three—280 total reps—35 percent	*Week Three*—297.5 total reps—35 percent
Week Four—120 total reps—15 percent	*Week Four*—127.5 total reps—15 percent

Figure 4.18 Novice Off-Season Cycles

You can see from the third and fourth week of the second off-season cycle, the math will rarely be clean in the breakdown of volume percentages.

In cases where the math ends up with fractions of repetitions, round up or down from the fractions of reps; being off by a handful of reps in a week or a session will not have an impact.

An advanced athlete will follow the same general pattern, but with different weekly percentages.

The first two months of the advanced off-season program might look like Figure 4.19.

ADVANCED-LEVEL BREAK-IN—FIRST OFF-SEASON CYCLE	ADVANCED-LEVEL SECOND OFF-SEASON CYCLE
1,000 reps	1,100 reps
Week One—220 total reps—22 percent	*Week One*—297 total reps—27 percent
Week Two—270 total reps—27 percent	*Week Two*—242 total reps—22 percent
Week Three—320 total reps—32 percent	*Week Three*—352 total reps—32 percent
Week Four—190 total reps—19 percent	*Week Four*—209 total reps—19 percent

Figure 4.19 Advanced Off-Season Cycles

PROGRESSION

This overall pattern applies to off-season training, where there are no significant sport or outside physical demands on the athletes. Under optimal conditions, there are at least four months of progressive training between the start of the off-season and the return to sport.

In the current sports environment, that is less of a reality, with athletes either engaged in multiple sports or with restrictions from collegiate and professional sports regarding the amount of time allowed for team activities.

The negative effects of this shortened training window are a hotly debated topic, and make the importance of a well-planned and executed program all the more critical.

In an ideal scenario, the monthly volume over the course of the off-season will steadily advance with a planned unloading month during the fourth month of training. In most cases, this will coincide with what we consider the preseason cycle, just before training camp for football athletes, and just prior to competition for other sports.

We will dive into the specifics of the preseason planning on page 237; however, the general progression for our two example athletes would look something like this:

NOVICE-LEVEL OFF-SEASON MONTHLY CYCLES	ADVANCED-LEVEL OFF-SEASON MONTHLY CYCLES
Cycle One—800 total reps Cycle Two—880 total reps *10 percent increase* Cycle Three—960 total reps *10 percent increase* Cycle Four—720 total reps *25 percent decrease from peak volume*	Cycle One—1,000 total reps Cycle Two—1,100 total reps *10 percent increase* Cycle Three—1,200 total reps *9 percent increase* Cycle Four—900 total reps *25 percent decreased from peak volume*

Figure 4.20 Off-Season Monthly Cycles

Two general rules should be followed when planning your volumes from cycle to cycle. First, any increase in training volume from one cycle to the next should not exceed 10 percent of the previous month's total volume. With the plan to continue to advance the training intensity throughout the off-season, adding too much volume on top of a higher work intensity is effectively burning the candle at both ends. You may see gains in the short term by pushing both volume and intensity higher, but long-term progress will suffer if the athletes are unable to recover from the added demands.

The second rule is that for cycle four—the unloading or preseason cycle—the total volume is reduced by roughly a quarter to a third of the total volume of the third cycle, which should be the peak of the off-season volume.

This allows for a continued high training intensity, yet the lower training volume helps buffer the recovery demands from the start of training camp or the preseason period.

That drop in training volume will also be due to the reduced frequency of weight-training days available as the fourth cycle leads into the start of training camp. If there are only two or three days available for weight work along with the practice schedule, it is impossible to squeeze a high volume of work into those workouts.

In the case of many collegiate athletes, there are only eight weeks for training in the off-season before the start of camp. In that case, we might not use the same sharp drop as is prescribed, and the preseason cycle might be skipped. We will cover that in more depth later.

When you plan for the following year's off-season, you can set the first cycle's total monthly volume based on the peak volume the athletes achieved the previous year.

The expectation is that each year, the strength and power of the athletes will not only improve, but their capacity to handle more work will also increase. A possible four-year plan for a high school football athlete could look something like this:

HIGH SCHOOL ATHLETE OFF-SEASON VOLUME				
	YEAR ONE	YEAR TWO	YEAR THREE	YEAR FOUR
CYCLE ONE	800 reps	850 reps	900 reps	1,000 reps
CYCLE TWO	850 reps	900 reps	975 reps	1,100 reps
CYCLE THREE	900 reps	960 reps	1,050 reps	1,200 reps
CYCLE FOUR	720 reps	750 reps	800 reps	900 reps

Figure 4.21 High School Off-Season Annual Volumes

There is nothing to say that athletes could not start the subsequent off-season at a higher volume. This sample is a conservative approach that should allow for steady gains.

In practice, you could even use the same program two years in a row with only adjusted volume totals and still expect to see gains in strength and power, particularly for younger and less-experienced lifters. While an advanced athlete can handle a more rapid progression of work, you want to "slow cook" your developing athletes.

HIGH SCHOOL ATHLETE OFF-SEASON WEEKLY VOLUMES PER CYCLE				
	YEAR ONE PERCENT	YEAR TWO PERCENT	YEAR THREE PERCENT	YEAR FOUR PERCENT
WEEKLY VOLUME	28–22–35–15	28–22–34–16	27–22–33–18	27–22–32–19

Figure 4.22 High School Off-Season Weekly Volumes

There is some wiggle room in the breakdown of the volume undulation between the weeks of a cycle. As a novice athlete matures and progresses through subsequent years of training within this system, the volume percentages can begin to slide toward the advanced level. For example, the cycle percentages for that same high school athlete could gradually change as the training years advance.

The weekly volumes gradually shift during the sophomore and junior years so that by the time the athletes have reached the senior year, they should be in the advanced level of training. This is not entirely necessary; it is another way to help physically prepare an athlete's body to handle the added training volume that will come with subsequent years of training in this style.

Starting with an idea of the total monthly volume to allocate to your athletes, the volume will be further broken down into exercise choices and our training weeks and session examples.

EXERCISE VOLUME PRINCIPLES

- *The total monthly training volume is distributed between seven primary movements: Squat—Clean—Press—Pulls—Snatch—Jerk—Posterior Chain.*

- *Do not exceed 25 percent of the total monthly volume in one particular exercise due to the overtraining effect.*

- *You need at least seven percent of the total monthly volume in a single exercise for a minimal training effect.*

With this programming, the total monthly volume is distributed across the fundamental movements.

The foundation of each training cycle is placed on the development and progression of the athlete's performance.

Squat—Clean—Press—Pulls—Snatch—Jerk—Posterior Chain

These lifts are the most critical in terms of carryover from the weightroom to performance in sports. The purpose of linking specific volumes to the lifts is to ensure the appropriate amount of work to elicit the greatest positive gains in strength and power while guarding against the risk of overtraining.

The movements that place the greatest physical demands on the nervous system and recovery and demand refined technique need to be tightly controlled. If there is no consideration for the total training volume in a month, week, or session, we run the risk of overtraining or sacrificing the quality of the work. The relative importance of some of the movements can and will change depending on the different levels of an athlete's experience.

Ideally, we distribute the monthly volume among the seven movements based on their relative importance in the training continuum, although all seven movements do not have to be trained within a given training cycle. Each movement lends itself to different qualities of power and strength for sports performance; however, depending on the goals of the training and the athlete's abilities, we can change the training values.

For example, a novice athlete may not be ready for loading the jerk due to deficits in technique and total-body strength and stability.

Perhaps the goal of a training cycle could be more directed toward absolute strength development, and the Olympic movements might be left out of that four-week period.

The coach's ultimate goal should be to incorporate all of the movements throughout the training lifetime of an athlete—always with consideration of the athlete's needs.

For each movement there is a defined volume range, which is largely due to the different demands and expectations for various levels of athletes. This should also incorporate what physical traits you are hoping to influence during that particular training cycle.

As you know, novice athletes require more emphasis on the strength-building movements, while advanced or elite athlete require and will be able to tolerate higher volumes of the Olympic lifts to generate maximal rates of force production.

The general monthly volume distributions we have found most effective are:

- ***Squat***—*18–25 percent of total volume*
- ***Clean***—*18–21 percent of total volume*
- ***Press***—*14–20 percent of total volume*
- ***Pulls***—*7–15 percent of total volume*
- ***Snatch***—*7–15 percent of total volume*
- ***Jerk***—*7–15 percent of total volume*
- ***Posterior Chain***—*7–18 percent of total volume*

The ranges of volume for each of the movements are not arbitrary. These came from Soviet guidelines, as well as our years of experimentation and the analysis of our programming and the eventual results.

We have made the mistake of dedicating too much volume to squats and cleans and too little volume to other movements, and ultimately found it best to operate somewhere within these adjusted ranges. We will delve deeper into the specific programming of the exercises for each level of athlete, yet it is important at this stage to clarify how to distribute the initial volume.

You will gain little from exceeding 25 percent of the total volume dedicated to one particular movement. Additionally, as noted earlier, there will not be enough total volume to stimulate progress with less than seven percent of the total volume for a movement.

If you are training all seven primary movements, exceeding that 25-percent volume threshold—particularly for cleans and squats—will enter the realm of overtraining and cause the repetitive strain injuries or nervous system fatigue that can kill any gains made in the gym. By designing the program within the narrow ranges of volume for each movement, we can optimally load an athlete with less concern of taxing the body's recovery systems beyond its limits.

Based on that, we could assume that the ceiling for total volume for squats would be 25 percent and the floor for posterior chain work would be seven percent. If you are training only four or five of the movements within a cycle, you can exceed that 25-percent cap. It would then be even more important to plan and vary your training intensity to avoid overtraining.

Taking a slightly conservative approach will never let you down when determining volume, and that will hold true here. In most cases, we want to come slightly off the extremes to find a sweet spot.

If we use the example of an advanced athlete's training cycle that allocates 1,000 repetitions for the entire month, we can then distribute those repetitions among the movements.

As a simple example, let us assume that for the month we want 20 percent of the total volume to be squats, 18 percent to be cleans, 16 percent as presses, 14 percent pulls, 12 percent snatches, 10 percent jerks, and 10 percent posterior chain movements.

Our 1,000-repetition month would look like this:

- *Squat*—*200 reps*
- *Clean*—*180 reps*
- *Press*—*160 reps*
- *Pulls*—*140 reps*
- *Snatch*—*120 reps*
- *Jerks*—*100 reps*
- *Posterior Chain*—*100 reps*

You can see how the total volume for the four-week training cycle is spread among the seven movements.

This says nothing about sets and reps or intensity level; it simply lays out the distribution of the work.

When beginning this type of programming, pick your exercise volume percentages and stick with them throughout the off-season and preseason period—in-season programming will be a different animal. When you have truly grasped the intricacies of The System, you can manipulate those percentages from cycle to cycle to address weaknesses or lagging movements. Still, do not make things more complex than they need to be.

These numbers, of course, are not set in stone. There can and will be manipulation of those percentages based on the particular demands of an athlete's sport, experience and ability, and the time of year.

Assuming this is the first time you are using this method of programming, we recommend beginning your program design with the general guidelines shown in Figure 4.23 for total monthly volume.

As you can see, we do not include the jerk in a novice athlete's program. The jerk is a highly technical lift with significant demands on strength and stability that the average novice lifter does not possess. For that reason, any volume that would be dedicated to the jerk can be allocated to the more fundamental strength-building movements to build a base. That same approach can and should be used for any other movements that are too advanced or less applicable for the particular sport demands of an athlete.

[CHAPTER FOUR—SYSTEMATIC PROGRAM DESIGN]

	NOVICE	ADVANCED	ELITE
SQUAT	24 percent	22 percent	18 percent
CLEAN	18 percent	19 percent	21 percent
PRESS	20 percent	17 percent	14 percent
PULLS	15 percent	11 percent	7 percent
JERK	0 percent	8 percent	12 percent
SNATCH	10 percent	13 percent	18 percent
POSTERIOR CHAIN	13 percent	10 percent	10 percent

Figure 4.23 Total Monthly Volume Examples

Changing the relative volumes and distribution is something best reserved for the coach who has put in the time to master the nuances of this style of programming and is comfortable with the various levels of the athletes.

You can see how as an athlete's level advances, more total volume is dedicated to the power movements and less is allocated to the strength movements. This is because we expect those loads to be significant, and a more-experienced lifter will generally respond well to lower-rep, higher-intensity work.

Another way to use the exercise percentages is through adjustment of the individual movements from cycle to cycle. As your athletes' strength levels increase and their efficiency with the Olympic movements improve, you can gradually shift a larger percentage of work toward those lifts. This is how we move from a more generalized strengthening plan toward a more power- and speed-directed focus.

For example, if a novice-level football player were to begin the first training cycle with the percentages listed, you could change successive cycles to emphasize different qualities.

143

NOVICE LEVEL	CYCLE ONE	CYCLE TWO	CYCLE THREE
SQUAT	24 percent	22 percent	21 percent
CLEAN	18 percent	18 percent	20 percent
PRESS	20 percent	22 percent	20 percent
PULLS	15 percent	15 percent	16 percent
JERK	0 percent	0 percent	0 percent
SNATCH	10 percent	12 percent	13 percent
POSTERIOR CHAIN	13 percent	11 percent	10 percent

Figure 4.24 Novice Cycles

As the off-season progresses, we could allocate more volume to the power movements to build the speed and explosiveness of the athlete as the season approaches. For the beginning lifter, it is possible to see good gains while keeping the total monthly volume relatively consistent and simply adjusting the volume and intensity of each movement, as well as changing the exercises. However, when implementing this style of programming for the first time, keeping things simple will serve you best.

WEEKLY VOLUME

The weekly volume breakdown should look familiar from the previous calculations. You will now use a similar wave pattern of loading to break the weekly volumes down into specific training session volumes.

As we are varying the volume with each workout, we again program in stress and recovery within the week.

NOVICE OR ADVANCED ATHLETE MONTHLY VOLUME	NOVICE OR ADVANCED ATHLETE WEEKLY VOLUME
Week One — 28 percent total reps	*Day One* — 28 percent weekly reps
Week Two — 22 percent total reps	*Day Two* — 22 percent weekly reps
Week Three — 35 percent total reps	*Day Three* — 35 percent weekly reps
Week Four — 15 percent total reps	*Day Four* — 15 percent weekly reps

Figure 4.25 750–1,000 Reps Monthly Volume

ADVANCED OR ELITE ATHLETE MONTHLY VOLUME	ADVANCED OR ELITE ATHLETE WEEKLY VOLUME
Week One — 27 percent total reps	*Day One* — 27 percent weekly reps
Week Two — 22 percent total reps	*Day Two* — 22 percent weekly reps
Week Three — 32 percent total reps	*Day Three* — 32 percent weekly reps
Week Four — 19 percent total reps	*Day Four* — 19 percent weekly reps

Figure 4.26 Greater than 1,000 Reps Monthly Volume

EYE OF THE COACH

If an athlete is excelling in strength movements but not the power movements, redistribute the percentages to allow for more volume in the power movements. Do this only when you are confident in your program design and the athlete's ability. Try to keep the exercise percentages constant and manipulate the total monthly training volume as a first option, and then change intensity before deviating too far from the baseline numbers.

For athletes who are unable to train on a four-day per week schedule, you can also use a three-day per week schedule with adjusted volume totals. However, training above the 1,000-rep monthly total on an abbreviated schedule can generate too high a demand on recovery, and might stall progress.

If it is necessary to use a three-day schedule, the total monthly volume should be constrained. Where we may like to set our monthly volume and then decide the frequency, more often than not, the frequency the athlete is able to train will dictate the monthly volume.

FEWER THAN 1,000 REPETITIONS MONTHLY VOLUME	FEWER THAN 1,000 REPETITIONS WEEKLY VOLUME
Week One—28 percent total reps *Week Two*—22 percent total reps *Week Three*—35 percent total reps *Week Four*—15 percent total reps	*Day One*—42 percent weekly reps *Day Two*—24 percent weekly reps *Day Three*—34 percent weekly reps

Figure 4.27 Three-Day Volume Example

SAMPLE TRAINING CYCLES

The math to determine an athlete's program is not particularly challenging; however, the mistake we see most often is incorrectly determining the training volume for each training session. You must first decide what the weekly total volume will be and then extrapolate the daily percentages from that number. More than a few coaches end up with a monthly total of 3,000 repetitions on their first pass because of simple math mistakes.

NOVICE MONTHLY VOLUME 750 REPETITIONS	VOLUME FOR WEEK THREE 262 REPETITIONS
Week One—28 percent is 210 reps *Week Two*—22 percent is 165 reps **Week Three—35 percent is 262 reps** *Week Four*—15 percent is 112 reps	**Three Sessions Per Week** *Day One*—42 percent is 110 reps *Day Two*—24 percent is 63 reps *Day Three*—34 percent is 89 reps

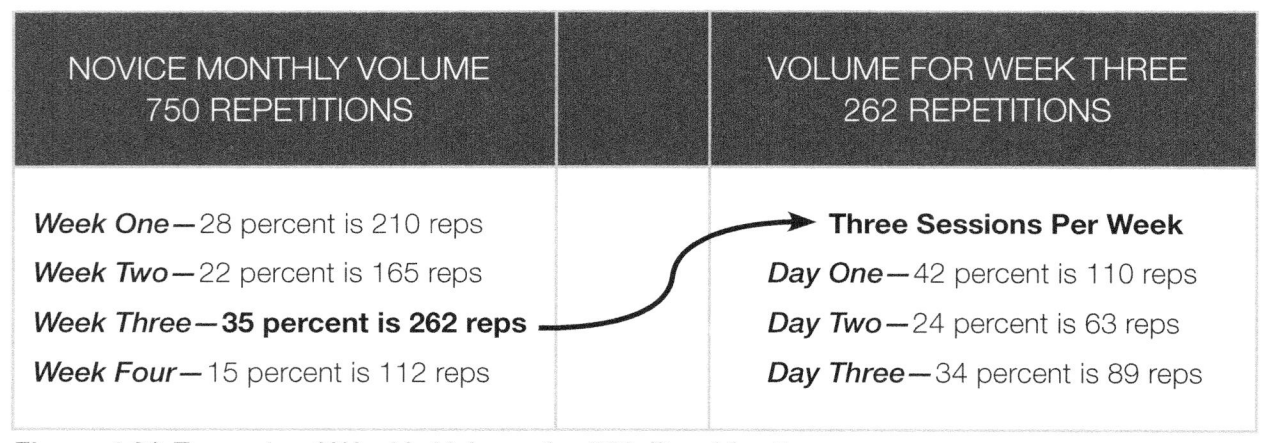

Figure 4.28 Example of Weekly Volume for 750-Rep Month

The weekly rep totals are inclusive of all the primary exercises performed that week, without counting the accessory work. Those 110 repetitions performed on day one will include some combination of movements from the fundamentals, as will days two and three. We determine the specific exercise volume by taking the volume percentage for the movement from the weekly total.

To paint a broader picture, let us use the example of an advanced athlete in a 1,000-rep month.

ADVANCED MONTHLY VOLUME 1,000 REPETITIONS
Week One—27 percent is 270 reps *Week Two*—22 percent is 220 reps *Week Three*—32 percent is 320 reps (detailed below) *Week Four*—19 percent is 190 reps

Figure 4.29 Example of Weekly Volume for 1,000-Rep Month

Using the advanced athlete baseline numbers for monthly exercise percentages we have:

- *Squat (22 percent) = 220 reps*
- *Clean (19 percent) = 190 reps*
- *Press (17 percent) = 170 reps*
- *Pull (11 percent) = 110 reps*
- *Snatch (13 percent) = 130 reps*
- *Posterior Chain (10 percent) = 100 reps*
- *Jerk (8 percent) = 80 reps*

In week three, 32 percent of the total monthly volume would equal 32 percent of the total reps for each movement performed within the week:

WEEK THREE = 320 TOTAL REPETITIONS		
70 Squat reps (70.4)	42 Snatch reps (41.6)	26 Jerk reps (25.9)
61 Clean reps (60.8)	35 Pull reps (35.2)	
54 Press reps (54.4)	32 Posterior Chain reps (32.0)	

Figure 4.30 Example of Week Three

We distribute the repetitions for each exercise across the training days. The 1000-rep example helps illustrate the decisions you need to make when the total volume falls on the margin of the three- or four-day per week training schedule.

You can program those 320 repetitions as either:

WITHIN-WEEK VOLUME WEEK THREE, 320 REPETITIONS	
Four Sessions Per Week	Three Sessions Per Week
Day One—27 percent is 86 reps	*Day One*—42 percent is 134 reps
Day Two—22 percent is 71 reps	*Day Two*—24 percent is 77 reps
Day Three—32 percent is 102 reps	*Day Three*—34 percent is 109 reps
Day Four—19 percent is 61 reps	

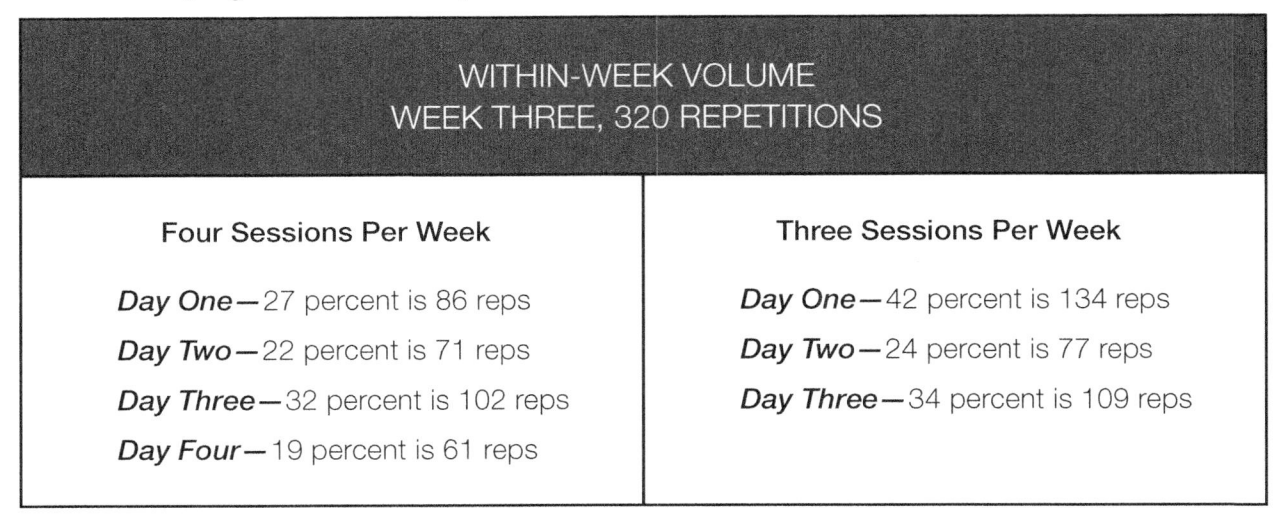

Figure 4.31 Example of Within-Week Volume

From this view, there is not much to dictate which design is better. The goal is always to optimize the training stimulus, while simultaneously building recovery into the system. Through classification of the training sessions based on volume, we can better appreciate which model works best.

WORKOUT CLASSIFICATIONS

With the total number of reps dedicated to each training session, there is another way to reframe the perspective of workout sessions based on individual volume.

The classification system works to categorize a workout as "Great," "Big," "Moderate," or "Light."

This is about balancing the training effect from session to session, so it is not max training every time. Using these classifications takes the decision of when to schedule a recovery session out of your hands. By providing another tool to systematically assess and build in the training volume, we remove some mental strain.

GREAT WORKOUT
150–175 TOTAL WORK REPS

Reserved for exceptional elite athletes

Rarely used due to physical demand

Greatest effect on strength, power, and psychological success

Will require increased recovery time

BIG WORKOUT
100–150 TOTAL WORK REPS

More commonly used due to positive gains

Great effect on strength, power, and some hypertrophy

Will ensure continued success

MODERATE WORKOUT
50–100 TOTAL WORK REPS

Used to maintain gains from the Big workouts

Can employ higher-intensity work due to slightly reduced total volume

LIGHT WORKOUT
UP TO 50 TOTAL WORK REPS

Active rest to aid recovery and recuperation in terms of volume

Allows rest to be programmed in rather than added at random

Can employ higher-intensity work with emphasis on technique and power production—particularly in-season

The rep volumes correspond to the "work" reps for the primary movements—anything above 50 percent of the 1RM. This does not include warmup sets or accessory work.

These terms allow us to assess the training volume of the sessions within the monthly cycle. Using our previous example, our 320-rep week will provide us with one Big workout, and three Moderate workouts.

This week is the highest volume week in the cycle.

WITHIN-WEEK VOLUME WEEK THREE, 320 REPETITIONS
Day One—86 reps *(Moderate)* *Day Two*—71 reps *(Moderate)* *Day Three*—102 reps *(Big)* *Day Four*—61 reps *(Moderate)*

Figure 4.32 Within-Week Volume for Four Sessions, Week Three

If we were to break down the other weeks, we would see more Light workouts scattered throughout. If a monthly cycle contains more Light workouts than Moderate or Big workouts, you are probably not applying enough stimuli to elicit gains.

This is why when dealing with the novice athlete who is training at lower training intensities, three sessions per week will be better in many cases. This will allow for more concentrated distribution of the volume. That same week in a three-session format would look like this:

WITHIN-WEEK VOLUME WEEK THREE, 320 REPETITIONS
Day One— 134 reps *(Big)*   *Day Two—* 77 reps *(Moderate)*   *Day Three—* 109 reps *(Big)*

Figure 4.33 Within-Week Volume for Three Sessions, Week Three

Here we have programmed in two Big workouts, which will elicit a greater training effect, yet will also demand more recovery. The following week will have a significantly reduced overall training volume, and will be our active recovery week with its Light and Moderate workouts.

Doing a comparison between the two options of four sessions versus three sessions for the training cycle, we see:

WEEK	FOUR SESSIONS PER WEEK	THREE SESSIONS PER WEEK
WEEK ONE 270 REPS	3 Moderate—73, 59, 87 reps 1 Light—51 reps	1 Big—113 reps 2 Moderate—65, 92 reps
WEEK TWO 220 REPS	2 Moderate—60, 70 reps 2 Light—48, 42 reps	3 Moderate—92, 53, 75 reps
WEEK THREE 320 REPS	1 Big—102 reps 3 Moderate—86, 71, 61 reps	2 Big—134, 109 reps 1 Moderate—77 reps
WEEK FOUR 190 REPS	2 Moderate—51, 61 reps 2 Light—42, 36 reps	2 Moderate—80, 65 reps 1 Light—46 reps
TOTALS	1 BIG 13 MODERATE 4 LIGHT	3 BIG 8 MODERATE 1 LIGHT

Figure 4.34 Four Sessions versus Three Sessions

Clearly, we can see the difference in the volume density with the three-session design. We are dealing with the same total monthly volume. However, the decreased frequency of training actually results in greater average volume per workout.

> **EYE OF THE COACH**
>
> *An athlete appearing moody, restless, with low energy, or a resting pulse or blood pressure 10 percent higher than baseline is likely overtrained. Sometimes, the signs of overtraining are more subtle than just flat-lined progress or an athlete's decreased output.*
>
> *If the effort in moving 100 pounds looks more like it should be 200 pounds, it is likely time to make a change and reduce the training volume or intensity. If you can train yourself to become effective at spotting the early signs of overtraining, you can change course at a plateau in performance before it becomes a downward slide.*
>
> *A quick test for overtraining is an athlete's vertical jump height. If there is greater than a 10-percent reduction in the athlete's normal vertical height, you should reduce the volume and intensity for that day's training. It helps if the athlete does not know you are testing unless you trust the athlete will give nothing less than a best effort.*

On the surface, it seems better to have more Big workouts to stimulate gains, yet this is a delicate line. Recent studies[44,45,46] demonstrate similar strength gains when training frequency was either three or six times per week if weekly volume and intensity were the same, with a stronger relationship between total volume and strength development. That would seem to favor having fewer sessions in a week to maximize recovery time, but there is certainly an opportunity for too much of a good thing. If the goal is to increase training volume to increase strength development, the athlete may not be ready for the demands of the greater density of volume in each training session.

The athlete's recovery ability is a major determinant in the frequency during the week. Too many high-volume days can take a toll on an athlete who may also be juggling outside factors that compromise the rate of recuperation following a workout. When performing training using 10RM weights, studies showed that most lifters recover their strength levels approximately 48 hours post-training, but even at 72 hours post-training, not all of the subjects demonstrated a full recovery in performance.[47,48]

Adding more training days during the week seemingly shortens that recovery window, but once the volume or training intensity begins to creep up, the four-session design becomes more favorable because otherwise there will be an overabundance of Big or possibly Great workouts without adequate Light recovery workouts. Those high-volume sessions are what demand the most recovery, so being able to spread the volume can help.

At this point, we have not factored in the training intensity for each workout, so it is difficult to say which model is more appropriate. Having light volume days does not mean those sessions will not employ higher-intensity lifts. This is something we will delve into more in the intensity section.

When in doubt, err on the side of gradually building the volume demands on both a monthly and a per-session basis with more frequent training but less volume within each session.

With volume, you will never end up on the wrong side if you take the conservative approach.

TRAINING SESSION VOLUME PRINCIPLES

To elicit a training effect, the minimal effective dose is 12 total exercise repetitions for a movement in a training session.

Being conservative with an athlete's recovery abilities, we will use a four-day per week training routine. Again, our specific exercise volume for week three is shown in Figure 4.35.

STRENGTH EXERCISE VOLUME

No more than 35 reps per exercise, plus or minus three

*10 reps per set—
best for hypertrophy,
less good for strength and power*

*4–7 reps per set—
equally good for strength,
hypertrophy, and power*

*1–3 reps per set—
better for strength and power,
not good for hypertrophy*

POWER AND SPEED EXERCISE VOLUME

No more than 25 reps per exercise, plus or minus three

*4–5 reps per set—
good for explosive strength
and technical training*

*2–3 reps per set—
good for explosive strength*

*1–2 reps per set—
good for maximal strength
and explosive strength*

[CHAPTER FOUR—SYSTEMATIC PROGRAM DESIGN]

WEEK THREE, 320 TOTAL REPETITIONS		
70 Squat reps	42 Snatch reps	26 Jerk reps
61 Clean reps	35 Pull reps	
54 Press reps	32 Posterior Chain reps	

Figure 4.35 Four Sessions Week Three

Now we can distribute those repetitions across our four-day per week training template. A possible breakdown of the weekly repetitions could look something like this:

	WEEK THREE REPS	SESSION ONE REPS	SESSION TWO REPS	SESSION THREE REPS	SESSION FOUR REPS
PREDICTED VOLUME	320	86 *27 percent total*	71 *22 percent total*	102 *32 percent total*	61 *19 percent total*
SQUAT	70	19	15	22	13
CLEAN	61	16	13	20	12
PRESS	54	15	12	17	10
SNATCH	42	11	9	13	8
PULLS	35	9	8	11	7
POSTERIOR CHAIN	32	8	7	10	6
JERK	26	7	6	8	5
TOTAL VOLUME	317*	85	70	101	61

Figure 4.36 Four-Day Training Template

*The total volume for the week differs slightly from the predicted total.

You can see that rounding of the volume percentages took two repetitions from the weekly total. This will be a natural occurrence of the math as you plan the weeks and months—losing a repetition here or there is not concerning.

Of course, in this model we are training every movement on each day, which is not an ideal option given the potential of repetitive strain injuries. We need more refining of the numbers to create a week to build up rather than break down the athletes.

The principles for programming exercise volumes in each training session are important. The described program was not just pulled from thin air. The movements we categorize as strength movements can be trained at a higher volume within a workout than can power movements—strength movements are the squat, press, and posterior chain, while the power movements are the clean, snatch, pulls, and jerk.

When programming the strength movements, we avoid volume greater than 35 reps—plus or minus three—in a training session, particularly when using higher-repetition sets.

Programming for power movements should avoid volumes greater than 25 reps per session—again, plus or minus three—to ensure that athletes maintain strict form for all reps. This lower volume is also due to the high demands those lifts place on the central nervous system.

Performing the Olympic lifts with significant loads of greater than 50 percent of an athlete's max will tax the largest motor neurons and the CNS as a whole. Adding volume requires more recovery between training sessions than may be available. Going to the well too many times can negatively impact performance in all areas, and can increase the risk of injury.

Depending on the goals for an athlete, factoring intensity into exercise volume will also play an important role.

Intensity ranges of 70 percent of 1RM or less generally allow 10 or more repetitions per set. These have been considered the primary training range to produce more hypertrophy or muscular endurance gains than significant increases in strength or power.[49,50]

Similarly, training above 85 percent of 1RM generally means fewer than six repetitions can be performed, which is the intensity range that produces the greatest benefit to maximal strength.

As we will discuss later in the intensity section, the intensity range where the bulk of our training takes place is between 70–85 percent of the athlete's 1RM to most efficiently stimulate both power and strength qualities, while also providing some hypertrophy benefits.

Think of the principles in terms of what we show in Figure 4.37.

STRENGTH MOVEMENTS—SQUAT, PRESS, POSTERIOR CHAIN	
No more than 35 reps per exercise each session, plus or minus three	
10 or more reps per set	Hypertrophy Emphasis
4–7 reps per set	Strength and Hypertrophy Emphasis
1–3 reps per set	Maximum Strength Emphasis

Figure 4.37 Strength Movement Reps

POWER AND SPEED MOVEMENTS—CLEAN, SNATCH, JERK, PULLS	
No more than 25 reps per exercise each session, plus or minus three	
4–5 reps per set	Explosive Strength or Technique Emphasis
2–3 reps per set	Explosive Strength Emphasis
1–2 reps per set	Maximal Load or Explosive Emphasis

Figure 4.38 Power and Speed Movement Reps

Although pulls may use higher loads than the power movements to develop more strength, we program them as power from the perspective of volume.

Knowing our goals for an athlete and using these guidelines, we can manipulate the daily intensity and volume per set to dictate the effects of the training in an undulating pattern. Providing this continuous, variable stimulation develops hypertrophy, strength, and power preferentially at different times over an extended period.

We will cover more specifics in the session design section beginning on page 177.

Of course, we have seen training systems use set-and-rep schemes exceeding the constraints we put on the movements. However, we are trying to find the effective dose that allows for the greatest gains with the lowest risk of overtraining.

When distributing repetitions throughout the week, we need to ensure that each movement has at the minimum 12 repetitions in a training session to elicit its training effect. That means we have the volume range from 12–35 repetitions per workout for strength movements and 12–25 for power movements—plus or minus three reps in both cases.

Returning to the previous example, there are sessions where we do not meet the minimum required reps for a movement. In those instances, we can redistribute those reps to other days, and can reallocate the movement volumes for each day.

The days in question are highlighted below:

	WEEK THREE REPS	SESSION ONE REPS	SESSION TWO REPS	SESSION THREE REPS	SESSION FOUR REPS
PREDICTED VOLUME	320	8 *27 percent total*	71 *22 percent total*	102 *32 percent total*	61 *19 percent total*
SQUAT	70	19	15	22	13
CLEAN	61	16	13	20	12
PRESS	54	15	12	17	**10**
SNATCH	42	11	**9**	13	**8**
PULLS	35	**9**	**8**	**11**	**7**
POSTERIOR CHAIN	32	**8**	7	10	6
JERK	26	**7**	**6**	**8**	**5**
TOTAL VOLUME	317	85	70	101	61

Figure 4.39 Distributing the Reps Per Exercise

The reps in bold denote volumes that fall below the 12-rep minimum.

Knowing that our goal is for strength movements to fall between 12–35 repetitions per session and power movements to be between 12–25 repetitions per session, we could reconfigure the week as shown in Figure 4.40.

	WEEK THREE REPS	SESSION ONE REPS	SESSION TWO REPS	SESSION THREE REPS	SESSION FOUR REPS
PREDICTED VOLUME	320	86 *27 percent total*	7 *22 percent total*	102 *32 percent total*	61 *19 percent total*
SQUAT	70	20	12	26	12
CLEAN	61	22	16	23	0
PRESS	54	27	0	27	0
SNATCH	42	0	22	0	19
PULLS	35	0	14	21	0
POSTERIOR CHAIN	32	17	0	0	14
JERK	26	0	13	0	13
TOTAL VOLUME	318	86	77	97	58

Figure 4.40 Redistributing the Reps

With the volume of each movement redistributed throughout the week, we have satisfied the constraints of the session volumes for the strength and power movements. Given the same scenario, two coaches might come up with slightly different combinations of movements for each session. Some of the difference would come from personal preferences of movement combinations or from the desired training effect; there is no right or wrong here.

If higher volumes are a concern, one method is to cluster exercises to allow for better distribution. One cluster we found beneficial from both a performance and a volume standpoint is cleans and presses on days one and three of a training week, and snatch and squats on days two and four. This can help distribute the relatively high volumes of squats and cleans on different days when concerned about the program taxing recovery.

We chose the week three example earlier because of the high volume of squats and cleans when we used a third day to appropriately distribute them. When the total volume for a particular movement exceeds 60 repetitions for a week, it is better to perform that movement over more than just two training sessions.

You saw how 70 reps of squats and 61 reps of cleans were spread over three days. We also added an extra session of snatches to spread out the volume. Conversely, we do all the posterior chain volume on a single day because a split of the volume would end up with one or two days below our 12-rep minimum.

Under ideal circumstances, when a particular movement is on the schedule two days a week, we try to program one day at a higher volume and the other at a lower volume. The total volume dictates some of this for the day it falls on, and also the other movements performed that day.

The higher-volume day will have more of a muscular stimulus, while the lower-volume day will have more of a CNS stimulus.

A secondary goal is to alternate the exercises on each day between a higher-volume exercise, followed by a lower-volume exercise and then a higher-volume exercise, although this will not always be possible.

The same plan can be determined for our novice-level athlete on a three-day-per-week training split. Assuming a starting volume with 850 total reps for the month:

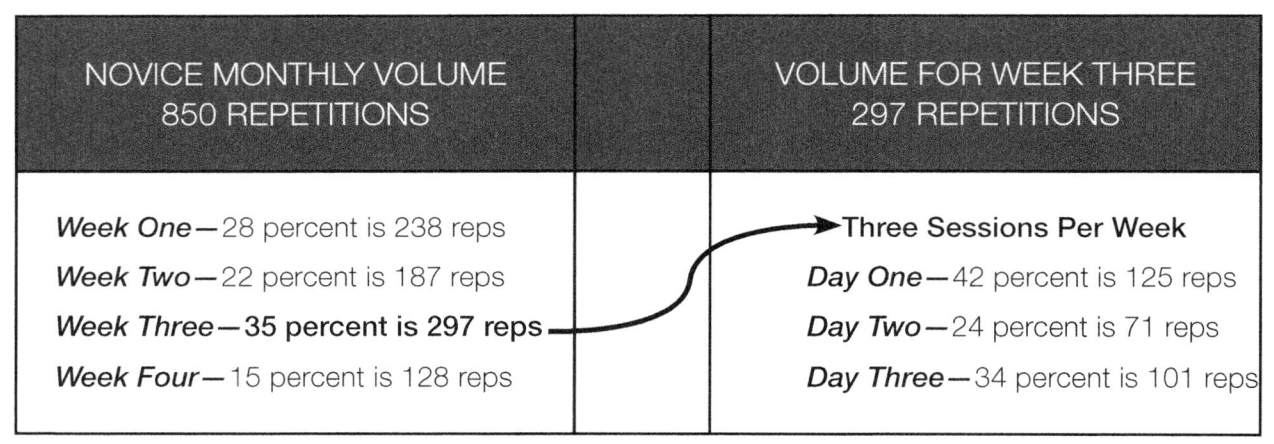

NOVICE MONTHLY VOLUME 850 REPETITIONS	VOLUME FOR WEEK THREE 297 REPETITIONS
Week One—28 percent is 238 reps	Three Sessions Per Week
Week Two—22 percent is 187 reps	*Day One*—42 percent is 125 reps
Week Three—35 percent is 297 reps	*Day Two*—24 percent is 71 reps
Week Four—15 percent is 128 reps	*Day Three*—34 percent is 101 reps

Figure 4.41 Novice-Level Three-Day Split

Our total monthly movement volume distribution would be:

- *Squat (24 percent) = 204 reps*
- *Clean (18 percent) = 153 reps*
- *Press (20 percent) = 170 reps*
- *Pull (15 percent) = 128 reps*
- *Snatch (10 percent) = 85 reps*
- *Jerk (0 percent) = 0 reps*
- *Posterior Chain (13 percent) = 110 reps*

[CHAPTER FOUR—SYSTEMATIC PROGRAM DESIGN]

WEEK THREE 297 TOTAL REPETITIONS		
71 Squat reps	45 Pull reps	0 Jerk reps
59 Press reps	38 Posterior Chain reps	
54 Clean reps	30 Snatch reps	

Figure 4.42 Week Three at 297 Total Repetitions

	WEEK THREE REPS	SESSION ONE REPS	SESSION TWO REPS	SESSION THREE REPS
PREDICTED VOLUME	297	125 *42 percent total*	71 *24 percent total*	101 *34 percent total*
SQUAT	71	30	17	24
PRESS	59	25	14	20
CLEAN	54	23	13	18
PULLS	45	19	11	15
POSTERIOR CHAIN	38	16	9	13
SNATCH	30	13	7	10
JERK	0	0	0	0
TOTAL VOLUME	297	126	71	100

Figure 4.43 Week Three Session Breakdown

159

With one less day during the week, you can see the comparatively high volumes within each session. This is why as the volume begins to climb, the fourth training day becomes so valuable in preventing overtraining.

By reallocating repetitions between days to meet our minimum volume requirements, an adapted week's volume would look like the next chart, Figure 4.44.

	WEEK THREE REPS	SESSION ONE REPS	SESSION TWO REPS	SESSION THREE REPS
PREDICTED VOLUME	297	125 *42 percent total*	71 *24 percent total*	101 *34 percent total*
SQUAT	71	31	18	22
PRESS	59	22	18	19
CLEAN	54	23	19	12
PULLS	45	23	0	22
POSTERIOR CHAIN	38	25	0	13
SNATCH	30	0	18	12
JERK	0	0	0	0
TOTAL VOLUME	297	124	73	100

Figure 4.44 Adapted Week Three Session Breakdown

[CHAPTER FOUR—SYSTEMATIC PROGRAM DESIGN]

> **EYE OF THE COACH**
>
> *If an athlete has to perform more than the principle volume for specific exercises—meaning greater than 35 reps for strength movements, less than 25 reps for power movements—an alternative method to facilitate recovery is to have them either:*
>
> *Perform the remaining reps at the end of the session*
>
> *Perform a second workout on the same day*

> **EYE OF THE COACH**
>
> *When determining what exercises to program on which day or how to distribute the reps, begin by setting the lowest total volume movement and the lowest total volume day. Then decide which movements need more than two days to accommodate the highest volumes, and allocate them to the higher total volume days.*
>
> *By first planning for the movements and days on the highest and lowest volume days, it becomes a little easier to make the numbers fit.*

This week, the squat, clean, and press are trained each training day, while the remaining movements are performed on two days. Few coaches feel comfortable training each of those movements in successive sessions for fear of overtraining. However, we still have not determined the training intensity or the specific variations of each movement over the course of the week. The relationship between the volume, intensity, and the movement dictates the choices to address the training goals for the athlete, while reducing the risk of overtraining or injury.

At this point, you should be able to program a month's cycle from a purely volume standpoint. Marrying the training volume to the training intensity is where the real benefits of this system become apparent.

INTENSITY

Keep exercise intensity within a narrow, undulating range for an efficient training stimulus.

One of the interesting findings that arose from the Soviet analysis of their strength programs was that the bulk of their training was within a relatively narrow range of intensity. A.S. Medvedyev's work found that around 68 percent of the volume of lifts were performed between 70–85 percent of the athlete's 1RM. Only five percent of the total volume of lifts were above 90 percent.[51] For some of the strongest Olympic athletes of the time, this certainly seems counterintuitive, particularly compared to the typical Western mindset.

There is little debate that the goal of most American strength coaches is usually to push their athletes' max lifts higher. It is a rare American weightroom that does not have a wallboard documenting the biggest lifts on the team, and it is a point of pride for people to maintain a position on the wall. To set the bar, most teams have a testing day to determine the benchmark for the athletes' 1RM.

We were some of the few coaches in the NFL who did not have a max testing day or even a board on the wall to mark the best lifts on the team. We rarely even had our players train above 95 percent of their predicted max.

Why? That is primarily because we have rarely seen a max lift performed with any semblance of proper form. We are not training powerlifters whose goal is to perform a single maximal repetition, and we believe it is more valuable to see the heaviest weight the athletes can move with speed and acceleration than the heaviest they can grind out.

With a testing day there is also always the risk that by the time you have seen a large number of squats or bench presses, you will end up okaying reps you normally would not count, and therefore end up with flawed information.

As always, our goals are injury prevention and maximizing on-the-field performance. Neither of those qualities are best addressed through training at the extreme of the intensity range with any regularity, so finding the percentages based more on quality than quantity serves our purposes better.

We adopted the same philosophy of the Soviet coaches by focusing the majority of our training within the narrow band of intensity at 70–85 percent of an athlete's max and emphasizing the speed of movement. In doing so, we saw significant gains in performance and a reduced incidence of injuries and fatigue from overtraining.

For an elite-level athlete, there is certainly a place for training above 85 percent; however, time and experience have shown us the value of reserving that intensity for the athletes who earn the right.

It is still important to motivate your athletes to push their training intensity higher, but seeing their names on the wall is not the end goal. Creating competition within the team is certainly beneficial in enhancing performance, yet putting emphasis on someone moving up the max board is not always in service of the actual goals of preventing injury and enhancing on-the-field performance.

As you will see repeated throughout this book: When in doubt, err on the side of being conservative in terms of both volume and intensity. It is always easier and preferable to gradually add weight or volume if an athlete is excelling in the weightroom, rather than adjusting down once the athlete begins to struggle in the gym or on the field.

DETERMINING PERCENTAGES

Despite the drawbacks of a true 1RM test, we need to determine an estimated maximum for each athlete in order to calculate target weights and percentages in our programming.

For those coaches who do not already have a tested 1RM for their athletes, and particularly those dealing with high school or novice athletes, we recommend a three-rep max test to determine the percentages. We also suggest this for coaches who are not comfortable assessing what a max-effort lift should look like.

Novice athletes are not technically proficient enough in the lifts to maximally load the bar; determining a 1RM will provide an inaccurate number at best. A week of nothing more than coaching technique would drastically alter that total.

By working up to what we call a "three-rep *almost* max," you can ensure proper form while you improve an athlete's feel for the weight and effort. With the three-rep test, you want to see the first rep accelerate upward and once the third rep drastically drops in speed, count that weight as the 3RM. Again, this is probably a conservative estimate; for our purposes, we consider that weight to be 80 percent of the athlete's 1RM.

The 1RM or 3RM tests have been shown to be reliable measures for unilateral strength in both trained and untrained men and women.[52]

This provides a starting point to determine the training loads, with some cushion to avoid over-extending an athlete's abilities too early.

One of the most impressive components of the Russian style of training was the involvement and education of the athlete in the feel for the weights. The intensity level can be controlled based on the energy level and "feel" of the athlete.

Once athletes have an idea of what 80 percent of the 1RM for three reps should feel like, they can better "tune" the weights from day to day. Combining self-regulation from an athlete with the "eye of the coach" is the secret to better controlling the day-to-day fluctuations in performance.

You will need a reference point to work from in exercise selection within each movement category. Spending time assessing and collecting a 1RM for every exercise movement is both tedious and pointless. By estimating max numbers for the core lifts, you can work backward to select the training load and intensity for the other lifts.

A quick reference chart might be as seen in Figure 4.45 on the next page.

CORE MOVEMENTS TRAINING INTENSITY DETERMINED FROM TESTED 1RM	TRAINING INTENSITY DETERMINED FROM PERCENTAGE OF CORE MOVEMENT 1RM
BACK SQUAT	Front Squat Step-Ups Lunges
BENCH PRESS	Incline Press Overhead Pressing— *Use percent of bodyweight rather than bench press max*
CLEAN	RDL Clean Pulls
SNATCH	Snatch Pulls

Figure 4.45 Exercise Selection

Basing percentages on bodyweight is another method of estimating a 1RM once novice athletes have experience handling progressively heavier weights. The following chart shows a general guideline we have used as both an overall relative strength goal as well as a 1RM predictor for the primary lifts.

MOVEMENT	ESTIMATED 1RM
SQUAT	Bodyweight times 1.5
CLEAN	Bodyweight times 1.25
OVERHEAD PRESS	Bodyweight
SNATCH	Bodyweight times .9

Figure 4.46 Estimating 1RM

With more training experience and physical development, many athletes' maximal strength will exceed these values, but we have seen significant improvements in physical performance with those developing athletes who can meet these marks.

INTENSITY AND VOLUME

To revisit Prilepin's chart covered beginning on page 39, we see the relationship of the reps-per-set scheme as it relates to the training intensity. As the intensity of the exercise increases, the reps in each set and the total repetitions performed will decrease.

PERCENT OF 1RM	REPS AND SETS	OPTIMAL NUMBER OF REPS	TOTAL VOLUME REP RANGES
55	3–6	30	18–30
60	3–6	26	18–30
65	3–6	24	18–30
70	3–6	20	12–24
75	3–6	18	12–24
80	2–4	15	10–20
85	2–4	12	10–20
90	1–2	6	4–10
95+	1–2	3	2–4

Figure 4.47 Training Intensity

Again, Prilepin's approach was specific to Olympic weightlifters, and the demands of team-sport athletes are significantly different. Those considerations mean you will slightly modify the approach to address other athletes' needs and the demands of a sport.

INTENSITY RANGE PERCENT 1RM	REP RANGE	POWER	STRENGTH	HYPERTROPHY
85 PERCENT OR GREATER	1–3	Moderate Effect	Large Effect	Minimal Effect
75–85 PERCENT	3–6	Moderate Effect	Moderate Effect	Small Effect
70–75 PERCENT	4–8	Moderate Effect	Small Effect	Moderate Effect
LESS THAN 70 PERCENT	10 reps	Small Effect	Minimal Effect	Large Effect

Figure 4.48 Effects of Intensity Ranges

When we know what qualities we want to emphasize, we can select both the optimal training intensity and the optimal rep-and-set range.

In the previous chapter, we covered the specific volumes per set for the strength and power exercises without addressing the intensity component. By appreciating the relationship between training intensity and volume per set, you should start to see the thread that ties The System together.

STRENGTH MOVEMENTS SQUAT, PRESS, POSTERIOR CHAIN, PULLS*	
NO MORE THAN 35 REPS PER EXERCISE EACH SESSION PLUS OR MINUS THREE	
10 or more reps per set	Hypertrophy Emphasis
4–7 reps per set	Strength and Hypertrophy Emphasis
1–3 reps per set	Maximum Strength Emphasis

Figure 4.49 Strength Movement Rep Ranges

*Pulls fall into both categories depending on the goal of programming.

[CHAPTER FOUR—SYSTEMATIC PROGRAM DESIGN]

POWER AND SPEED MOVEMENTS CLEAN, SNATCH, JERK, PULLS*	
NO MORE THAN 25 REPS PER EXERCISE EACH SESSION PLUS OR MINUS THREE	
4–5 reps per set	Explosive Strength or Technique Emphasis
2–3 reps per set	Explosive Strength Emphasis
1–2 reps per set	Maximal Strength/Power Emphasis

Figure 4.50 Power and Speed Movement Rep Ranges

Now we start to see where the intensity and rep and set relationships come into play. The only major modification made to Prilepin's chart is in our inclusion of slightly higher set and exercise volumes to produce more hypertrophy when necessary. Just as with the Russians, technique and speed of the bar take top priority with all training.

The primary goals for a strength coach involved in athletics is to improve strength and power and reduce the risk of injury in the most efficient manner. A strength coach cannot afford to let one training quality suffer at the expense of another, which is why the 70–85 percent intensity range is the optimal range for efficiency in influencing strength and power without sacrificing one over the other.

EYE OF THE COACH

We have observed that some athletes with a high genetic power potential tend to be proportionally smaller in the midsection and low back. These are the type of athletes who, without much weight training or gym strength, exhibit a naturally high power output in jumping or running. Despite their high output, many of these athletes tend to have lower work capacity due to this structural build.

Be careful to not overextend their capacity in your set-and-rep programming. Instead of three sets of five reps, they may respond better to five sets of three reps. This maintains the same total volume while programming to their ability to help avoid injuries.

EXERCISE INTENSITY PRINCIPLES

- *As the load increases, the velocity and power of movement begins to decline.*
- *The majority of training should be within a narrow range of intensity at 70–85 percent 1RM to most efficiently enhance both strength and power.*
- *Novice athletes will train the majority of the work sets at lower intensity levels than advanced and elite athletes.*

THE ZONES OF INTENSITY

We determine the appropriate intensity level for the training movements under the umbrella of the six Zones of Intensity. Each zone encompasses an intensity range to provide a different stimulus in our programming for particular training qualities.

ZONE ONE—50–59 PERCENT 1RM

This is the range of intensity we generally use in the warmup. Weights in this range should be light enough that an athlete can perform in excess of 10 repetitions. The purpose is to increase body temperature and the pliability of the soft tissue. In the case of novice athletes, this zone will actually encompass more than the warmup because it will help refine technique and build work capacity for a beginner.

ZONE TWO—60–69 PERCENT 1RM

We use this range to prepare the nervous and musculoskeletal systems for the main workout. These are the warmup sets for the main movements, where the emphasis should be on perfecting the form and speed qualities of the lifts.

With the novice athlete, we again use this range heavily in perfecting technique and building a foundation of strength and speed of the bar for progression into more intensive training.

ZONE THREE—70–79 PERCENT 1RM

This range is where athletes begin to better develop the strength and speed-strength qualities. The bulk of the training volume occurs in this range as athletes progress through the first year or two of training in The System.

ZONE FOUR—80–89 PERCENT 1RM

Extending into this range of intensity further develops an athlete's maximal strength qualities. Novice-level athletes may progress into this training intensity if they demonstrate the physical ability to handle these loads. Advanced and elite-level athletes train into the upper range of Zone Four to enhance their explosive abilities.

ZONES FIVE AND SIX—90–99 PERCENT AND GREATER THAN 100 PERCENT 1RM

We use this maximal range of training sparingly, primarily to perfect psychological and maximal strength development. Training successfully with loads greater than 90 percent of max requires a high degree of concentration and movement quality. We reserve this range of training for athletes who have earned it.

With a primary focus on improving the qualities of strength and power, the majority of the training load should fall between Zones Two and Four: 70–89 percent. Rarely will the training load venture north of 90 percent of the 1RM, and the goal of setting a PR does not enter into the equation. Your athletes will not get stronger by testing and setting records in the weightroom; they get stronger by training.

USING THE ZONES

When an athlete achieves an appropriate level of training experience and efficiency of movement, you will implement speed training in Zones Two to Four, with the bulk of the work done in Zones Two and Three.

Reserve Zone Four for those with exceptional athletic ability, as the emphasis of any sport training should always focus maximal acceleration of the weight. Extending into the 80-percent range is certainly beneficial to further develop strength and power, yet will generally be met with too extreme of a reduction in bar speed to be optimal for athletic enhancement.

If a particular sport demands maximal strength development, training into the 90-percent range of the 1RM will play a more prominent role. However, it will still encompass a small percentage of the total volume of work.

RELATIVE INTENSITY

It is important to recognize the *relative intensity* of the work when analyzing a program and determining the training intensity. Over the course of a training session, a movement will be performed at different intensity levels, for different reps within each set. A series of back squats based on a 1RM percentage might be 50x6, 60x4, 70x4, 70x4, and 75x4. Of those 22 repetitions, the athlete would perform six reps in Zone One, four reps in Zone Two, and 12 reps in Zone Three.

Relative intensity takes into account the repetitions in relation to the performance intensity to provide an average training intensity for the movement. We need to determine the total work performed and divide it by the total number of repetitions.

(50 percent x 6) + (60 percent x 4)
+ (70 percent x 4) + (70 percent x 4)
+ (75 percent x 4)

↓

(300) + (240) + (280) + (280) + (300)

↓

= 1,400 / 22 reps = **63.6 percent 1RM**

The relative training intensity for a squat workout of 63 percent falls within Zone Two. By keeping the same intensity for each set but reallocating our repetitions, we see the relative intensity of the session will change.

(50 percent x 4) + (60 percent x 3)
+ (70 percent x 5) + (70 percent x 5)
+ (75 percent x 5)

↓

(200) + (180) + (350) + (350) + (375)

↓

= 1,455 / 22 reps = **66.1 percent 1RM**

This does not seem like a profound change with about a two-percent increase in relative intensity. That will become important as an athlete is moving more weight when the intensity increases along with the added sets and reps.

Simultaneously increasing the training intensity and volume is a touchy balancing act as we work to prevent overtraining. In this case, where the goal for the athlete is to train more sets in desired intensity range at 70–75 percent to elicit strength and power gains, allocating additional repetitions at lower intensities pulls down the overall training intensity.

If the goal is to introduce higher-intensity sets in Zone Four at 80–89 percent while maintaining the training volume and average training intensity, the repetitions can be redistributed to balance out the training effect.

(50 percent x 5) + (60 percent x 3)
+ (70 percent x 4) + (70 percent x 4)
+ (75 percent x 4) + (80 percent x 2)

↓

(250) + (180) + (280) + (280) + (300) + (160)

↓

= 1,450 / 22 reps = **65.9 percent 1RM**

The first set of five reps performed at 50 percent of 1RM allows for a warmup and technique work, and the second set at 60 percent only needs two or three reps for a gradual progression and feel for the movement with more load. The goal is still for the bulk of the work to fall in the 70–79 percent range, with the final set extending up to 80 percent.

When the reps per set are less than four, an athlete should be striving to accelerate the bar and focus more on the power aspect of the movement. By manipulating the reps per set, you can expose the athlete to higher-intensity work while maintaining the total volume and relative intensity.

Relative intensity will be important as you drill down into the programming to determine the desired training intensity of a movement or session.

SELECTING TRAINING LOADS

An effective training system will ultimately employ work through all the Zones; however, your athletes have to justify their right to advance the training intensity and load.

The goal of training is not only about moving your athletes as quickly as possible into higher intensities, particularly in the case of novice athletes.

Quality should always come before quantity in both volume and intensity.

NOVICE ATHLETE

Primarily Zones of Intensity Two or Three—
60–75 percent 1RM and occasionally into Zone Four

Figure 4.51 Novice Athlete Intensity Zones

For novices, put your priority on teaching the movements and allowing enough repetition to first engrain good movement patterns and develop strength. Novices have to do sufficient reps in a set to get the feel of the movement and allow for corrections. Advance too quickly into higher intensities, and all of their effort will be spent on handling the weight instead of perfecting the movement. When cleans start looking like reverse curls combined with a limbo maneuver or they are leaning back to finish a military press, it is time to reduce the load.

In addition, with the novice lifter, each training session should focus on technique for one primary lift at a time. Trying to teach technique of multiple movements in the same training session leads to limited retention.

For example, in the first year of high school, we recommend almost all of the work should be done in Zones One and Two, with some forays into Zone Three. That is mostly 50–70 percent of max, but that allows for sets of higher reps and incursions into the four- to seven-rep range to improve their feel and allow them enough reps to correct in response to your coaching.

The secondary benefit of this approach is developing hypertrophy as they progress and their bodies grow and develop, which is obviously important for football and other contact sports. Because we expect this level of athlete to be relatively new to strength training, the weight used at those 50–70 percent intensities should steadily increase as they gain time under the bar. As we said, these athletes can often use the same general programming for the first two years of training and still see continued improvements in strength and power.

ADVANCED OR ELITE ATHLETE

Primarily Zones of Intensity Three and Four—
70–89 percent 1RM and occasionally into Zones Five and Six

Figure 4.52 Advanced or Elite Athlete Intensity Zones

You will progress the training of more advanced athletes into Zones Four and Five as they demonstrate successful gains in strength and power and appropriate recovery. These athletes will make some jumps into the 90–100 percent intensities every once in a while; however, that will still be the exception rather than the rule.

Unless you work with professional or very proficient athletes, you will get 98 percent of the training effect in the 70–85 intensity window. That last 10 percent of the intensity range is the difference in the last two percent of performance for the cream of the crop.

Some of the strongest athletes in the world train above 90 percent of their max sparingly. Pushing the training envelope is a privilege and not a right for the advanced or elite athlete. As your athletes mature in training age, they generally respond better to lower reps per set and higher total volume when training for strength gains.

In the Soviet style of training, they did not care how an athlete felt on a particular day in regard to how much work was done. Even if an athlete was jumping through the roof with energy, plates were rattling as the bar was flying, and 80 percent of max looked more like 50 percent, that athlete did not push the volume or intensity level higher than prescribed for the day. It was a rigid system they believed over the long term would lead to optimal gains in performance. The stereotypical Eastern strength coach did not care about the athlete's feelings.

For the less-experienced strength coach, tightly adhering to the prescribed intensity or volume numbers can be a valuable method. This removes some of the guesswork and variability of adopting this style of program design and is a conservative track to follow.

That can be a challenge for a coach because it goes against every impulse we have to push the limits at every opportunity and to see continued gains from week to week. The athletes may have to leave the weightroom feeling as if they cheated themselves, frustrated about being held back or not hitting a new PR. We have been conditioned to think that walking away from a workout without feeling completely exhausted is a waste.

The problem is, the short-term gratification of increasing the volume for the athletes' sake or forcing them to strain under a load they cannot handle that day will impact the long-term pattern of training and recovery that allows for steady progress.

Some days they will feel like they could do more…and that is okay. This philosophy is about taking a big-picture view of where your athletes need to go as you stick to a tightly prescribed plan. With time and experience, you will recognize when and where to be flexible and push the envelope.

> ### EYE OF THE COACH
>
> *In our practice, we have used high-performance days to allow the athletes to slightly increase the weight on the bar, but never at the expense of speed of the lift. You need to refine your "eye of the coach" to see when athletes can be pushed and when to dial things back.*
>
> *Because we are tying the percentages to the desired rep ranges for a particular training effect, if your athletes are able to perform a lift at a heavier weight within the prescribed intensity and rep range, let them go.*
>
> *However, if one of those athletes comes in another day looking lethargic and straining with the warmup sets, expect that athlete to still put in the work for the day, but at a reduced intensity level. Those symptoms can be the body demonstrating that the CNS might not be firing on all cylinders, and it is time to take the foot off the gas pedal.*

When determining a Zone of Intensity for training, we base the weights on the most recent numbers we have for previous training sessions or our determined "easy" three-rep max and the goals of the training session—power, strength, or hypertrophy development. As the cycles progress and your athletes improve their movement efficiency and output, you will still use the Zones of Intensity and reps per set, but the emphasis falls to what you see in the day's performance.

Any number of variables can impact an athlete's performance on a given day, particularly with high school or college athletes. A late night studying, relationship drama, or not eating breakfast or lunch can all lead to drops in performance in the weightroom.

The program may call for sets of three reps at 80 percent of 1RM for bench press and the prescribed weight may be 225 pounds. Base the determination of load for that workout on what the athlete can handle that day…on what you see. If an athlete is struggling to move a weight, you need to adjust to allow some level of success. That does not preclude the athletes from giving their best possible efforts that day, but there is no sense in beating a dead horse.

If a movement looks slow or the only way the bar is making it up is through some creative contortions, that is not an 80-percent day.

We want to see controlled, explosive movement for all the fundamental lifts. We want to hear the plates rattle as the bar accelerates through the motion.

If we can only achieve that with 180 pounds on a particular day, that is where we train. The goal is to hit the volume target and fall within the rep-per-set and intensity range for the desired training effect. That will often be a moving target. Always defer to what you see rather than what the plan calls for on a specific day.

We sympathize with coaches who are not comfortable assessing an athlete's performance to know when it is time to dial things back, because it took us years to master that. It also takes courage and control to convince athletes to back off the weights for a session or an entire week. Anyone who sets foot in the weightroom wants to see the numbers climb, and it is hard to not be a slave to those numbers.

It took us a long time to trust what we saw. Being uncompromising on the quantity and quality of work may impact gains in the short term, but will lead to success in the long term.

COUNTING REPS

Once you have determined the desired Zone of Intensity for the work sets of a particular movement or session, it is important to understand when to count the reps. Inconsistency in tracking the work sets can significantly impact the total volume and lead to under- or overtraining.

We always recommend at least one or two warmup sets of progressive loading to perfect technique and speed of a movement. Once the intensity hits 50 percent of the 1RM, the reps count toward the volume total.

> ## EYE OF THE COACH
>
> *As the training intensity increases and the work includes more low-rep sets, if an athlete hits a PR, hold off on further reps and move on to the next exercise.*
>
> *When an athlete takes the body to a point it hasn't previously been, there will be a training effect. Allowing an athlete to over-reach in the next set at an even higher load can lead to bad motor patterns, overtraining, and injury, particularly with less-experienced lifters. The goal is to get stronger and if that goal is met for the day, move on.*

As an athlete progresses through the sets, you should generally stick to no more than a 10-percent increase in intensity from set to set. For example, you could assign one set at 50 percent, one set at 60 percent, one at 65 percent, and then one set at 70 percent. Beyond 70 percent, intensity increases should not be greater than 10 percent per set. Jumping straight from 70 percent to 80 percent or 80 percent to 90 percent can produce too large of a drop-off in the speed of the lift.

Of course, speed will decrease as the loads get heavier, but there should not be a huge drop off from set to set.

If you begin counting the total rep volume at intensities that are below 50 percent, the more warmup sets your athletes do, the fewer reps there are for work sets. The opposite can happen when coaches do not begin counting reps until the athletes are at 60, 65, or even 70 percent of the 1RM.

If you do not begin counting reps until athletes reach those higher intensities, you are adding volume on top of higher relative intensity. In a single training session, it is a minor issue, but if a coach or athlete consistently miscounts the total repetitions, it can begin to erode progress as overtraining sets in. It is important to be meticulous when choosing training loads.

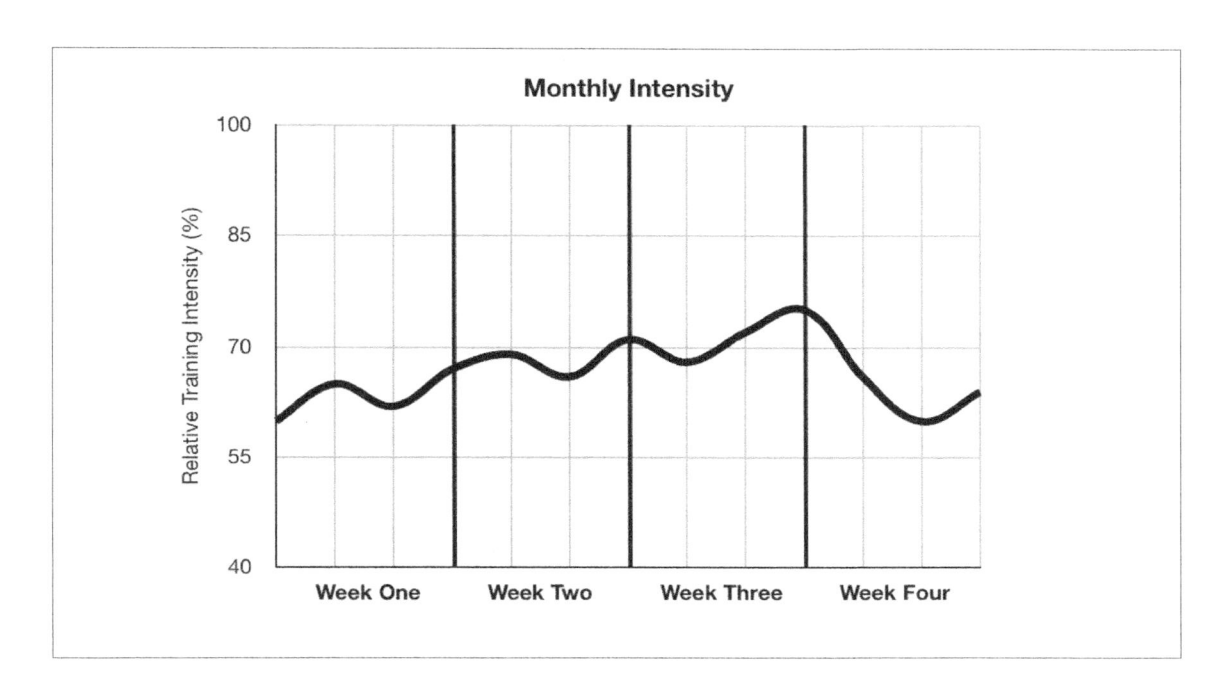

Figure 4.53 Monthly Intensity Per Week

In the same way the volume undulates over the course of a training cycle, the overall relative intensity will also undulate to provide a varied training response.

As you can see in Figure 4.53, over the course of the three weeks, the relative training intensity progresses to include a higher quality of work, and the fourth week sees a drop in the relative intensity.

When the next monthly cycle begins, the first week's relative intensity would be at a higher level than the corresponding week from the previous month.

The previous graph shows a more rapid increase in relative intensity than you may use with your novice athletes, but it should paint a picture that the quality of work is variable but increasing. For the novice athlete, the slope of this line is much more gradual, with a greater emphasis on increasing training volume first and intensity second.

One important aspect we have not addressed in selecting the appropriate training intensity applies to the effect of the athlete's bodyweight on the loads used for the squat, which we will cover next.

SQUAT PROGRAMMING

Determining the appropriate Zone of Intensity is particularly important when training the squat, especially with advanced or elite athletes. Because the squat variations entail moving the weight of the bar and also the weight of the body through the range of motion, we recommend using the bodyweight of the athlete when selecting the appropriate training intensity. We focus more on an athlete's relative strength to bodyweight over absolute strength—the maximal load lifted.

When we encounter stories of football players squatting 500 or 600 pounds, we often debate whether the risk of pushing the loads higher is worth the reward. Obviously, if the sport is powerlifting or Olympic lifting, the load is what matters. For most other sports, the purpose of weight training is to enhance athleticism.

In one example, Coach Goldstein was visiting us at Giants Stadium, where a Giants football player, David Meggett, had easily squatted 427 pounds at a bodyweight of 178. When we asked Coach Goldstein how to make Meggett stronger, he replied, "You do not have to make him any stronger; you have to make him faster."

This comment had a profound impact on our training moving forward and reminded us not to chase higher intensity when it is not necessary.

A 300-pound offensive lineman and a 150-pound wide receiver squatting with 150 pounds on their backs are not moving the same absolute weight. We expect the lineman would be able to handle higher total loads.

However, as we are always looking to manage training intensity, we have to consider the relative work being done. Despite the load being the same, the heavier athlete is moving over 100 pounds more with each repetition. If both athletes are training at 70 percent of max, the larger athlete is likely moving more weight on the bar, as well as more absolute weight. That will require longer recovery times for the heavier athlete because of the additional workload.

For larger advanced or elite athletes who weigh more than 250 pounds, we train approximately 50 percent of the volume for the squat in Zones Two and Three, with the remainder in the higher zones. The smaller advanced or elite athletes weighing less than 240 pounds will train at approximately 50-percent volume in Zones Three and Four.

This does not imply that the larger as well as the smaller athlete will not perform exercise repetitions in all of the Zones of Intensity. When considering heavier body weights, the

Zones of Intensity IV and V must be appropriately programmed and carefully monitored. This consideration is to warrant adequate recovery and the avoidance of excessive fatigue, thus reducing the risk of injury while ensuring continued optimal training and athletic performance.

Just because the training intensity is less for the heavier athlete does not mean we make a sacrifice to the speed of the movement or effort. The goal remains developing explosive strength.

With a small tweak in programming, you will reap the benefits and reduce the risk of overtraining with one of the more physically demanding movements that forms the bedrock of your programs.

PROGRAM DESIGN PRINCIPLES

- *Desired Zones of Intensity should be distributed throughout the training week.*
- *The specific exercise intensity undulates over the course of a training week.*
- *Training intensity is significantly reduced as a planned unload during the final week of a training cycle.*
- *Intensity levels will progress from cycle to cycle over the course of the season.*

Before we dive too deeply into the specifics of planning a training week or session, we need to take an overall view of training intensity as it pertains to the goals for your athletes.

In the chapter on volume, the emphasis was on calculating total volume for months, weeks, sessions, and movements. We mentioned its connection to the training intensity for the week, but without giving any specifics.

The intensity undulates throughout the week during each four-week cycle, with the intensity levels changing from workout to workout for each movement.

The general plan is to perform each movement at least two times per week. With that in mind, the aim is to have one workout of the movement as an intensity day with higher relative intensity, and a volume day at lower relative intensity.

For an intensity day, we generally focus the work sets on the upper reaches of the Zones of Intensity. With a novice athlete, that means ideally sets in the 70–75 percent range, and for advanced or elite athletes it would be in the range of 80–85 percent or higher. Remembering Prilepin's chart, most of the sets are in the three to six reps-per-set range to ideally stimulate strength and power while preserving form.

Looking back at the advanced athlete example, the volume for the week's movements shifted between the days to make sure the daily volumes fell within the minimum and maximum ranges.

The choices for the days and the volumes were not random, because the goal was to have one day at a higher volume for the movement and one day at a lower volume.

This set the week to include one day that could be the intensity day and one as the volume day.

The volume numbers will not always provide an orderly distribution. Some massaging of the values should get you in the neighborhood.

	WEEK THREE REPS	SESSION ONE REPS	SESSION TWO REPS	SESSION THREE REPS	SESSION FOUR REPS
PREDICTED VOLUME	320	86 *27 percent total*	71 *22 percent total*	102 *32 percent total*	61 *19 percent total*
SQUAT	70	20	12	26	12
CLEAN	61	22	16	23	0
PRESS	54	27	0	27	0
SNATCH	42	0	22	0	19
PULLS	35	0	14	21	0
POSTERIOR CHAIN	32	17	0	0	14
JERK	26	0	13	0	13
TOTAL VOLUME	318	86	77	97	58

Figure 4.54 Four Sessions Per Week

Because of the high volume of cleans in week three and with our desire to keep the total reps below 25 in each training session, we distribute the movement across three training days rather than two. We still plan for those reps as part of the day one and day three workouts, as either a volume or intensity day, and the third day is at our discretion. We decide the training intensity for that day based on the other movements being trained.

On day one, we could perform 22 reps; on day three we could call for 23 reps, and include 16 reps on day two to reach our total of 61. We would plan days one and three as volume days, and day two as an intensity day due to its lower total volume.

Accounting for our desired Zones of Intensity, the training sessions could then look like:

Day One
Volume Day, 22 reps

50/4, 60/4, 70/4, 70/4, 75/3, 75/3

Day Two
Intensity Day, 16 reps

55/3, 65/3, 70/3, 75/3, 80/2, 80/2

Day Three
Volume Day, 23 reps

50/3, 60/4, 70/4, 70/4, 70/4, 70/4

*The above are percent of 1RM and number of repetitions—
for example, 50/5 = 50% of 1RM for 5 repetitions.*

DAY ONE 22 REPS	DAY TWO 16 REPS	DAY THREE 23 REPS
Zone One 50–59 percent, 4 reps **Zone Two** 60–69 percent, 4 reps **Zone Three** 70–79 percent, 14 reps **Zone Four** 80–89 percent, 0 reps	**Zone One** 50–59 percent, 3 reps **Zone Two** 60–69 percent, 3 reps **Zone Three** 70–79 percent, 6 reps **Zone Four** 80–89 percent, 4 reps	**Zone One** 50–59 percent, 3 reps **Zone Two** 60–69 percent, 4 reps **Zone Three** 70–79 percent, 16 reps **Zone Four** 80–89 percent, 0 reps
RELATIVE INTENSITY 65.9 PERCENT	RELATIVE INTENSITY 69.6 PERCENT	RELATIVE INTENSITY 65.6 PERCENT

Figure 4.55 Relative Intensity over Three Sessions

With this distribution, the intensity day actually includes one work set in Zone Four, with the volume days primarily emphasizing Zone Three.

Despite the fact that we are training the same movement three days during the week, by working in the different intensity and repetition ranges with a varying volume from session to session, we are able to reduce the risk of overtraining and manage the strain to the nervous and muscular systems.

Showing the breakdown of the Zones of Intensity in relation to the overall weekly volume, it is clear the bulk of the work falls within Zone Three (70–79 percent of 1RM), which is our optimal range to stimulate the qualities of power and strength.

WEEK THREE
CLEANS, 61 TOTAL REPETITIONS

Zone One
50–59 percent — 10 reps

Zone Two
60–69 percent — 11 reps

Zone Three
70–79 percent — 36 reps

Zone Four
80–89 percent) — 4 reps

Figure 4.56 Intensity Zones for Cleans in Week Three

EYE OF THE COACH

Here, the intensity-to-rep relationship will not be as strict as it was in our previous charts. For this advanced-level athlete, we want to provide enough repetition to first emphasize speed and still train the technique of the movements.

At the lower Zones of Intensity, they could certainly perform more reps if they wanted, but, the goal is not to train to failure with each set. It is about taking the long view of the work done to spur progress over the course of the weeks and months.

As you continue to design training sessions, ideally try to alternate one exercise on an intensity day with the next exercise on a volume day, and vice versa. This creates a constantly varying training effect as you undulate the intensity and volume for each exercise throughout the week, as well as within each session. Planned variation of the training variables allows us to simplify the exercise selection and place constant focus on the most important movements.

A sample week of training sessions could look like this:

SAMPLE TRAINING WEEK	
Day One 27 percent, 86 repetitions Clean—Volume Pulls—Intensity Squat—Intensity Press—Volume	**Day Two** 22 percent, 71 repetitions Snatch—Intensity Jerk—Volume Clean—Intensity Pulls—Volume
Day Three 32 percent, 102 repetitions Snatch—Volume Clean—Volume Squat—Volume Press—Intensity	**Day Four** 19 percent, 61 repetitions Snatch—Intensity Jerk—Intensity Squat—Intensity Posterior Chain—Volume

Figure 4.57 Sample Training Week

You can see it will not always hold to the pattern. Do not try to force it. Similarly, if you have two days with low or comparable training volumes, one can be with fewer reps and sets and the other with higher reps and sets, yet at a lower relative intensity to get a similar undulating effect. Just make sure you are programming variation into the lifts and days as it pertains to volume and intensity so there are ebbs and flows of the training stimulus.

This pattern will repeat for the first three weeks of the training cycle. Then, for the fourth week of the month, which from a volume perspective would be the unloading week, we also unload the intensity.

By following the same general volume waves, yet restraining the training intensity to less than 75 percent of an athlete's 1RM, we have created an active recovery week.

Despite the technical challenges inherent in adopting a more quantitative method of programming than is the norm, from a psychological standpoint, the unloading week will be the most challenging aspect for both the strength coach and athlete.

THE UNLOAD

No aspect requires more restraint than the planned unload. The impulse of both the coach and athlete will often be to push for more volume on the intensity days and more intensity on the volume days, particularly if the athlete is feeling good and the bar is moving fast. As the strength coach, the approach you take here is possibly the most critical factor to long-term success in developing powerful athletes.

The fourth week of each training cycle has a significant reduction in the overall volume—just 15 or 19 percent of the total monthly volume—and the training loads will not exceed 75 percent of the 1RM. As strength coaches, we recognize the importance of an unload to prevent progress from stalling or keep athletes from burning out. Unfortunately, it is usually something we push further back or treat as an afterthought, rather than an integral part of programming.

A programmed unload operates as one of the checks and balances of The System. It allows continued training of the fundamental movements and helps us refine technique and speed in the lifting. By restricting both the total volume and the training intensity, we allow the body to recover from the heavier training loads of the month and to compensate in response, yet we do this in an active manner.

Too often, strength coaches think of recovery in terms of passive recovery, whether that be ice, sleep, stretching, or low-threshold aerobic work. All of those activities are integral to promoting an environment where a body can replenish and rebuild. These should absolutely be considered and addressed with your athletes. However, by continuing to train through an unload week in the lower Zones One, Two, or Three, we do not risk the loss of gains in strength and power, and can still keep the athletes fresh.

This is where a coach will have to get comfortable being personally uncomfortable. This unload week will often have athletes leaving the weightroom not tired, not sweaty, laughing, joking, and potentially unfocused as compared to the typical week. We are still asking them to lift and move explosively, yet the lighter loads and minimal volume will feel easy.

Many of the "workers" on the team will either lobby you or attempt to lift heavier or do more work. They might even feel cheated. Other coaches from the "break them down to build them back up" school may be angry or frustrated that you are not pushing the athletes hard enough. That is where the job of focusing, coaching, and educating your athletes and coaches will be critical in creating buy-in.

There is no easy fix, but as the weights on the bar steadily go up, the speeds on the field climb, and the energy levels of the team grow higher, they cannot help but get on board.

PROGRESSION

Like standard periodization models, the system entails a progressive increase in the training intensity over the course of the training timeline. We do it with a more flexible approach to planning intensity, allowing us to avoid the relative decrease in intensity during the competitive season that often appears in linear programs.

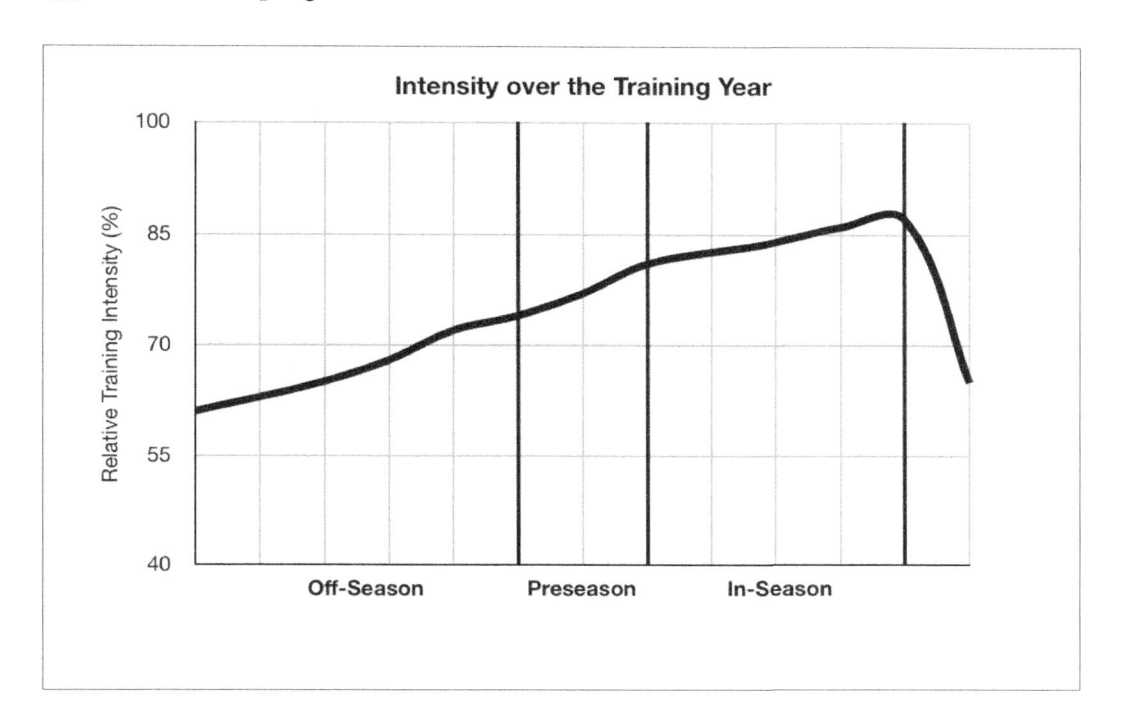

Figure 4.58 Training Year Intensity

Linear periodization models often pick a particular point in time to "peak," such as an athlete training for a peak performance to occur at the Olympic Games. When dealing with sports in which the season spans multiple months, where do you choose to have performance peak? The start of the season? The midpoint? The playoffs?

Our goal is to continue to increase or maintain training intensity over an extended period, and that requires small undulations in the progression of the training intensity.

From a macro view, the previous chart looks like a relatively straight, linear progression from the start of the off-season through the competitive season. However, a better representation of the progression of training intensity is to look at the periodization graph as if it were a graph of the stock market.

The stock market provides a better mental image of progression of training intensity because it represents both the short-term and long-term view of progression over a training year and an athlete's future training.

If we look back over the entire history of the stock market, we see an upward trending line from its inception to the levels it has reached today.

However, zoom in on any particular span of time of that seemingly smooth line, and you see a highly variable line of highs and lows as the market went up and down.

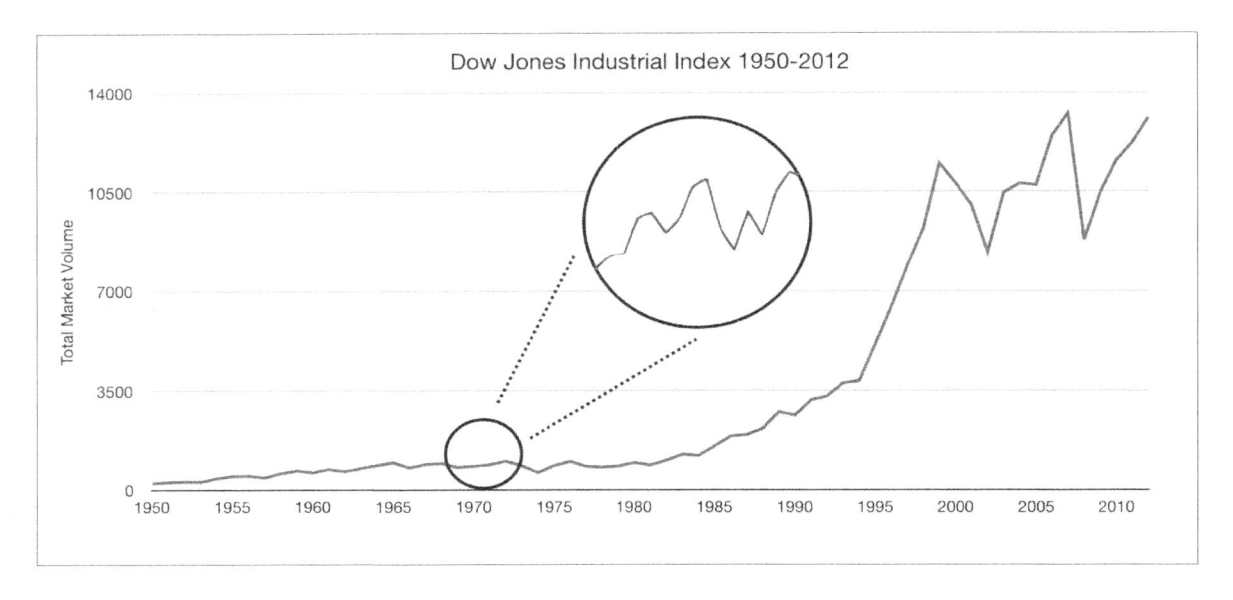

Figure 4.59 Dow Jones 1950–2012

Your program design will look much the same. Over the span of a training year and over the lifetime of an athlete, training intensity should be gradually trending upward. As the months and years pass, the athlete is training at higher Zones of Intensity to develop maximal power and strength for a sport.

Just as with the stock market graph, there will be dips. Some are planned to unload and allow recovery, and some will inevitably arise when an athlete cannot handle the prescribed training intensity or when other factors interfere with the training schedule.

The goal is always to be trending in an upward direction when you zoom out and look at the timeline as a whole.

There will be the small, planned undulations throughout the training year. Once the competitive season is complete, the intensity level will precipitously drop to a lower level and then resume its climb toward the next training year. The wave repeats, with each year seeing the quality of work slowly climb as an athlete matures.

Maintaining the overall training volume and progressing the quality of the work is one of the easiest ways to develop an athlete. For example, for an advanced athlete such as a collegiate freshman, the first cycle of the off-season may begin with 1,000 repetitions spread among the Zones of Intensity in the pattern shown in Figure 4.60.

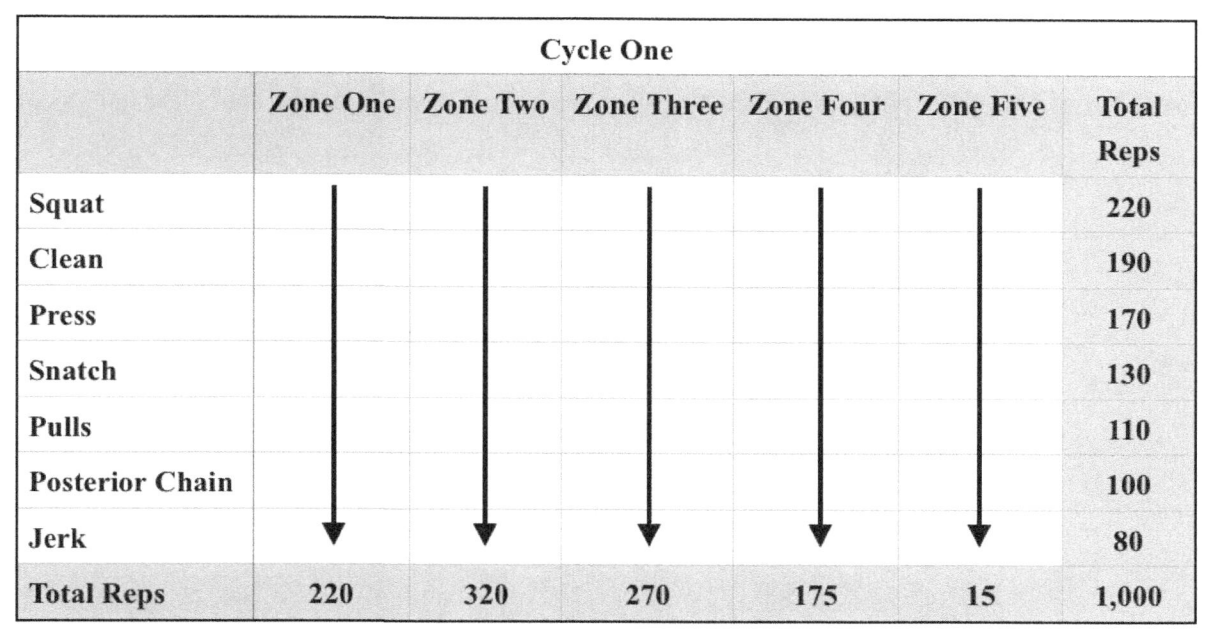

Cycle One						
	Zone One	Zone Two	Zone Three	Zone Four	Zone Five	Total Reps
Squat	↓	↓	↓	↓	↓	220
Clean						190
Press						170
Snatch						130
Pulls						110
Posterior Chain						100
Jerk						80
Total Reps	220	320	270	175	15	1,000

Figure 4.60 Example of Cycle One

For simplicity, we want you to focus on the total volume of repetitions under each zone for all movements combined.

The bulk of the training volume (320 reps) falls within Zone Two—60–69% of 1RM—but over the successive cycles, the graph will shift to the right as the athlete achieves a higher quality of work or intensity per repetition. If the total monthly volume is maintained at 1,000 reps, a higher total number of reps would be performed in the higher zones, resulting in a higher quality of work and improved overall performance.

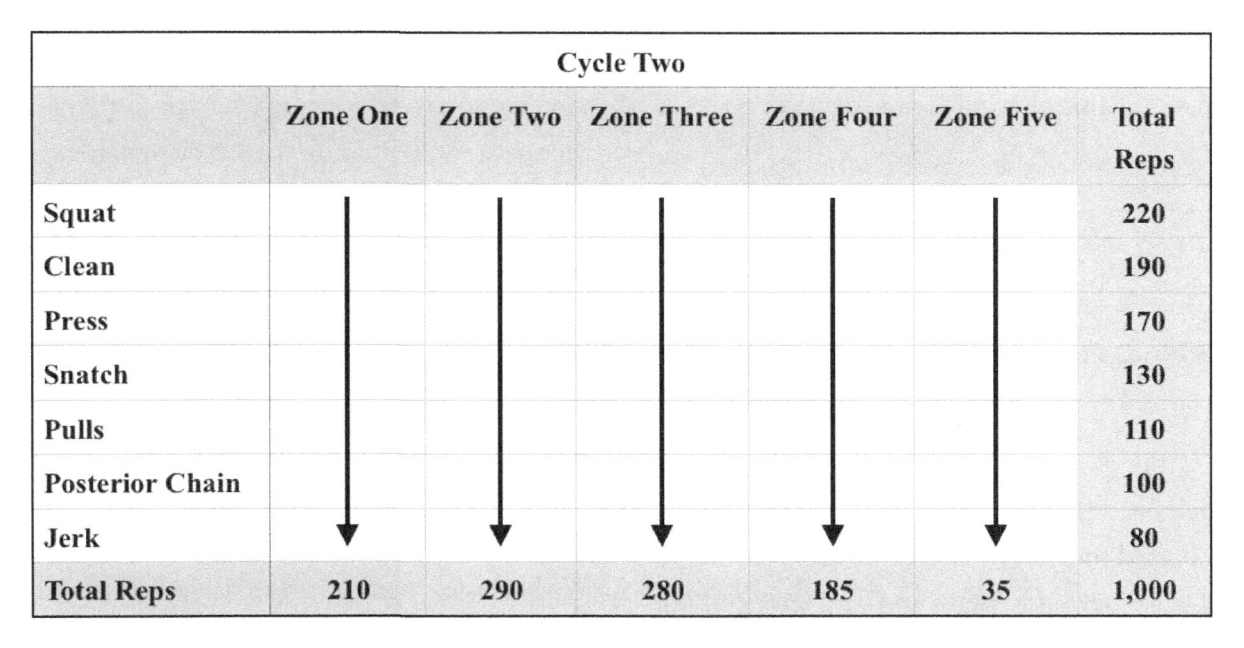

Cycle Two						
	Zone One	Zone Two	Zone Three	Zone Four	Zone Five	Total Reps
Squat	↓	↓	↓	↓	↓	220
Clean						190
Press						170
Snatch						130
Pulls						110
Posterior Chain						100
Jerk						80
Total Reps	210	290	280	185	35	1,000

Figure 4.61 Example of Cycle Two

Note the shifting total volume of reps into the higher intensity zones.

Viewed another way, if we were looking at a single movement such as squats over the off-season cycles, the repetition distribution for the movement could look similar to this:

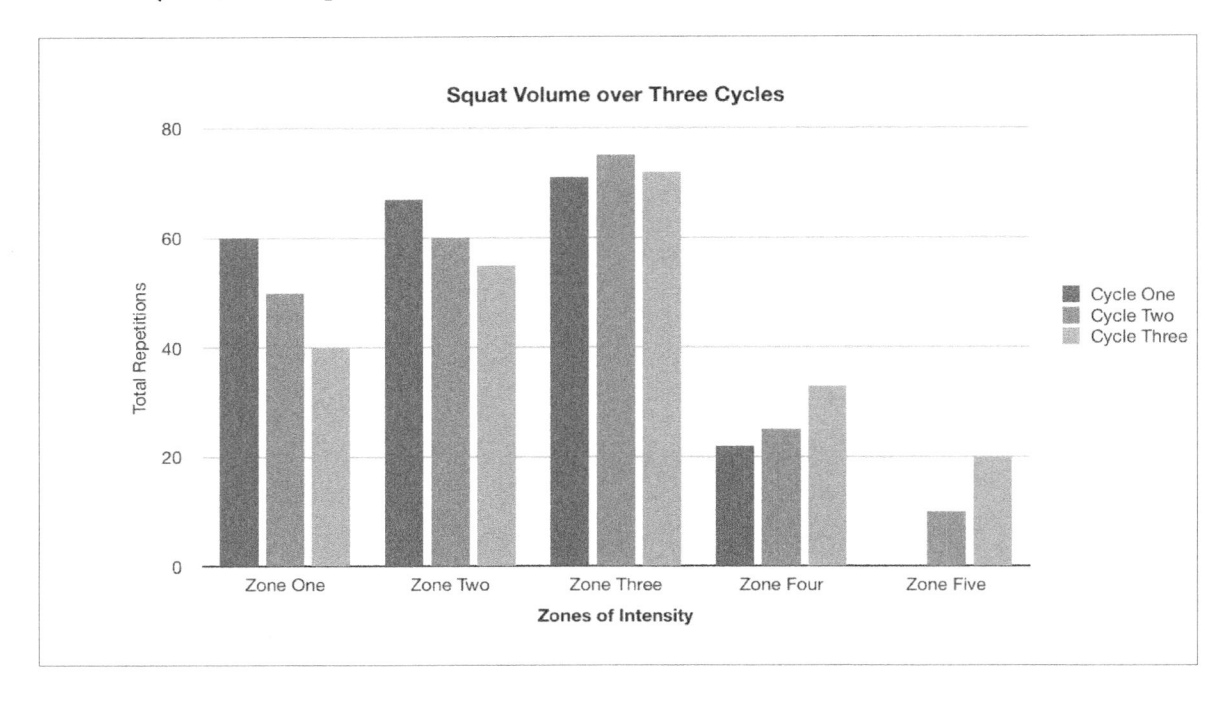

Figure 4.62 Squat Volume over Three-Month Cycle

The relative volume of training performed in Zone One steadily decreases while Zones Three to Five gradually increase. Again in this example, the total volume of squats remains constant from month to month.

Remember the caveat to this design: The relative intensity climbs over the course of the training cycles, but not in a linear fashion. Within the training cycles, we program small elevations and dips of intensity. Some will be planned and some will be out of necessity.

This is where developing the eye of the coach becomes indispensable. Using a percentage-based model and the guidance of Prilepin's chart for selecting reps and sets gives us the most accurate planning and tracking of the training loads.

However, we must recognize that basing the loads strictly off percentages is still a flawed method. With rapid gains in strength, a novice athlete's 1RM may go up in a couple weeks. The maximal reps at a given percentage are inconsistent from athlete to athlete; where one athlete can perform five reps at 80%, another may only be able to perform three or four. Even a week of poor sleep from studying for finals or travel may mean that 75% 1RM for that day will be less than the "true" 75%.

This is where becoming a slave to the numbers leads to frustration as you struggle to find the "perfect" program that fits every individual. We have designed "perfect" programs that had to be tossed in the trash because of outside variables—a delayed cross-country plane flight following a game, a physical double-overtime game the players literally limped away from, a stomach virus working its way through the locker room.

Despite the limitations in percentage-based training, focusing on quality first will serve to iron out inconsistencies. Plan your sets, reps, and intensity based on the goal of training at that time and let the speed of the bar dictate whether the load matches your estimated percentage. If you can develop your eye of the coach and quickly recognize when it is time to dial back the intensity, you will become more comfortable coaching to the individual rather than coaching to your program.

Over the course of weeks and months and years of training, something will inevitably arise to challenge the best laid plans, but the principle of progressing training intensity while remaining flexible in your approach should hold true.

Program design on paper rarely translates into reality. We still try.

FREQUENCY

As we discussed earlier in the section covering volume, we determine the ideal training frequency based on total monthly volume. If there are greater than 1,000 repetitions, we will have four sessions per week; under 1,000 generally means three sessions per week. This ideal scenario most often applies to off-season training when the training schedule is most open and flexible.

However, more often than not, volume does not dictate frequency—frequency dictates volume. If there is more time available to train, training frequency should increase, allowing for a higher training volume. If time is limited, training volume decreases because the training frequency is lower. Trying to squeeze more work into a smaller time window leads to breakdowns as the workouts and volume begin to pile up.

In the case of in-season training, which will be covered later, priority goes toward maintaining energy levels and output on the field above all else. There are demands for practice, games, film study, and meetings, and time for training becomes a precious commodity. That reduced training time inevitably means fewer workouts and a reduced training volume. However, there must be a minimum of two training sessions per week to sustain the training effect of power and strength throughout the competitive season.

In football where there is only one game per week, we usually have a Monday workout the day after a game, and the second workout will be Thursday or Friday, with at least one recovery day before a game. With sports that have multiple games per week, maintaining the twice-per-week frequency can be a challenge when considering the need to include recovery time. The best option in these cases is to have one workout immediately following a game.

Clearly, as it pertains to high-intensity training, training in an already fatigued state is far from an ideal situation.

However, allowing training to fall by the wayside because of less-than-ideal conditions shows up on the field. Programming higher-intensity work throughout the season pays dividends in performance as long as the volume is appropriately controlled.

In the case of Coach Parker's athletes, multiple New York Giants players set PRs two days before a playoff game, and went on to dominate on the field.

It is important to maintain strength and power gains from the off-season into the competitive season, and also to strive to continue to enhance those qualities.

TRAINING EFFICIENCY

Whether training using The System or another periodization plan, the goal is to maximize the training effect while minimizing the risks of overtraining. Research on the best methods to stimulate testosterone and other hormone production with resistance training is conflicting to say the least.[53]

Intensity, volume, exercise order and selection, and rest periods all factor into the degree of hormonal release with training. Due to the spike and then gradual decrease in free testosterone and other hormones during an exercise session, we keep the training time to 60 minutes, plus or minus 15 minutes.

Bulgarian coaches stressed to us that after 45 minutes of training, testosterone levels dropped by up to 80%. For this reason, they would break their training into multiple sessions each day, although the evidence for their findings is difficult to uncover.

If the goal is maximizing muscle fatigue for bodybuilding, allowing a training session to drag into a two-hour running conversation between sets and exercises may not present a particularly negative effect on the training stimulus.

However, weight training for athletes is ultimately focused on training intensity over training volume. We want the movements to be explosive and powerful, and longer rest periods may be required to allow for more complete CNS recovery, particularly on heavy days.

Too often the recovery time between sets drags from two or three minutes to 10 minutes. An athlete's goal should be to attack a workout with efficiency and intensity. Get in; get out. It is important to ensure recovery between sets for maximal output, but training under a state of mild fatigue can also develop physical and mental toughness that carries out onto the field.

When we plan a 60-minute training session, we are not counting the time spent warming up or cooling down, and we are not counting warmup sets. The workout time begins as soon as an athlete enters the selected Zone of Intensity with the first exercise and begins counting reps.

Particularly in-season, time spent in the weightroom is time that could be used in meetings or working on sport skills or technique. For in-season training, we have even restricted the training time to 20–45 minutes to keep the routine brutally efficient. In the changing landscape of collegiate athletics, athletes are severely limited in the amount of time they are allowed to spend in team activities. Time comes at a premium.

In the struggle to squeeze more work into less time, we have seen instances of supersetting of movements—performing two non-competing movements back to back—to improve time efficiency.

We sometimes see coaches cutting rest breaks down to where the training looks more like a CrossFit® workout. These methods can be employed in certain instances with accessory work to help build work capacity. However, to perform an entire training session this way will not create the best environment to develop high-level power and strength, which is our main goal.

When dealing with a constrained environment or if we are trying to program in-season for sports that have more than one game per week, the goal is to find the minimum effective dose of frequency, intensity, and volume, and maximize our results within that framework. When time and recovery are in short supply and performance on the field is the number one priority, the focus should always be on quality work performed intensely.

Focusing on the major movements and approaching your program design with sound principles will help streamline your work in a challenging environment.

DESIGNING THE TRAINING SESSION

- *Train all physical qualities throughout the training year to a varying degree.*
- *Exercise selection should reflect the athlete's training level, the point in the season, and the training emphasis for each cycle.*
- *Exercises change each four-week cycle to allow for variation in stress.*
- *Progress the program from simple to complex.*
- *The training session should be structured as:*

Warmup

Power or fastest exercise

Absolute strength movements

Exercises of local effect

Abs, grip, neck, or supplementary work

ADDRESS ALL QUALITIES

To varying degrees, address all the physical qualities of work capacity, strength, power, and speed throughout the training cycle.

This core principle regarding exercise selection is what makes this system such an efficient method of program design. The exercises are tied to the monthly variation in the percentage of each training movement. The reason there are ranges of total volume for each movement is because multiple factors influence the volume for each movement.

As earlier discussed, a novice athlete requires more total volume in the strength movements of the squat, clean, press, and posterior chain work to build a foundation of strength.

Dedicate the bulk of the training volume to those movements for these athletes; however, the goal is to still maintain some thread of the power and explosive movements of the snatch with the eventual addition of the jerk.

Following the hierarchy, we always dedicate some work to each physical quality to maintain gains. Speed training may be the pinnacle of the training hierarchy, yet even the novice athlete needs a minimal effective dose to train that quality.

Priority goes to the qualities forming the foundation of the pyramid; however, just as dedicating too much emphasis to one component can have negative impacts on the others, completely forsaking one component can also negatively impact progress.

As a novice athlete matures and gains strength and proficiency in the lifts, the more complex lifts begin to assume a larger portion of the total training volume.

TIME OF SEASON

If there is one specific pattern we follow, it is that as the off-season advances and the competitive season grows closer, the intensity level gradually progresses with an increased emphasis on explosive or power movements for carryover to the sport. This does not vary significantly from most other periodization models in use today. The qualities to highlight will shift over the weeks and cycles, with the exercises changing every four weeks, but the overall goal and progression of athletic development are the same for the novice, advanced, and elite athlete.

Although the starting volumes of the primary movements differ based on the experience of the athletes, the emphasis on the higher qualities in the hierarchy increases as the season arrives.

Everything exists on a continuum, with fluctuations and shifts based on a coach's decisions and an athlete's needs. That is the challenge and also the benefit of The System. The continuous variability and shifting training effects of the general framework can appear daunting in design. This ultimately spurs consistent gains in the athlete's performance and avoids prolonged plateaus.

[CHAPTER FOUR—SYSTEMATIC PROGRAM DESIGN]

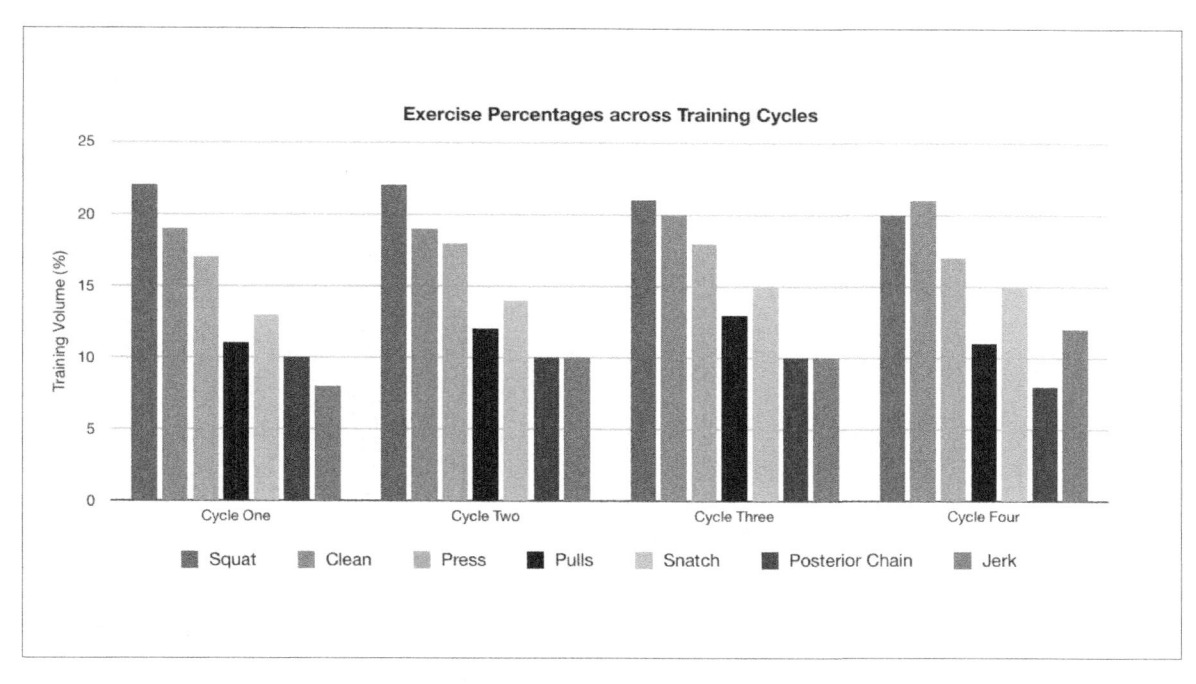

Figure 4.63 Example of Exercise Percentages

SESSION STRUCTURE

The design of a training session was one of the most beneficial takeaways from our time spent with the Soviet coaches. We had previously been performing a general warmup and stretching, and then diving into the training without deep thought into exercise order or determining what sequence would enhance the performance of each lift.

There were also times when we fell into the trap of splitting our workouts into upper- or lower-body days, as you would see in a typical bodybuilding program. There are no upper- and lower-body days when playing sports, and we shifted to the idea that each training session should consist of total-body movements.

The warmup should be more than just random movement prep and build-up sets of the main lifts. Increasing body temperature and blood flow are the top priorities to improve the extensibility and mobility of the soft tissue and joints.

We also want to activate the central nervous system and prime the movement patterns to be trained. There are plenty of options of exercises you can use to warm up; however, we have found the following to be incredibly fast and effective movements for a full-body prep, which you will see in Figure 4.64.

FULL-BODY PREP MOVEMENTS	
Overhead Squat—1x6	Hyperextension and Reverse Hyper—x 20
Shrugs—3x8	Toe Touches with a Bar—x 20
Around The World—6 each way	Kettlebell Swing—x 15
Single-Leg Squat—1x6, each leg (for athletes weighting less than 250 pounds)	Lateral Step-Ups—x 20, each leg
	Hanging Knee-Ups—x 10–15

Figure 4.64 Prep Movement Rep Ranges

Generally, we select two or three movements depending on the workout, and all of the movements are performed with no more than 50 percent of an athlete's 1RM if performed with load.

Overhead and single-leg squats, which we use as our screening movements, improve flexibility and balance for greater depth and body control for squatting and the Olympic lifts. The other movements improve activation of the posterior chain and postural musculature to prepare an athlete to handle the training loads. If you chose to design your own warmup, remember the purpose is preparing the body for the training movements to follow. Every choice should have a purpose.

Javorek's Complex One from page 65 is another valuable inclusion in a warmup. By using a load less than 50 percent of an athlete's max for low reps, will also prime the nervous system for explosiveness and build in more reps for technique on the Olympic lifts. In addition, low-rep box or vertical jumps prior to the main lifts also prepare the CNS and lower extremities for rapid movement. We have found that five or six repetitions of jumps or plyometrics are often enough to trigger improved force output in the subsequent lifts.

The first primary lift should always be the fastest or most explosive exercise. Beginning the training session with the Olympic lifts "charges" the nervous system through the high demand of the speed of the lift and full-body coordination. Calling the high-threshold motor units of the nervous system into action first ensures they will be primed for the subsequent lifts and will not be excessively fatigued for the movements that require more technical proficiency.

Athletes can perform a heavy squat with good form in a fatigued state, yet a heavy snatch done at less-than-full capacity will end up, at best, with some creative compensations and at worst, injury.

Consider the technique demands of the movements, with the snatch and jerk being more technically demanding than a clean as an example. It is more appropriate to program these first.

The next lifts should be the absolute strength movements. In this case, squats, presses, or posterior chain work follow the first explosive lift. This does not mean the absolute strength movements are not performed explosively. However, because they are less technically demanding and will often entail higher-rep work, they should follow the initial lifts.

We also found it best to perform each movement for all the sets and reps before moving to the next movement. Some strength coaches superset opposing movements to increase the density and efficiency of a training session, but program design is not always about cramming more work into a smaller window. Making athletes focus on form, speed, and the technical aspects of one movement at a time will improve their proficiency and performance in the short and long term, especially with novice athletes who may be developing the particular movement patterns for the first time.

For the novice lifter training on a three-day-per-week cycle, days one and three will consist of a minimum of four main lifts, and day two will consist of at least three. There will be significant variations in where the exercises fall because we have one less training day than the typical advanced or elite program.

The week's total volume and a particular movement's volume dictates which exercises fall on each day. Often, the volumes for the week may be so low that a particular movement will only be trained once or only on day two, which is a low total volume day and may have only three or four main lifts.

Looking back to our example athletes, the structure for the novice lifter in week three could be:

SAMPLE WEEK NOVICE		
Day One	**Day Two**	**Day Three**
Clean	Snatch	Snatch
Pull	Clean	Clean
Squat	Squat	Pull
Press	Press	Squat
Posterior Chain		Press
		Posterior Chain

Figure 4.65 Sample Exercise Selections over Three Sessions, Novice

For the advanced or elite athlete, we follow the same pattern spread over the four days, with days one and three consisting of four or five main lifts, and days two and four of at least three. This, again, is a general starting point. As the total monthly and weekly volume increases, there will be instances when additional movement volume needs to be trained on a third day and can be distributed where there are "extra" reps to be used for the training day.

The advanced example from the higher-volume week three could look something like Figure 4.66.

SAMPLE WEEK ADVANCED			
Day One	**Day Two**	**Day Three**	**Day Four**
Snatch	Jerk	Snatch	Jerk
Clean	Clean	Clean	Clean
Pull	Squat	Pull	Squat
Squat	Press	Squat	Posterior Chain
Press		Press	

Figure 4.66 Sample Exercise Selections over Four Sessions, Advanced

Once the primary movements are completed, the accessory work or exercises of local effect can be performed. This accessory work serves to support the larger movements by bringing up weak areas and can be tailored to the specific position or sport demands of the athletes.

Here is where you have a little more license to get creative and program work to enhance the performance for a particular sport. Athletes are only as strong as their weakest links. Being able to spot deficiencies and address them through accessory work enhances their overall performance.

Accessory work is not included under the monthly volume total because we do not anticipate it taking as significant a toll on an athlete's nervous system or recovery abilities due to the limited volume performed.

This does not mean you should program five or six accessory lifts that produce additional soreness or muscle fatigue just to squeeze in more work. Hold yourself to the same lean and efficient approach of the larger program and choose two targeted exercises, train them with intensity, and then move on. Pullups, bent-over rows, or dedicated biceps or triceps work would fall under the category of accessory work.

We reserve the last portion of a training session for the supplementary work of abdominal, grip, or neck strengthening, and then recovery.

The goal is to keep a session lean and short, with a high degree of intensity throughout the time in the weightroom. Do not let training sessions drag on with extended rest breaks or conversation. We are not training Olympic lifters with five-minute breaks between lifts to allow for full recovery.

Sports do not generally allow the athletes to fully recover between activities; once they feel ready, they should be back under the bar.

You should now have an idea of the general principles of planning a training cycle accounting for volume and intensity. You have the basic tools to program the weight training by starting from the perspective of the overall off-season training period, and drilling down to the months, weeks, days, and individual sessions to enhance strength and power.

CHAPTER FIVE
SPRINTING AND JUMPING

When training athletes for power and speed in a sport, lifting in the weightroom is not the only component required to maximize performance. Integrating sprint and jump training into the overall program is a critical piece to translate gains in the weightroom onto the field. This can be where many strength coaches fall down when designing effective programming. They sometimes do not know what they are trying to develop or how to do it.

Luckily, our fundamental principles of programming hold true when integrating sprinting and jumping.

SPRINTING AND JUMPING PRINCIPLES

Returning again to the Hierarchy of Development, we see where speed and elastic, reactive strength development comprise the top of the pyramid.

All of the lower qualities need to be sufficiently developed if we hope to maximize an athlete's speed qualities. Through weight training, we develop some baseline work capacity, strength, and explosive strength.

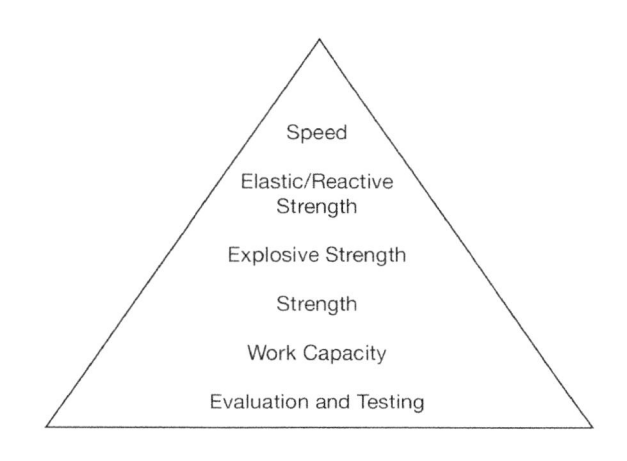

Figure 5.1 Quality Development Hierarchy

When it comes time to program running or speed work, often it is just something pulled from a track and field program intended for sprinters or endurance athletes but added to the lifting program.

Strength coaches trying to develop athletes' full potential should dedicate the same amount of time and mental effort creating and refining the speed and plyometric work as they do the weight programming. That can sometimes be more challenging because of the huge spectrum of options, training devices, and methods available to improve speed.

As it is with all things, the first step is to revisit the principles of training to figure out the *what* and *why* of the training needs. Then, base your decisions off that. From there, you can apply the same method to develop the speed component of training alongside the strength and power components.

True speed and reactive strength training can be particularly taxing on the CNS and the muscular system as a whole. Without a solid foundation of full-body strength and work capacity, it is more likely an athlete will break down rather than progress. We are all likely guilty at one time or another of throwing athletes into 30-, 40-, or 50-yard sprints, or having them jumping on and off boxes before building a physical base. Falling into that trap consistently only increases the odds of strains, sprains, or worse.

If the volume of speed work increases too quickly and there is no appreciation for the demands on an athlete's recovery on top of weight training or practices, there will be too much stress on the system, and performance will suffer.

This is about sensible and progressive loading to ensure long-term success.

SPORT SPEED

A tremendous amount of what we learned and implemented in our speed training came from Olympic track coaches Charlie Francis, Loren Seagrave, and Ben Tabachnik. They were or are extremely smart men, and we called on them on more than a few occasions to analyze what we were doing and how we were coaching. Their input was always tremendously valuable, and shaped our approach and perspective.

We took a lot of the work Coach Francis did[54] and implemented it straight into our training. Before we did that, we first had to first look at his goals for training and compare those with our goals to see where they matched up and where they deviated.

He dedicated the bulk of his coaching to track and field athletes, and in particular Olympic sprinters. Although his results were outstanding, the best methods for training his Olympic sprinters were not necessarily ideal for training our football athletes. Recognizing the similarities and differences between the demands of our particular sports directed our approach in choosing what to borrow and what to modify to our specific needs.

As an example, football presents a unique problem in that it has different positions with different demands for speed. Other than the obvious differences of receivers and defensive backs performing a greater volume of sprinting compared to linemen, even the basics of the body mechanics of the different positions are different.

Linemen start in a crouched, two- or three-point stance; linebackers and running backs start in a squared stance with hands on their knees; and wide receivers and defensive backs stand up in a staggered, forward-leaning stance. Once the ball is snapped, each position starts moving in a different way, and all of them differently than a sprinter starting out of blocks.

At the same time, think of how much time a football player, or even a basketball or baseball player actually "sprints." The opportunities to get to a full-speed straight-line sprint in those sports may be in covering kickoffs or punts, or chasing down a fly ball, and these will almost never be a 100-meter straight-line run. Being able to improve an athlete's maximal speed is important, yet it is not the most important. To improve on-the-field speed, the most critical and most trainable quality is *acceleration*.

Obviously, a sprinter's ability to accelerate off the blocks is crucial to success; but, it is also about reaching and sustaining the maximum speed through the race. Usain Bolt is rarely the fastest to accelerate to his top speed. However, once he is there, he can sustain it longer than his competitors to pull away from the pack.

Bolt's world record is 9.58 seconds in the 100-meter dash as of this writing, and he does most of his damage over the final 50 meters. The average length of a football play is roughly 5.5 seconds. Home plate to first base is only 90 feet. Even a soccer player chasing down a perfectly placed pass on a breakaway is probably covering a maximum of 20 meters at full speed.

Most sports do not allow athletes to hit their top speed unless they are breaking off a massive run or catch. However, the players who can accelerate the fastest are those who are terrorizing quarterbacks or blowing past defenders on a consistent basis.

That is why with most sports, rather than dedicating efforts on improving the time of a 40- or 100-yard sprint, you should spend an inordinate amount of time on the first 10 to 20 yards of sprinting to create the most explosive athletes over that short distance. From our perspective, sprint programming should always start from this point, and then expand in intensity and complexity.

For most team sports, the demands of various positions and directions of movement are drastically different from a track and field athlete, but many coaches fail to adjust their programming around those differences.

THE SPEED HIERARCHY

Just like with weight training, we need to build the foundation and then develop the higher-level qualities of speed. Running, jumping, and plyometric training all require the same approach as weight training, with a logical progression in volume, intensity, and complexity to achieve optimal results.

Sprinting is a physically demanding activity on the musculoskeletal and nervous system. Before you start running your athletes into the ground, you need to refine technique, build work capacity and training volume, develop explosive strength—starting strength and strength-speed—and then increase intensity and speed-strength and maximal speed work.

You can see that the language and terms used in the speed hierarchy is different then the initial hierarchy of development. This is primarily to provide a different perspective on training qualities as it pertains to performance in sport.

Starting strength is closely linked to absolute strength, or the ability to maximally generate the impulse to initiate movement. At its most basic, strength-speed is lifting a heavy(er) weight as fast as possible (think 60–80 percent 1RM), while speed-strength is more focused on maximizing speed using lighter loads (20–50 percent 1RM). Although they seem similar in nature, they are two distinctive qualities that need to be addressed separately.[55,56]

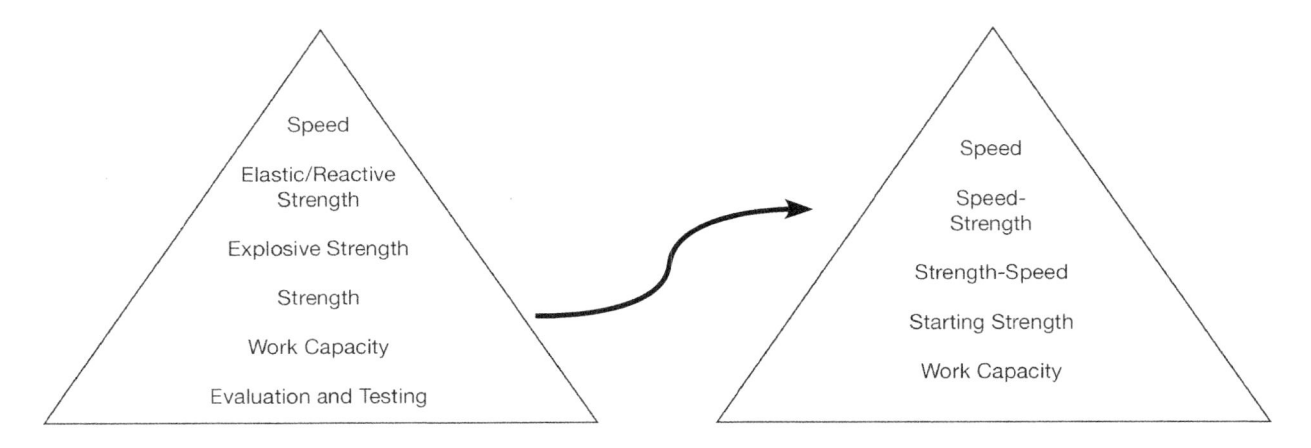

Pyramid 1 (bottom to top): Evaluation and Testing, Work Capacity, Strength, Explosive Strength, Elastic/Reactive Strength, Speed

Pyramid 2 (bottom to top): Work Capacity, Starting Strength, Strength-Speed, Speed-Strength, Speed

Figure 5.2 Shifting the Hierarchy

We initially addressed sprinting and jumping in the prep phase at a relatively lower volume and intensity to introduce or reintroduce these higher-level qualities. Progressing those qualities over the subsequent off-season cycles will take the same approach as the overall weight training plan.

WORK CAPACITY— BUILDING TECHNIQUE AND MOVEMENT ECONOMY

Regardless of position or sport, the most critical aspect of sprinting and speed work is the stance and start. Teaching speed improvement and acceleration should always be focused on this aspect. Whether coming out of the blocks, the batter's box, or off the line of scrimmage, how the body moves during the first 10 yards is critical to on-the-field success.

Therefore, we are going to build the bulk of our speed training on those first 10 to 20 yards. More work and more corrections can be made in a 10-yard dash than can be made in the 40-yard dash—any good track coach will tell you that. If you want to improve an athlete's 40-yard dash time, improve the first 10. Athletes need to learn how to run and accelerate first and foremost.

Our weight training should have developed improved explosive qualities through the emphasis on the speed of the lifts and the Olympic variations. This really goes hand-in-hand with speed work, but we need repetition of the running motion to have that power translate into a sport.

The drills outlined in the prep phase section on page 72 are intended to refine an athlete's ability to maintain a body position—a forward lean of the trunk with acceleration and an upright trunk at full speed. This will maximize the force delivered into the ground and minimize the amount of time the foot is spent on the ground. Both will serve to direct momentum forward and take advantage of the elastic qualities of the muscular system.

- *Mach Sprint Drills— A-Skips, A-Runs, page 72*
- *Hurry Go Get Em, page 84*
- *Wall Marches, page 75*
- *20-Yard Dash, page 85*
- *Tempo Runs, page 76*
- *150 Yards The Hard Way, described at right*

Speed is on the top of our pyramid, but as with the lifting, we need to first build a base of work capacity. Work capacity training stresses different energy systems than sprint training, and at a higher relative volume. A body will be tapping into all the various energy pathways, to different extents at different times. Including work to stress the aerobic pathways will help shorten recovery from the anaerobic, high-intensity work that comes with speed work.

One of the most valuable tools we learned from Charlie Francis was the tempo run drill.[57] Tempo runs allow us to amass a lot of volume, while at the same time providing an opportunity to teach an athlete how to run, and how to run economically. You can easily coach tempo runs from the middle of the field and take care of many athletes at the same time. These are not about refining the technical nuances of sprinting, but the general body mechanics and simple cues to teach efficient motion with foot strike and arm carriage.

We want to coach the foot strike through the forefoot, and discourage the heel strike that is so common with submaximal running. For the arms and torso, it is about limiting extraneous motion that bleeds efficiency from the movement. Reinforcing these mechanics at a slower relative velocity carries over as the intensity of the speed training progresses. Also, coaching to keep the eyes 15 yards ahead at full speed will maintain a level body position. Looking up or down will alter the hip position and result in leaning too far forward or backward.

150 YARDS "THE HARD WAY"

"The Hard Way" is a conditioning drill intended to build work capacity with an added competitive element. Divide your group of players into lines of five athletes. Prior to the start, go down the rows and divide the five-person teams evenly based on speed. If you have extra people, create a line of three or four, but understand the order of finish will be faster than the lines of five. These smaller groups should be the less conditioned or heavier athletes.

Place one cone at the starting line in front of each group and another cone 15 yards away. Explain that all athletes are to stay to the right side of the cone.

Three athletes will stand to the right side of the cone at the starting line, and the other two will walk 15 yards to the right side of the other cone facing the rest of their group. When all groups are properly lined up, explain that each person starts in a three-point stance and sprints by the cone at the other end. As the first person sprints past the cone, the first person at the opposite cone will sprint back toward the starting line.

After completing each sprint, the athlete quickly gets in line behind the other two members of the group. All athletes will continue running this 15-yard sprint until each has completed 10 sprints.

The first team to finish the final sprint are the winners. The entire drill takes three or four minutes and provides 150 yards of high-tempo competitive sprinting done in fast succession. This gives a quality of endurance to the speed workouts and will allow you to observe each athlete under the stress of sprinting the 15 yards while competing with the other groups.

Watch how your athletes handle the 10 sprints for 15 yards. If their energy is high and they are not doubled over in complete exhaustion, you may want to schedule another round after a 10-minute rest and recovery period. You can also use 20, 25, 30 or more yards as you see fit, but remember you are effectively "adding weights to the bar" when calling for more distance.

Start short and simple and then move to complex, because there can certainly be too much of a good thing.

EYE OF THE COACH

One of the most effective and simple cues we use is "Pick your pocket; pick your nose" to train the synchronization of the arm motion.

By giving two external reference points, it is easier for the athletes to learn the motion, rather than bombarding them with a stream of feedback.

Never coach the athlete to make a fist. Squeezing the hands closed tenses the shoulder and neck muscles and increases the heart rate from the overflow of the nervous system.

Keeping the thumb and index finger together and the other fingers relaxed allows the neck and shoulder muscles to remain relaxed and the shoulders and arms to move fluidly.

THE STRENGTH CONTINUUM—ACCELERATION

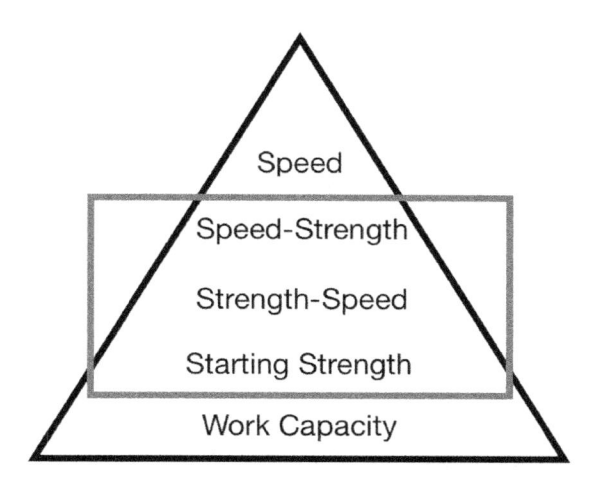

Figure 5.3 The Strength Continuum—Acceleration

Emphasizing acceleration during the concentric portion of strength movements addresses the ability to overcome inertia and redirect force that is critical in initiating movement in running or jumping. The power movements performed in the weightroom will impact the speed of initiating movement. They can also improve speed and acceleration over slightly longer distances of 20 to 30 yards because we are further enhancing the rate of force development.

Research has shown that increasing maximal squat strength improves sprinting times for 10- and 40-yard runs,[58] and there is a significant difference for the athlete who can squat greater than two times bodyweight compared to even 1.9 times bodyweight.

The weightroom work lays the base for improving the efficiency of the CNS and muscular system for explosive force production. The weightroom helps build starting strength, which is the strength to overcome resistance and initiate movement. Many shot-putters and throwers who perform very little sprint work, if any, can accelerate just as effectively for the first 10–15 yards of a sprint as do most runners because of the volume of explosive lifting they perform.

Many of these drills used in progressing from strength to speed development use weighted and unweighted sprinting and jumping in succession. The goal of alternating loaded and unloaded movements is to "trick" the CNS. Following a loaded sprint or jump, the nervous system is anticipating the need for a higher output; by removing the load, we use that increased motor unit recruitment for improved performance.

We can get a similar effect with lifting by performing a movement with 80-percent 1RM, then performing a set at 90-percent 1RM, and then another at 80-percent 1RM.

RESISTED RUNNING

When carrying that same strength and power focus into sprint training, resisted running will translate those qualities onto the field. The nature of resisted running causes the foot to maintain contact with the ground longer with the body in a forward leaning acceleration position. This necessitates more time spent elongating the leg and delivering force through a larger range of motion.

You can run your athletes with all kinds of implements, whether pushing or pulling sleds, running stadium stairs or hills, or even short dashes. Each tool will provide opportunities for the athletes to learn how to overcome resistance and accelerate. As the athletes progress and the emphasis shifts toward speed-strength, you can increase the distance of sprinting to 20–30 yard sprints with gradually increasing volume.

HILLS AND STAIRS

Hill sprinting is excellent for novice or heavier athletes, as it limits the impact forces as compared to running stairs. Even for advanced or elite athletes, using a combination of uphill and downhill running on slopes of roughly three degrees has been shown to increase maximal sprint speed and step rate.[59]

RESISTED RUNNING WITH SLEDS

Sled work should not include more than 20 percent of bodyweight, as the added weight will impact body position too much and will limit speed capabilities. Heavier sled pushes or drags can be used for work capacity development, but when speed is the goal, limiting the load will carry over more effectively.

This is a timed competitive sprint for 20 yards. Pair off athletes of roughly the same weight. Have one partner walk 30 yards from the start. All athletes with sleds line up in a three-point stance waiting for the coach's whistle. Depending on the maturity of the athletes and the load used, the finish time should not be much more than 3.5 seconds.

As they athletes finish, they will walk back to the original starting line while their partners get into a harness and readies for the next 20-yard dash. The rest period should be one minute for each second spent running—the rest should be two-and-a-half to three minutes between runs.

After three runs, have the athletes remove the harness and sled and run 20 yards. At this point, they will walk, jog, stretch, and take water for up to 10 minutes, and then repeat another series of four rounds of 20-yard sprints without weight.

JUMP TRAINING FOR STRENGTH-SPEED AND SPEED-STRENGTH

In the jump training in the prep phase starting on page 78, we touched on the standing long jump and vertical and box jumps to develop the explosive force from a static position. Moving from simple to complex as we move into speed-strength, the most critical aspect of jump training is to move from vertical jumping to linear jumping, and to add repetition to stimulate reactive strength qualities. The linear component adds both impact and shear forces to the knees and ankles, and requires a much higher level of eccentric strength to control momentum.

As the athlete's strength improves, the single jumps can be progressed into jumps performed in succession to address reactive and elastic force development that is critical to maximal speed. Emphasizing an athlete's ability to absorb and redirect force rapidly through repeated jumping moves us into a speed-strength focus, where the emphasis begins to shift away from load and toward velocity.

As the velocity and repetitions increase, the contribution of the elastic and reactive strength of the tendons and nervous system becomes critical to maintain a sustained high rate of force production. The jumping drills every strength coach should utilize are listed below.

- *Goal Post Touches, page 81*
- *Rockets, page 82*
- *Hopping, page 80*
- *Standing Long Jump, page 79*
- *Triple Jumps, page 79*
- *Box Jumps, page 82*

EYE OF THE COACH

When you run your athletes uphill or resisted, such as stadiums or sled pulls, always finish with two or three max sprints at the same distance as the hill or resisted runs. You have to re-teach what you want the body to learn that day. Running the stadium stairs or pulling the sled is not the same as what athletes do on the field; you want that rhythmical motion reinstated, just like practicing a golf put or shooting a free throw.

Performing sprints afterward will engrain the ideal mechanics in a fatigued state, the way they will be called upon in competition.

ABSOLUTE SPEED— MAXIMAL SPRINTING AND JUMPING

Speed sits at the pinnacle of the hierarchy because it requires the maximal power and reactive strength output of the nervous and muscular systems. It is the confluence of all the physical qualities addressed in the lower levels of the pyramid. For that reason, it can be one of the more challenging and slower qualities for the strength coach to address with consistent success.

Many strength coaches advocate that an athlete be able to squat at least one-and-a-half times bodyweight to reduce the incidence of injury in speed training. Since three-to-five times bodyweight hits the leg with every stride during running, an adequate base of strength in the lower body needs to be present when including high-intensity work such as bounding or depth jumps.

We can still dedicate time to sprint or speed training before athletes hit that benchmark. However, if we are hoping to reach an athlete's full potential, we need to consider those strength goals. This time is where we build the base of the pyramid to support the upper levels.

SPEED WORK

When the emphasis shifts to maximal speed training, we need to make a slight shift in programming to provide a different training stimulus. For every second athletes run in a full-speed sprint, they need to rest at least one minute afterward. If a 10-yard dash were to take one second to complete, there should be at least a minute of rest following it.

What we are training with true speed work is different from tempo runs or resisted running. With work capacity drills, an athlete never stops moving and with strength and speed-strength, we are working at a submaximal intensity for repetition. Those provide a conditioning effect to improve an athlete's output.

When training pure speed, we are asking for absolute maximal output of the muscles and nervous system. We need to make sure the tank is full concerning energy systems and recovery if we want to improve the speed quality. If you want to train max output, you need to produce max output. Too many coaches talk about what a great speed workout they put their athletes through…that consisted of a series of gassers.

Sprint training and conditioning are very different. Running your athletes into the ground without adequate recovery will not improve sprint speed. That is punishment, both literally and figuratively.

Sprint programming holds to the same principles as weight training. We keep the volume of the Olympic lifts or power movements lower than strength movements to preserve technique and speed of the movement. The emphasis is to maximize the nervous system output—and the same holds true for max sprint work. The intensity is high and the volume is low. Based on our experience, you should not exceed 600 yards of maximal speed work in a single training session.

Once technique or speed begins to fall apart and we keep dipping into the well of max effort, we end up with a negative training effect…or worse, a training room full of strained hamstrings and an angry coaching staff.

Some of the best drills for developing top-end speed entail a flying start. A flying start means an athlete is already moving, and then accelerates to full speed. The emphasis is less on acceleration as it is on reaching and sustaining maximum speed over distance.

The following are some of our favorite speed work drills.

- *Ins and outs*
- *Parachute training*
- *Build-ups*
- *Pure sprinting 30–40 yards*

INS AND OUTS

Ins and Outs are an excellent drill to teach how to accelerate, run at peak speed, and decelerate. This drill is done at any distance, but these are usually best introduced at 15-yard increments. You will use three cones in a row at 15, 30, and 45 yards. The athletes build up speed over the first 15 yards, hit maximum speed over the second 15 or 30 yards, and then decelerate over the final 15 yards.

More benefit can come from watching rather than timing the drill, as you watch for an upright posture at max speed. If you see athletes "shrink" in height over the second 15 yards, they are fighting the forward momentum and self-limiting the speed.

PARACHUTE TRAINING

Parachute training improves foot speed and top speed. Running into the wind forces athletes to reach their maximum velocity more quickly as they fight the drag from the parachute.

This is not intended for less-experienced athletes, but for those who have demonstrated good progress in sprinting form and have a solid foundation of strength through the weight program. Prepare for some serious hamstring soreness afterward.

BUILD-UPS

Build-ups are similar in design to the Ins and Outs drill where we are using a flying start to build into a max sprint, but without the deceleration. The total distance covered is 40–50 yards, with the goal of increasing the speed every 10 yards. The final 10 yards should be the fastest, where athletes are at their max sprint speed.

PURE SPRINTING

Pure sprinting is any sprint work focusing exclusively on going from a dead stop to maximal speed over 30–40 yards. With these drills, it is important to emphasize good starting position and mechanics initiating the movement, and translating your coaching into performance.

Photos 5.1 a–d Sprint Starting Positions

A four-point, three-point, and staggered starting position for sprint training

Depending on the sport or position athletes play, the starting stance or cue to start can be made more specific to the demands they will encounter in a game or competition. Track athletes will benefit from starting in a four-point stance, football linemen in a three-point stance, while wide receivers or basketball players should use a staggered, upright stance.

No matter what choices you make, pure sprinting is where we try to engrain all the previous training into maximal speed on the field.

EYE OF THE COACH

In many team sports, there is some aspect of running backward or in a non-linear direction, such as defensive backs, basketball players, and outfielders. Be sure to incorporate sprint work that involves moving backward.

The CNS is the hardest nut to crack and will require a number of elements to develop maximal output. Especially when you train a group of athletes, it is hard in a team environment to pick the right method for everyone. Try to separate groups as closely as possible in the run drills for each day, depending upon the athletes' major muscle fiber types—"fast twitch" athletes: receivers, running backs, defensive backs; "slow-twitch" athletes: linemen, tight ends, quarterbacks. Running linebackers and defensive ends with the fast-twitch group can further enhance competitive qualities.

JUMP TRAINING FOR SPEED

Jump training to emphasize speed is where the integration of bounding and plyometrics come into play. You should progressively build the base of simple jumps and repetitive straight-line jumping so your athletes can tolerate the demands of non-linear or high-speed jumping.

Many of the injuries sustained in sports come from movement in the transverse or frontal plane when doing cutting or twisting motions on one leg.

Although these planes of motion need to be trained to reduce injury risk, athletes also need adequate elastic strength and reactivity in the legs before adding too much intensity or volume to high-level jumping or bounding. We need to train the body's ability to absorb and eccentrically accept the load, and then redirect the force in the opposite direction.

The natural progression of linear-jumping exercises is to first add volume and then intensity through jumping in succession, moving from two-leg to single-leg jumping or adding height in the case of box jumps. Your coaching emphasis should always be toward shortening the amount of time an athlete spends in contact with the ground.

As an athlete progresses up the pyramid from general to specific training, jumping should begin to look more like the demands of the sport itself. Bounding drills add multiple jumps in succession to further train the reactivity needed for high-speed jumping in sport.

The longer a foot is in contact with the ground between the concentric and eccentric phase during jumping or sprinting, the less power is generated. Think of the Olympic triple-jumper or basketball point guard effortlessly springing off the ground from foot to foot. Once the foot hits the ground, any amount of time beyond a quarter-second of contact means lost elastic strength and reactivity and less force output.

Plyometrics are the top of the heap in jump training. They demand a high degree of coordination and body control. An athlete needs a high degree of absolute and reactive strength—especially eccentrically—to absorb and redirect the forces with a reduced risk of injury.

It can be hard to program specific intensity and volume of plyometric and high-speed jumping drills. We need to use common sense when it comes to introducing jumps.

It will ultimately be more of a qualitative decision regarding the maximum of your plyometric training. Once quality degrades and the foot is not coming off the ground quickly or the heel is striking, it is time to stop.

For heavier athletes, just as with squatting, the combination of bodyweight on top of the impact forces causes greater stress to the body than the same work for lighter athletes. It is a safer route to decrease the overall volume and intensity of jumps and plyometrics for heavier athletes and to emphasize footwork, lateral quickness, and minimize contact time. Taking a less-is-more approach with larger athletes will still improve their explosiveness and reactive strength without the added risk of injury or additional recovery demands.

A simple progression for introducing jump training for your athletes should follow the general guidelines in Figure 5.4 on the following page.

JUMPING PROGRESSION GUIDELINES	
Standing Jumps *Four weeks minimum*	Box Jump *straight, side, turning* Vertical Jump Broad Jump
Advanced Jumps	Weighted Box Jumps *with vests or dumbbells* Box Drops *"stick" the landing—* *for building eccentric strength* Consecutive Broad Jumps *two or three reps* Standing Triple Jump Line Hops Double and Single-Leg Hops Side-to-Side Box Jumps
Depth Jumps *First, assess the athlete's maximum jump height from a standing vertical jump. When performing a depth jump, the height of the rebounding jump should be no less than the maximum height reached on the vertical jump.*	**Box Height** *minimum of 24 inches for men and 18 inches for women[60]* * *If the athlete cannot demonstrate appropriate jump height from the minimum height, you can go lower, but it may be more beneficial to first focus on improving general lower-body strength.* **Max Height** *45 inches for dynamic strength* * *Any greater height changes the landing mechanism so that neither reactivity nor strength is gained.* * *Be particularly careful with untrained athletes and athletes over 220 pounds.*
Bounding and Hurdles	*Should be able to back squat at least 1.5 times bodyweight before initiating bounding and hurdles.*

Figure 5.4 Example of Jumping Progression

The goal of the training will dictate when to perform plyometrics or jumping in a training session. Train pure speed and elastic strength first when the athlete is fresh.

The CNS output and reactivity of the muscles is at its highest in a primed and non-fatigued state. This is about putting the body in the best position to succeed in maximum force generation.

Because athletes still need to be explosive when tired in a game situation, you can include some plyos at the end of a training session to develop explosive movement in a fatigued state.

When performed in a fatigued state, the volume and intensity of plyos should be reduced to avoid knee or ankle injury. When fatigued, preference should go to more simple exercise variations.

DEPTH JUMPS

Depth jumps, or "shock training" as the Soviets called these, are one of the more advanced jumping drills that can enhance power output and maximal speed. The benefit of this method of training is believed to be from improving stiffness, elasticity, and power development that improves speed-strength and maximal speed.

Start with a 14–18-inch box height for an absolute novice, and focus first on depth drops, where the athlete steps off the box and attempts to "stick" the landing with a forward trunk lean, a bend in the knees, and the weight on the balls of the foot. The landing position should look like the athlete is preparing to jump back up in the air.

Once good form can be attained, progress to the depth jump where the goal is to minimize contact time with the ground—the amortization phase—and rapidly explode up from impact into a vertical or horizontal jump without the heels touching the ground.

Photos 5.2 a–c Depth Jumps
Too deep of a squat when landing as shown above limits the elastic/reactive component of depth jumps. Coaching a quick and explosive reaction off the floor will enhance the training effect.

We are teaching athletes to accept impact fluidly with the feet, ankles, knees, hips, trunk, and arms and train the stretch-reflex to efficiently transfer momentum and energy into a countermovement. The landing should not be rigid or stiff, and the athlete should see a slightly greater vertical jump height than the person's normal height as the body is absorbing momentum and kinetic energy and redirecting the force.

As the height of the box increases, so too do the impact forces, which is why we reserve this drill for athletes with a squat weight of at least 1.5 times bodyweight.

LATERAL PLYOMETRIC BOX JUMPS

Lateral plyometric box jumps are another valuable drill to train lateral motion and speed, with a particular emphasis on maintaining body position and control. It is best performed with a 12-inch height box that is two feet by two feet wide.

The athlete stands in the middle of the box and upon the coach's whistle, jumps with both feet to either side of the box. Upon hitting the ground, the athlete rebound jumps to the middle of box and continues by jumping to the other side, then jumping side to side for 10 seconds.

This is a good drill for a group, allowing you to boost effort or reward high performers. Have at least three players in each group and rotate between sets to allow recovery. The goal is for the athlete to perform greater than one crossover per second, landing on the forefoot and exploding quickly in the opposite direction.

[CHAPTER FIVE—SPRINTING AND JUMPING]

Photos 5.3 a–d Lateral Box Jumps
The athlete must stay on the balls of the feet to successfully complete this drill.

This drill is a valuable return-to-sport test. Athletic trainer and strength coach Don Chu recommends that an athlete to achieve greater than 90 foot contacts in 90 seconds before being cleared to return to play.[61]

BOUNDING

Bounding is extremely simple to perform, but is another poorly utilized drill for many coaches. Your athletes will leap off one leg, attempting to propel the body forward as far as possible. As they land on the opposite foot, the goal is to immediately explode into the next bound. This is effectively "springing off the ground."

It can be performed forward, like an exaggerated sprint stride, or laterally, like a speed skater pushing off.

The error we most often see in the performance of bounds is that focusing on distance often extends the amount of time the foot is in contact with the ground. Focusing on shortening the foot contact often detracts from maximal force and the distance covered.

We recommend introducing bounding over short distances of about 20 yards, with the focus on limiting the contact time of the

213

foot with the ground, and cueing the athletes to forcefully throw their arms forward in front of their faces in an exaggerated running motion.

If you can train the athletes to quickly turnover their feet and drive their arms, you will see the distance covered improve. Work up to 50 yards, depending on the athletes.

> ### EYE OF THE COACH
>
> *Plyometrics develop speed. Direct the bulk of your coaching at minimizing the time spent in contact with the ground and maximizing output. Planning a recovery period of 5:1 for plyometric drills allows the greatest expression of speed without sacrificing quality.*
>
> *Remember, if your athletes train slow, they will be slow.*

AGILITY

We dedicate most of the training emphasis to sagittal-plane strength and power development, yet training the body to move efficiently in every plane of motion is what ultimately allows athleticism to translate onto the field.

Coaches like doing agility drills in some form, either to teach movement patterns or increase foot quickness. There is no shortage of options in training quickness and agility.

The following are a few drills we have found to be productive for nearly all athletes in all sports.

FOUR CORNERS

Place four cones five yards apart in a square and position a line of players on one side of the square while you stay on the opposite side. Give a command or signal; the first runner sprints to the middle of the square and rapidly moves the feet while staying in one place.

Point to a cone. The athlete in the middle moves as fast as possible to that cone, but before reaching the cone, you will point to another cone. The player continues to move as fast as possible between cones as you direct the action. Observe the foot movement pattern and stop to make corrections when needed.

Four to six movements are sufficient. Then give a hand signal for the athlete to finish with a run past you and out of the square. The drill continues with the next athlete; reps are usually three to six series of four to six movements. If you think about all the movements you can require a player to do, this touches on just about all the movement patterns—lateral, forward, backward, rotation.

Once athletes get good at the five-yard square—especially for defensive backs, linebackers, and wide receivers in football—widen the space to 10 yards. Ten yards is too wide for lineman or heavier athletes, but it works great for basketball, baseball, volleyball, and soccer players.

[Chapter Five—Sprinting and Jumping]

> **EYE OF THE COACH**
>
> *You can also make this drill more challenging by adding a mental reaction component by "naming" each cone and calling out the name of the cone you want the athlete to run to rather than pointing. This adds another element of reactivity where the athlete cannot guess at a visual cue and has to receive the verbal cue, internalize it, and then react.*

LATERAL SHUFFLES

Most coaches reading this will think we have lost it at this point because this is such a simple drill. Trust us: There are a few often-overlooked points to lateral shuffles that make it a staple for nearly everyone.

In a lateral shuffle, pay close attention to the first step of the lead leg when the drill begins. The toe of the lead foot must not turn out as this will change the entire direction of speed. Have your athletes keep their toes pointed forward at all times. The speed and direction of movement will always coincide with the direction the toes are facing.

When touching the designated line and returning to the starting point, make sure your athletes do not step under the body with what is now the lead foot. When the foot touches the line, the athletes should explode back toward the origin.

If the trailing leg ends up under the body, it now takes two steps to change the movement and get the lead leg back ahead of the body. There are many plays made and missed due to a single step; this is how we train that.

ZIG-ZAG RUN

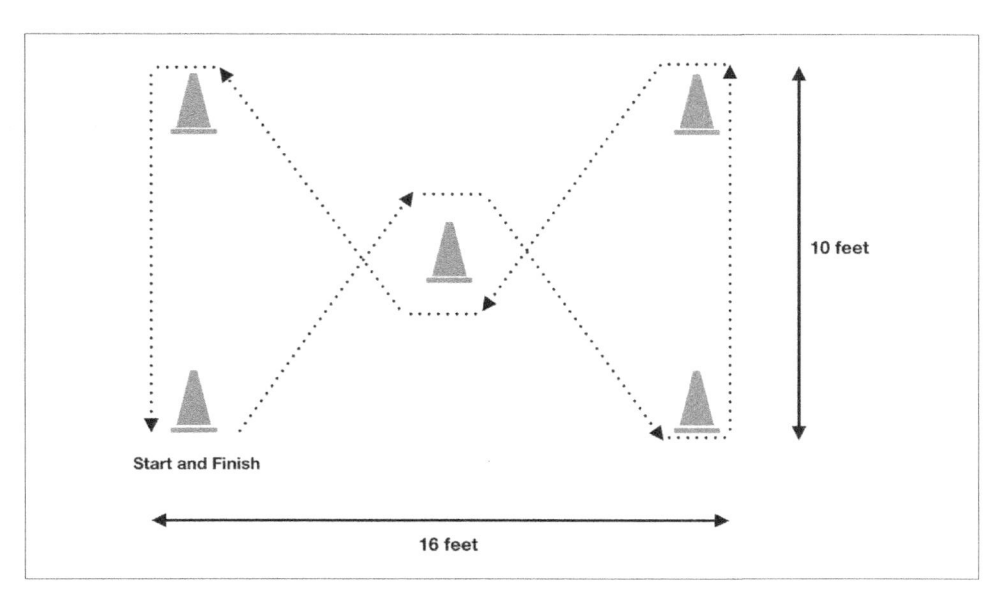

Figure 5.5 Zig-Zag Run Cone Set-up
A diagram explains better than words how to set up the drill using cones.

- *On the whistle or signal, the athletes will sprint to the first cone, quickly turn to point their feet and body toward the next cone, sprint to the next cone, quickly turn the body and feet toward the next cone and continue until returning to the original starting cone.*

- *Athletes run the drill one at a time, and we suggest timing each run. An athlete is covering 30 or more yards per run.*

Zig-Zag runs are meant to train athletes to control the body through foot movement and body position, not with chopping steps.

When they arrive at a cone, they should rapidly lower their center of gravity and turn, taking the least number of steps as possible.

The Zig-Zag run is applicable to all sports and all positions, especially larger athletes like offensive linemen.

There are many offensive linemen who release on a screen pass and while moving downfield to block a defender, totally whiff due to lack of body and foot control. It is also a great drill for punt and kickoff coverage.

The options and choices can seem endless when programming jumping and running drills. That's only a bad thing if you lose sight of why you are selecting a particular drill for your athletes. Knowing what qualities will be impacted by the choice of exercises is what separates the best coaches from the average.

Coach Don Chu, who literally wrote the book on plyometrics,[62] designed a simple reference chart based on the evidence for which qualities are improved through the various plyometric exercises.

EYE OF THE COACH

Run your athletes around cones and tell them not to chop their steps. They control the body by foot movement and body position. You will notice great improvements after a month of work on this drill.

When programming agility work, it is best to schedule the drills after jumping or running.

More often than not, the demands of agility and directional changes that arise in a game do not happen when athletes are rested and recovered. By providing rest between jump or running drills and then working agility, we can simulate a more realistic training environment of performance under fatigue.

QUALITIES IMPACTED BY DIFFERENT PLYOMETRIC EXERCISES						
	JUMPS IN PLACE	STANDING JUMPS	MULTIPLE JUMPS	BOX DRILLS	BOUNDING	DEPTH JUMPS
STARTING SPEED	X	X	X			X
ACCELERATION			X	X	X	
CHANGE OF DIRECTION		X	X	X		X
VERTICAL JUMP	X	X	X	X		X
HORIZONTAL JUMP		X	X	X	X	

Figure 5.6 Impacts of Plyometric Exercises
Adapted with permission from Don Chu[63]

INTEGRATING RUNNING AND JUMPING

Integrating sprint and jump training into a training program does not have to be as challenging as it is often made out to be. Just as this system employs volume and intensity days when planning the weekly weight-training sessions, the same approach applies to sprint and jump work. The goal is to train in the gym and on the track at a high level, without one detracting from the performance of the other. Splitting the week into days dedicated to lifting and days dedicated to sprinting and jumping has proven most beneficial for us.

On lifting days, the emphasis is on the work done in the weightroom. Some simple jumping, such as tuck jumps and box jumps, is beneficial prior to lifting to help prime the CNS. However, rarely do we program more than five or six reps—adding that little bit of explosive work just before the lifts helps improve an athlete's overall elastic qualities. The primary running performed on a lift day should, for the most part, be for work capacity.

Here is where the tempo runs are an effective tool following the weight work to help develop an athlete's endurance. The intensity level for tempo runs is moderate, at roughly 70 percent of an athlete's max sprint speed, and the focus is to work on mechanics.

After weight training can often be a valuable time to work on tempo runs because they are done with the athlete in a fatigued state, which more closely mirrors in-game conditions as it further develops work capacity.

In a team environment, it is still most useful to use the starting time guidelines of 15–16–17 seconds described on page 77 for each 100 yards of tempo runs based on each athlete's size and ability. Trying to determine 70 percent of each individual's max is tedious and probably unnecessary for most team sports.

Following the broader time guidelines and adjusting higher or lower on a case by case basis makes things simple for you and your athletes.

The non-lifting days contain the bulk of the volume of sprinting and jumping. Speed and elastic strength work live at the top of the pyramid of development and require high degrees of CNS and muscular output to truly develop those qualities.

Unlike the primary lifting movements, we do not ascribe to specific volume totals for the different exercises for sprints and jumps. Taking a slightly more qualitative approach to volume will serve you better than hard and fast numbers. Quality comes first. If you start to see the amplitude or frequency of the jumps significantly decrease, or if the speed or quality of the sprints rapidly declines, it is time to stop.

With that in mind, the sequencing of the drills on a sprint day should also maximize an athlete's movement and energy systems to allow for maximal output and the most effective training stimulus. The best structure for sprint days is:

- *A thorough full-body warmup*
- *Technique drills—done first for good motor patterning*
- *Jump and sprint drills—with maximal output and effort while fresh*
- *Strength-speed or agility—fatiguing and emphasize more sustained effort*
- *Work capacity—if needed, these are performed last as they have the lowest physical and technical demands*

Following this general structure ensures good mechanics that carry over into the max-effort work, which is most important.

The strength-speed work helps to further develop rapid force development—this might include sled work, hills, or stadiums. It is not training maximal speed quality, and you can train it effectively in a slightly fatigued state.

You can program agility work early in a session to emphasize rapid ground contact, or in a fatigued state to better simulate game conditions.

Finally, any additional work capacity should come last, since it is low-to-moderate intensity and poses the lowest risk of injury when performed while fatigued. Lower intensity work has been shown to be positive for recovery as well, as it is assumed that it assists in clearance of blood lactate.[64]

> ### EYE OF THE COACH
>
> *The objective is not to have your athletes doubled over and puking or straining and flailing across the goal line. Everything serves a purpose; if speed or form starts to deteriorate, it is time to stop.*
>
> *"Work capacity" does not mean to run them until they cannot run anymore.*

SPRINT RESETS

The one caveat to the structure of the sprint work is that following any of the strength-speed work such as sled pulls, stadiums, and hills, there should be some higher-intensity sprints after resting. The goal of these sprints is to re-establish good mechanics with 90-percent intensity or above, and at the same distance as the resisted running.

Much of speed is predicated on mechanics, so any of the drills or activities that may cause a deviation from proper form should be followed by technical or form work at full speed.

If the schedule dictates that lifting and speed work have to be done on the same day, the sprinting and speed work should always precede the lifting. Speed is the top of the pyramid; we do not want anything detracting from the performance of true speed work. It is better to sacrifice a little in the weightroom than to sacrifice anything on the field.

MONTHLY VOLUME

The sprint and jump training also follows a similar four-week cycle that corresponds with the lifting. The primary difference is in the determination of the volume of work with the weeks distributed into a moderate, moderate-heavy, heavy, or light, recovery volume week.

The distribution of the weekly volume should encompass all of the qualities of speed development—work capacity, technique, strength-speed and speed-strength, speed, and agility. The relative amount of the weekly volume emphasizes the most important qualities depending on the athlete's level, abilities, and the time of the year.

Generally, a novice requires more volume on technique, work capacity, and strength-speed to develop a solid base.

There is still some higher-intensity jump and sprint work to be done; however, it will be low volume and focused on the simplest variations—single jumps, short sprints, and lateral box jumps for 10–20 seconds.

Advanced and elite athletes should have already established a solid foundation, and should be able to tolerate more strength-speed and max-speed work.

As a general guideline for volume, assume these ranges in planning:

TRAINING VOLUME RANGES FOR SPRINTING OR JUMPING		
QUALITY	DAILY RANGE	WEEKLY RANGE
WORK CAPACITY	400–2,400 yards	1,000–4,400 yards
STRENGTH-SPEED AND SPEED-STRENGTH	50–200 reps or yards	100–400 reps or yards
SPEED	100–600 yards	200–1,500 yards

Figure 5.7 Sprinting or Jumping Training Volume Ranges

From Vermeil's Sports and Fitness Training System for Enhancing Athletic Performance, Al Vermeil, M.S., C.S.C.S

Those numbers represent the entire span of training volume for all levels of athletes. The upper ranges of volume are for the elite-level athletes with at least 10 years of consistent training and development. We reserve 2,400 yards of tempo work or 600 yards of speed work in a single session for the highest-level athletes.

We cannot stress this enough: These extreme ranges of volume for the elite-level athlete are for world-class athletes and for those athletes whose primary sport is running or jumping. Unless you are training track athletes who are exclusively running or jumping, pushing the volume of sprinting and jumping toward those upper ranges requires more recovery time and will likely detract from other areas of training.

For example, a good benchmark is to limit jumps to 310 a month or an average of 10 per day. Coach Don Chu, who is arguably one of the most successful American coaches when it comes to programming jumpers and track athletes, tells us to train no more than 120 jumps in a day for an elite athlete. That represents the max of the max.

That does not sound like a tremendous amount of volume, but this is more than enough when weightlifting, running, sprinting, and skill practice are all included in the workload. That 120 daily rep max would be appropriate for people whom that is about all they do—such as high jumpers or long jumpers. Jumps are intense on the body. Do less, not more.

As with weightlifting, if we have a clear goal for our *primary* training emphasis, it is possible to expand outward to the training cycle and weeks to determine the appropriate volume for each quality.

Coach Vermeil has a great chart to demonstrate the shifting volumes for each quality depending on the training emphasis, which you'll find in Figure 5.8 on the following page.

As the training emphasis shifts toward speed, the relative volumes of work capacity, strength, and speed-strength go down. The lower qualities are still trained to maintain a certain level of development; however, the bulk of the volume is dedicated to higher-intensity training.

No matter the level of athlete, as the off-season progresses and you reach the pre-season and in-season phases, the intensity level and amount of higher-intensity work should gradually increase. It is no different from the lifting program where the volume of work gradually moves toward the more explosive power movements as the season approaches.

VOLUME GUIDELINE PER WEEK
BASED ON COMPONENT TO BE EMPHASIZED

QUALITY	WORK CAPACITY EMPHASIS	STRENGTH EMPHASIS	STRENGTH-SPEED EMPHASIS	SPEED-STRENGTH EMPHASIS	SPEED EMPHASIS
WORK CAPACITY TEMPO RUNS	3,200–4,400 yards	1,000–2,400 yards	1,000–2,000 reps	Variable, for recovery	Variable, for recovery
STRENGTH	150–175 reps or yards	150–320 reps or yards	100–250 reps or yards	75–150 reps or yards 70–80 percent max	50–100 reps or yards 70–80 percent max
STRENGTH-SPEED	50–70 reps or yards	50–100 reps or yards	75–100 reps or yards	50–100 reps or yards 70–80 percent max	50–100 reps or yards 70–80 percent max
SPEED-STRENGTH	200–400 reps or yards Low Intensity	150–300 reps or yards Low–Medium Intensity	100–300 reps or yards Low–Medium Intensity	75–200 reps or yards Medium–High Intensity	50–150 reps or yards Medium–High Intensity
SPEED	200–400 yards	200–600 yards	300–600 yards	400–1,000 yards	500–1,500 yards

The shaded blocks represent the primary quality emphasized.

Figure 5.8 Volume Guidelines

From Vermeil's Sports and Fitness Training System for Enhancing Athletic Performance, Al Vermeil, M.S., C.S.C.S

The following would be a more appropriate representation of those volume ranges for the different levels of athletes for a given training session.

[CHAPTER FIVE—SPRINTING AND JUMPING]

TRAINING VOLUME RANGES PER TRAINING SESSION			
QUALITY	NOVICE	ADVANCED	ELITE
WORK CAPACITY	400–1,500 yards	1,000–2,000 yards	Up to 2,400 yards
STRENGTH-SPEED AND SPEED-STRENGTH	50–100 reps or yards	100–200 reps or yards	Up to 200 reps or yards
SPEED	100–250 yards	250–500 yards	Up to 600 yards

Figure 5.9 Training Volumes Per Session

From Vermeil's Sports and Fitness Training System for Enhancing Athletic Performance,
Al Vermeil, M.S., C.S.C.S

EYE OF THE COACH

Approach running and jumping just as you do lifting. You can always keep the volume of running the same but drop the finishing times, which is similar to adding more weight to the bar while keeping volume the same. Too much volume is always a killer to progress.

WEEKLY VOLUME

Whatever you determine the monthly volumes to be based on the time of year and the training goals, that total volume is again broken down into weekly totals. You can follow the same undulating volume pattern used with the lifting—28-22-35-15 percent or 27-22-32-19 percent monthly volume as described beginning on page 136—or you can take a more general approach to the sprinting and jumping.

You can use a four-week cycle of moderate, moderate-heavy, heavy, and light recovery weeks based on the volume ranges to provide a little more flexibility in your programming. This same general approach will come into play with in-season programming.

Using the novice athlete example again, let us assume it is early in the off-season, with emphasis on work capacity as the primary training quality.

A weekly breakdown using a linear progression to build up an athlete's tolerance may look something like:

WEEKLY VOLUME TOTALS FOR SPRINTING OR JUMPING WORK CAPACITY EMPHASIS			
WEEK	WORK CAPACITY	STRENGTH-SPEED AND SPEED-STRENGTH	SPEED
MODERATE	2,700 yards	60 reps or yards	120 yards
MODERATE HEAVY	2,800 yards	70 reps or yards	160 yards
HEAVY	3,000 yards	80 reps or yards	320 yards
LIGHT RECOVERY	2,300 yards	50 reps or yards	100 yards

Figure 5.10 Work Capacity Weekly Volumes for Sprinting or Jumping

From Vermeil's Sports and Fitness Training System for Enhancing Athletic Performance, Al Vermeil, M.S., C.S.C.S

Within those weeks, it is best to restrict the session volume to the ranges we noted to ensure recovery. There is no sense in burning athletes out by excessive running, and then spending two weeks waiting for them to fully recover. Programming lower volume allows recovery and progression.

Not exceeding 100–250 yards of sprinting per session and focusing the tempo work between 400–1,000 yards allows athletes to get accustomed to the initial work level. Track athletes can handle higher volumes or distances as needed for a particular event. Start low and progress based on how they perform.

As the off-season progresses and the training volume increases, there should be a shift toward more speed-strength and speed work as the season approaches and the emphasis of the training changes. Once the first training cycle is complete in a linear progression, you can use the same undulating volume pattern as the lifting. This will simplify the planning and structure of the programming and sync the recovery weeks of running and weightlifting.

COMPARISON OF WEEKLY VOLUMES OF LIFTING VERSUS RUNNING AND JUMPING			
LINEAR PROGRESSION		UNDULATING PROGRESSION	
LIFTING	RUNNING	LIFTING	RUNNING
22% volume	Moderate volume	27% volume	Moderate-heavy volume
27% volume	Moderate-heavy volume	22% volume	Moderate volume
32% volume	Heavy volume	32% volume	Heavy volume
19% volume	Light volume	19% volume	Light volume

Figure 5.11 Comparing Lifting, Running, and Jumping Volumes

After two cycles, a novice-level athlete may be using an undulating pattern more in line with the following:

WEEKLY VOLUME TOTALS FOR SPRINTING OR JUMPING— SPEED-STRENGTH OR SPEED EMPHASIS			
WEEK VOLUME	WORK CAPACITY	SPEED-STRENGTH	SPEED
MODERATE-HEAVY	1,900 yards	90 reps or yards	325 yards
MODERATE	1,500 yards	80 reps or yards	275 yards
HEAVY	2,100 yards	100 reps or yards	450 yards
LIGHT RECOVERY	1,300 yards	60 reps or yards	200 yards

Figure 5.12 Volumes for Sprinting or Jumping, Speed-Strength or Speed

From Vermeil's Sports and Fitness Training System for Enhancing Athletic Performance, Al Vermeil, M.S., C.S.C.S

You can see that the total volume of speed-strength and speed work increases significantly as the training cycles progress. There is a decrease in the volume of work capacity to allow more high-intensity work. You still need some general development of endurance, especially for novice-level athletes.

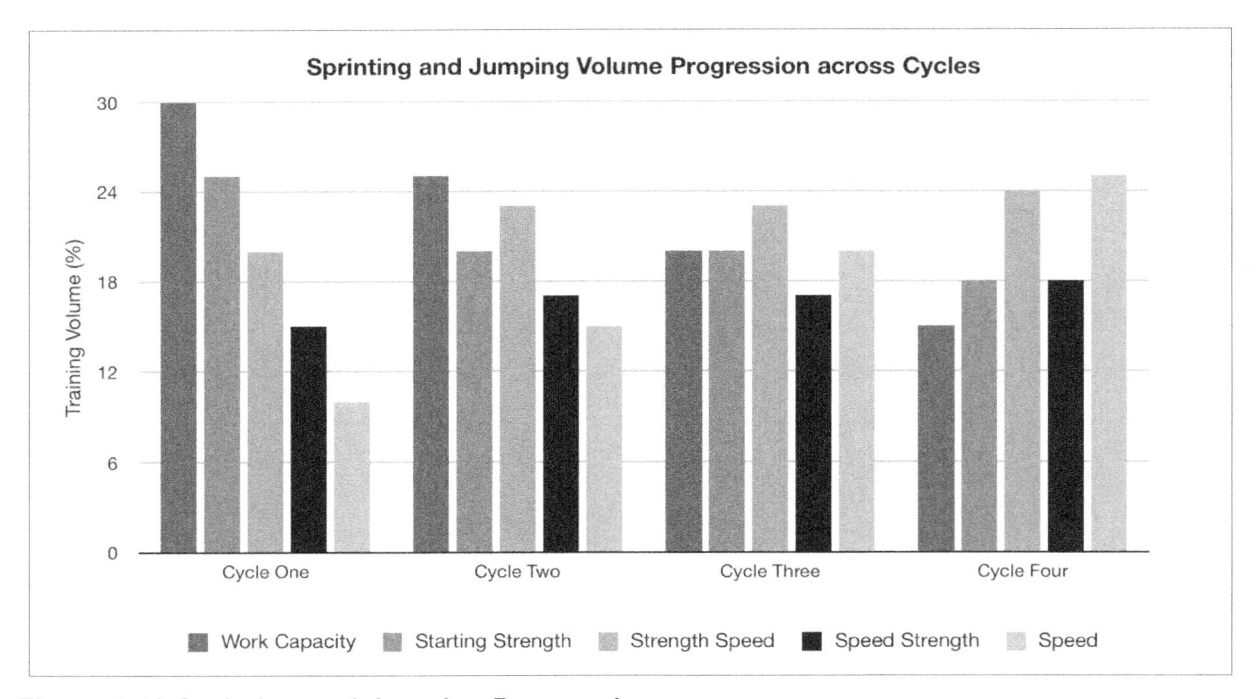

Figure 5.13 Sprinting and Jumping Progression

Our goal is to peak in sprinting and jumping intensity as the season arrives. We achieve that by shifting the training emphasis and volume toward higher-intensity or speed work just prior to the start of competition.

Because of the increasing recovery demands of the high-intensity work during the fourth cycle, front-loading the monthly volume in the preseason cycle was one option that served us well to ensure the athletes peak leading to the start of competition. By shifting to a *heavy—moderate—moderate-heavy—light* progression, athletes maintain their training intensity, but have a lower training volume over the two weeks leading into the start of practice.

This often resulted in the team arriving fresher and more energized.

SPRINTING AND JUMPING SESSION DESIGN

In an ideal program design for team sports, there should be two days per week dedicated to just sprinting and jumping. Mirroring the lifting, one day would be an intensity day more dedicated to jumps or sprints, and the other a volume day with more technique or strength-speed work. The goal is to optimize the training effect with a lower risk of injury. There is no set rule for which should fall when during a week.

The split we found most effective is to schedule the higher-intensity workout early in the week, and the higher-volume workout later in the week. The only rule you should follow is to make sure the high-intensity sprint workout does not follow a day with a high volume of dedicated hamstring or posterior chain work.

If the training session the day before a high-intensity sprint day involved a high volume of dedicated hamstring work, there should be at least 24 hours and two meals between the lifting and sprint sessions.

When the focus is on speed and the athletes are working above 90 percent of their maximum for speed work, it is imperative that the hamstrings not be significantly fatigued or tight from the previous day's training.

Given enough recovery time and a thorough warmup and build-up sets, the risk of a hamstring strain is reduced; however, a back-to-back schedule is still less than ideal. There is nothing more frustrating than injuries caused by training, and although injuries are inevitable in athletics, smart planning can make them the exception rather than the rule. For that reason, we often try to reserve the bulk of RDLs or hamstring work until the second half of the week, specifically Fridays, whenever possible.

A novice athlete's week of training may look something like:

MONDAY	TUESDAY *INTENSITY*	WEDNESDAY	THURSDAY *VOLUME*	FRIDAY
Lift *42 percent weekly volume* Tempo Runs	Mach Run Drills Jumps Technique Sprints Speed-Strength *Sleds, hills, etc* Sprint Resets	Lift *24 percent weekly volume* Tempo Runs	Mach Run Drills Jumps Technique 10-yard sprints Tempo Runs	Lift *34 percent weekly volume* Tempo Runs

Figure 5.14 Novice Athlete Training Week Example

The intensity of work on Tuesday is higher than Thursday, and the total volume in distance is significantly less in the higher-intensity session. The high-intensity Tuesday session is followed by the Wednesday workout, which is the lowest total volume lifting day.

This allows some recovery from the running work, and then the higher volume of distance work through sprinting, jumping, and work capacity occurs in the Thursday session.

MONDAY	TUESDAY	WEDNESDAY	THURSDAY	FRIDAY
High Volume Lifting	Lower Volume, Higher Intensity Sprints and Jumps	Low-Volume Lifting	Higher Volume, Lower Intensity Sprints and Jumps	Moderate Volume Lifting

Figure 5.15 Comparing the Intensity of the Sessions

As is the case throughout our programming, there is built-in recovery through the varying volume and intensity levels of the work. Rather than having multiple days in succession of high volume or high intensity work, the undulating pattern overloads and stresses different training qualities on different days.

By applying the same rationale of the weightlifting program to sprinting and jumping, you can easily progress athletes through the months and years of training. Sprints and jumps should be approached just like the higher intensity "power" movements of the clean, snatch, or jerk where the reps per set are kept under six or eight and the total volume in each training session are tightly monitored.

Treating sprint work, plyometrics, or jumps as an afterthought, or just making up volume or intensity as you go will rarely produce the best result. Every component of training impacts some other quality, and the fusion of lifting, conditioning, sprinting, and jumping will not happen on its own.

EYE OF THE COACH

Jumps can be included on running days. They can also be programmed into the lifting days. Spreading the volume over each day also provides increased frequency and repetition to ensure good technique and output.

On lifting days, you can add jumps after the warmup and before lifting to stimulate central nervous system output, after leg work to train explosive qualities under some fatigue, or after the last exercise and before tempo runs to re-establish coordination prior to running.

CHAPTER SIX
SEASONAL PROGRAM DESIGN

*"In preparing for battle,
I have always found that plans are useless,
but planning is indispensable."*
~ Dwight D. Eisenhower

In programming for athletic performance, it is important to distinguish the specific demands of different sports, and in particular individual versus team sports.

We previously mentioned how the Soviet coaches planned multiple years of an athlete's training in advance, all the way down to the percentages and specific volumes. They were largely training individual sport athletes for the Olympics with well-defined competition schedules. That allows for much more rigid programming and control over the training variables to improve the most important physical qualities of an event.

As an example, a shot putter needs a high degree of power and strength to throw the shot. Those qualities can be consistently trained at the expense of other qualities such as endurance or multidirectional agility work.

The competitions that shot putters participate in are predictable and reasonably spaced apart, with a long off-season building to a short competitive season. Even within a competition, there may be only three repetitions of throwing the shot in each of three to six rounds.

It is a specific and constrained event, with possibly 18 maximal efforts and adequate rest in between. Using the foundational principles, developing a comprehensive and refined training program for these athletes is relatively straightforward.

In the case of team sports, there is often a demand for a much broader range of physical qualities and skills. Team sports are often performed in uncontrolled and variable environments that demand endurance, strength, power, and speed almost simultaneously.

Elite-level soccer midfielders need to have the power and speed to accelerate and chase the ball, and they will also run an average of seven to nine miles over the course of a single match.

During the course of a game, basketball players may end up running two miles and NFL cornerbacks and wide receivers can run over a mile, all while needing to push and pull on their opponents, jump, change direction, and withstand physical contact.

On top of that, the demands are different for the different positions or the body types common to a particular role on a team, such as linemen versus wide receivers. Although the team is drinking from the same well of training, each athlete will not fit into a preplanned sport-specific program.

That would be challenging enough; however, in addition to the need for a broader training approach for team sports, a high school athlete's season may span three or four months, while collegiate and professional seasons can stretch even longer with playoffs and championships. A Super Bowl champion team's season stretches from training camp in August to the championship game in February!

A successful strength coach needs to be able to prepare the athletes for the rigors of the season—in shorter and shorter time spans of an off-season—and also to maintain and continue to develop the physical qualities throughout the season. A delayed bus or plane trip home after a game or the varying practice schedule during the season makes even the most meticulously designed program impossible to sustain.

This valuable graphic from Coach Al Vermeil sums up the challenge of programming from the beginning of the off-season to the in-season for different athletes.

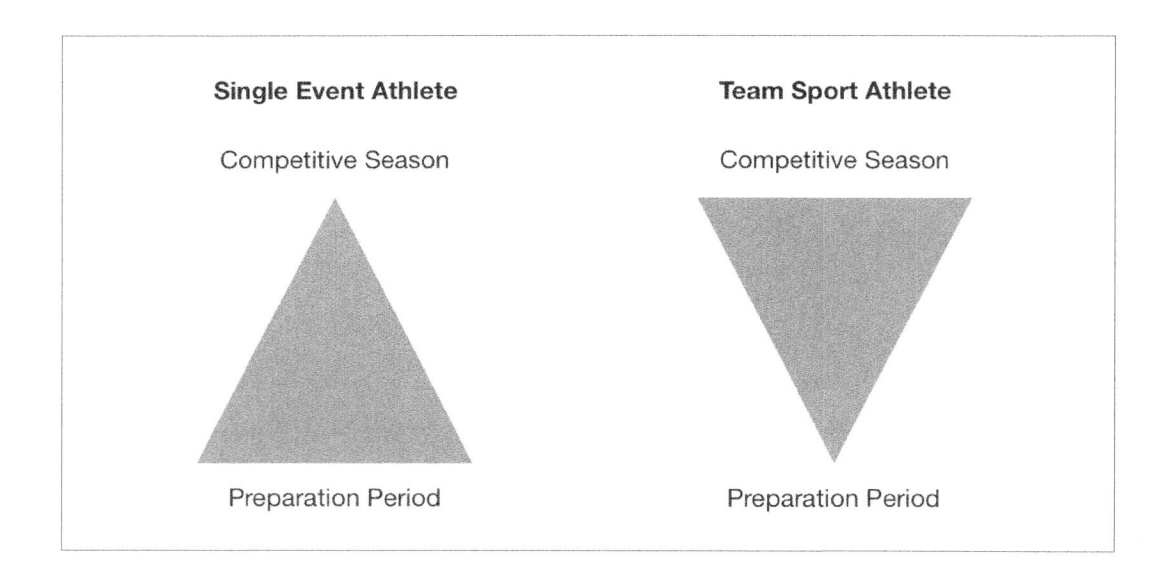

Figure 6.1 Programming for Single Events versus Team Sports

From Vermeil's Sports and Fitness Training System for Enhancing Athletic Performance, Al Vermeil, M.S., C.S.C.S

That is a tall order to fill.

It would certainly be easier to throw our hands up, admit defeat, and try to adapt a training plan on the fly to fit the day's or week's demands, hoping for the best, particularly during a sport season.

Obviously, this would be both unsustainable and impossible.

This does not mean there should not be a plan in place. It just means there needs to be a framework that enhances all of the physical qualities while allowing for flexibility.

All the exercise physiology and technical skills at your disposal will only get you halfway there when it comes to building a sustainable and successful system of training. That will come from the art of programming and refining your eye of the coach to know when to push the envelope and when to dial back the intensity or volume to make sure your athletes' performance peaks when it matters the most.

We need to create a framework of programming using the principles laid out to point us in the right direction. There will always be room for variation, substitution, and adaptation based on what the universe throws at you. That is the strength of using the undulating pattern to manipulate the training variables.

By starting with a flexible structure, we can adapt the plan as the need arises while keeping the final objective in sight. A perfectly designed and scripted training program is guaranteed to change as the weeks and months pass. Going through the process and consistently applying the principles to a master plan will make it easier to make adjustments when the time comes.

It is always valuable to first zoom out and take a wider perspective on the entire training timeline to map out the larger training blocks and the goals of training for athletes.

Depending on the sport and an athlete's needs, you should determine the relative importance of the different qualities and the amount of time to devote to each, depending on the timeline of training and on your goals.

No matter what, the general progression of emphasis over time should move in this direction:

Work Capacity > Hypertrophy > Strength > Power > Speed and Agility

The focus of the training for any particular month or block dictates the *why* and *how* of selecting the parameters of volume, intensity, and exercise selection. By starting from the standpoint of our goals for each block or macrocycle, we can start our planning from the *why*.

For the sake of simplicity, we approach the training timeline in terms of three simple and general blocks or macrocycles:

Off-Season, Preseason, and In-season

In a perfect world, the off-season would span at least 12 weeks, broken into four-week microcycles. The preseason would consist of one four-week microcycle, and the in-season would depend on the length of the competitive season.

We can employ the same general strategy of the standard periodization blocks, with initially lower-intensity and higher-volume work directed at building work capacity or hypertrophy, and gradually increasing the training intensity.

By using the undulating model, instead of dedicating an entire cycle to a single training goal, we program the cycles based on the *primary* and *secondary* qualities we need to address.

The primary training for the given cycles mirrors the standard periodization approach, but the difference is in maintaining the thread of all the qualities as the cycles advance.

	CYCLE ONE	CYCLE TWO	CYCLE THREE	CYCLE FOUR
PRIMARY EMPHASIS	Work Capacity Hypertrophy*	Strength Hypertrophy*	Power	Speed
SECONDARY EMPHASIS	Strength Power Speed	Work Capacity Power Speed	Strength Speed Work Capacity	Power Strength Work Capacity

Figure 6.1 Programming for Single Events versus Team Sports

In instances where hypertrophy is a desired goal of training

With the undulating pattern, it is possible to gradually develop each of the physical qualities while simultaneously increasing the athlete's work capacity and maintaining more of the gains leading up to the start of competition. Therein lays the real benefit of The System compared to most other programming models.

Knowing the primary and secondary goals of the microcycles, we can begin to program the training variables of volume, intensity, and frequency for the larger training blocks so we can develop a plan for the training year.

OFF-SEASON TRAINING CYCLE

GOALS

Restore or build work capacity

Progress training volume and intensity to develop the primary qualities of hypertrophy, strength, power, and speed

Volume
Progressively increases over the course of the off-season

Intensity
Progressively increases

Exercise Selection
Emphasis on strength movements, progressing toward power

Frequency
Three or four training sessions per week, depending on total volume

Once a competitive season is over, there is generally a mass exodus from the facility and weightroom as the athletes decompress from the rigors of the season. In most cases, no one is in a rush to get back into the gym. By that point, they need a break from us as much as they do from the weights.

We generally advocate for no more than one or two weeks completely off of training. This guidance depends on the length of the season, how the season ends, and the athletes' health and injury status at the end of the year, but, really, it is mostly for energy.

The problems start to arise when one or two weeks of rest and recovery starts to stretch into a month or more and conditioning, strength, and power start to erode.

A period of active rest and recovery programmed into the training is more beneficial for bouncing back and correcting movement or strength deficits following the season than completely shutting down training and then attempting to start from scratch.

The first two to four weeks of the off-season should consist of the prep phase outlined earlier on page 60. Novice athletes can follow the sample program, while advanced or elite athletes will spend two to four weeks of simple lifting consisting of the complexes, squats, pulls, RDLs, presses, and initiation of work capacity development for running and jumping.

Using a three-day per week lifting schedule provides enough stimulus to work up to handling three or four series with the prescribed weights in the complexes and some lower volume strength work (12–20 total reps) and Olympic lifts (12–15 total reps).

Even with elite-level NFL athletes, it is never wrong to re-establish the base of work capacity and movement competency that comes from a prep phase.

VOLUME

Athletes begin their progression at the low end of their respective monthly volume ranges. From year to year, the ideal goal is to begin the off-season at roughly 10 percent of the prior year's peak volume. This way, there's no question of where to begin because you can use the prior year's numbers to set the new baseline.

A novice who began the first year of training at 750 total reps and ended the off-season at 900 could start the second year at 800 reps. When taking this approach, they never peak too quickly when coming back, but are already a month ahead of where they started the prior off-season.

They can also handle programming that includes more complex lifting, running, and jumping, as they have already been exposed to and can tolerate the added demands.

After a one or two cycles, the athletes should be able to start progressing beyond the previous year's max by the midpoint of the off-season.

If the advanced or elite athletes' program starts with a four-day per week program and in the previous year, they reached 1,300 reps in the final off-season cycle, they could start the next year with something like 1,175 reps for the first cycle.

Using this method assumes you have three to four months of an off-season to build up to and beyond the 1,300 mark. By following this build-up pattern, you assure yourself of no problems with small injuries curtailing development.

You then allow the program to take the athletes where you want them to be.

PROGRESSION

You can undertake three possible progression patterns with your athletes:

- *Monthly volume increases, while the quality of the work remains the same*
- *Monthly volume remains the same, while the quality of the work increases*
- *Monthly volume and the quality of the work increases—be careful*

For a novice, the quality of work—the intensity—naturally progresses as the athlete matures and gains efficiency of movement. Seventy percent of a novice athlete's 1RM in the first cycle will be drastically different in the third cycle simply due to rapid physical adaptation.

Because of this, a novice athlete should generally follow a gradual progression of the monthly volume with a consistent undulation of the intensity pattern within the narrow range of Zones One to Three as described on page 168.

As athletes mature and gain experience, the relative training intensity can and should be increased, but the increase in monthly volume should never be greater than 10 percent of the previous month's total.

Intensity will gradually advance from Zone Two into Zone Three as the off-season progresses. Exercise selection begins with more emphasis on the strength movements, such as squats, presses, and RDLs, and then advances toward the Olympic lifts as the preseason approaches. This provides an early hypertrophy and strength emphasis that gradually moves toward more explosive strength and power.

Keeping in mind the developmental hierarchy, we are moving the emphasis from the base of strength and work capacity toward the peak of power and speed.

As you gradually increase the month-to-month volumes and your athletes' ability to handle a progressively higher training intensity, you will ultimately have to make a decision. There is a finite range of training volume that will provide a training effect without elevating the risk of overtraining. What we found in our time with the New York Giants is that we could only add so much volume before it became counterproductive.

In one off-season, we progressed from 1,200 reps in the first month to 1,400…to 1,600…to 1,800 reps.

By the time we reached 1,800 reps, the athletes were hurting—we were burning the candle at both ends.

Even if you are effectively varying the training intensity, if the intensity and the volume of the training continue to increase, it is difficult to effectively determine which variable is negatively impacting performance.

Even the most genetically gifted athletes can be easily overtrained, so it stands to reason that the less experienced or less physically mature athletes are at an even greater risk of breaking down from an aggressive training program.

RUNNING, JUMPING, AND CONDITIONING

As we covered previously, the approach to sprinting, jumping, and conditioning should follow the same pattern as the weight training.

The volume and intensity of sprint or plyometric work should gradually increase as the off-season progresses, while the volume of tempo runs and lower intensity work gradually decreases.

It is important to remember that even though the volume of tempo runs or conditioning decreases over the off-season, the speed at which the runs are performed should get faster (relative intensity).

PROGRESSION OVER THE OFF-SEASON

JUMPS

- *Complexity—moving from single jumps to jumps in succession, or from double-leg to single-leg variants as broad jumps progress to bounding*

- *Intensity—moving from emphasis on amplitude in height or distance to speed and reactivity*

SPRINTS

- *Complexity—moving from short sprints or technical work to multi-directional or change of direction*

- *Intensity—moving from speed-strength toward maximal speed emphasis*

CONDITIONING

- *Adding volume and/or increasing the speed and intensity to build speed endurance, depending on the demands of the sport*

EYE OF THE COACH

What we ultimately found is that for many athletes, 1,200–1,400 reps are the sweet spot of training volume. If you can progress your athletes into this range of monthly volume, the focus should then shift to increasing the intensity of the work.

You could, in many cases, perform two cycles in succession with the same volume—say 1,300 reps—and just focus on progressing the Zones of Intensity to see very good progress.

PRESEASON TRAINING CYCLE PRIOR TO THE START OF TRAINING CAMP

GOALS

Enhance power and speed development for carryover to the sport

Prepare athletes for the increased demands of sport practice and competition

Volume
At least a one-third reduction from peak off-season volume, maybe closer to 40 percent lower

Intensity
Increasing emphasis on explosive strength and speed over absolute strength

Exercise Selection
Strength movements progressing toward power movements

Frequency
Three or four training sessions per week, depending on total volume

As you approach a competitive season, there should be a reduction in the training volume and a shift in the emphasis from strength movements toward exercises that emphasize speed and power.

Many programs spend a tremendous amount of time emphasizing strength, power, and speed development during the off-season, and then fail to maintain those qualities once competition begins. All those months of hard work are for nothing if you cannot translate it into the season.

In football, the preseason is the month just prior to the start of training camp, before the demands of practice and meetings fill the daily schedule. The preseason priority is to increase the training intensity in preparation for performing in practice and on the field as athletes transition into sport.

This phase will gradually reduce the training load through less volume while priming power and speed heading into the season. Weight training during the season will take somewhat of a backseat to serve in a supporting role to skill practice and team activities for the sport.

VOLUME

You should reach the peak off-season volume for the cycle just prior to the preseason. In this four-week cycle, the volume will be reduced by at least a third to allow the athletes to start training camp a little more fresh.

If advanced athletes reach 1,300 reps in the final month of the off-season, the preseason volume should be no more than 910 reps. A novice athlete who reaches 1,000 reps may drop the volume even more, to something closer to 600 reps.

This number may seem low compared with the baselines set earlier. The increasing training intensity on top of the added sport demands can make recovery challenging for a younger or less-experienced athlete. There is no precise formula because each athlete's recovery ability is different. As always, when in doubt, err on a little less volume.

Another successful programming change is to alter the undulating volume pattern for the preseason cycle, where the volume is front-loaded and then tapered over the second half of the month.

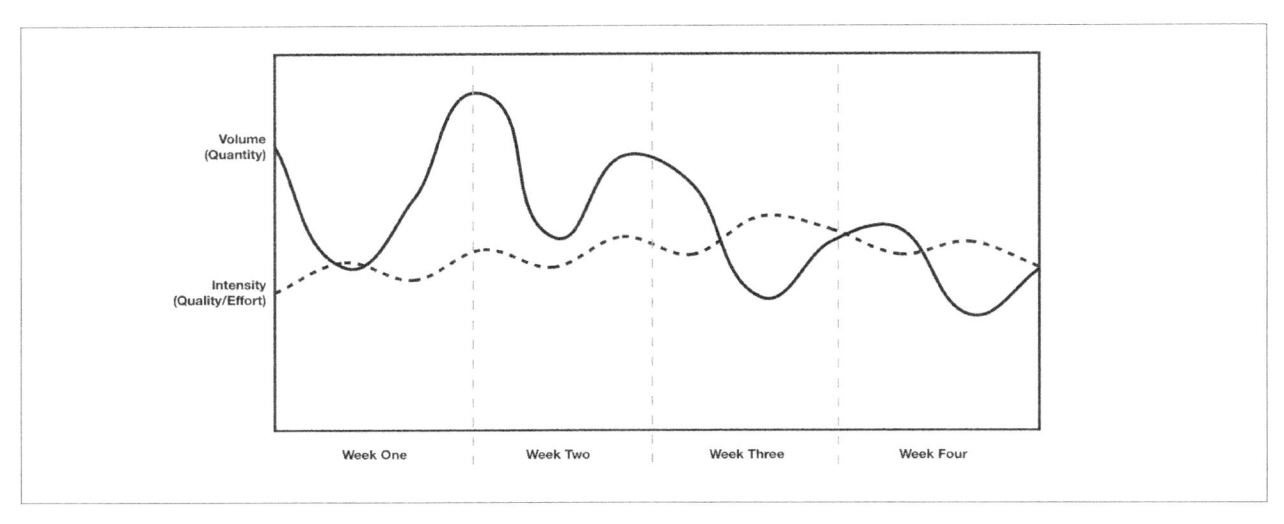

Figure 6.2 Undulating Preseason Volume

Rather than taking the typical wave of *27 percent—22 percent—32 percent—19 percent* or *28 percent—22 percent—35 percent—15 percent*, you can flip weeks two and three. This would provide an early peak in the month and then a reduction of the volume to let the athletes head into camp fresh.

This same pattern can be used leading up to a big meet or event for other sports where you want to peak just before the competition.

[CHAPTER SIX—SEASONAL PROGRAM DESIGN]

TYPICAL OFF-SEASON AND PRESEASON VOLUME UNDULATION	TAPERED PRESEASON VOLUME UNDULATION
Novice	**Novice**
27 percent—22 percent—32 percent—19 percent	*27 percent—32 percent—22 percent—19 percent*
Advanced or Elite	**Advanced or Elite**
28 percent—22 percent—35 percent—15 percent	*28 percent—35 percent—22 percent—15 percent*

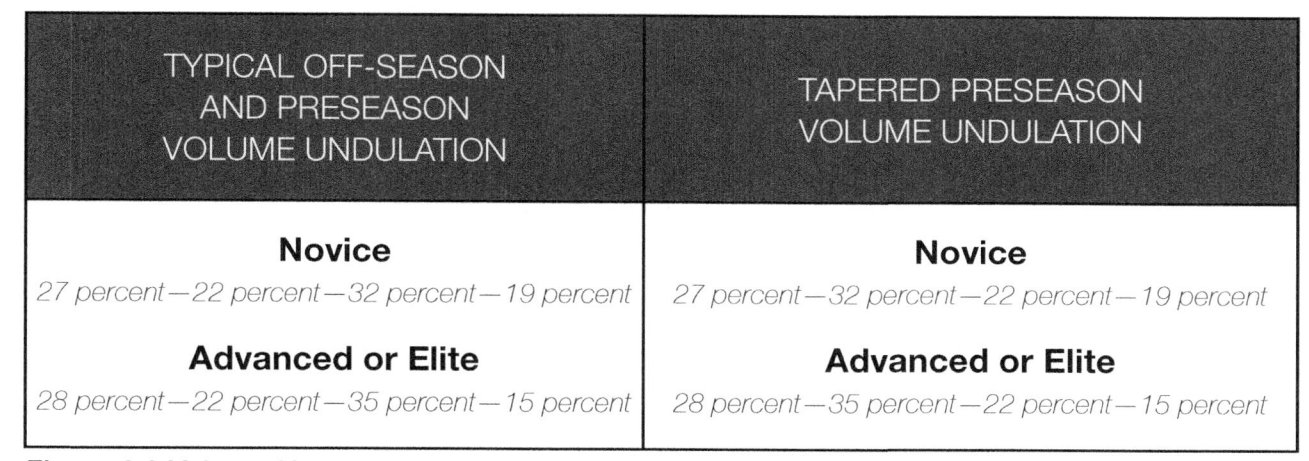

Figure 6.3 Volume Undulation over the Seasons

SHORTENED OFF-SEASON

Unfortunately, the changing landscape of athletics places increased challenges to planning a preseason phase. The preseason phase exists under ideal circumstances; if the off-season is short—say, 12 weeks or fewer—there will have to be a shift in the approach to the preseason cycle.

The athletes will just be making significant gains around week eight when the volume is drastically dropped for the preseason cycle. Too big of a drop will stall progress if there were only two off-season cycles of progression prior to the start of camp. In that scenario, the preseason volume should only be dropped by 15–20 percent from the peak off-season volume, and the training intensity should continue to progress as competition begins.

This is where utilizing the front-loaded volume approach can be especially helpful. This way the training intensity can remain high and the taper of volume over the preseason cycle can allow for added recovery leading into the start of training camp. It is taking advantage of the super-compensation effect, where the expectation is to see a bump in performance as the volume falls over the final two weeks.

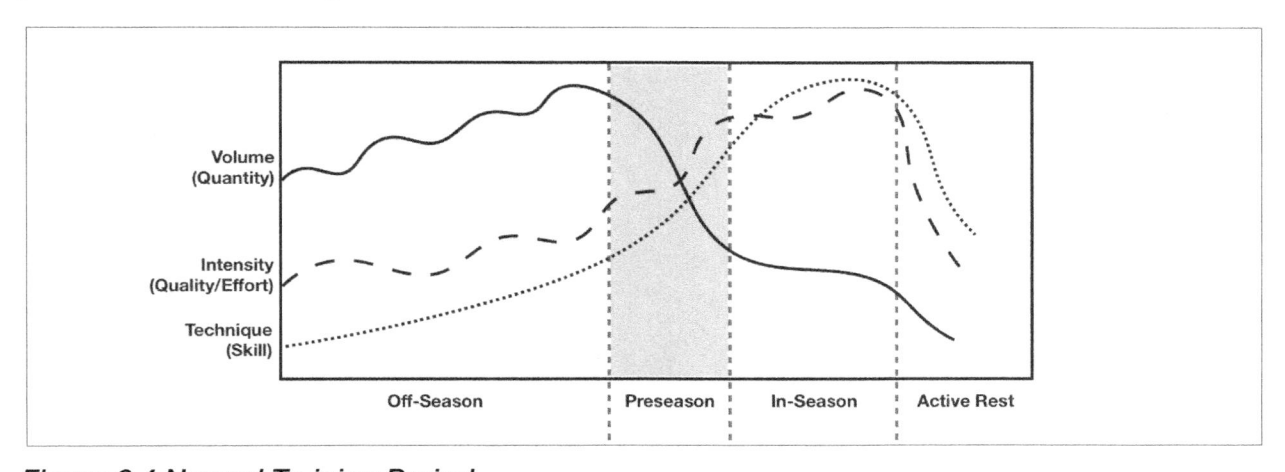

Figure 6.4 Normal Training Period

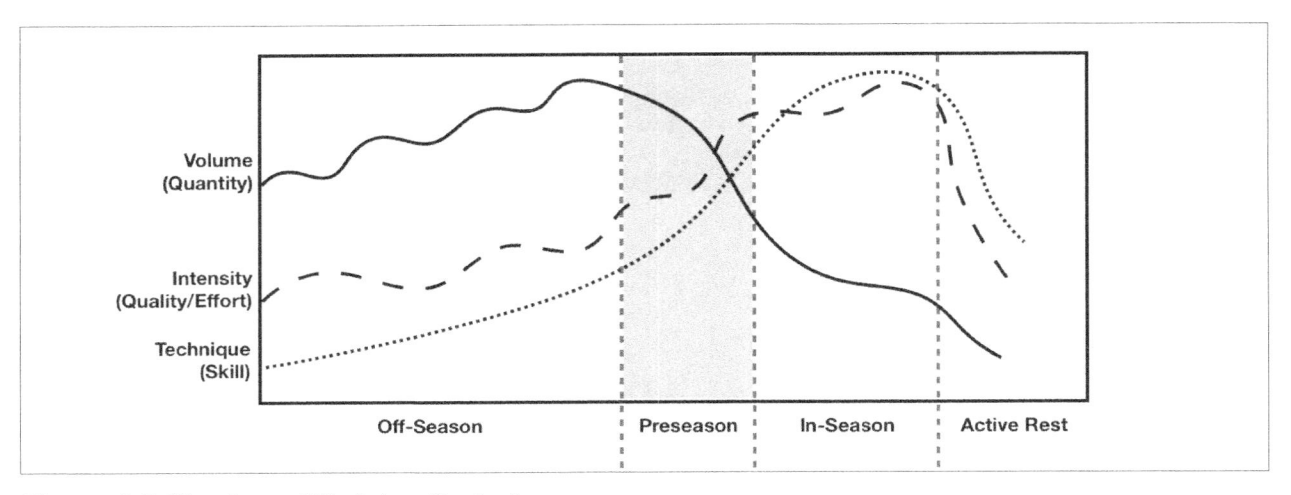

Figure 6.5 Shortened Training Period
Notice the decreased slope of volume reduction

This is far from ideal, but with the restrictions placed on organized team activities and off-season training periods, it is unfortunately becoming more the norm than the exception. In a perfect world, the athletes would independently begin their training prior to the start of the organized off-season team workouts to buy more time to prepare. However, that in itself is a challenge.

PROGRESSION

The intensity of training should increase as the total volume drops during this phase. The majority of the training intensity should be in the higher zones of Zone Three for novices into the more advanced Zone Four, with sets in the three-to-six rep range.

The foundation of exercises continues to be based on the strength movements of squats and presses; however, there will be increased emphasis on exercises that develop speed of muscle contraction. The volume of Olympic lifts is boosted to create a shift from absolute strength into power and speed training that translates onto the field.

For example, the volume of military presses may go down and be replaced with more push-presses or jerks. The goal is to continue to see progress in the weights and the speed of the lifts, but with the reduction in training volume off-setting the higher intensity of work.

The goal is to not only maintain the gains made in the off-season, but to also increase strength and power into and through the season.

There is nothing worse than peaking going into the first week of the season, starting fast, and then watching as progress in the weightroom and on the field flat lines or fades over the course of the year. The athletes should be handling heavier weights and pushing themselves, while the reduced volume takes enough strain off the system to prevent overtraining.

RUNNING, JUMPING, AND CONDITIONING

Along with the reduction in the volume of weight training, in this phase the volume of the sprinting and jumping should also decline. The goal is to be peaking the explosive speed emphasis of the work, with higher intensity and more complex running and jumping in the pre-season cycle just before the start of camp.

For jumping, novice athletes should now be performing multiple jumps in succession, and advanced athletes should be performing bounding or high-level plyometrics. Sprinting should be focused on maximal speed and acceleration.

Rather than placing the emphasis on jumping higher or running farther, your programming here should be directed toward increasing the speed of movement. With the shift in programming, your coaching should also shift to develop quickness and reactivity. Adding drills that stress changes in direction, minimizing ground contact, and the speed of reaction to unexpected stimuli will improve those qualities at the start of training camp.

The one exception is with the conditioning work through the tempo runs. For most team sports, the goal is not to create long-distance runners, so there is generally a ceiling of volume dedicated to the tempo runs. Tempo runs should peak in volume and intensity just prior to the start of camp.

Over the course of the off-season, most athletes should have worked up the tempo run volume to around 12–16 cycles in the 100-yard runs, depending on their level and ability, while the speed of the runs should increase to develop endurance with speed.

This should prepare them for the demands of practice and game situations once camp opens, without the need to "work them into shape" once they arrive.

Successful programming leading up to the start of the season should produce athletes who are stronger, faster, and more explosive in their respective sports. There are many paths of periodization that can effectively produce this outcome.

The challenge for most coaches is in transitioning the approach from preparing athletes to compete to maintaining their performance throughout a competitive season. This can often produce that inevitable question of "what's next" in terms of progression or volume or intensity.

Here is where understanding and applying the principles and methods we outlined can spell the difference between those teams that gradually fall by the wayside as the season wears on versus those who only seem to get stronger as the stakes get higher.

IN-SEASON TRAINING CYCLE

GOALS
Progress the qualities of strength, power, and speed throughout the competitive season

Facilitate recovery from competition

Volume
Very low, need to manage total volume carefully, but no specific number

Intensity
Highest, with the primary emphasis on gaining strength and explosive qualities

Exercise Selection
Power, speed, and strength

Frequency
Two times per week

In-season programming can be the most daunting and challenging task for strength coaches, yet may be one of the last advantages strength coaches have available to employ against their opponents.

Thousands of training programs do a good job of developing strength, power, and speed during the off-season, and then fall terribly short in maintaining those qualities during the season when it matters most.

There is no magic program for in-season training because if there was, every coach would know about it and would be using it with great success. Through diligent trial and error, we learned the hard way that a beautifully planned and coordinated training program falls apart in the first week of the season.

It is critical to remain flexible in your approach to training during the competitive season to facilitate recovery, reduce the risk of injury, and continue to support performance on the field.

The strategy many coaches take is to focus solely on reducing the incidence of injury and maintaining performance of the off-season. Some coaches limit the exercise intensity to 80 percent of the off-season peak to avoid overload.

This training philosophy is perplexing, because why would any coach be satisfied with a 20-percent deficit in an athlete's physical qualities after extreme physical efforts during the off-season produced these improvements?

Why is it desirable for athletes to be 20-percent weaker at a time they are required to perform at optimal levels? Would any coach be satisfied with an 80-percent effort and skill level on game day?

If approached appropriately, training during the season can not only maintain, but can continue to develop strength and power qualities throughout the competitive season. You will have to commit a lot of thought to training volume and timing, with responsible monitoring of your athletes to look for signs of overtraining. You will inevitably need to adapt the training to each athlete instead of the athletes to the training, but a prepared coach should not be afraid to push athletes during the season.

There will often be times during the competitive season when a head sport coach or strength and conditioning professional will make the statement, "We need to keep our players fresh." This usually means having the players rest or perform "easy" workouts at a low, submaximal intensity to not "wear the players out," so to speak.

There are certainly times through a long and physically taxing season when that thought process may be practical. However, to adhere to this philosophy for an extended period will prove costly. Barring injury or a situation where performance in the weightroom is significantly hampered or counter-productive, you should have an expectation of continued effort and dedication to training during the season. Mental and physical toughness is a difficult quality to measure; allowing athletes off the hook of hard training during the season does not instill a mindset of grit and perseverance.

Avoiding appropriately planned and timed high-intensity, low-volume training in-season will contribute to a gradual deconditioning of your athletes and a forfeiture of the strength and power qualities they possessed at the start of the season. Maintaining or enhancing strength and power qualities in-season is what elevates the teams that roll through opponents as the season wears on.

It never failed that in Coach Parker's New York Giants weightroom, players commented how much stronger they felt versus the same divisional opponent later in the season, as well as how much easier they handled those opponents the second time around.

The most common mistake we see with in-season programming is to sacrifice weight on the bar to reduce the *perceived* risk of injury. Repetitive strain injuries—not training intensity—are the number one injury mechanism in athletics, other than an in-game injury.

If you choose to drastically reduce the training intensity, remember that there must be an increase in training volume if there is any hope of creating a training stimulus. Adding more training volume to compensate for lower intensity weight training on top of practice and game volume leads to far more issues than adding weight to the bar while reducing the overall sets and reps. As long as you are tracking the fatigue levels of the athletes and adjusting accordingly, you can keep gradually pushing intensity up throughout the season.

You do not want your team peaking in week one of the season when you have months of games ahead. You want that peak as the season wears on and the competition falls behind.

There is nothing more frustrating than coming out of the gates firing, and then watching performance slowly dissolve as the weeks pass.

Coach Parker's in-season weight programs placed emphasis on not only maintaining strength and power qualities during the season, but also on *improving* those physical qualities as the season progressed. There was no expectation of coasting to the finish line.

During one championship season with the New York Giants, 35 of his players hit a PR in at least one lift during the week prior to the start of the playoffs. Giants running back Joe Morris set a PR in the power clean on a Wednesday prior to a Saturday playoff game, and went on to rush for 202 yards in that game. What coach would not want players to continue to get stronger into the last month of the season?

The secret is to create an environment that promotes lifting heavy during the season. There is an element of mental and physical toughness we must develop to cut through the aches and pains and energy swings that come during a season. There are big variations between athletes' energy and conditioning levels throughout the season, and nowhere is the eye of the coach more relevant than in successfully navigating the nuances of in-season programming.

We have all made the mistake of meticulously designing in-season programming for our various teams and sports…down to the specific percentages and volumes for each position and player.

In almost every case, that painstakingly designed plan went out the window within the first week. A delayed flight home, a sickness working its way through the team, or a particularly brutal game will tax the athletes' recovery and ability to perform in the weightroom.

If there was a perfect model or plan for in-season training, we would all be doing it. What has served us best is taking a more flexible approach to allow planned progression of intensity throughout the season, but with room to maneuver and adjust.

VOLUME

Compared with the off-season and preseason, in-season volume is drastically reduced, both from a standpoint of total training volume, as well as volume within the training sessions. The total volume is reduced by at least a third entering the preseason phase and another third in-season.

Similar to our off-season planning, the volume undulates throughout the monthly cycle, yet a little more generalized than before. The focus is on the weekly volume as it pertains to each exercise, categorized as medium-heavy, medium, heavy, and light volume.

IN-SEASON CYCLE—WEEKLY VOLUME

Week One
Medium-Heavy, 14–17 reps per exercise

Week Two
Medium, 12–15 reps per exercise

Week Three
Heavy, 17–20 reps per exercise

Week Four
Light, 10–12 reps per exercise

These training sessions should be short, intense, and efficient. Your goal is to complete the workouts in 30–60 minutes, which means to focus your exercise selection on the few essential movements that provide the greatest training effect. This is why in-season squats, presses, and cleans should make up the foundation of the programming, including pulls or snatches as needed.

Squats and presses maintain and build strength, while cleans provide continued development of explosive power. In contact sports, pulls play a particularly important role during in-season training because they are easier on the hands and wrists than Olympic lifts and allow for heavier loading than the Olympic lifts. Snatch high pulls or clean pulls allow athletes to train the same explosive full-body movement of a clean or snatch, but without the stress of catching the bar at the finish.

The exercises will be from the same "family" for each day, but they will not be the same exercises from day to day. Novice athletes need less variety of exercises compared with advanced athletes. There should not be any more than three to six exercises on a single day, and that includes any supplementary work of abs, neck, or accessory exercises, such as triceps or lat work for linemen, or position or role-specific work.

Rather than setting a target monthly volume and then performing the math to break down the weeks and workouts as we did during the off-season, in-season training follows a less-rigid model. Total volume continues to undulate from week to week; however, the volume for each exercise is restricted within specific ranges per workout.

Here, the terms of "medium-heavy," "medium," "heavy," and "light" refer to the *training volume for the week*, rather than the intensity levels of training, and provide the same varying stimulus response as the off-season programming. Once you select the training movements, there is a narrow range of volume for each session and you can set the training intensity and reps and set based on the goal of training.

With the constrained in-season exercise selection, each training session places primary emphasis on two or three movements. Going back to Prilepin's chart and our goals of developing strength and power, the overall reps and sets for any of the movements should fall between one and six reps.

Sets of two and three reps for the primary movements evolve to an increased number of single-rep sets as the season progresses. With the reduced overall volume, those smaller rep and set numbers are a lot less taxing on musculoskeletal recovery than higher-rep work. Any accessory lifts will then use fewer sets and lighter intensities to reach the desired volume.

The absolute minimum training frequency is two times per week if you have any hope of maintaining or improving strength and power qualities.[65] Those two weekly sessions will be brief, efficient, and very intense. This is all about maximizing gains while minimizing the time allotment that takes away from practice, meetings, and recovery.

The approach we use most often for football is to program two or possibly three workouts during the week. The higher-volume workout is on Monday and the lower-volume workout on Wednesday or Thursday. By scheduling the bigger workout early in the week, there is more time for recovery before the next game.

The split we like is Monday and Wednesday for skill positions or Monday and Thursday or Friday for linemen, assuming the games are on Sundays.

SAMPLE TWO DAY PER WEEK PLAN	
BIG DAY—HIGHER VOLUME 30–45 MINUTES	LESSER DAY—LOWER VOLUME 20–30 MINUTES
Warmup *See page 192* Cleans Military Press Squats Low Back, Abs, and Neck	Warmup Dumbbell Cleans Bench Press *Or something different from the earlier workout* Abs, Neck

Figure 6.6 Two Session Example

Another approach we used with success is to think of the training week in terms of recovery, strength, and power. The volume and intensity for the week moves in an inverse relationship, where Monday's workout is a higher-volume but slightly lower-intensity session for recovery. Wednesday or Thursday is a higher-intensity workout but lower-volume for strength and power, and a third, brief workout on Friday is very low volume but high intensity for the upper body.

Coach Miller used these Friday workouts to add additional upper-body pressing and pulling for the linemen or athletes who needed more shoulder strengthening or protection. Most of the lifts were performed seated or lying to save the legs for the upcoming game.

This three-session per week approach provided our athletes a little easier entry into the week to work out soreness or stiffness from the weekend's game, and still get in higher-intensity work as the week progressed.

SAMPLE THREE DAY PER WEEK PLAN		
RECOVERY SESSION LOWER INTENSITY 20–30 MINUTES	STRENGTH AND POWER SESSION HIGHER INTENSITY 30–45 MINUTES	UPPER-BODY SESSION 20–30 MINUTES
Warmup Squat Press Abs, Neck, Low Back	Warmup Clean Squat Press Abs, Neck, Low Back	Warmup Press Row Variations Abs, Neck, Low Back

Figure 6.7 Three Session Example

By higher volume, we mean higher reps and sets with a slightly reduced intensity. During the season, the training intensity should be high to maintain and progress strength and power, but the higher-volume days may employ sets of four or five repetitions, where the lower-volume days use heavy triple, double, or single-rep sets.

It is possible to perform a single training session with the focus of maximum explosive strength training moving high-weight loads (90% of 1RM) at least one or two days before competition because of the shorter regeneration times and potentiating effects.

Compared with lifting light loads at high speed (30% of 1RM), this method has been shown to provide statistically superior gains in maximal strength, peak power, impulse size, and explosive strength.[66]

Planning for football or a sport with one game per week is certainly easier than a sport with multiple competitions in a week.

For the strength coaches with multiple weekly games, it is still important to include high-intensity work throughout the season, but managing volume for those athletes becomes even more critical.

Coach Vermeil is an example of how some strength coaches in these sports program high-intensity training not only during the in-season weeks, but also preparing athletes with high intensity and low-volume workouts *on game day* as well. Some of his athletes would even perform short, high intensity workouts *prior* to a game.

The championship teams Coach Vermeil helped develop in football, baseball, and basketball are a testament to the importance of continuing to train at a high intensity throughout a competitive season.

PROGRESSION

If the goal of an in-season program is to continue to advance the training intensity, the question inevitably arises of how to select the best intensity when taking into account recovery, the game schedule, how much the athletes have been playing or practicing, and the intensity of the games.

If we determine intensity purely off percentages, the loads will be too heavy for some, too light for some, and just right for some. We would be overtraining a third of the team, under-training a third, and appropriately training the rest.

EYE OF THE COACH

The coach needs to listen and observe the athletes. Recognize who your best-conditioned players are and know that when these athletes are fatigued, it is likely many others are fatigued as well.

If your leaders in the weightroom begin to drag, it is a cardinal sign that you need to take your foot off the gas and allow for more recovery.

In our years of implementing this philosophy of training, not one of us ever heard players say they were too fatigued to continue to train in this type of in-season program.

Keeping a finely tuned eye for overt signs of fatigue will help ensure your players' success.

This is a less-than-ideal outcome, likely to result in declining performance for the majority of the team.

By choosing a starting weight we know everyone can handle and then letting them self-regulate based on the reps and sets of the work sets, we can hold a larger percentage of the team within their ideal intensity ranges. The reserve athletes who are fresher and less beat up can push a little harder, while the starters who are feeling the effects of a brutal game can dial the intensity back a bit.

As a coach, you should still program for the specific percentages and weights you would ideally like to see based on previous performances. As long as there are no compromises in effort and speed of the lifts, building in a slightly more flexible plan may save you from yourself.

Athletes need intensity in their work, not just "work." When appropriate, incorporate weight intensities of 90 percent to 95 percent in each of the squat, clean, and press categories twice monthly. This will provide your athletes the opportunity to perform six high-intensity lifts distributed across 30 days.

The intensity variation over the course of the month will largely mirror the undulating wave utilized during the off-season. The relative training intensity of the lifts should undulate through the higher Zones of Intensity, ideally above 80 percent of the 1RM over the first three weeks, and then fall back to between 70–75 percent of 1RM for the fourth week.

That fourth week again serves as an unload, with both lighter volume and intensity, before resuming higher-intensity work with a new mix of exercises in the following month.

The concept of extending into high-intensity sets during the season is easy to comprehend, but difficult for many strength coaches to trust. A 90 to 95-percent effort is still *submaximal.*

For example, if an athlete has the ability to sprint a 10-second 100 meters and trains running an 11-second 100 meters—a 90-percent effort—it is an "easier" effort, yet still provides a stimulus for improvement.

Let us consider an athlete who has performed a successful, technically proficient 500-pound max back squat. The following table shows a comparison of the work performed as stress on the body utilizing two different in-season training sessions.

Assume the athlete warmed up and then worked up to a set of squats at 80 percent of the PR. Utilizing the mathematical formula for work—*work = force x distance*—where the force is the weight intensity and the distance we will assume to be six feet—three feet in both the descent and ascent of the squat motion.

Based on a 500-pound squat, the work performed of a limited 80-percent daily routine versus a 90–95-percent bimonthly daily routine is presented in Figure 6.8 on the following page.

80-PERCENT SQUAT 3X3 ROUTINE					
SET	FORCE	TOTAL DISTANCE	REPS PER SET	WORK PERFORMED PER EXERCISE SET IN FOOT-POUNDS
ONE	400 pounds *80 percent*	6 feet	3	7,200 foot-pounds
TWO	400 pounds *80 percent*	6 feet	3	7,200 foot-pounds
THREE	400 pounds *80 percent*	6 feet	3	7,200 foot-pounds
TOTAL			9	**21,600 foot-pounds**

Figure 6.8 Comparison of Work Performed at 80 Percent

80–95 PERCENT SQUAT ROUTINE					
SET	FORCE	TOTAL DISTANCE	REPS PER SET	WORK PERFORMED PER EXERCISE SET IN FOOT-POUNDS
ONE	400 pounds *80 percent*	6 feet	2	4,800 foot-pounds
TWO	400 pounds *80 percent*	6 feet	2	4,800 foot-pounds
THREE	425 pounds *85 percent*	6 feet	2	5,100 foot-pounds
FOUR	450 pounds *90 percent*	6 feet	1	2,700 foot-pounds
FIVE	475 pounds *95 percent*	6 feet	1	2,850 foot-pounds
TOTAL			8	**20,250 foot-pounds**

Figure 6.9 Comparison of Work Performed at 80-95 Percent

The total work performed for the second routine is 20,250 foot-pounds, which is 1,350 foot-pounds less than the first routine. To elicit a better training response, we would assume that more work is better. However, if we compare the two routines, the quality of the work per squat rep in the first routine is 5.3 percent less when compared to each squat rep performed in the second routine—400 pounds versus 422 pounds, respectively.

What has been accomplished with the second approach is a greater physiologic demand from the heavier sets, but less total work performed, which could impact recovery. The principle applies to all stages of training, but especially in-season training—maximize the stimulus while minimizing the needed recovery.

Athletes who are well coached and technically proficient in exercise performance use less energy in executing a heavy lift. This means technically sound, high-intensity lifts performed at low volumes result in a stimulus for adaptation and improvement, rather than being wasted energy and contributing to excessive fatigue. One huge point here:

You need to have athletes and coaches you trust to successfully train this way.

If you have a group of athletes you know will work, compete, and respond to coaching, and who are not going to abuse every opportunity of autonomy, you can dedicate your focus to coaching and refining technique. If they demonstrate a good self-awareness and self-assessment of their physical abilities, they can be trusted with the difficulty of the work this type of training entails.

The same goes for the head coach, who must support the strength coach and this type of training. Just like with lifting and conditioning, scheduling high tempo and succinct practice sessions as opposed to prolonged and drawn-out practices helps train intensity and limits excessive fatigue in the athletes over time.

Practice volume is the same as training volume. Not adjusting one or the other during the season places a limitation on the athletes' physical abilities in the weightroom, and in practice and game day performance as well. We haven't encountered many coaches who were happy to reduce their practice time, which means efficiency in the training aspect becomes critical.

DEDICATED HAMSTRING WORK

One particular area we learned to address through trial and error is to take care with dedicated hamstring work during the season. The direct hamstring work that makes up the foundational movements during the off-season should taper prior to the start of the season. We recommend being very conservative during the season, particularly with defensive backs, wide receivers, or athletes performing a large volume of sprinting.

Glute-ham raises and RDLs are incredibly valuable exercises. However, taxing the hamstrings directly in the weightroom and then asking athletes to perform at a high level in practice or game situations can increase the likelihood of hamstring strains.

The back and hamstrings go through a lot of stress during the season and although the RDL is an outstanding exercise, including it in-season along with cleans, squats, and pulls can do more harm than good.

If the posterior chain is adequately strengthened during the off-season, it will continue to get more than enough attention from the inclusion of complexes as a warmup, hyperextensions, reverse hyperextensions, and occasional glute-ham raises.

IN-SEASON CONDITIONING

When it comes to in-season conditioning for football, we found the most effective method for maintaining conditioning is to increase the pace of the sessions and practices rather than adding conditioning exercises.

All of the running, jumping, and sprinting leading up to the competitive season is meant to prepare athletes to perform the specific sport skills. At that point, practicing and playing the sport should be enough to maintain those qualities for the season.

Your job is to provide the sport coaches a product that is ready to roll. Adding more running or high-intensity running and jumping will only drain the athletes' tanks.

One method that has proven valuable is working closely with the coaching staff to regulate the volume and intensity of drills and practice to create the same undulating training effect when training camp begins. Mixing longer, less-intense practices with shorter, more-intense practices can help develop the on-the-field skills while building in recovery.

During the season, working with the coaches to maintain a high tempo and to limit rest between plays to 30 or maybe 40 seconds in some practices can do several things.

First, there is no standing around so players do not get bored and are more engaged. Second, the most effective conditioning for carryover into the sport is to practice with intensity.

The goal is not to have a clinic out on the field; teams have meetings for that. Players are not on their feet as long, and as the season wears on, they are not on the field more than an hour or 90 minutes. This builds toughness on top of game endurance.

Practicing with minimal breaks and sustained intensity will translate onto the field as opponents struggle to keep pace.

[CHAPTER SIX—SEASONAL PROGRAM DESIGN]

EYE OF THE COACH

Although it is not as big of an issue with high school and college athletics, there is another challenge that can impact in-season programming for those coaching baseball, basketball, or athletes with long seasons relative to the off-season.

The NBA's Golden State Warriors championship season of 2016-17 began with training camp the last week of September and ended with the championship game on June 12, 2017. The MLB World Series champions will have to sustain strength and conditioning from February through October.

It takes a special breed of coach to succeed in preparing and developing athletes and then sustaining those gains over nine or ten months of competition. This is why we consider the work and insight of Coach Al Vermeil so valuable in developing athletes.

In almost any scenario, we stick with two or three days of training for 30 to 60 minutes and focus on no more than three to six exercises, with sets in the one-to-six rep range during the season. It is a simple but effective approach.

Operating within that framework and sharpening your ability to identify the athletes' needs and adapt your plan to their acute condition will ultimately dictate your success.

SECTION THREE
IMPLEMENTING THE SYSTEM

CHAPTER SEVEN—
PUTTING IT ALL TOGETHER

PLANNING YOUR PROGRAMS

In the Foundation section beginning on page 19, we covered the sequential order of training different qualities under Coach Al Vermeil's Hierarchy of Athletic Development. The sequential order of qualities does not mean addressing only one quality at a time—that sometimes gets lost in the implementation of that system.

You can simultaneously direct the training at different qualities, but there should be an emphasis on a single component, depending on an athlete's needs. It is appropriate to maintain a thread of all the elements within a cycle to maintain your athletes' hard-earned gains.

The System is built with that principle in mind. The variety in volume and intensity ensures the maintenance of strength, power, speed, and hypertrophy throughout the cycle while allowing continued progress. It will not maximally develop one quality, but will provide steady gains without the need for complete shifts in the training.

There is an art and science to the programming and, like anything of value, it takes time to master and become efficient. The first time we were tasked with creating a 16-week program, Coach Goldstein told us it would take 40 hours to design, including the appropriate volume and intensities. Despite our best attempts and years of experience, he was almost right.

You need to approach this next step with that same mindset: Anything of value takes time to acquire. Michael Jordan and Larry Bird did not develop their abilities through only team practice. Tom Brady was not born with the ability to assess and dissect a defense. Vince Lombardi and Bear Bryant were not instantly successful at coaching and developing some of the greatest dynasties in football history. All of these people took years of refining their craft and styles and dedicating time away from competition to learn, test, refine, and retest their methods.

There is no difference when it comes to learning the art and science of strength programming for sports. This is what it will take to become a successful strength coach.

It will be challenging and your first attempt will be a little painful—and probably even the second and third. The more repetition, the more efficient you will become. This skill will come with time. You will see the true benefits of this programming method when your athletes continue to get stronger and faster on the field into and even throughout a competitive season.

Now, the high school coach with 40 kids cannot have 40 different programs. We do not suggest the impossible task of creating a highly technical and nuanced program for each athlete. However, once you grasp the concepts and principles, it will become easier to create programming that is flexible in its approach and progression.

With that in mind, take the bird's-eye view of the principles within The System to start down your programming path. It will be easier to have an over-arching plan for your team and then make the minor adjustments necessary for the particular athlete.

DESIGNING A PROGRAM

This system allows the strength coach to create a template of training that allows for planning and progress over the span of years rather than months.

This is not a 16-week football program or an off-season hypertrophy program. This is a way of assessing, planning, and implementing a training regimen to develop strength, power, and speed that is second to none.

Once you are comfortable with the general concepts and design of a single training cycle, it will be far less daunting to plan an athlete's off-season or long-term training plan.

The specifics can be daunting when initially reviewed. There is an art and science to effective programming, and although there seems to be a lot of moving parts in undulating patterns, once you have laid out one or two training cycles, it will become more intuitive.

In this section, we will detail two examples of common athletes and the programs we would design for each.

We assume the vast majority of coaches reading this book are working with high school and collegiate-level athletes. Therefore, to show the process, we will present programs designed for the absolute novice and for a typical advanced-level athlete. By the end of these examples, you will have the tools you need to design anything between or beyond these two levels.

Although both of the sample programs are for football players, once you appreciate the process and structure, it will only require a small shift to develop individual programs for different athletes and sports.

The rep numbers will rarely split evenly when you determine the percentages. Take the grade school approach and round up if there is more than half a rep left over and down if it is less than half.

The week and daily session totals may end up a few repetitions off the ideal rep total. Taken over the course of months and years, these minor variations will smooth out.

[CHAPTER SEVEN—PUTTING IT ALL TOGETHER]

THE NOVICE ATHLETE

The athlete in this example is a 180-pound high school junior linebacker who has completed a year of formal training using The System. During that year, he demonstrated good technique with the Javorek Complex and has a base of work capacity to tolerate higher-intensity training.

As we begin the program, it is the summer off-season. He has no history of injury or medical concerns, and has trained with weights in some capacity for two years. He has already completed one four-week prep phase cycle as shown beginning on page 87, where the intensity level was kept between Zones One and Two at 50–69 percent of 1RM.

Our primary training variables are:

Volume
800 total repetitions for the month

Intensity
Training will take place primarily within Zones One and Three at 50–79 percent 1RM

Frequency
Three times per week due to low total volume

The hierarchy of the primary movements for the novice-level athlete from most important to least important is: *Squat—Press—Clean—Pulls—Posterior Chain—Snatch—Jerk*. For the four-week training cycle, the total volume per exercise will be:

MOVEMENT	PERCENT TOTAL VOLUME	MONTHLY VOLUME
SQUAT	24 percent	192 reps
PRESS	20 percent	160 reps
CLEAN	18 percent	144 reps
PULLS	15 percent	120 reps
POSTERIOR CHAIN	13 percent	104 reps
SNATCH	10 percent	80 reps
JERK	0 percent	0 reps

Figure 7.1 Monthly Volume Per Exercise

MONTHLY VOLUME BREAKDOWN				
	WEEK ONE REPS	WEEK TWO REPS	WEEK THREE REPS	WEEK FOUR REPS
PREDICTED VOLUME	224 *28 percent total*	176 *22 percent total*	256 *32 percent total*	144 *18 percent total*
SQUAT	54	42	62	36
PRESS	45	35	51	29
CLEAN	40	32	46	26
PULLS	33	26	38	22
POSTERIOR CHAIN	29	23	33	19
SNATCH	22	17	26	14
JERK	0	0	0	0
TOTAL VOLUME	**223**	**175**	**256**	**146**

Figure 7.2 Exercise Reps Per Week

WEEKLY VOLUME BREAKDOWN				
	SESSION ONE 42 PERCENT	SESSION TWO 24 PERCENT	SESSION THREE 34 PERCENT	TOTAL REPS
WEEK ONE	94	53	76	**223**
WEEK TWO	74	42	59	**175**
WEEK THREE	108	61	87	**256**
WEEK FOUR	61	35	50	**146**

Figure 7.3 Session Volume Per Week

[CHAPTER SEVEN—PUTTING IT ALL TOGETHER]

	WEEK ONE REPS	SESSION ONE REPS	SESSION TWO REPS	SESSION THREE REPS
TRAINING SESSION VOLUMES				
PREDICTED VOLUME	224	94 *42 percent total*	53 *24 percent total*	76 *34 percent total*
SQUAT	54	23	13	18
PRESS	45	19	11	15
CLEAN	41	17	10*	14
PULLS	33	14	8*	11
POSTERIOR CHAIN	29	12	7*	10
SNATCH	22	9*	5*	7*
JERK	0	0	0	0
TOTAL VOLUME	**224**	**94**	**54**	**75**

Figure 7.4 Predicted Exercise Volume

The asterisks above denote volume falling below the minimum 12-rep threshold.

The week one table in Figure 7.4 shows a perfect example of the need to be flexible with your approach when it comes to programming. Given a novice athlete performing a low monthly volume, it is unlikely the repetitions for each movement will be nicely distributed between each of the three training sessions in the week.

For some of the movements, there are not enough repetitions on some of the training days within our minimum of 12 repetitions to elicit a training effect.

It is acceptable to have a few sessions where the movement volume falls below the minimum effective dose. However, for the pulls and posterior chain, there would only be one session that hit the mark under the strict guidelines. The snatch would not have a single session with enough reps.

With that in mind, you can make some modifications to the general distribution to create a more efficient and effective training template.

[CHAPTER SEVEN—PUTTING IT ALL TOGETHER]

	WEEK ONE REPS	SESSION ONE REPS	SESSION TWO REPS	SESSION THREE REPS
TRAINING SESSION VOLUMES				
PREDICTED VOLUME	223	94 *42 percent total*	53 *24 percent total*	76 *34 percent total*
SQUAT	54	23	13	18
PRESS	45	19	11	15
CLEAN	41	17	12 (+2)	12 (-2)
PULLS	33	18 (+4)	0	15 (+4)
POSTERIOR CHAIN	29	16 (+4)	0	13 (+3)
SNATCH	22	0	12 (+7)	9 (+2)
JERK	0	0	0	0
TOTAL VOLUME	**223**	**93**	**48**	**82**

Figure 7.5 Modified Distribution Template

Parentheses denote a change in the total repetitions from redistribution.

By manipulating the repetitions between the training sessions, the volume percentages will skew away from the "ideal" 42–24–34 percent split. As long as the total weekly volume remains the same—plus or minus a few reps—there should be little concern.

It is fine to shift a movement from one session to another to recalibrate the distribution, and often moving it to the lightest volume day helps maintain the overall design. In this case, the low total number of snatch repetitions meant redistributing them where in one session we have only nine total reps.

In theory, those nine repetitions could be shifted to session two so the daily volumes would be closer to the predicted totals. Having two separate days to train a movement can help the novice athletes learn a movement due to the increased frequency.

If carried through for the remaining three weeks of the cycle, the need to redistribute repetitions throughout the week will again be an issue, particularly for the lower volume weeks two and four.

It is more important to be rigid in the larger scale of the programming and flexible in the nuances to help maintain both your sanity and your time. The weekly routine can be roughed out with the particular sessions and order of movements.

Remembering that the movement sequence should include the fastest movements first and the strength movements second, that first week of the cycle would look like this:

SESSION ONE	SESSION TWO	SESSION THREE
Clean 17 reps	**Snatch** 12 reps	**Snatch** 9 reps
Pull 18 reps	**Clean** 12 reps	**Clean** 12 reps
Squat 23 reps	**Squat** 13 reps	**Pull** 15 reps
Press 20 reps	**Press** 12 reps	**Squat** 18 reps
Posterior Chain 16 reps		**Press** 15 reps
		Posterior Chain 13 reps

Figure 7.6 First Week Sessions

Before diving into determining training intensity, you should consider the specifics of each training movement. The exercise selection for the week holds constant throughout the four-week cycle, with the variations in volume and intensity providing the stimulus rather than constantly changing exercises.

To ensure all of your athletes' needs are being addressed, you have to determine the exercises, the starting position, and each athlete's ability.

You also need to consider your long view of progression of the movements over the successive cycles. You cannot indefinitely clean, back squat, bench press, and deadlift your way forward.

For the novice athlete introduced above, a sample first cycle could look like this:

SESSION ONE	SESSION TWO	SESSION THREE
Clean 17 reps, *hang at mid-thigh*	**Snatch** 12 reps, *hang at mid-thigh*	**Snatch** 9 reps, *rack at mid-thigh*
Snatch High Pull 18 reps, *from the power rack, bar above the knee*	**Clean** 12 reps, *rack at mid-thigh*	**Clean** 12 reps, *hang at mid-thigh*
Back Squat 23 reps	**Step-Ups** 13 reps	**Clean Pull** 15 reps, *from the power rack, bar above the knee*
Bench Press 20 reps	**Military Press** 12 reps, *standing*	**Front Squat** 18 reps
RDL 16 reps		**Incline Press** 15 reps
		RDL 13 reps

Figure 7.7 Novice Athlete First Cycle Sample

Emphasizing the primary barbell lifts develops full-body strength without the added stability demands of more complex movements or implements. Starting the Olympic movements from the mid-thigh above-the-knee position allows the athlete to master the technique over a shorter range of motion.

Once you have chosen the weekly volumes, you can then determine the exercise reps and sets based on the Zones of Intensity and each athlete's developmental needs—work capacity, hypertrophy, strength, or power.

As previously noted, the novice athlete needs the bulk of the sets to fall within Zones One to Three to build a base of strength and work capacity, but with the understanding of the bleed-over of qualities between the Zones. Adjusting the reps and sets along with the intensity helps fine-tune the training effect with each athlete's goals in mind.

For the novice-level athlete, more emphasis goes on the lower Zones of Intensity between the ranges of 50–79 percent of the 1RM. The first week's intensity could look like this:

CLEANS IN WEEK ONE 41 TOTAL REPS	
Zone One at 50–59 percent 1RM—3 reps	Zone Four at 80–89 percent 1RM—0 reps
Zone Two at 60–69 percent 1RM—11 reps	Zone Five at 90–99 percent 1RM—0 reps
Zone Three at 70–79 percent 1RM—27 reps	Zone Six at 100 percent 1RM or greater—0 reps
Total Volume **Zone One is 7 percent** **Zone Two is 27 percent** **Zone Three is 66 percent**	

Figure 7.8 Novice Athlete Intensity Zones, Week One

The goal is to progress the work into Zone Three to stimulate greater strength and power gains. Moving through the cycle, the relative intensity level undulates, with Zones One and Two making up a larger percentage of the work in the lower volume weeks and a smaller percentage in the higher volume weeks.

However, the bulk of the work should fall between Zones Two and Three.

[CHAPTER SEVEN—PUTTING IT ALL TOGETHER]

WEEK TWO 32 TOTAL REPS	
Zone One at 50–59 percent 1RM—7 reps	Zone Four at 80–89 percent 1RM—0 reps
Zone Two at 60–69 percent 1RM—7 reps	Zone Five at 90–99 percent 1RM—0 reps
Zone Three at 70–79 percent 1RM—18 reps	Zone Six at 100 percent 1RM or greater—0 reps
Total Volume **Zone One is 22 percent** **Zone Two is 22 percent** **Zone Three is 56 percent**	

Figure 7.9 Novice Athlete Intensity Zones, Week Two

WEEK THREE 46 REPS	
Zone One at 50–59 percent 1RM—3 reps	*Zone Four at 80–89 percent 1RM—2 reps
Zone Two at 60–69 percent 1RM—10 reps	Zone Five at 90–99 percent 1RM—0 reps
Zone Three at 70–79 percent 1RM—31 reps	Zone Six at 100 percent 1RM or greater—0 reps
Total Volume **Zone One is 7 percent** **Zone Two is 22 percent** **Zone Three is 67 percent** **Zone Four is 4 percent**	

Figure 7.10 Novice Athlete Intensity Zones, Week Three

* Exposing an athlete to a small dose of higher-intensity work into Zone Four provides confidence and experience handling heavier weights to set the stage for later cycles.

WEEK FOUR 26 REPS	
Zone One at 50–59 percent 1RM — 7 reps	Zone Four at 80–89 percent 1RM — 0 reps
Zone Two at 60–69 percent 1RM — 6 reps	Zone Five at 90–99 percent 1RM — 0 reps
Zone Three at 70–79 percent 1RM — 13 reps	Zone Six at 100 percent 1RM or greater — 0 reps
Total Volume **Zone One is 27 percent** **Zone Two is 23 percent** **Zone Three is 50 percent**	

Figure 7.11 Novice Athlete Intensity Zones, Week Four

When programming the weekly sessions, you can distribute the intensity, reps, and sets based on your goals for each movement as an intensity or volume day. Following the pattern described, the exercises ideally alternate as either intensity or volume between training days, and within each training session.

Using the weekly volumes from above, a possible week one could look like this:

SESSION ONE	SESSION TWO	SESSION THREE
Clean — 17 reps **(V)** Pull — 18 reps **(V)** Squat — 23 reps **(V)** Press — 20 reps **(V)** Posterior Chain — 16 reps **(V)**	Snatch — 12 reps **(V)** Clean — 12 reps **(I)** Squat — 13 reps **(I)** Press — 12 reps **(I)**	Snatch — 9 reps **(I)** Clean — 12 reps **(I)** Pull — 15 reps **(I)** Squat — 18 reps **(V)** Press — 15 reps **(V)** Posterior Chain — 13 reps **(I)**

Figure 7.12 Session Examples Based on Volumes: (I) Intensity Day; (V) Volume Day

We would follow the Zones of Intensity determinations for each movement for the week and month, and then distribute those repetitions across the training days.

Knowing that for our novice-level athlete we are going to have the majority of the work falling between Zones One to Three, the sets and reps can be programmed for the week according to whether it is an intensity or volume day.

EXAMPLE WEEK ONE—223 TOTAL REPS

Squat—54 reps   Posterior Chain—29 reps

Press—45 reps   Snatch—22 reps

Clean—41 reps   Jerk—0 reps

Pull—33 reps

(V) Volume Day   **(I)** Intensity Day   **(RI)** Relative Intensity
50/3 means 50 percent of 1RM x 3 repetitions

DAY ONE 93 TOTAL REPS	REPS	RELATIVE INTENSITY
Clean (V) 50/3, 60/3, 70/3, 70/3, 70/3, 70/2	17	64.7 percent
Snatch High Pull (V) 60/5, 70/5, 75/4, 75/4	18	69.4 percent
Back Squat (V) 50/5, 60/3, 70/5, 75/5, 75/5	23	66.5 percent
Bench Press (V) 50/5, 60/3, 70/6, 70/6	20	63.5 percent
RDL (V) *percent clean 1RM* 55/4, 55/4, 65/4, 65/4	16	60 percent

Figure 7.13 Day One Example

DAY TWO 48 TOTAL REPS	REPS	RELATIVE INTENSITY
Snatch (V) 50/3, 60/3, 70/3, 70/3	12	62.5 percent
Clean (I) 60/4, 70/4, 70/4	12	66.6 percent
Step-Ups (I) *percent back squat 1RM* 20/5+5, 25/5+5, 30/3+3	13	24.2 percent
Military Press (I) *percent bodyweight* 50/6, 50/6	12	50 percent

Figure 7.14 Day Two Example

DAY THREE 82 TOTAL REPS	REPS	RELATIVE INTENSITY
Snatch (I) 50/3, 60/3, 70/3	9	60 percent
Clean (I) 60/4, 70/4, 75/4	12	68.3 percent
Clean Pull (I) *percent clean 1RM* 75/5, 80/5, 80/5	15	78.3 percent
Front Squat (V) *percent back squat 1RM* 40/5, 45/5, 50/4, 50/4	18	45.8 percent
Incline Press (V) *percent bench press 1RM* 45/5, 55/5, 60/5	15	52.6 percent
RDL (I) *percent clean 1RM* 55/5, 65/5, 70/3	13	61.5 percent

Figure 7.15 Day Three Example

From this example, we can see the relative breakdown of the volume and intensities for a novice-level athlete. The majority of the work sets fall within the three-to-six rep range to place the focus on strength development with some hypertrophy gains.

[CHAPTER SEVEN—PUTTING IT ALL TOGETHER]

We do not exceed the 75-percent intensity threshold, other than for a couple of sets of cleans. This allows more repetitions to improve technique and provide a feel for the movements.

When all of the reps, sets, and intensities are compared, we see the relative training intensity falls squarely in Zone Two for most of the movements. For the novice athlete training with a low total monthly volume, that should be the sweet spot.

To look at just cleans, we can see the relationship between the Zones of Intensity and the relative training intensity over the course of the cycle.

CLEANS—RELATIVE INTENSITY (RI)				
	WEEK ONE	WEEK TWO	WEEK THREE	WEEK FOUR
SESSION ONE HANG, MID-THIGH	50/3 60/3 70/3 x 4 sets **65 percent RI** **18 reps**	50/3 60/3 70/3 75/3 x 3 sets **67.5 percent RI** **18 reps**	50/3 60/2 70/3 x 2 sets 80/1 70/3 80/1 75/3 **67.6 percent RI** **19 reps**	50/4 60/3 70/3 75/2 x 2 sets **63.5 percent RI** **14 reps**
SESSION TWO RACK, ABOVE KNEE	60/4 70/4 x 2 sets **66.6 percent RI** **12 reps**	0 *redistributed*	60/4 70/4 70/3 **66.4 percent RI** **11 reps**	0 *redistributed*
SESSION THREE HANG, MID-THIGH	60/4 70/4 75/4 **68.3 percent RI** **12 reps**	50/4 60/4 70/4 75/2 **62 percent RI** **14 reps**	60/4 70/4 75/4 x 2 sets **70 percent RI** **16 reps**	50/3 60/3 70/3 x 2 sets **62.5 percent RI** **12 reps**

Figure 7.15 Relative Intensity of Cleans

271

PROGRESSION AT THE END OF THE CYCLE

When you reach the end of a training cycle, you have two choices of progression. You can either increase the training volume by no more than 10 percent for the next month, or you can maintain the training volume but increase the work quality—*the intensity.*

There is some flexibility that will ultimately depend on your "eye of the coach." The primary way to sabotage your athletes' progress is to simultaneously increase both the training volume *and* the intensity too quickly, particularly with novice athletes. You need to be particularly conscious of the signs of overtraining to avoid stalled progress or, in the worst-case scenario, regression.

For the novice-level athlete, the most effective method of progression is to first increase the training volume.

As a beginning lifter needs to continue to build work capacity along with baseline strength, gradually adding volume is the safest and simplest approach. For these athletes, you could add 40 repetitions to the monthly total to reach 840 total monthly reps.

Another progression option is to slightly shift the specific exercise volumes to emphasize more strength or power movements, depending on the time of the season or the goals.

For example, taking one or two percent of the volume from squats and adding those reps to snatches allows more work to enhance technique while progressing the athletes towards more explosive training.

The expectation for a novice lifter is that strength gains will be rapid compared to a more experienced lifter, just as a byproduct of resistance training. Even training at the same intensity will ultimately result in heavier loads being used as efficiency and output improves. You could effectively leave the total training volume and relative training intensity the same for the following month and shift the work into more complex movements and see progress in explosive strength and power.

The goal with a novice lifter is to gradually increase the work capacity and volume of training and to introduce higher-intensity sets and more of a power and speed emphasis as the season approaches. Even with higher-intensity work, the relative intensity of the training continues to fall largely between 60–80 percent. The novice athlete can hopefully handle progressively heavier weights within those intensity ranges as strength and technique improves from month to month.

As an example, over the course of an off-season, a novice athlete's exercise volume breakdown could progress as follows:

MOVEMENT	CYCLE ONE PERCENT TOTAL VOLUME	CYCLE TWO PERCENT TOTAL VOLUME	CYCLE THREE PERCENT TOTAL VOLUME
SQUAT	24 percent	22 percent	20 percent
PRESS	20 percent	20 percent	18 percent
CLEAN	18 percent	19 percent	20 percent
PULLS	15 percent	15 percent	16 percent
POSTERIOR CHAIN	13 percent	12 percent	12 percent
SNATCH	10 percent	12 percent	14 percent
JERK	0 percent	0 percent	0 percent

Figure 7.16 Percent of Total Volume Per Cycle

Depending on the ability of the athletes and the quality of your eye, you can use one or both of those progressions to add a new stimulus in the next cycle.

No matter which option you choose, changing the specific exercises for each primary movement in the next cycle is straightforward. If an athlete is able to perform a lift with good technique and control, the complexity of the movement can be progressed.

In this example, if the athlete demonstrated good ability with the power clean from the mid-thigh position, you could choose to alter the exercise in the next cycle by having the athlete perform the lift from just above the knee.

It does not require a wholesale change of an exercise to continue to spur gains because the athlete is still gaining proficiency in the lifts. Increasing the range of a lift requires greater muscle activation and the development of new motor pathways from a more complex motion.

Just remember, accelerating the complexity of movement, especially with explosive lifts for a novice athlete is the most surefire way to cause injury or develop undesirable compensations if they are not physically ready.

THE ADVANCED ATHLETE

The athlete in this example is a 200-pound college freshman wide receiver who has completed a four-week prep phase, with the appropriate strength benchmarks met with sound technique. The athlete is currently in the beginning of the off-season program. There is no history of injury or medical concerns, and he has trained in a strength and power program with Olympic lifting for four years. He has been able to build a progressive level of strength and power and can physically tolerate a higher total monthly training volume as well as a higher relative volume for the power movements compared to a novice athlete.

Our primary training variables are:

Volume
1,000 total repetitions for the month

Intensity
Training takes place within Zones Three or Four at 70–85 percent 1RM

Frequency
Three or four workouts per week entering the 1,000-rep range

The hierarchy of the primary movements for an advanced-level athlete from most important to least important is: *Squat—Clean—Press—Snatch—Pulls—Jerk—Posterior Chain.*

MOVEMENT	PERCENT TOTAL VOLUME	MONTHLY VOLUME
SQUAT	22 percent	220 reps
CLEAN	19 percent	190 reps
PRESS	17 percent	170 reps
SNATCH	13 percent	130 reps
PULLS	11 percent	110 reps
POSTERIOR CHAIN	10 percent	100 reps
JERK	8 percent	80 reps

Figure 7.17 Percent of Total Volume Per Movement

[CHAPTER SEVEN—PUTTING IT ALL TOGETHER]

	WEEK ONE REPS	WEEK TWO REPS	WEEK THREE REPS	WEEK FOUR REPS
PREDICTED VOLUME	**270** *27 percent total*	**220** *22 percent total*	**320** *32 percent total*	**190** *19 percent total*
SQUAT	59	48	70	42
CLEAN	51	42	61	36
PRESS	46	38	54	32
SNATCH	35	29	42	25
PULLS	30	24	35	21
POSTERIOR CHAIN	27	22	32	19
JERK	22	18	26	15
TOTAL VOLUME	**270**	**221**	**320**	**190**

Figure 7.18 Predicted Volume Per Week

WEEKLY VOLUME BREAKDOWN					
	SESSION ONE 27 PERCENT	SESSION TWO 22 PERCENT	SESSION THREE 32 PERCENT	SESSION FOUR 19 PERCENT	TOTAL REPS
WEEK ONE	73	59	86	51	269
WEEK TWO	59	49	70	42	220
WEEK THREE	86	71	102	61	320
WEEK FOUR	51	42	61	36	190

Figure 7.19 Weekly Volume Breakdown

TRAINING SESSION VOLUMES					
	WEEK ONE REPS	SESSION ONE REPS	SESSION TWO REPS	SESSION THREE REPS	SESSION FOUR REPS
PREDICTED VOLUME	270	73 *27 percent total*	59 *22 percent total*	86 *32 percent total*	51 *19 percent total*
SQUAT	59	16	13	19	11
CLEAN	51	14	11	16	10
PRESS	46	13	10	15	8*
SNATCH	35	9*	8*	11*	7*
PULLS	30	8*	7*	10*	5*
POSTERIOR CHAIN	27	7*	6*	9*	5*
JERK	22	6*	5*	7*	4*
TOTAL VOLUME	272	74	59	87	52

Figure 7.20 Training Session Volumes

An asterisk denotes volume falling below the minimum 12-rep threshold.

Those daily volumes that fall below the minimal volume threshold for a particular movement need to be adjusted across the other training days as shown next.

[CHAPTER SEVEN—PUTTING IT ALL TOGETHER]

	WEEK ONE REPS	SESSION ONE REPS	SESSION TWO REPS	SESSION THREE REPS	SESSION FOUR REPS
TRAINING SESSION VOLUMES					
PREDICTED VOLUME	270	73 *27 percent total*	59 *22 percent total*	86 *32 percent total*	51 *19 percent total*
SQUAT	59	17 (+1)	13	17 (-2)	12 (+1)
CLEAN	51	14	12 (+1)	13 (-3)	12 (+2)
PRESS	46	13	18 (+8)	15	0 (-8)
SNATCH	35	17 (+8)	0 (-8)	18 (+7)	0 (-7)
PULLS	30	0 (-8)	0 (-7)	18 (+8)	12 (+7)
POSTERIOR CHAIN	27	15 (+8)	0 (-6)	0 (-9)	12 (+7)
JERK	22	0 (-6)	11 (+6)	0 (-7)	11 (+7)
TOTAL VOLUME	270	76	54	81	59

Figure 7.21 Modified Session Volume Distribution

The figures in parentheses denote changes in total repetitions after redistribution.

Looking at those volume numbers in the week one training sessions and ordering the movements with the fastest movement first, followed by the strength movements, the week's plan could look like this:

SESSION BREAKDOWN	
SESSION ONE—76 REPS	**SESSION TWO—54 REPS**
Power Snatch 17 reps, hang above knee **Power Clean** 14 reps, hang above knee **Back Squat** 17 reps **Military Press** 13 reps **RDL** 15 reps	**Split Jerk** 11 reps **Power Clean** 12 reps, rack above the knee **Front Squat** 13 reps **DB Incline Press** 18 reps
SESSION THREE—81 REPS	**SESSION FOUR—59 REPS**
Power Snatch 18 reps, hang above knee **Power Clean** 13 reps, rack above knee **Snatch Pull** 18 reps, rack above knee **Step-Ups** 17 reps **Military Press** 15 reps	**Split Jerk** 11 reps **Power Clean** 12 reps, hang mid-thigh **Clean Pull** 12 reps, rack below knee **Back Squat** 12 reps **RDL** 12 reps

Figure 7.22 Session Breakdown

[CHAPTER SEVEN—PUTTING IT ALL TOGETHER]

For an advanced-level athlete, you want to place more work in the middle Zones of Intensity to develop more strength and power. The distribution of training intensities for the week could be as follows:

CLEANS IN WEEK ONE 51 TOTAL REPS	
Zone One Warmup—11 reps *50–59 percent 1RM*	**Zone Four** Power—7 reps *80–89 percent 1RM*
Zone Two Hypertrophy—11 reps *60–69 percent 1RM*	**Zone Five** Power—0 reps *90–99 percent 1RM*
Zone Three Strength—22 reps *70–79 percent 1RM*	**Zone Six** Power—0 reps *100 percent 1RM, or greater*

Figure 7.23 Training Intensity for Advanced Athletes

Although this athlete is only performing 11 more cleans reps in week one compared with the novice-level athlete, you can clearly see the difference in the training intensity levels.

NOVICE ATHLETE CLEANS 40 REPS	ADVANCED ATHLETE CLEANS 51 REPS
Zone One 50–59 percent—3 reps	**Zone One** 50–59 percent—11 reps
Zone Two 60–69 percent—11 reps	**Zone Two** 60–69 percent—11 reps
Zone Three 70–79 percent—27 reps	**Zone Three** 70–79 percent—22 reps
Zone Four 80–89 percent—0 reps	**Zone Four** 80–89 percent—7 reps

Figure 7.24 Training Intensity of Cleans, Novice Versus Advanced

Our weekly session breakdown will then look like this:

SESSION ONE—76 REPS	SESSION TWO—54 REPS
Power Snatch—17 reps **(V)**	Split Jerk—11 reps **(V)**
Power Clean—14 reps **(V)**	Power Clean—12 reps **(I)**
Back Squat—17 reps **(V)**	Front Squat—13 reps **(I)**
Military Press—13 reps **(I)**	DB Incline Press—18 reps **(V)**
RDL—15 reps **(V)**	

SESSION THREE—81 REPS	SESSION FOUR—59 REPS
Power Snatch—18 reps **(I)**	Split Jerk—11 reps **(I)**
Power Clean—13 reps **(V)**	Power Clean—12 reps **(I)**
Snatch Pull—18 reps **(I)**	Clean Pull—12 reps **(V)**
Step-Ups—17 reps **(V)**	Back Squat—12 reps **(I)**
Military Press—15 reps **(I)**	RDL—12 reps **(V)**

Figure 7.24 Weekly Session Breakdown—(V) Volume Day, (I) Intensity Day

EXAMPLE WEEK ONE—270 TOTAL REPS

ADVANCED LEVEL

Squat—59 reps   Pull—30 reps

Clean—51 reps   Posterior Chain—27 reps

Press—46 reps   Jerk—22 reps

Snatch—35 reps

(I) *Intensity*   **(V)** *Volume*   **(RI)** *Relative Intensity*

50/3 means 50 percent of 1RM x 3 repetitions

DAY ONE—76 TOTAL REPS	REPS	RELATIVE INTENSITY
Power Snatch (V) 50/3, 60/3, 70/3, 70/3, 70/3, 75/2	17	65.3 percent
Power Clean (V) 50/3, 60/2, 70/3, 70/3, 70/3	14	64.3 percent
Back Squat (V) 60/5, 70/4, 70/4, 70/4	17	67.1 percent
Military Press (I) 60/3, 70/4, 75/3, 75/3	13	70 percent
RDL (V) 60/5, 70/5, 70/5	15	66.6 percent

Figure 7.25 Day One

DAY TWO—54 TOTAL REPS	REPS	RELATIVE INTENSITY
Split Jerk (V) 55/2, 65/3, 70/3, 70/3	11	65 percent
Power Clean (I) 55/2, 65/3, 75/3, 80/2, 75/2	12	69.2 percent
Front Squat (I) 55/3, 65/3, 75/3, 75/2, 75/2	13	63.1 percent
DB Incline Press (V) 50/3, 60/3, 70/4, 70/4, 70/4	18	65 percent

Figure 7.26 Day Two

DAY THREE—81 TOTAL REPS	REPS	RELATIVE INTENSITY
Power Snatch (I) 50/3, 60/3, 70/3, 75/3, 80/2, 75/2, 80/2	18	68.6 percent
Power Clean (V) 50/2, 60/3, 70/4, 70/4	13	64.6 percent
Snatch Pull (I) 55/3, 65/3, 75/3, 75/3, 80/2, 75/2, 80/2	18	70.5 percent
Step-Ups (V) 50/5, 60/4, 70/4, 70/4	17	61.8 percent
Military Press (I) 60/3, 70/3, 75/3, 80/3, 75/3	15	72 percent

Figure 7.27 Day Three

DAY FOUR—59 TOTAL REPS	REPS	RELATIVE INTENSITY
Split Jerk (I) 55/3, 65/3, 75/2, 80/2, 80/1	11	67.3 percent
Power Clean (I) 55/3, 65/3, 75/3, 80/3	12	68.8 percent
Clean Pull (V) 55/3, 65/3, 70/3, 70/3	12	64.2 percent
Back Squat (I) 55/3, 65/3, 75/3, 80/3	12	67.9 percent
RDL (V) 60/4, 70/4, 70/4	12	66.6 percent

Figure 7.28 Day Four

Looking again at the cleans, you can see the Zone of Intensity breakdowns are as follows:

SESSION ONE 14 REPS VOLUME DAY	SESSION TWO 12 REPS INTENSITY DAY	SESSION THREE 13 REPS VOLUME DAY	SESSION FOUR 12 REPS INTENSITY DAY
Zone One—3 reps	Zone One—2 reps	Zone One—2 reps	Zone One—3 reps
Zone Two—2 reps	Zone Two—3 reps	Zone Two—3 reps	Zone Two—3 reps
Zone Three—9 reps	Zone Three—5 reps	Zone Three—8 reps	Zone Three—3 reps
Zone Four—0 reps	Zone Four—2 reps	Zone Four—0 reps	Zone Four—3 reps

Figure 7.29 Zones of Intensity

With two intensity days in the week, we can reach into the range of Zone Four, but again, the bulk of the training volume falls in Zones Two and Three.

As you progress into weeks two and three, the relative training intensity should gradually increase, with more reps filling the Zone Four category. To facilitate some recovery from the heavier loads, the fourth week unload will not have any work extending beyond Zone Three.

In the final week of the training cycle, there will be nothing in excess of 75 percent of 1RM. When the next cycle begins, the training intensity can again be gradually advanced, with more work occurring in Zones Three and Four. With continued development and more time spent under the bar, your athletes' training will steadily fill Zones Three to Six for the elite level as we chase strength and power gains in the more mature athletes.

We have left out accessory or assistance work from the planning because that will be largely dictated by your athletes' needs. Generally, we include two assistance exercises, along with neck, grip, and abdominal training in each workout. We do not factor the volume of these exercises into the monthly totals, but it is no less important to success of the athletes.

For our football athletes, generally additional triceps and lat work serves the purpose of improving pushing and gripping or pulling strength needed on the field. With other sports, you should assess the needs of the athletes and the sport and then program accordingly.

You can now follow the same progression to determine the remaining exercise or movement values and weeks when it comes to volume and training intensity in a four-week cycle.

Although it can seem tedious and labor intensive, following this step-wise approach will help you track progress and guard against overtraining. It will also provide a system of checks and balances to make sure you are training in the manner you think you are.

Our experience with this gave us the uncomfortable realization that our programming was nowhere near what we believed it to be. This approach pulls the curtain back on how you are actually designing your training and, more often than not, the initial results will be painful.

PROGRESSION AT THE END OF THE CYCLE

Now we face the question of how to advance the programming into the next month. With the advanced-level athlete, the first option is to increase the monthly volume. Adding no more than 10 percent of the previous month's total should again spur progress, particularly early in the off-season.

The other option with advanced athletes is to make a minimal change to the monthly volume, possibly increasing it by no more than two or three percent, and to increase the quality or intensity of the work. You would modify the exercises to change the stimulus and increase the relative amount of volume within the higher Zones of Intensity.

This is where a delicate balancing act takes place, when increasing both the quality *and* the quantity of work. Your athletes should have at least two years of experience training under this programming style, and you should have a firm grasp of both the programming and your athletes' abilities before you begin simultaneously advancing both variables.

For experienced advanced and elite-level athletes and the strength coach who has mastered programming with this system, you can also progress by changing the relative volume for each training movement from cycle to cycle.

We covered that as a method for novice-level athletes; however, this can be taken a step further with highly trained athletes. This method provides another layer of variability to the training, as each movement can undergo fluctuation from month to month to place even greater emphasis on power movements such as the snatch or jerks to maximally train explosive power.

While it is effective, it requires a high level of performance and competency of both the athlete and the strength coach. That competency is required if you are to meet with success and avoid the pitfall of too much volume for movements that are incredibly taxing to the nervous system.

PROGRAMMING ELITE ATHLETES

We have not included an elite-level example or sample program in this book for several reasons.

First, the coaches who are working with truly elite-level athletes are a small minority of the coaching world. To avoid application of a high-level program to an unprepared athlete by an over-enthusiastic coach, we decided to remove the option altogether.

What we covered in this book is a collection of principles and processes to logically and systematically construct a training program for athletic development and performance enhancement. When you understand and implement the basic principles and methods we have outlined, designing a training plan for an elite-level athlete is merely an exercise in progression of the fundamentals.

Every training variable and progression logically flows into the next, and as long as you are consistently monitoring and adjusting based on your athletes' performance and timeline, you can create a multiple-year training plan that will ensure steady progress.

CHAPTER EIGHT—
FOOTBALL PROGRAMMING

With our collective years of training dedicated most deeply to football, we have included two sample programs for the novice and advanced-level football athlete. The programs cover the first two cycles of the off-season plan using the guidelines outlined earlier. Our hope is that seeing the design process provides a model for you to build your own programs.

OFF-SEASON EIGHT-WEEK TRAINING PLAN

THREE-DAY PER WEEK NOVICE PROGRAM

This sample program is for a high school sophomore athlete who has one year of training in The System.

This is the first strength cycle for the high school sophomore player after completing the work capacity phase. In this program, we create strength first and foremost, as well as teaching the Olympic lifts. These are still novice lifters and simple is the best way to start.

CYCLE ONE—STRENGTH EMPHASIS

Monthly Volume
800 reps

Weekly Volumes
28 percent—22 percent—32 percent—18 percent*

Daily Volumes
42 percent—24 percent—34 percent

*Because this is the athlete's second year of training under this style of programming, this sample takes a small variation in the weekly volumes to place a little more volume into the recovery week.

MOVEMENT	EXERCISE VOLUME	MONTHLY VOLUME	WEEKLY VOLUME WEEKS 1–2–3–4
SQUAT	24 percent	192 total reps	54–42–62–36
CLEAN	18 percent	144 total reps	40–32–46–26
PRESS	20 percent	160 total reps	45–35–51–29
PULLS	15 percent	120 total reps	33–26–38–22
JERK	*0 percent	0 total reps	0–0–0–0
SNATCH	10 percent	80 total reps	22–17–26–14
POSTERIOR CHAIN	13 percent	104 total reps	29–23–33–19
TOTAL	**100 percent**	**800 total reps**	**223–175–265–146**

Figure 8.1 Novice Strength Cycle Volumes

[CHAPTER EIGHT—FOOTBALL PROGRAMMING]

MOVEMENT	WEEKLY VOLUME	DAILY VOLUMES	MOVEMENT	WEEKLY VOLUME	DAILY VOLUMES
SQUAT 24 PERCENT	54	23–13–18	JERK 0 PERCENT	0	0
	42	18–10–14		0	0
	62	26–15–21		0	0
	36	20–0–16		0	0
CLEAN 18 PERCENT	40	17–10–14 (17–12–12)	SNATCH 10 PERCENT	22	9–5–7 (12–0–9)
	32	13–8–11 (18–0–14)		17	7–4–6 (0–17–0)
	46	19–11–16		26	11–6–9 (0–14–12)
	26	11–6–9 (14–0–12)		14	6–3–5 (0–14–0)
PRESS 20 PERCENT	45	19–11–15	POSTERIOR CHAIN 13 PERCENT	29	12–7–10 (16–0–13)
	35	15–8–12		23	10–6–8 (13–0–11)
	51	21–12–17		33	14–8–11 (18–0–14)
	29	12–7–10 (16–0–13)		19	8–5–7 (12–0–8)
PULLS 15 PERCENT	33	14–8–11 (18–0–15)			
	26	11–6–9 (14–0–12)			
	38	16–9–13			
	22	9–5–7 (0–21–0)			

Figure 8.2 Novice Cycle One Strength Breakdown

The numbers in parentheses represent adjusted daily volumes.

As you can see with many of the days, you do not have enough reps assigned to reach the 12 needed for a response to take place. This is where, when you have younger players starting out as novice lifters and less of a total monthly volume as in the case of 800 monthly totals, you will have days with fewer than 12 reps.

Our suggestion is to take the day with fewer reps and distribute those reps to the other days. Remembering the heavy volume day and moderate-volume days, you can assign the light day of 24 percent to the other lifts by totals. This will in some weeks shorten Wednesday's workout, but that should be the lightest day of the week.

All lifts are denoted as percent max and number of reps, so 50/5 is 50 percent of the 1RM for five repetitions.

[CHAPTER EIGHT—FOOTBALL PROGRAMMING]

WEEK ONE

DAY ONE

Physioball Jackknife and Pushup: 1x10+10

Hanging Knee-Up, eyes down: 1x10

Single-Leg Squat: 1x6+6

Complex One, percent bodyweight: 40–45–50 1x3 reps

Clean, hang from mid-thigh: 50/3, 60/3, 70/3 x 4 sets

*Snatch High Pull: 60/5, 70/5, 75/4, 75/4
percent of max snatch, rack above the kne*

Back Squat: 50/5, 60/3, 70/5, 70/5, 70/5

Bench Press: 50/5, 60/3, 70/6, 70/6

RDL, percent of max clean: 55/4x2, 65/4, 65/4

Ab Work

Neck

Tempo Run: 4x100 at 14–15–16-second pace

DAY TWO

Snatch Squat: 1x6 with bar or dowel

Hyperextension: x8—select appropriate load

Complex One, percent bodyweight: 40–45–50, 1x3 reps

Snatch, hang from mid-thigh: 50/3, 60/3, 70/3, 70/3

Clean, rack at mid-thigh: 60/4, 70/4, 70/4

Step-Up, percent max back squat: 20/5+5, 25/5+5, 30/3+3

Standing Military Press, percent bodyweight: 50/6, 50/6

Ab Work

Tempo Run: 4x100 at 14–15–16-second pace

DAY THREE

Lying Leg Twist: 1x5+5

Reverse Hyper: 1x10—select appropriate load

Hanging Alternate Knee-Up: 1x6+6

Box Jump: x6

Complex One, percent bodyweight: 40–45–50, 1x3

Snatch, rack mid-thigh: 50/3, 60/3, 70/3

Clean, hang mid-thigh: 60/4, 70/4, 75/4

Clean Pull: 75/5, 80/5, 80/5
percent of max clean, rack above the knee

Front Squat, percent max back squat: 40/5, 45/5, 50/4, 50/4

Incline Press, percent of max bench: 45/5, 55/5, 60/5

RDL, percent of max clean: 55/5, 65/5, 70/3

Ab Work

Neck

Tempo Run: 4x100 at 14–15–16-second pace

WEEK TWO

DAY ONE

Physioball Jackknife and Pushup: 1x10+10

Hanging Knee-Up, eyes down: 1x12

Single-Leg Squat: 1x6+6

Complex One, percent bodyweight: 40–45–50, 1x3

Clean, hang from mid-thigh: 50/3, 60/3, 70/3, 75/3 x 3 sets

Snatch High Pull: 65/5, 75/5, 80/4
percent of max snatch, rack above knee

Back Squat: 50/5, 60/2, 70/6, 75/5

Bench Press: 50/5, 60/2, 70/4, 75/4

RDL, percent of max clean: 55/4, 65/4, 70/5

Ab Work

Neck

Tempo Run: 4x100 at 14–15–16-second pace

DAY TWO

Snatch Squat, bar or dowel: 1x6

Hyperextension: x8 (select appropriate load)

Complex One, percent bodyweight: 40–45–50, 1x3

Snatch, hang mid-thigh: 50/3, 60/3, 70/3, 75/3, 75/3, 75/2

Step-Up, percent max back squat: 20/4+4, 25/3+3, 30/3+3

Standing Military Press, percent bodyweight: 50/5, 50/5

Ab Work

Tempo Run: 6x100 at 14–15–16-second pace

DAY THREE

Lying Leg Twist: 1x6+6

Reverse Hyper: 1x10—select appropriate load

Hanging Alternate Knee-Up: 1x7+7

Box Jump: x6

Complex One, percent bodyweight: 40–45–50, 1x3

Clean, rack mid-thigh: 50/4, 60/4, 70/4, 75/2

Clean Pull: 75/4, 80/4, 80/4
percent of max clean, rack above knee

Front Squat, percent of max squat: 40/4, 45/4, 50/3, 55/3

Incline Press, percent of max bench: 45/4, 55/4, 60/4

RDL, percent of max clean: 55/5, 65/6

Ab Work

Neck

Tempo Run: 4x100 at 14–15–16-second pace

WEEK THREE

DAY ONE

Physioball Jackknife and Pushup: 1x10+10

Hanging Knee-Up: x15

Single-Leg Squat: 1x5+5

Complex One, percent bodyweight: 40–45–50, 1x3

Clean, hang from thigh: 50/3, 60/2, 70/3x2, 80/1, 70/3, 80/1, 75/3

Snatch High Pull, rack above knee: 70/4x2, 80/4, 80/4

Back Squat: 50/5, 60/2, 70/4, 75/5 x 3 sets

Bench Press: 50/5, 60/2, 70/2, 75/6, 75/6

RDL, percent of max clean: 55/6, 65/6, 65/6

Ab Work

Neck

Tempo Run: 4x100 at 14–15–16-second pace

DAY TWO

Snatch Squat, bar: 1x6

Hyperextension: 1x8 — select appropriate load

Complex One, percent bodyweight: 40–45–50, 1x3

Snatch, hang mid-thigh: 50/3, 60/3, 70/3, 75/3, 75/2

Clean, rack mid-thigh: 60/4, 70/4, 70/3

Step-Up, percent of max back squat: 20/5+5, 25/5+5, 30/5+5

Standing Military Press, percent bodyweight: 50/4, 55/4, 55/4

Ab Work

Tempos Run: 4x100 at 14–15–16-second pace

DAY THREE

Lying Leg Twist: 1x7+7

Reverse Hyper: x10 — select appropriate load

Hanging Alternate Knee-Up: 1x8+8

Box Jump: x7

Complex One, percent bodyweight: 40–45–50, 1x3reps

Snatch, rack mid-thigh: 50/3, 60/3, 70/3, 70/3

Clean, hang mid-thigh: 60/4, 70/4, 75/4, 75/4

Front Squat, percent of max back squat: 40/4, 45/4, 50/4, 55/3 x 3 sets

Incline Press, percent of max bench: 45/5, 55/6, 60/6

RDL, percent of max clean: 55/5, 65/5, 70/4

Ab Work

Neck

Tempo Run: 4x100 at 14–15–16-second pace

WEEK FOUR

DAY ONE

Physioball Jackknife and Pushup: 1x10+10

Hanging Knee-Up: x12

Single-Leg Squat: 1x4+4

Complex One, percent bodyweight: 40–45–50, 1x3

Clean, hang mid-thigh: 50/4, 60/3, 70/3, 75/2, 75/2

Back Squat: 50/5, 60/5, 70/5, 70/5

Bench Press: 50/5, 60/2, 70/5, 75/4

RDL, percent of max clean: 55/6, 65/6

Ab Work

Neck

Tempo Run: 4x100 at 14–15–16-second pace

DAY TWO

Snatch Squat, bar: 1x6

Hyperextension: x8 — select appropriate load

Complex One, percent bodyweight: 40-45-50, 1x3

Snatch, hang from thigh: 50/4, 60/4, 70/3, 75/3

Clean Pull, percent of max clean, rack above knee: 60/6, 70/5x2, 80/5

Ab Work

Tempo Run: 4x100 at 14–15–16-second pace

DAY THREE

Lying Leg Twist: 1x5+5

Reverse Hyper: x10 — select appropriate load

Hanging Alternate Knee-Up: 1x8+8

Box Jump: x5

Complex One, percent bodyweight: 40–45–50, 1x3

Clean, rack mid-thigh: 50/3, 60/3, 70/3, 70/3

Front Squat, percent of max back squat: 40/3, 45/3, 50/3, 55/3

Incline Press, percent of max bench press: 45/5, 55/3, 60/5

RDL, percent of max clean: 55/4, 65/4

Ab Work

Neck

Tempo Run: 4x100 at 14–15–16-second pace

CYCLE TWO—POWER EMPHASIS

We will shift the percentages on some lifts to continue to create gains in this area, but never completely doing away with the other lifts.

Monthly Volume
840 reps

Weekly Volumes
32 percent—22 percent—28 percent—18 percent*
* flipping weeks one and three to provide another small training stimulus

Daily Volumes
42 percent—24 percent—34 percent

MOVEMENT	EXERCISE VOLUME	MONTHLY VOLUME	WEEKLY VOLUME WEEKS 1-2-3-4
SQUAT	22 percent	185 total reps	59-41-52-33
CLEAN	18 percent	151 total reps	48-33-42-27
PRESS	22 percent	185 total reps	59-41-52-33
PULLS	15 percent	126 total reps	40-28-35-23
JERK	0 percent	0 total reps	0-0-0-0
SNATCH	12 percent	101 total reps	32-22-28-18
POSTERIOR CHAIN	11 percent	92 total reps	29-21-26-17
TOTAL	**100 percent**	**840 total reps**	**267-186-235-151**

Figure 8.3 Novice Power Cycle Volumes

The numbers in parentheses represent adjusted daily volumes.

MOVEMENT	WEEKLY VOLUME	DAILY VOLUMES	MOVEMENT	WEEKLY VOLUME	DAILY VOLUMES
SQUAT 22 PERCENT	59	25–14–20	JERK 0 PERCENT	0	0
	41	17–10–14		0	0
	52	22–13–18		0	0
	33	14–8–11 (18–0–15)		0	0
CLEAN 18 PERCENT	48	20–12–16	SNATCH 12 PERCENT	32	13–8–11 (0–17–15)
	33	14–8–11 (18–0–15)		22	10–5–7 (12–0–10)
	42	18–11–14		28	12–7–10 (0–16–13)
	27	11–6–9 (14–0–12)		18	8–4–6 (0–12–6)
PRESS 22 PERCENT	59	25–14–20	POSTERIOR CHAIN 11 PERCENT	29	12–7–10 (16–0–13)
	41	17–10–14		21	9–5–7 (20–0–0)
	52	22–13–18		26	11–6–9 (14–0–12)
	33	14–8–11		17	7–4–6 (18–0–0)
PULLS 15 PERCENT	40	17–10–14 (22–0–19)			
	28	12–7–10 (16–0–13)			
	35	15–8–12 (19–0–16)			
	23	10–6–8 (13–0–11)			

Figure 8.4 Novice Cycle Two Power Breakdown

Here we change the Olympic lifts from mid-thigh to above the knee and the clean pulls to below the knee. The simpler pulls will always be one position below the position of the Olympic lifts to assist the learning curve.

We are adding the push-press on Wednesdays to ready the athletes for progression to the jerk. You will also see in-place tuck jumps at the beginning to prime the CNS.

Have your athletes pause the first rep of the bench press and incline press on the chest for each set. This creates two things—a slowed eccentric momentum of the bar and a little more strength from the bottom position at the chest.

WEEK ONE

DAY ONE

Hanging Knee-Up, eyes down: 1x14

Hyperextension: x8 — select appropriate load

Snatch Squat, with bar: 1x6

Complex One, percent bodyweight: 40–45–50 1x2 reps

Clean, hang above the knee: 50/4, 60/3, 70/3, 75/3 x 3 sets, 80/1

Clean Pull, rack below knee: 75/5, 75/5, 80/4, 80/4, 85/4

Back Squat: 50/5, 60/3, 70/5, 70/5 80/4 x 3 sets

Bench Press, pause first rep each set: 50/5, 60/3, 70/5, 80/4 x 3 sets

RDL percent of max clean: 60/4, 70/4, 70/4, 75/4

Ab Work

Neck

Tempo Run: 4x100 at 14–15–16-second pace

DAY TWO

Physioball Jackknife and Pushup: 1x10+10

Reverse Hyper: x10–select appropriate load

Single-Leg Squat: 1x6+6

In-Place Tuck Jumps: x10

Complex One, percent bodyweight: 40–45–50 1x2 reps

Snatch, hang above the knee: 50/4, 60/3, 70/3, 75/3, 75/3, 80/1

Clean, rack above the knee: 50/3, 60/3, 70/3, 75/3

Push-Press, percent of bodyweight: 55/4, 60/4, 65/3, 65/3

Step-Up, percent of max back squat: 20/4+4, 25/4+4, 30/3+3, 35/3+3

Ab Work

Tempo Run: 4x100 at 14–15–16-second pace

DAY THREE

Hanging Knee-Up, medicine ball between the knees: 1x10

Snatch Squat, with bar: 1x6

In-Place Tuck Jump: x10

Complex One, percent bodyweight: 40–45–50 1x2 reps

Snatch, rack above the knee: 50/3, 60/3, 70/3, 70/3, 80/1 x 3 sets

Clean, hang above the knee: 55/4, 65/4, 75/4, 75/4

Snatch High Pull, percent of max snatch, rack above the knee: 75/5, 75/5, 85/3 x 3 sets

Front Squat, percent of max back squat: 40/4, 50/4, 55/3, 55/3 60/3, 60/3

Incline Press, percent of max bench press: 45/5, 55/2, 60/5, 60/5, 65/3

RDL, percent of max clean: 60/5, 70/4, 75/4

Ab Work

Neck

Tempo Run: 4x100 at 14–15–16-second pace

WEEK TWO

DAY ONE

Hanging Knee-Up: x14

Hyperextension: x8—select appropriate load

Snatch Squat, with bar: 1x6

Complex One, percent bodyweight: 40–45–50 1x2 reps

Clean, hang above the knee: 50/4, 60/4, 70/3, 75/3, 80/2, 80/2

Clean Pull, percent of max clean, rack below the knee: 75/4, 80/4, 85/4, 85/4

Back Squat: 50/4, 60/4, 70/4, 80/4

Bench Press, pause first rep: 50/5, 60/2, 70/5, 80/5

RDL, percent of max clean: 60/6, 70/5, 75/5, 75/5

Ab Work

Neck

Tempo Run: 4x100 at 14–15–16-second pace

DAY TWO

Physioball Jackknife and Pushup: 1x10+10

Reverse Hyper: x10—select appropriate load

Single-Leg Squat: 1x4+4

In-Place Tuck Jump: x10

Complex One, percent bodyweight: 40–45–50 1x2 reps

Snatch, hang above the knee: 50/3, 60/3, 70/3, 80/2, 80/1

Step-Up, percent of max back squat: 20/3+3, 25/4+4, 30/4+4

Push-Press, percent of bodyweight: 55/3, 60/3, 65/3, 70/2

Ab Work

Tempo Run: 5x100 at 14–15–16-second pace

DAY THREE

Hanging Knee-Up, with medicine ball: 1x10

Snatch Squat, with bar: 1x6

In-Place Tuck Jump: x10

Complex One, percent bodyweight: 40–45–50 1x2 reps

Snatch, rack above knee: 50/3, 60/3, 70/3, 80/2

Clean, hang above the knee: 60/4, 70/3, 70/3 80/3, 85/1, 85/1

Snatch High Pull, percent of max snatch, rack above the knee: 65/5, 75/4, 85/4

Front Squat, percent of max back squat: 45/4, 55/4, 60/3, 60/3

Incline Press, percent of max bench, pause first rep: 45/5, 55/2, 60/4, 60/3

Ab Work

Neck

Tempo Run: 4x100 at 14–15–16-second pace

WEEK THREE

DAY ONE

Hanging Knee-Up: 1x15

Hyperextension: x8—select appropriate load

Snatch Squat, with bar: 1x6

Complex One, percent bodyweight: 40–45–50 1x2 reps

Clean, hang above the knee: 50/3, 60/3, 70/3, 75/3, 80/2, 75/3*, 85/1*

*By reducing the intensity for one set and then raising it for the next, we can "trick" the nervous system to get a greater output for the last set.

Clean Pull, percent of max clean, rack below the knee: 75/5, 80/5, 85/5, 85/4

Back Squat: 50/5, 60/2, 70/3, 75/6, 75/6

Bench Press, pause first rep: 50/5, 60/2, 70/5, 80/5, 80/5

RDL, percent of max clean: 60/5, 70/5, 75/4

Ab Work

Neck

Tempo Run: 4x100 at 14–15–16-second pace

DAY TWO

Physioball Jackknife and Pushup: 1x10+10

Reverse Hyper: x10—select appropriate load

Single-Leg Squat: 1x6+6

In-Place Tuck Jump: x10

Complex One, percent bodyweight: 40–45–50 1x2 reps

Snatch, hang above the knee: 50/3, 60/3, 70/3, 75/3, 75/3, 80/1

Clean, rack above the knee: 60/3, 70/3, 75/3, 80/3

Step-Up, percent of max back squat: 20/4+4, 25/4+4, 30/3+3, 35/2+2

Push-Press, percent of bodyweight: 55/4, 60/3, 65/3, 70/3

Ab Work

Tempo Run: 4x100at 14–15–16-second pace

DAY THREE

Hanging Knee-Up, with medicine ball: 1x12

Snatch Squat, with bar: 1x6

In-Place Tuck Jump: x12

Complex One, percent bodyweight: 40–45–50 1x2 reps

Snatch, rack above the knee: 50/3, 60/3, 70/3, 75/2, 75/2

Clean, hang above the knee: 50/3, 60/3, 70/3, 75/3, 75/2

Snatch High Pull, percent of max snatch, rack above the knee: 65/4, 75/4, 85/4, 85/4

Front Squat, percent of max back squat: 40/3, 50/3, 60/3 x 4 sets

Incline Press, percent of max bench: 45/5, 55/2, 60/4, 60/4, 65/3

Ab Work

Neck

Tempo Run: 4x100 at 14–15–16-second pace

[CHAPTER EIGHT—FOOTBALL PROGRAMMING]

WEEK FOUR

DAY ONE

Hang Knee-Up: x10

Hyperextension: x6—select appropriate load

Snatch Squat, with bar: 1x6

Complex One, percent bodyweight: 40–45–50 1x2 reps

Clean, hang above the knee: 50/4, 60/4, 70/3, 70/3

Clean Pull, percent of max clean, rack below the knee: 70/4, 70/4, 80/5

Back Squat: 50/6, 60/6, 70/6

Bench Press: 50/4, 60/2, 70/6, 70/6

RDL, percent of max clean: 60/6, 70/6

Ab Work

Neck

Tempo Run: 4x100 at 14–15–16-second pace

DAY TWO

Physioball Jackknife and Pushup: 1x10+10

Reverse Hyper: x7—select appropriate load

Single-Leg Squat—1x4+4

In-Place Tuck Jump: x7

Complex One, percent bodyweight: 40–45–50 1x2 reps

Snatch, hang above the knee: 50/4, 60/4, 70/4, 75/3, 75/3

Push-Press, percent bodyweight: 55/3, 60/3, 65/3

Ab Work

Tempo Runs: 4x100 at 14–15–16-second pace

DAY THREE

Hanging Knee-Up, with medicine ball: 1x10

Snatch Squat, with bar: 1x6

In-Place Tuck Jump: x8

Complex One, percent bodyweight: 40–45–50 1x2 reps

Clean, hang above the knee: 50/3, 60/3, 70/3, 75/3

Snatch High Pulls, percent of max snatch, rack above the knee: 65/4, 75/4, 80/4

Front Squat, percent of max back squat: 40/4, 50/4, 55/4, 60/3

Incline Press, percent of max bench, pause first rep: 45/4, 55/2, 60/6

Ab Work

Neck

Tempo Run: 4x100 at 14–15–16-second pace

OFF-SEASON EIGHT-WEEK TRAINING PLAN

THREE-DAY PER WEEK ADVANCED PROGRAM

*High school senior athlete transitioning to college
who has three years of training in The System*

This example would be the first off-season cycle with the emphasis on strength and power development for a graduating high school senior who will be competing in college.

We again assume this athlete has completed the work-capacity phase, and the expectation is that with three years of training under this style of programming, the athlete should have a firm grasp of technique with the fundamental movements.

Through this program, you will see the progression of the complexity of exercises, with cleans performed from a start at the floor, and a combination of exercises, such as a snatch and overhead squat, performed as a complex.

CYCLE ONE—STRENGTH EMPHASIS

Monthly Volume
900 reps

Weekly Volumes
27 percent—22 percent—32 percent—19 percent

Daily Volumes
42 percent—24 percent—34 percent

MOVEMENT	EXERCISE VOLUME	MONTHLY VOLUME	WEEKLY VOLUME WEEKS 1–2–3–4
SQUAT	23 percent	207 total reps	56–46–66–39
CLEAN	21 percent	189 total reps	51–42–61–36
PRESS	21 percent	189 total reps	51–42–61–36
PULLS	0 percent	0 total reps	0–0–0–0
JERK	7 percent	63 total reps	17–14–20–12
SNATCH	7 percent	63 total reps	17–14–20–12
POSTERIOR CHAIN	21 percent	189 total reps	51–42–61–36
TOTAL	**100 percent**	**900 total reps**	**243–200–289–171**

Figure 8.5 Advanced Strength Cycle Volumes

[CHAPTER EIGHT—FOOTBALL PROGRAMMING]

MOVEMENT	WEEKLY VOLUME	DAILY VOLUMES	MOVEMENT	WEEKLY VOLUME	DAILY VOLUMES
SQUAT 23 PERCENT	56	24–13–19	JERK 7 PERCENT	17	7–4–6 (0–17–0)
	46	19–11–16 (20–12–15)		14	6–3–5 (0–14–0)
	66	28–16–22 (28–17–22)		20	8–5–7 (0–20–0)
	39	16–9–13 (16–10–12)		12	5–4–3 (0–12–0)
CLEAN 21 PERCENT	51	22–12–17	SNATCH 7 PERCENT	17	7–4–6 (0–0–17)
	42	18–10–14		14	6–3–5 (0–0–14)
	61	26–15–21 (25–15–22)		20	8–5–7 (0–0–20)
	36	15–9–12 (16–10–12)		12	5–4–3 (0–0–12)
PRESS 21 PERCENT	51	22–12–17 (32–0–21)	POSTERIOR CHAIN 21 PERCENT	51	22–12–17 (24–15–12)
	42	18–10–14 (26–0–16)		42	18–10–14 (16–12–12)
	61	26–15–21 (35–0–26)		61	26–15–21 (26–20–16)
	36	15–9–12 (22–0–15)		36	15–9–12 (15–10–12)
PULLS 0 PERCENT	0	0–0–0			
	0	0–0–0			
	0	0–0–0			
	0	0–0–0			

Figure 8.6 Advanced Cycle One Strength Breakdown

The numbers in parentheses represent adjusted daily volumes.

The math will be slightly easier for this advanced athlete, as the larger monthly volumes allow for a more normal distribution of reps between the training sessions.

You will see, however, that in some weeks, one or two repetitions were added to the totals when necessary. Starting at 900 repetitions and advancing to 1,000 reps in the second cycle will still lend itself to a three-day per week structure, but with increased density of work on those three days.

We have also included triceps and lat work to this program to provide an idea of the set and rep scheme based on our goals. These reps are not included in the totals as this is considered accessory work.

All lifts are denoted as percent max times reps, meaning 50/5 is 50 percent of the 1RM for five repetitions.

WEEK ONE

DAY ONE

Power Clean, from the floor: 50/5, 60/5, 70/4, 70/4, 70/4

Dumbbell Bench Press: 55/6, 65/6, 70/5 x 4 sets

Back Squat: 50/6, 60/6, 70/4, 70/4, 70/4

Hyperextensions: 4x6—select appropriate load

Lat Pulldown or Pull-ups: 3x8

Triceps: 3x10

Ab Work

Neck

DAY TWO

Power Clean, from the hang position: 50/3, 60/3, 70/2, 70/2, 70/2

Split Jerk: 50/3, 50/3, 60/3, 70/2, 70/2, 70/2, 75/2

Trap Bar Deadlift, percent of max clean: 60/4, 70/4, 70/4, 75/3

Front Squat, percent of max back squat: 50/4, 60/3, 60/3, 60/3

Ab Work

DAY THREE

Snatch with Overhead Squat: 50/4+4, 60/3+3

Power Clean, from the hang position: 50/4, 60/4, 75/3 x 3 sets

Dumbbell Incline Press: 50/6, 65/6, 75/3, 75/3, 75/3

Back Squat: 50/4, 60/3, 75/3 x 4 sets

Good Morning, percent of max clean: 50/6, 60/6

Bent-over Row: 4x8

Triceps: 4x8

Ab Work

Neck

WEEK TWO

DAY ONE

Power Clean, from the floor: 50/3, 65/3, 75/3 x 4 sets

Dumbbell Bench Press: 50/6, 60/5, 70/3, 80/3, 70/3, 80/3, 70/3

Back Squat: 50/4, 65/4, 75/4, 75/4, 75/4

Hyperextensions: 4x4—select appropriate load

Lat Pulldown or Pull-ups: 3x10

Triceps: 3x8

Ab Work

Neck

DAY TWO

Power Clean, from the hang position: 50/2, 65/2, 75/2, 75/2, 75/2

Split Jerk: 50/3, 65/3, 70/2, 75/2, 75/2, 75/2

Trap Bar Deadlift, percent of max clean: 50/4, 65/4, 75/4

Front Squat, percent of max back squat: 50/4, 65/4, 75/4

Ab Work

DAY THREE

Snatch with Overhead Squat: 50/3+3, 60/3+3, 70/3+3, 70/3+3, 75/2+2

Power Clean, from the hang position: 50/3, 60/3, 70/2, 80/2, 80/2, 80/2

Dumbbell Incline Press: 65/4, 75/3 x 4 sets

Back Squat: 55/3, 65/3, 75/3 x 3 sets

Good Morning, percent of max clean: 55/6, 65/6

Bent-over Row: 4x6

Triceps: 4x8

Ab Work

Neck

WEEK THREE

DAY ONE

Power Clean, from the floor: 50/5, 65/5, 75/3 x 5 sets

Dumbbell Bench Press: 55/5, 55/5, 65/5, 75/5 x 4 sets

Back Squat: 55/6, 65/6, 75/4 x 4 sets

Hyperextensions: 1x6, 4x5—select appropriate load

Lat Pulldown or Pull-ups: 3x12

Triceps: 3x12

Ab Work

Neck

DAY TWO

Power Clean, from the hang position: 50/3, 60/3, 70/3, 70/3, 70/3

Split Jerk: 55/4, 65/4, 75/3 x 4 sets

Trap Bar Deadlift, percent of max clean: 60/5, 70/5, 80/5, 80/5

Front Squat, percent of back squat: 50/4, 65/4, 75/3, 75/3, 75/3

Ab Work

DAY THREE

Snatch with Overhead Squat: 50/4+4, 60/4+4, 75/3+3 x 4 sets

Power Clean, from the hang position: 50/3, 50/3, 60/3, 60/3, 75/2, 75/2, 75/2, 80/2, 80/2

Dumbbell Incline Press: 50/5, 60/5, 75/4 x 4 sets

Back Squat: 50/3, 65/3, 75/3, 75/3, 80/2, 80/2, 80/2, 80/2, 80/2

Good Morning, percent of max clean: 60/4, 70/4, 70/4, 70/4

Bent-over Row: 4x8

Triceps: 4x8

Ab Work

Neck

WEEK FOUR

DAY ONE

Power Clean, from the floor: 50/4, 50/4, 65/4, 65/4

Dumbbell Bench Press: 50/5, 60/5, 70/4, 70/4, 70/4

Back Squat: 50/4, 65/4, 65/4, 65/4

Hyperextensions: 3x5—select appropriate load

Lat Pulldown or Pull-ups: 3x6

Triceps: 3x6

Ab Work

Neck

DAY TWO

Power Clean, from the hang position: 50/2, 65/2 x 4 sets

Split Jerk: 50/2, 60/2, 60/2, 70/2, 70/2, 70/2

Trap Bar Deadlift, percent of max clean: 55/4, 70/3, 70/3

Front Squat, percent of max back squat: 50/4, 65/3, 65/3

Ab Work

DAY THREE

Snatch with Overhead Squat: 50/2+2, 65/2+2 x 5 sets

Power Clean, from the hang position: 50/2, 60/2, 70/2 x 4 sets

Dumbbell Incline Press: 50/3, 60/3, 70/3, 70/3, 70/3

Back Squat: 50/3, 60/3, 70/3, 70/3

Good Morning, percent of max clean: 60/6, 60/6

Ab Work

Neck

CYCLE TWO—POWER EMPHASIS

Monthly Volume
1,000 reps

Weekly Volumes
27 percent—22 percent—32 percent—19 percent

Daily Volumes
42 percent—24 percent—34 percent

MOVEMENT	EXERCISE VOLUME	MONTHLY VOLUME	WEEKLY VOLUME WEEKS 1-2-3-4
SQUAT	23 percent	230 total reps	62-51-74-44
CLEAN	21 percent	210 total reps	57-46-67-40
PRESS	21 percent	210 total reps	57-46-67-40
PULLS	0 percent	0 total reps	0-0-0-0
JERK	7 percent	70 total reps	19-15-23-13
SNATCH	7 percent	70 total reps	19-15-23-13
POSTERIOR CHAIN	21 percent	210 total reps	57-46-67-40
TOTAL	**100 percent**	**1,000 total reps**	**270-220-320-190**

Figure 8.7 Advanced Power Cycle Volumes

MOVEMENT	WEEKLY VOLUME	DAILY VOLUMES	MOVEMENT	WEEKLY VOLUME	DAILY VOLUMES
SQUAT 23 PERCENT	62	26–15–21	JERK 7 PERCENT	19	8–5–6 (19–0–0)
	51	21–12–17			
	74	31–18–25		15	6–4–5 (15–0–0)
	44	18–11–15 (18–12–15)			
				23	9–6–8 (23–0–0)
				13	6–3–4 (13–0–0)
CLEAN 21 PERCENT	57	24–14–19	SNATCH 7 PERCENT	19	8–5–6 (0–19–0)
	46	19–11–16 (22–0–24)		15	6–4–5 (0–15–0)
	67	28–16–23 (24–19–24)		23	9–6–8 (0–23–0)
	40	17–10–13 (18–0–22)		13	6–3–4 (0–13–0)
PRESS 21 PERCENT	57	24–14–19	POSTERIOR CHAIN 21 PERCENT	57	24–14–19 (20–12–25)
	46	19–11–16 (19–12–16)		46	19–11–16 (19–12–15)
	67	28–16–23		67	28–16–23 (24–0–33)
	40	17–10–13 (16–10–14)		40	17–10–13 (15–12–13)
PULL 0 PERCENT	0	0–0–0			
	0	0–0–0			
	0	0–0–0			
	0	0–0–0			

Figure 8.8 Advanced Cycle Two Power Breakdown

The numbers in parentheses represent adjusted daily volumes.

WEEK ONE

DAY ONE

Power Clean, from the hang position: 50/3, 50/3, 60/3, 60/3, 70/2, 80/2 x 5 sets

Split Jerk: 50/3, 50/3, 60/3, 70/2, 70/2, 80/2, 80/2, 80/2

Back Squat: 50/4, 60/4, 70/3, 80/3 x 5 sets

Alternate Dumbbell Military Press: 55/6+6, 55/6+6, 65/4+4 x 3 sets

Twisting Hyperextensions: 1x5, 5x3 — select appropriate load

Dumbbell Row, on bench: 3x6

Triceps: 3x8

Ab Work

Neck

DAY TWO

Split Snatch: 50/3, 50/3, 65/3, 65/2, 70/2, 75/2, 75/2, 75/2

Clean, from the hang position: 50/3, 60/3, 70/3, 70/3, 75/2

Trap Bar Deadlift, percent of max clean: 60/3, 75/3, 80/3, 80/3

Front Squat, percent of max back squat: 55/5, 65/5, 75/5

Alternate Dumbbell Incline Press: 65/4+4, 70/4+4, 75/3+3 x 2 sets

Ab Work

DAY THREE

Power Clean, from below the knees: 50/3, 50/3, 65/3, 70/2, 80/2, 85/1, 85/1, 80/2, 80/2

Push-Press, percent bodyweight: 55/4, 65/5, 75/5, 75/5

Back Squat: 50/3, 60/3, 75/3, 85/3, 80/3, 85/3, 80/3

Hyperextensions: 2x6, 6x3 — select appropriate load

Cable Shoulder Extensions: 4x6

Triceps: 3x8

Ab Work

Neck

WEEK TWO

DAY ONE

Clean, from the hang position: 50/3, 50/3, 60/3, 60/3, 70/2, 80/2, 85/2 x 3 sets

Split Jerk: 50/3, 65/3, 70/3, 75/2 x 3 sets

Back Squat: 50/3, 60/3, 70/3, 75/3 x 4 sets

Alternate Dumbbell Military Press: 60/4+4, 70/5+5 x 3 sets

Twisting Hyperextensions: 6x3—select appropriate load

Dumbbell Row, on bench: 3x8

Triceps: 4x6

Ab Work

Neck

DAY TWO

Split Snatch: 50/3, 60/3, 65/3, 70/2 x 3 sets

Trap Bar Deadlift, percent of max clean: 60/4, 75/4, 75/4

Front Squat, percent of max back squat: 50/2, 60/2, 70/2, 80/2, 80/2, 80/2

Alternate Dumbbell Incline Press: 65/6+6, 75/6+6

Ab Work

DAY THREE

Power Clean, from below the knees: 50/4, 60/4, 60/4, 70/3 x 4 sets

Push-Press, percent bodyweight: 50/3, 50/3, 65/3, 65/3, 75/2, 75/2

Back Squat: 50/3, 60/3, 70/3, 80/2, 85/2, 85/2, 85/2

Hyperextensions: 3x5—select appropriate load

Cable Shoulder Extensions: 3x8

Triceps: 3x8

Ab Work

Neck

WEEK THREE

DAY ONE

Power Clean, from the hang position: 50/3, 50/3, 60/3, 60/3, 70/2, 80/2, 85/2, 85/2, 80/2, 80/2

Split Jerk: 50/3, 50/3, 65/3, 65/3, 75/2, 75/2, 85/1, 85/1, 80/2, 75/3

Back Squat: 50/6, 60/5, 70/5, 80/3 x 5 sets

Alternate Dumbbell Military Press: 50/5+5, 60/5+5, 70/4+4, 75/3+3 x 4 sets

Twisting Hyperextensions: 1x6, 6x4 — select appropriate load

Dumbbell Row, on bench: 3x10

Triceps: 3x12

Ab Work

Neck

DAY TWO

Split Snatch: 50/3, 50/3, 60/3, 60/3, 65/3, 70/2 x 4 sets

Clean, from the hang position: 50/4, 60/4, 60/4, 70/4, 75/3

Front Squat, percent of max back squat: 50/4, 60/3, 70/3, 75/2, 80/2, 80/2, 80/2

Alternate Dumbbell Incline Press: 70/4+4 x 4 sets

Ab Work

DAY THREE

Power Clean, from below the knees: 50/4, 60/4, 60/4, 70/3 x 4 sets

Push-Press, percent bodyweight: 55/5, 65/5, 75/4, 75/4, 80/3, 80/2

Back Squat: 50/4, 50/4, 60/4, 70/4, 75/3, 80/2, 85/2, 85/2

Hyperextensions: 3x15

Cable Shoulder Extensions: 4x6

Triceps: 4x6

Ab Work

Neck

WEEK FOUR

DAY ONE

Clean, from the hang position: 50/3, 60/3, 70/3 x 4 sets

Split Jerk: 50/4, 65/3, 65/3, 65/3

Back Squat: 50/3, 65/3, 75/3 x 4 sets

Alternate Dumbbell Military Press: 50/5+5, 60/5+5, 75/3+3, 75/3+3

Twisting Hyperextensions: 5x3—select appropriate load

Dumbbell Row, on bench: 3x6

Triceps: 3x8

Ab Work

Neck

DAY TWO

Power Snatch, from below the knees: 50/3, 60/2, 70/2, 70/2, 70/2, 70/2

Trap Bar Deadlift, percent of max clean: 50/3, 60/3, 70/3, 70/3

Front Squat, percent of max back squat: 50/3, 60/3, 70/3, 75/3

Alternate Dumbbell Incline Press: 50/2+2, 60/2+2, 70/2+2, 75/2+2, 75/2+2

Ab Work

DAY THREE

Power Clean, from below the knees: 50/3, 50/3, 60/3, 60/3, 70/3, 70/3, 75/2, 75/2

Push-Press, percent bodyweight: 50/4, 60/4, 70/3, 70/3

Back Squat: 55/5, 65/5, 65/5

Hyperextensions: 1x5, 4x2—select appropriate load

Neck

PRESEASON FOUR-WEEK TRAINING PLAN

FOUR-DAY PER WEEK ADVANCED PROGRAM

Collegiate junior athlete with five years of training experience

This is the final cycle for a college junior before the start of training camp. In this scenario, the athlete completed successive cycles of 1,200, 1,300, 1,450 reps in each month. With the preseason cycle, the peak volume of 1,450 reps is cut by about 25 percent to set the month's volume at 1,100 total reps.

In this example, we will use the four-day-per-week model to provide a better understanding of the volume distribution with an extra training day during the week.

As previously noted, the volume for this month is weighted toward the beginning of the month in a 32–22–27–19 percent pattern to allow for a slight taper in volume leading into the start of practice and competition.

The training intensity for this phase should always be high, with an emphasis on maximal strength and power development to ensure carryover to sport.

With the four-day per week design, we run into multiple instances of days with fewer than our 12-rep "minimum." Hitting those daily volumes is the ideal situation because this is a high-level athlete who is training at sufficiently high intensity, with most of the movements trained at least two days in the week. Still, that 12-rep mark is a little more flexible.

As you know, a more adapted or experienced lifter will often respond better to higher intensity and lower volume relative to a novice or inexperienced lifter.

Monthly Volume
1,100 reps

Weekly Volumes
32 percent—22 percent—27 percent—19 percent

Daily Volumes
27 percent—22 percent—32 percent—19 percent

MOVEMENT	EXERCISE VOLUME	MONTHLY VOLUME	WEEKLY VOLUME WEEKS 1–2–3–4
SQUAT	22 percent	244 total reps	79–54–65–46
CLEAN	16 percent	177 total reps	57–40–48–32
PRESS	16 percent	178 total reps	56–41–48–33
PULLS	14 percent	154 total reps	49–34–42–29
JERK	7 percent	72 total reps	22–16–20–14
SNATCH	15 percent	166 total reps	52–37–45–32
POSTERIOR CHAIN	10 percent	110 total reps	35–24–30–21
TOTAL	**100 percent**	**1,100 total reps**	

Figure 8.9 Advanced Four-Day Exercise Volumes

[CHAPTER EIGHT—FOOTBALL PROGRAMMING]

MOVEMENT	WEEKLY VOLUME	DAILY VOLUMES	MOVEMENT	WEEKLY VOLUME	DAILY VOLUMES
SQUAT 22 PERCENT	79	18–20–26–15	JERK 7 PERCENT	22	0–22–0–0
	54	18–10–16–10		16	0–16–0–0
	65	18–12–20–15		20	0–20–0–0
	46	15–10–12–9		14	0–14–0–0
CLEAN 16 PERCENT	57	17–16–24–0	SNATCH 15 PERCENT	52	16–0–16–20
	40	10–12–18–0		37	12–0–13–12
	48	12–16–20–0		45	15–0–12–18
	32	10–10–12–0		32	10–0–10–12
PRESS 16 PERCENT	56	24–0–17–15	POSTERIOR CHAIN 10 PERCENT	35	24–0–0–11
	41	16–0–10–15		24	12–0–0–12
	48	18–0–18–12		30	15–0–0–15
	33	12–0–12–19		21	8–0–0–13
PULLS 14 PERCENT	49	18–15–16–0			
	34	12–12–10–0			
	42	15–15–12–0			
	29	10–9–10–0			

Figure 8.10 Advanced Four-Day Rep Breakdown

WEEK ONE

DAY ONE (MONDAY)

Power Snatch, from the hang position: 50/3, 60/3, 70/2 x 5 sets

Split Clean, from the hang position: 50/2, 50/2, 60/2, 60/2, 70/2, 75/2, 85/2, 95/1, 75/2

Clean Pull, percent of max clean, from below the knees: 80/3, 80/3, 90/3 x 3 sets

Dumbbell Bench Press: 25/3+3, 30/3+3, 35/3+3, 40/3+3

Back Squat: 50/3, 60/3, 70/3, 80/3, 85/2, 90/1, 95/1, 90/1, 95/1

Good Morning, percent of max clean: 50/6, 60/5, 70/6, 70/6

Ab Work

Neck

DAY TWO (TUESDAY)

Power Clean, from a box below the knees: 50/3, 60/3, 70/2 x 5 sets

Split Jerk: 50/3, 50/3, 65/2, 65/2, 75/2 x 6 sets

Clean Pull, percent of max clean, from the hang position, straight legs: 80/4, 80/4, 90/4, 90/4

Step-Up, percent of max back squat: 30/3+3, 40/3+3, 50/2+2, 50/2+2

Ab Work

DAY THREE (THURSDAY)

Split Snatch, from above the knees: 50/3, 60/3, 70/2, 80/2 x 4 sets

Snatch Pull, percent of max snatch, below the knees: 70/3, 70/3, 80/3, 80/3, 90/3, 90/3

Dumbbell Clean: 25/3+3, 30/3+3, 35/3+3, 40/3+3

Bench Press: 55/3, 60/3, 70/3, 80/3, 90/2, 75/3

Back Squat: 50/5, 60/5, 70/4, 80/3 x 4 sets

Neck

Ab Work

DAY FOUR (FRIDAY)

Dumbbell Snatch: 25/3+3, 30/3+3, 35/2+2 x 2 sets

Incline Press, percent of max bench: 50/3, 60/3, 70/3 x 3 sets

Front Squat, percent of max back squat: 50/3, 60/3, 70/3 x 3 sets

Good Morning, percent of max clean: 55/6, 65/5

Ab Work

Neck

WEEK TWO

DAY ONE (MONDAY)

Power Snatch, from the hang position: 50/3, 60/3, 70/2 x 3 sets

Split Clean, from the hang position: 50/2, 60/2, 70/2, 80/2, 80/2

Clean Pull, percent of max clean, from blocks below the knee: 80/3, 90/3 x 3 sets

Dumbbell Bench Press: 25/2+2, 30/2+2, 35/2+2, 40/2+2

Back Squat: 50/3, 60/3, 70/3, 80/3, 80/3, 80/3

Good Morning, percent of max clean: 50/4, 60/4, 60/4

Ab Work

Neck

DAY TWO (TUESDAY)

Jumps: 2x10

Power Clean, from a box below the knees: 50/2, 60/2, 70/2 x 4 sets

Split Jerk: 50/2, 60/2, 70/2 x 6 sets

Clean Pull, from the hang position, straight legs: 75/4, 85/3, 85/3

Leg Press: 30/3+3, 40/2+2

Ab Work

DAY THREE (THURSDAY)

Split Snatch, from the hang position: 50/3, 60/3, 70/2, 80/2, 90/1, 95/1, 75/1

Snatch Pull, percent of max snatch, from below the knees: 85/3, 85/3, 90/2, 90/2, 95/2

Dumbbell Clean: 25/3+3, 35/3+3, 40/3+3

Bench Press: 60/3, 70/3, 80/2, 80/2

Back Squat: 50/4, 60/4, 70/4, 80/4

Ab Work

Neck

DAY FOUR (FRIDAY)

Dumbbell Snatch: 25/3+3, 30/3+3

Incline Press, percent of max bench: 50/3, 60/3, 70/3, 70/3, 70/3

Front Squat, percent of max back squat: 50/3, 60/3, 70/2, 70/2

Good Morning, percent of max clean: 50/4, 60/4, 70/4

Ab Work

WEEK THREE

DAY ONE (MONDAY)

Power Snatch, from the hang position: 50/3, 65/3, 75/3 x 3 sets

Split Clean, from the hang position: 50/2, 60/2, 70/2, 80/2, 85/2, 85/2

Clean Pull, percent of max clean, from box below the knees: 75/3, 80/3, 85/3 x 3 sets

Dumbbell Bench Press: 25/3+3, 35/3+3, 40/3+3

Back Squat: 50/3, 65/3, 75/3, 80/3, 85/3, 85/3

Seated Good Morning, percent of max clean: 50/5, 60/5, 70/5

Ab Work

Neck

DAY TWO (TUESDAY)

Jumps: 2x10

Power Clean, from a box below the knees: 50/3, 65/3, 75/2 x 5 sets

Split Jerk: 50/2, 50/2, 60/2, 60/2, 70/2, 70/2, 80/2 x 4 sets

Clean Pull, from the hang position, straight legs: 70/4, 80/4, 90/4

Step-Up, percent of max back squat: 40/2+2, 45/2+2, 55/2+2

Ab Work

DAY THREE (THURSDAY)

Split Snatch, from the hang position: 50/2, 60/2, 70/2, 80/2, 80/2, 80/2

Snatch Pull, percent of max snatch, from the hang position: 65/3, 75/3, 85/3, 85/3, 95/3

Dumbbell Clean: 25/3+3, 35/3+3, 40/2+2, 45/2+2

Bench Press: 60/3, 75/3, 85/3 x 4 sets

Back Squat: 55/4, 70/4, 80/4, 80/4, 80/4

Ab Work

Neck

DAY FOUR (FRIDAY)

Dumbbell Snatch: 30/3+3, 35/3+3, 40/2+2, 45/2+2

Incline Press, percent of max bench: 50/3, 65/3, 75/2, 75/2, 75/2

Front Squat, percent of max back squat: 50/3, 60/3, 70/3, 70/3, 70/3

Good Morning, percent of max clean: 50/5, 60/5, 70/5

Ab Work

WEEK FOUR

DAY ONE (MONDAY)

Power Snatch, from the hang position: 50/2, 60/2, 70/2, 70/2, 70/2

Split Clean, from the hang position: 50/2, 65/2, 75/2, 75/2, 75/2

Clean Pull, percent of clean max, from box at the knees: 60/3, 70/2, 80/2

Dumbbell Bench Press: 25/2+2, 30/2+2, 35/2+2

Back Squat: 50/3, 65/3, 75/3, 75/3, 75/3

Seated Good Morning, percent of max clean: 50/4, 60/4

Ab Work

Neck

DAY TWO (TUESDAY)

Jumps: 2x10

Power Clean, from a box at the knees: 50/2, 60/2, 70/2, 70/2, 70/2

Split Jerk: 50/2, 60/2, 65/2 x 5 sets

Clean Pull, from the hang position, straight legs: 70/4, 75/3, 75/3

Step-Up, percent of max back squat: 35/5+5

Ab Work

DAY THREE (THURSDAY)

Split Snatch, from the hang position: 50/2, 60/2, 75/2, 75/2, 75/2

Snatch Pull, percent of max snatch, from the hang position: 60/3, 70/3, 80/2, 80/2

Dumbbell Clean: 25/2+2, 35/2+2, 35/2+2

Bench Press: 60/4, 75/4, 75/4

Back Squat: 50/4, 60/4, 70/4

Ab Work

Neck

DAY FOUR (FRIDAY)

Dumbbell Snatch: 25/3+3, 35/3+3

Incline Press, percent of max bench: 50/3, 60/3, 60/3

Front Squat, percent of max back squat: 50/3, 65/3, 65/3

Good Morning, percent of max clean: 55/5, 65/4, 65/4

Ab Work

IN-SEASON TRAINING PLAN

Principles apply for novice, advanced, and elite-level athletes

The final two examples are of in-season programming based on a two- or three-day training week. Here we assume normal weeks when athletes are at home and not playing an away game with travel late in the week.

With some of the above-mentioned problems in setting up a plan, you need to adjust as you see fit, but understand that shorter weeks need to first address recovery more than anything else.

You will see tempo runs included on day one of each week, which is intended to help accelerate recovery with low volume, low-to-moderate intensity running. Remember that the training movements are going to be kept to a minimum—clean, squat, press, pull—including accessory work, and the total training volume will also be comparatively low. For that reason, we are not going to get overly concerned with exact training volumes for each movement or week.

Training Volume for Each Movement

Week One
Medium–Heavy (14–17 reps per exercise)

Week Two
Medium (12–15 reps per exercise)

Week Three
Heavy (17–20 reps per exercise)

Week Four
Light (10–12 reps per exercise)

TWO DAYS PER WEEK PROGRAM
WEEK ONE

DAY ONE (MONDAY)

Single-Leg Squat: 2x5 each leg

Hanging Knee-Up, eyes looking down: x10

Power Clean, hang above the knee, percent of max clean: 55/4, 65/3, 75/3, 75/3, 80/2

Back Squat, percent of max squat: 55/5, 65/4, 75/3, 80/3

Military Press, percent of bodyweight: 55/4, 65/4, 75/3, 75/3, 75/3

Ab work: not much volume, low intensity

Hyperextension: 2x8

Neck

Tempo Run: 4x100 yards

Stretch

DAY TWO (WEDNESDAY)

Shrugs 2x8

Kettlebell or Dumbbell Swing: 1x8

Dumbbell Power Clean, from the hang above the knee, percent of max clean: 50/3, 60/3, 70/3, 75/2, 75/2

Dumbbell Bench Press, percent of max bench: 55/5, 65/4, 75/4, 75/4

Lat work, moderate weight – 2x8

Triceps work, moderate weight – 2x8

Abs, planks or variation

Stretch

WEEK TWO

DAY ONE (MONDAY)

Single-Leg Squat: 2x5 each leg

Hanging Knee-Up, eyes looking down: x10

Power Clean, hang above the knee, percent of max clean:
55/3, 65/3, 75/2, 75/2, 80/1, 80/1, 85/1

Back Squat, percent of max squat: 55/4, 65/3, 75/3, 80/2, 85/1, 80/1

Military Press, percent of bodyweight: 55/4, 65/4, 75/4, 80/2

Ab work: not much volume, low intensity

Hyperextension: 2x8

Neck

Tempo Run: 4x100 yards

Stretch

DAY TWO (WEDNESDAY)

Shrugs 2x8

Kettlebell or Dumbbell Swing: 1x8

Dumbbell Power Clean, from the hang above the knee, percent of max clean:
50/3, 60/3, 70/2, 75/2, 75/2

Dumbbell Bench Press, percent of max bench: 55/4, 65/4, 75/4, 80/2

Lat work, moderate-heavy weight – 2x7

Triceps work, moderate-heavy weight – 2x7

Abs, planks or variation

Stretch

[CHAPTER EIGHT—FOOTBALL PROGRAMMING]

THREE DAYS PER WEEK IN-SEASON PROGRAM

Here you will see the slight variations in programming on a three-day schedule in-season. This program was written by Coach Miller, who differs slightly from Coach Parker's approach. You will see his inclusion of low-volume hamstring work on Mondays, which he feels assists in improving blood flow to the hamstrings to accelerate recovery from a Sunday game.

WEEK ONE

DAY ONE (MONDAY)

Hyperextension: 1x10

Single-Leg Squat: 2x5 each leg

Hanging Knee-Up, eyes looking down: x10

Complex One
45-percent bodyweight 3x3 reps each for skill position—
Receivers and defensive backs
40-percent bodyweight 3x3 reps each for mid-skill positions—
Linebackers, tight-ends, running backs, quarterbacks, and kickers
35-percent bodyweight 3x3 reps each for linemen

Step-Up—percent of max squat
Skill and mid-skill: 75lb/4+4, 95lb/4+4, 110lb/4+4
Linemen: 95/4+4, 110/4+4, 125/4+4

Bench Press—percent of max bench
Skill and mid-skill: 50/6, 60/5, 70/4, 70/4
Linemen: 45/6, 50/5, 55/4, 55/4

Leg Curl
2x8 moderate weight—do on Monday, as players have Tuesday off.
These can help identify problems from the game and speed recovery.

Ab work: not much volume, low intensity

Stretch

* Highly suggest a 45-minute massage or soft tissue work for recovery

DAY TWO (WEDNESDAY)

Glute/Ham Hyperextension: 1x8

Kettlebell or Dumbbell Swing: 1x8

Clean, from the hang above the knee, percent of max clean: 50/3, 60/2, 70/3, 75/2, 80/1, 80/1

Back Squat, percent of max squat: 50/4, 60/3, 70/3, 75/3

Standing Military Press, percent of bodyweight: 45/5, 50/5, 55/4, 55/4

Abs, planks or variation: 1:30 seconds

Stretch

DAY THREE (FRIDAY)

Here we program additional upper-body bench, incline, or overhead pressing along with rows or pulldowns for linemen, linebackers, tight ends, and running backs who may need more shoulder protection. If players did flat bench on Monday, they will do standing dumbbell presses for four sets of four reps using mod-heavy weight.

Have the others do

Bench Press, percent of max bench: 50/6, 60/3, 70/3, 75/1, 80/1, 85/1

Seated Row, moderate-heavy weight: 2x8

Again, we highly suggest massage or soft tissue work to help speed recovery from a week of practice and lead up to a game.

WEEK TWO

DAY ONE (MONDAY)

Reverse Hyperextension: x10

Slider Squat, backward or lateral using furniture movers or a slideboard—
Skill and mid-skill: 75lb/4+4, 95lb/4+4, 110lb/4+4
Linemen: 95lb/4+4, 110lb/4+4, 125lb/4+4

Complex One with dumbbells—
45-percent bodyweight 3x3 reps each for skill position
40-percent bodyweight 3x3 reps each for mid-skill position
35-percent bodyweight 3x3 reps each for linemen

Single-Leg Dumbbell Squat, rear foot elevated: 55lbs/4+4, 65lbs/4+4, 75lbs/4+4

Standing Military Press, percent of bodyweight: 55/4, 65/4, 70/4, 75/4

DAY TWO (WEDNESDAY)

Glute/Ham Hyperextension: 1x8

Clean Pull, rack below the knee, percent of max clean: 50/4, 60/4, 70/4, 80/2, 85/2

Front Squat, percent of max back squat: 40/3, 50/3, 55/3 ,60/3, 60/3

or

Step-Up, percent of max back squat: 20/2+2, 25/2+2, 30/2+2, 35/1+1, 40/1+1, 40/1+1

Dumbbell Bench Press, percent of max bench: 55/4, 65/4, 65/4, 70/4

DAY THREE (FRIDAY)

If any players did flat bench on Monday, have them do standing dumbbell press for four sets of four reps using moderate-heavy weight.

Have the others do

Bench Press, percent of max bench: 50/5, 60/3, 70/2, 75/1, 80/1, 85/1, 85/1

Seated Row, moderate-heavy weight: 2x6

Massage or soft tissue work for recovery

Every three weeks, you can drop reps to one or two per set and move to heavier percentages. Singles and doubles will not fatigue your athletes unless you get the total rep count too high. This is a great way to see where their strength is during certain times of a season.

In-season training will always be the greatest challenge for a strength coach because there will inevitably be a lot of things out of your control that impact your athletes' status and abilities.

However, there is no excuse to significantly dial back the training intensity. Volume can always be managed to limit the overall stress to the body, but sacrificing intensity in the weightroom will ultimately mean sacrificing intensity on the field.

CHAPTER NINE—
INTEGRATING SPRINTING AND JUMPING

You should at this point have a better understanding of the design of a three-day and four-day per week training plan for lifting. To truly address full athletic development, the missing components are conditioning, sprinting, and jumping.

Building a comprehensive running and jumping plan is as important as the weight program to fully integrate all the work performed in the weightroom onto the field.

This sample program coincides with the novice program example found on page 259. The purpose of this four-week block is to teach a novice athlete how to run properly and to start developing acceleration and speed at the foundational level.

For the younger athlete, there is often much more to teach in the stance and start of a sprint than any other facet. It is about teaching how to rapidly apply force into the ground to build more explosive and powerful athletes over the first 0–20 yards.

This program assumes the athletes have completed the break-in cycle of running and jumping, demonstrating good control and form. During each new phase, as the athletes show you they are ready for more, the program needs to take steps to deliver the same thing as the weight program with increases in volume, intensity, and complexity.

You must make changes to elicit the correct aspect of speed you desire to achieve with the athletes. You also need to understand where the athletes are with all other phases before moving forward. They will only be as fast or explosive as their weakest link, and if their strength or power or mechanics are not up to the task, performance will suffer.

EYE OF THE COACH

The standing triple long jump teaches how to quickly absorb and explode from the correct landing position. It will increase body awareness, teach how to land properly in the athletic ready stance, all the while moving in a linear direction. The goal is to minimize contact time with the ground, which means the heels should not hit down.

OFF-SEASON FOUR-WEEK SPRINT AND JUMP TRAINING PLAN WEEK ONE—MODERATE VOLUME

DAY ONE

Lift

Tempo Run—*5x100 yards at 16–15–14-second pace, as described on page 77*

DAY TWO

Continuous Warmup of 30 Yards

Start with simple movements and always integrate some 75–80–85 percent runs, followed by the same speed backward runs. Introduce and teach new movement patterns at this stage, and try to integrate components of what you will be training that day. The warmup should be 15 to 20 minutes of continuous movement, stretches, and running.

Mach Run Drills—*3x15 yards each*

Standing Triple Long Jump—
3 series of three jumps

This is same as the single jump, but once the athletes hit the ground, they continue into jumps two and three. At the end of the third jump, note where the athlete lands, as 10 yards is the distance you want to see. Larger players will have a harder time reaching this. The larger players should try to reach between 8.5 to 9 yards in three jumps.

Three-Step Wall March—
5 reps of 3 steps per set, 3 sets

This is the same drill as described in the prep phase, but now the athletes take three fast and explosive steps while maintaining the correct body position.

Hurry Go Get Em—*10 yards x 3 sets*

Walk-Jog Recovery—
Stretch and water, a 6–8 minute rest

Sled Pulls, Stadiums, or Hill Runs,
depending on the tools you have—
3 sets of 20 yards with 15–20 percent bodyweight of athlete

After three runs, have the athletes remove the harness and sled and run 20 yards. At this point, they will walk, jog, stretch, and take water for up to 10 minutes, and then repeat another series.

Flat Surface Sprint—
100 percent for a minimum of 20 yards, for at least two reps

This allows the body to re-establish the correct movement pattern of running in a normal fashion, particularly needed after running hills or stadiums. Flat runs without sleds at the end of the segment will suffice if the athletes did sled work.

Walk-Jog Recovery and Stretch

DAY THREE

Lift

Tempo Run—
5x100 yards at 16–15–14-second pace

DAY FOUR

Continuous Warmup of 30 Yards

Mach Run Drills—*3x20 yards each*

Lateral Box Jump, *12-inch box—*
Four series of 10 seconds, a minimum of 10 reps of contact to top of box

Falling 20s—*5x20 yards*

Light Stretch and Water—
6–8 minutes rest

Tempo Run—
12 rounds of 4x100 yards at 15–14–13-second pace, walk 100-yard recovery; 4x100 yards at 15–14–13-second pace, walk 100 yard recovery; 4x100 yards at 15–14–13-second pace

Walk-Jog Recovery and Stretch

DAY FIVE

Lift

Tempo Run—
5x100 yards at 16–15–14-second pace

FALLING 20s

Photos 9.1 a–b Falling 20s

The athlete should allow gravity to pull them forward and down while maintaining a good neutral posture before explosively driving their arms and leg into a sprint.

From a standing stance with both feet together, the athletes lean forward, try to keep from bending over at the waist, and sprint 20 yards. Athletes go in single-file; critique their technique and body position.

This drill is to teach the removal of the wall from the wall marches and apply to a real sprint. They will do a slow walk back for recovery.

WEEK TWO
MODERATE-HEAVY VOLUME

DAY ONE

Lift

Tempo Run—*5x100 yards at 16–15–14-second pace*

DAY TWO

Continuous Warmup—*x 30 yards*

Mach Run Drill—*4x15 yards*

Triple Standing Long Jump—*4 series of three jumps*

Hurry Go Get Em—*3x10 yards*

Sled Pull—*20 yards x 2 with sled, 1 without sled, 1 with sled, 1 without sled*

Walk-Jog Recovery—*stretch and water, a 6–8 minute rest*

Sled Pull—*2x20 yards, 1x20 yards without the sled, 1x20 yards with the sled, 1x20 yards without the sled*

Sprints—*100 percent—2x20 yards*

Walk-Jog Recovery and Stretch

DAY THREE

Lift

Tempo Run—*4x100 yards at 15–14–13-second pace*

Notice slight increase in intensity with a drop in volume

DAY FOUR

Continuous Warmup—*x 30 yards*

Mach Run Drill—*4x20 yards*

Lateral Box Jumps, *from a 12-inch box—5x10 seconds*

Three-Step Wall March—*4 series x 3 steps*

Sprint, timed 10-yards—*6x10 yards with two minutes rest and recovery between reps*

Tempo Run—*15 rounds of 4x100 yards at 15–14–13-second pace, walk 100 yards; 4x100 at 15–14–13-second pace, walk 100 yards; 4x100 yards at 15–14–13-second pace, walk 100 yards; 3x100 at 15–14–13-second pace*

Walk-Jog Recovery and Stretch

DAY FIVE

Lift

Tempo Run—*4x100 yards at 15–14–13-second pace*

[CHAPTER NINE—INTEGRATING SPRINTING AND JUMPING]

WEEK THREE
HEAVY VOLUME

DAY ONE

Lift

Tempo Run—*5x100 yards at 15–14–13-second pace*

DAY TWO

Continuous Warmup—*x 30 yards*

Mach Run Drill—*5x15 yards*

Triple Standing Long Jump—*4 series x 3 jumps*

Hurry Go Get Em—*3x10 yards*

Sprint, timed 20-yards—*8x20 yards with a minimum of 2 minutes rest between runs*

Walk-Jog Recovery—*stretch and water, a 8–10 minute rest*

Timed 20-Yard Sprints—*8x20 yards with minimum of 2 minutes rest between runs*

Walk-Jog Recovery and Stretch

DAY THREE

Lift

Tempo Run—*5x100 yards at 15–14–13-second pace*

DAY FOUR

Continuous Warmup—*x 30 yards*

Mach Run Drill—*4x20 yards each*

Lateral Box Jump *from a 12-inch box—4x15 seconds*

Three-Step Wall March—*4 series of three steps*

Hurry Go Get Em—*3x10 yards*

150 "The Hard Way"—*150 yards*

Walk-Jog Recovery and Stretch

DAY FIVE

Lift

Tempo Run—*5x100 yards at 15–14–13-second pace*

WEEK FOUR
RECOVERY VOLUME

DAY ONE

Lift

Tempo Run—
4x100 yards at 15–14–13-second pace

DAY TWO

Continuous Warmup—*x 30 yards*

Mach Run Drill—*3x15 yards each*

Triple Standing Long Jump—
3 series of three jumps

Three-Step Wall March—
3 series of three steps

Hurry Go Get Em—*3x10 yards*

Sled Pull—*2x20 yards with sled and 1x20 yards without sled*

Rest—*6–8 minutes*

Sled Pull—*2x20 yards with sled and 1x20 yards without sled*

Falling 20s—*4x20 yards*

Walk-Jog Recovery and Stretch

DAY THREE

Lift

Tempo Run—*4x100 yards at 15–14–13-second pace*

DAY FOUR

Continuous Warmup—*x 30 yards*

Mach Run Drill—*3x20 yards*

Lateral Box Jump, *from a 12-inch box—4x10 seconds*

Hurry Go Get Em—*3x10 yards*

Tempo Run—*11 rounds of 4x100 yards at 16–15–14-second pace, walk 100; 4x100 yards at 16–15–14-second pace, walk 100; 3x100 yards at 16–15–14-second pace*

Walk-Jog Recovery and Stretch

DAY FIVE

Lift

Tempo Run—*4x100 yards at 15–14–13-second pace*

Just as with the previous programs, our hope is that these examples will provide the outline for your own program development. The specific needs, abilities, and limitations of your athletes and your schedule will always dictate the structure of your programming.

By providing you with a holistic picture of lifting, running, and jumping, our goal is to illustrate the changing intensity, volume, and complexity of the training variables and provide you with the knowledge you need to effectively plan your training.

CHAPTER TEN—
FINAL THOUGHTS

This book is in no way an exhaustive review of every nuance of our system of programming and periodization. However, it does include the basic principles of this method of programming and our hope was to provide you with the essential components of the process that served us well in our careers so you could benefit as much as we have.

Even with as much technical information as we have given, your ultimate success with this style of programming will come from putting the knowledge into action, and then consistently evaluating your coaching choices.

The art and science of coaching cannot be pulled from a book; it has to be earned in the trenches. Even when they are presented as such, there are only so many "rules" that hold up consistently in strength and conditioning.

Although it takes time to develop, your "eye of the coach" is the most valuable tool that will always trump whatever percentages or sets or reps are on a page.

Utilizing The System results in a logical, reproducible "checks and balances" structure of programming that provides a consistent progression of training for athletes in all sports. We spent our careers working to refine the specifics of this programming system to ensure optimal results, but that does not mean this is a one-size-fits-all program.

Despite the three of us working closely together for so long and testing and adapting these methods countless times, over time we have each taken slightly different approaches under the umbrella of The System. This is not a failing, but rather an additional advantage of this type of programming.

If nothing else, we hope this book provides you with new tools and a perspective to assess your programs. You can apply the principles broadly for a team or group, and refine the nuances for the individual needs of each athlete, or you can experiment on your own to find the variables that best fit your athletes or sport. Hopefully, you will take the same approach as the Soviet coaches who guided us and never stop analyzing your pursuit of developing the best athletes.

To the younger strength coaches, there are some final thoughts we would like to impart.

We learned these lessons through much blood, sweat, tears, and long days spent in the trenches. We hope these points can help you avoid some of the pitfalls and hurdles we encountered and help you achieve the success we were so fortunate to have.

- *You will gain the trust and respect of your athletes by having them understand that you as a coach are there to get the best out of them, and that you are willing to do that on the days when they are not. Demonstrating to your athletes that you care will inspire more effort and loyalty than showing how much you know.*

- *Many strength coaches are intent on displaying how much they know, even if subconsciously. This is a mistake; do your best to tamp down that urge. Approach every opportunity as a chance to learn.*

- *There is nothing more important than establishing a positive team culture. Creating consistency in building a culture of toughness, self-denial, and teamwork will create an addicting and successful environment.*

- *No coach should have to coach effort. Set a tone from the first day and be sure the athletes know exactly what you expect of them. Your athletes should be clear on the attendance and punctuality policy, academics if appropriate, and their efforts as members of the team. This message should be firm and clear. Players want organization, structure, and to be led.*

- *As coaches, we are not creating weightlifters or world-class sprinters—unless we are actually coaching weightlifters or world-class sprinters. We are utilizing principles and exercises to enhance athleticism. Your choice of tools and coaching should reflect that.*

- *We do not coach weights or sprinting—we coach people. The greatest coaches know how to build a team by not only coaching, but also developing individuals.*

- *Always provide your athletes with tasks in which they can succeed. Failure teaches many valuable lessons; however, successes will inspire them to continue to work and grow. Place your emphasis on continually challenging and improving both yourself as a coach and your athletes.*

- *Surround yourself with winners. Learn how to pick them for yourself. You are the average of the people you spend the most time with; making sure your circle is made up of inspired and successful individuals will be of benefit in both your career and your life.*

- *We all want to reach the pinnacle of the coaching ranks, but success is not all about where you coach. It is about who you coach for and with. Some of our greatest days in coaching were working with junior high and high school athletes.*

Legendary Coach Bear Bryant made a statement one day that really stuck, as it applies to all walks of life. Now that our coaching careers are largely over, we can readily see his wisdom yet again. He likely was speaking of his own life, but it applies to all of us—

"As you go through the journey, you will find in the end that you will have lost some of the rings and spent most of the money, but you are left with the memories."

Coach Bryant was absolutely right.

Make a commitment each and every day to avoid the dangers of routine and make it a day of success and not failure. Do this one thing and we promise the memories of satisfaction and joy will far outnumber and outshine any lingering memories of regret or loss.

Johnny Parker

Al Miller

Rob Panariello

APPENDICES

APPENDIX A — ATHLETE PROFILES

APPENDIX B — PROGRAMMING PRINCIPLES

APPENDIX C — LISTS OF GRAPHS, TABLES, AND IMAGES

REFERENCES

INDEX

AUTHOR BIOGRAPHIES

APPENDIX A— ATHLETE PROFILES

NOVICE-LEVEL ATHLETES
Fewer than two years of consistent strength training or who are physically immature

GOALS
*Teach and refine basic movement quality and technique—
lifting, running, jumping*

Prepare the body and build a base of work capacity with the initial emphasis on progressing training volume (work quantity), rather than intensity (work quality)

VOLUME
Recommended starting exercise percentages

Squat—24 percent	Posterior Chain—13 percent
Clean—18 percent	Snatch—10 percent
Press—20 percent	Jerk—0 percent
Pulls—15 percent	

Strength movements take emphasis here to build a foundation with slightly higher reps and sets to improve technique and motor control. Once the athletes establish sufficient work capacity, the emphasis shifts to quality of work rather than quantity.

INTENSITY

For an absolute novice, the first four weeks generally do not exceed Zones One or Two—50-69 percent 1RM—and the majority of intensity may remain primarily in Zone Two for one or two years, depending on performance and development.

Novice athletes with one or two years of training experience will progress into Zone Three—70-79 percent 1RM—or possibly Zone Four at 80-89 percent. However, performance will dictate whether these athletes may or may not enter Zone Three training for at least the first five to twelve weeks.

ADVANCED-LEVEL ATHLETES

Greater than two years of training experience, increased physical maturity, with an adequate base of work capacity and lifting quality and technique

GOALS

Further refine technique and complexity of movements— power movements, sprinting

Develop strength, power, and speed qualities with shifting emphasis toward maximal strength and speed work

Emphasis stays on progressing the training volume until the athletes have reached the 1,100–1,200 reps per month range, where primary emphasis should shift toward progressing training intensity

VOLUME

Recommended starting exercise percentages

Squat—22 percent *Snatch—13 percent*

Clean—19 percent *Posterior Chain—10 percent*

Press—17 percent *Jerk—8 percent*

Pulls—11 percent

An increasing percentage of the training volume now shifts toward the higher intensity Olympic lifts.

INTENSITY

Training intensity will increase relative to the novice, with these athletes training primarily in Zones Three and Four, with work into Zones Five or Six when appropriate.

ELITE-LEVEL ATHLETES

Professional level, greater than eight years of training experience, with high work, strength, and power capacities

GOALS

Develop maximal strength and maximal power and speed qualities

Emphasis on progressing training intensity with sufficient volume to stimulate gains

VOLUME

Recommended starting exercise percentages

Squat—18 percent

Jerk—12 percent

Cleans—21 percent

Snatch—18 percent

Press—14 percent

Posterior Chain—10 percent

Pulls—7 percent

Here the emphasis moves to increased volume on maximal and explosive strength and power movements.

INTENSITY

These athletes will train primarily in Zones Three and Four, with increased work into Zone Five at 90–100 percent 1RM and, when appropriate, into Zone Six at 100 percent 1RM or greater.

APPENDIX B—
PROGRAMMING PRINCIPLES

VOLUME PLANNING

Determine the initial total monthly volume—
based on an athlete's training level, prior experience, injury status, prior year's peak volume, and other factors.

- *Novice athlete—less than 1,000 reps (minimum of 750 reps)*
- *Advanced or elite athlete— generally more than 1,000 reps, unless returning from an injury or a de-conditioned state*

Distribute the total monthly volume among the fundamental movements—
based on the exercise percentages for the athlete's level.

Determine the total weekly volumes—
based on an athlete's training level and phase of training, and whether returning to training or off-season.

- *Novice athlete:*
- *Return to training: 22–28–35–15 percent of total monthly volume*
- *Off-season: 28–22–35–15 percent or 35–22–28–15 percent of total monthly volume*
- *Advanced or elite athlete:*
- *Return to training: 22–27–32–19 percent of total monthly volume*
- *Off-season: 27–22–32–19 percent or 32–22–27–19 percent of total monthly volume*

**Determine the frequency of weekly training sessions—
based on the total weekly volume and workout classifications.**

- *Generally three days per week when less than 1,000 reps for the month*
- *Four days per week is optimal when more than 1,000 reps for the month*

**Determine the total volume for each training sessions—
based on the weekly percentage and session volume percentage.**

- *Three training sessions per week: 42–24–34 percent of weekly volume*
- *Four training sessions per week: 28–22–35–15 percent or 27–22–32–19 percent of weekly volume*

**Determine the weekly volume for each fundamental movement—
based on the total weekly volume.**

- *Weeks with very high volume of a particular exercise (>60 reps) may need that exercise performed in three or four workout days.*

**Determine the exercise volume for each training session—
based on the weekly exercise volume.**

- *Higher-volume days may need more exercises than lower-volume days.*
- *Training sessions should include both strength and power movements.*
- *Strength movements are no more than 35 plus or minus three reps per movement per session.*
- *Power movements are no more than 25 plus or minus three reps per movement per session.*

**Monthly volume gradually builds over the course of the off-season—
not more than 10 percent month to month.**

**Monthly volume falls by at least one-third of the peak into the preseason
and will be reduced in-season by another third.**

**Training frequency will also be reduced to two times per week in-season
due to a significant reduction in volume.**

INTENSITY PLANNING

Determine the target Zones of Intensity
based on an athlete's level of training and the desired training effect.

- *Novice athletes*

- *Primarily Zones One and Two at 50–69 percent 1RM and into Zone Three at 70–79 percent*

- *Advanced or Elite*

- *Primarily Zones Three and Four at 70–85 percent 1RM and into Zones Five or Six at 90 percent or greater*

   > **The majority of work should fall between the 70–85 percent of 1RM range of intensity for the program as a whole.*

Determine the reps and sets based on the goal of training—
work capacity, hypertrophy, strength, power, or speed.

- *Use Prilepin's Chart on pages 40–41 to help determine the ideal reps and sets based on percent of the athlete's 1RM.*

Determine the undulation of intensity for each movement
over the course of the week and month.

- *Weekly*

- *Ideally, program each movement for two days: one a high-intensity day, and the other a lower-intensity higher-volume day.*

- *Use an undulating pattern for movements and training sessions*

- *Monthly*

- *Relative intensity should increase from week to week.*

- *Overall intensity should not exceed 50–65 percent 1RM for novice or 70-75 percent 1RM for advanced athletes during unloading in week four.*

Determine the progression of the relative intensity level of training
over the course of the off-season and into the preseason and in-season.

Relative training intensity should gradually advance leading up to the
start of competition and through the season.

EXERCISE SELECTION

Select exercises emphasizing whole-body strength and power development

- *Utilize squats, presses, cleans, pulls, snatches, jerks, and posterior chain work above all else*

- *Accessory work is intended to supplement the fundamental movements for more targeted training related to the athlete or sport*

Progress from simple to complex

Novice

- *Emphasize primarily strength movements and progress into power movements*

- *Begin with simple variations of the fundamental lifts and running/jumping drills to master technique and motor control*

Advanced/Elite

- *Can perform higher volume of power movements*

- *Will benefit from more variety of exercises, and should employ more complex variants to stimulate greater physical gains*

Develop work capacity, strength, power, and speed in that order

- *Follow the progression of the hierarchy of athletic development in selecting the primary training emphasis*

- *Applies for both weight training as well as sprinting and jumping*

Never compromise quality of movement

APPENDIX C— TABLES, GRAPHS, AND PHOTOS

TABLES AND GRAPHS

Figure 1.1 Al Vermeil's Hierarchy of Athletic Development 23

Figure 1.2 Quality Development 27

Figure 1.3 Developmental Hierarchy 28

Figure 2.1 Continuum of Recovery 35

Figure 2.2 Maximum Repetition Percentages 38

Figure 2.3 Intensity and Repetition Ranges 39

Figure 2.4 Simplified Prilepin's Chart 40

Figure 2.5 Refined Prilepin's Chart 41

Figure 2.6 Speed–Velocity Curve 44

Figure 2.7 Force–Velocity Curve 45

Figure 2.8 Adaptation to Resistance Training 46

Figure 2.9 Typical Linear Periodization Model 49

Figure 2.10 Verkhoshansky's Standard Model for the Main Adaptation Cycle Model 50

Figure 2.11 General Adaptation Syndrome 51

Figure 3.1 Javorek Complex One 66

Figure 3.2 Examples of Loading 68

Figure 3.3 Example of "Hardgainer" Preparation Plan 70

Figure 4.1 Linear Periodization Model 96

Figure 4.2 The System's Undulating Periodization Model 96

Figure 4.3 Example of Four-Week Program 97

Figure 4.4 Novice Progression 98

Figure 4.5 Squat Teaching Progression 107

Figure 4.6 Press Teaching Progression 111

Figure 4.7 Posterior Chain Teaching Progression 113

Figure 4.8 Pull Teaching Progression 117

Figure 4.9 Clean Teaching Progression 119

Figure 4.10 Snatch Teaching Progression 122

Figure 4.11 Jerk Teaching Progression 124

Figure 4.12 Progression from Simple to Complex Variations 126

Figure 4.13 Example Movement Progression 128

Figure 4.14 Example of Volume Ranges 132

Figure 4.15 Return-to-Training Break-in Cycle 134

Figure 4.16 Football Break-in Cycle 135

Figure 4.17 Weekly and Monthly Volumes 136

Figure 4.18 Novice Off-Season Cycles 136

Figure 4.19 Advanced Off-Season Cycles 137

Figure 4.20 Off-Season Monthly Cycles 138

Figure 4.21 High School Off-Season Annual Volumes 139

Figure 4.22 High School Off-Season Weekly Volumes 139

Figure 4.23 Total Monthly Volume Examples 143

Figure 4.24 Novice Cycles 144

Figure 4.25 750–1,000 Reps Monthly Volume 145

Figure 4.26 Greater than 1,000 Reps Monthly Volume 145

Figure 4.27 Three-Day Volume Example 146

Figure 4.28 Example of Weekly Volume for 750-Rep Month 146

Figure 4.29 Example of Weekly Volume for 1,000-Rep Month 147

Figure 4.30 Example of Week Three 147

Figure 4.31 Example of Within-Week Volume 148

Figure 4.32 Within-Week Volume for Four Sessions, Week Three 149

Figure 4.33 Within-Week Volume for Three Sessions, Week Three 150

Figure 4.34 Four Sessions versus Three Sessions 150

Figure 4.35 Four Sessions Week Three 153

Figure 4.36 Four-Day Training Template 153

Figure 4.37 Strength Movement Reps 155

Figure 4.38 Power and Speed Movement Reps 155

Figure 4.39 Distributing the Reps per Exercise 156

Figure 4.40 Redistributing the Reps 157

Figure 4.41 Novice-Level Three-Day Split 158

Figure 4.42 Week Three at 297 Total Repetitions 159

Figure 4.43 Week Three Session Breakdown 159

Figure 4.44 Adapted Week Three Session Breakdown 160

Figure 4.45 Exercise Selection 164

Figure 4.46 Estimating 1RM 164

Figure 4.47 Training Intensity 165

Figure 4.48 Effects of Intensity Ranges 166

Figure 4.49 Strength Movement Rep Ranges 166

Figure 4.50 Power and Speed Movement Rep Ranges 167

Figure 4.51 Novice Athlete Intensity Zones 171

Figure 4.52 Advances or Elite Athlete Intensity Zones 172

[APPENDIX C—TABLES, GRAPHS, AND PHOTOS]

Figure 4.53 Monthly Intensity per Week 175
Figure 4.54 Four Sessions per Week 178
Figure 4.55 Relative Intensity over Three Sessions 179
Figure 4.56 Intensity Zones for Cleans in Week Three 180
Figure 4.57 Sample Training Week 181
Figure 4.58 Training Year Intensity 183
Figure 4.59 Dow Jones 1950–2012 184
Figure 4.60 Example of Cycle One 185
Figure 4.61 Example of Cycle Two 185
Figure 4.62 Squat Volume over Three-Month Cycle 186
Figure 4.63 Example of Exercise Percentages 191
Figure 4.64 Prep Movement Rep Ranges 192
Figure 4.65 Sample Exercise Selections over Three Sessions, Novice 193
Figure 4.66 Sample Exercise Selections over Three Sessions, Advanced 194
Figure 5.1 Quality Development Hierarchy 197
Figure 5.2 Shifting the Hierarch y200
Figure 5.3 The Strength Continuum—Acceleration 203
Figure 5.4 Example of Jumping Progression 210
Figure 5.5 Zig-Zag Run Cone Set-up 215
Figure 5.6 Impacts of Plyometric Exercises 217
Figure 5.7 Sprinting or Jumping Training Volume Ranges 220
Figure 5.8 Volume Guidelines 222
Figure 5.9 Training Volumes per Session 223
Figure 5.10 Work Capacity Weekly Volumes for Sprinting of Jumping 224
Figure 5.11 Comparing Lifting, Running, and Jumping Volumes 225
Figure 5.12 Volumes for Sprinting or Jumping, Speed-Strength or Speed 225
Figure 5.13 Sprinting and Jumping Progression 226
Figure 5.14 Novice Athlete Training Week Example 227
Figure 5.15 Comparing the Intensity of the Sessions 228
Figure 6.1 Programming for Single Events versus Team Sports 230, 232
Figure 6.2 Undulating Preseason Volume 238
Figure 6.3 Volume Undulation over the Seasons 239
Figure 6.4 Normal Training Period 239
Figure 6.5 Shortened Training Period 240
Figure 6.6 Two Session Example 246
Figure 6.7 Three Session Example 247
Figure 6.8 Comparison of Work Performed at 80 Percent 250
Figure 6.9 Comparison of Work Performed at 80-95 Percent 250
Figure 7.1 Monthly Volume per Exercise 259

Figure 7.2 Exercise Reps per Week 260

Figure 7.3 Session Volume per Week 260

Figure 7.4 Predicted Exercise Volume 261

Figure 7.5 Modified Distribution Template 263

Figure 7.6 First Week Sessions 264

Figure 7.7 Novice Athlete First Cycle Sample 265

Figure 7.8 Novice Athlete Intensity Zones, Week One 266

Figure 7.9 Novice Athlete Intensity Zones, Week Two 267

Figure 7.10 Novice Athlete Intensity Zones, Week Three 267

Figure 7.11 Novice Athlete Intensity Zones, Week Four 268

Figure 7.12 Session Examples Based on Volumes 268

Figure 7.13 Day One Example 269

Figure 7.14 Day Two Example 270

Figure 7.15 Day Three Example 270

Figure 7.15 Relative Intensity of Cleans 271

Figure 7.16 Percent of Total Volume per Cycle 273

Figure 7.17 Percent of Total Volume per Movement 274

Figure 7.18 Predicted Volume per Week 275

Figure 7.19 Weekly Volume Breakdown 275

Figure 7.20 Training Session Volumes 276

Figure 7.21 Modified Session Volume Distribution 277

Figure 7.22 Session Breakdown 278

Figure 7.23 Training Intensity for Advanced Athletes 279

Figure 7.24 Training Intensity of Cleans, Novice versus Advanced 279

Figure 7.24 Weekly Session Breakdown(V) Volume Day; (I) Intensity Day 280

Figure 7.25 Day One 281

Figure 7.26 Day Two 281

Figure 7.27 Day Three 282

Figure 7.28 Day Four 282

Figure 7.29 Zones of Intensity 282

Figure 8.1 Novice Strength Cycle Volumes 286

Figure 8.2 Novice Cycle One Strength Breakdown 287

Figure 8.3 Novice Power Cycle Volumes 297

Figure 8.4 Novice Cycle Two Power Breakdown 298

Figure 8.5 Advanced Strength Cycle Volumes 308

Figure 8.6 Advanced Cycle One Strength Breakdown 309

Figure 8.7 Advanced Power Cycle Volumes 315

Figure 8.8 Advanced Cycle Two Power Breakdown 319

Figure 8.9 Advanced Four-Day Exercise Volumes 322

Figure 8.10 Advanced Four-Day Rep Breakdown 323

PHOTOS

Photo 3.1 Overhead Squat 63

Photo 3.2 Single-Leg Squat, Top 64

Photo 3.3 Single-Leg Squat, Bottom 65

Photo 3.4 A-Skip 73

Photos 3.5 a–b A-Run 74

Photo 3.6 Butt Kicks 75

Photos 3.7 a–b Wall March 76

Photos 3.8 a–d Standing Long Jump 79

Photos 3.9 a–d Hops 80

Photos 3.10 a–c Goalpost Touch 81

Photos 3.11 a–b Box Jump and Landing 83

Photos 3.12 a–b Hurry Go Get Em 84

Photo 4.1 Using Olympic Lifts 102

Photo 4.2 The Back Squat 104

Photo 4.3 The Front Squat 105

Photos 4.4 a–d The Split Squat 106

Photos 4.5 a–f The Overhead Press 108

Photos 4.6 a–d The Push Press 109

Photos 4.7 a–b The Romanian Deadlift 112

Photo 4.8 The Trap Bar Deadlift 112

Photos 4.9 a–c The Glue-Ham Hyperextension 113

Photos 4.10 a–c The Clean Pull 114

Photos 4.11 a–c The Snatch Pull 115

Photos 4.12 a–d Pull Start Positions 116

Photos 4.13 a–d The Clean 118

Photos 4.14 a–d The Power Snatch 121

Photos 4.15 a–g The Jerk 123

Photos 5.1 a–d Sprint Starting Positions 207

Photos 5.2 a–c Depth Jumps 211

Photos 5.3 a–d Lateral Box Jumps 213

Photos 9.1 a–b Falling 20s 341

REFERENCES

1 http://www.verkhoshansky.com/CVBibliography/tabid/71/Default.aspx

2 http://www.dynamicfitnessequipment.com/category-s/1823.htm

3 http://www.strengthpowerspeed.com/store/al-vermeil-comprehensive-strength-coach-series/

4 Roos KG, Marshall SW, Kerr ZY, et al. Epidemiology of Overuse Injuries in Collegiate and High School Athletics in the United States. *Am J Sports Med.* 2015 Jul. 43 (7):1790-7.

5 Schroeder AN, Comstock RD, Collins CL, Everhart J, Flanigan D, Best TM. Epidemiology of overuse injuries among high-school athletes in the United States. *J Pediatr.* 2015 Mar. 166 (3):600-6.

6 Laurent, CM, et al., "Sex-specific responses to self-paced, high-intensity interval training with variable recovery periods," *Journal of Strength and Conditioning Research,* 2014, 28(4), 920-927.

7 Ratamess NA, Alvar BA, Evetoch TK, Housh TJ, Kibler WB, Kraemer WJ, et al. American college of sports medicine position stand. Progression models in resistance training for healthy adults. *Med. Sci. Sports Exerc.* 2009;41:687.

8 Bompa, Tudor O. *Periodization Training for Sports.* Champaign, IL: Human Kinetics; 1999.

9 Rodrigues Pereira, MI, Chagas Gomes, PS. Muscular strength and endurance tests: reliability and prediction of one repetition maximum—review and new evidences. *Rev Bras Med Esporte.* 2003, 9(5), 336-346.

10 Mayhew, JL, Johnson, BD, LaMonte, MJ, Lauber, D, and Kemmler, W. Accuracy of prediction equations for determining one repetition maximum bench press in women before and after resistance training. *J Strength Cond Res* 2008, 22(5), 1570–1577.

11 Cormie P, McGuigan MR, Newton RU. Developing maximal neuromuscular power: part 2 - training considerations for improving maximal power production. *Sports Med.* 2011;41(2):125-146.

12 Newton RU, Kraemer WJ. Developing explosive muscular power: implications for a mixed methods training strategy. *Strength Conditioning Journal* . 1994; 16: 20-31.

13 Medvedyev, AS., 1986. A System of Multi-Year Training in Weightlifting: Sistema Mnogoletnyei Trenirovki V Tyazheloi Atletikye. Sportivny Press.

14 Prilepin, A.S., Scientific–Practical Contribution to the Intensification of the Modern Training of Weightlifters, Petr Poletayev, Sportivny Press, Andrew Charniga, Jr. translation, http://www.sportivnypress.com/documents/75.html accessed 2/16/2018.

15 Oliver, JM, Jagim, AR, Sanchez, AC, Mardock, MA, Kelly, KA, Meredith, HJ, Smith, GL, Greenwood, M, Parker, JL, Riechman, SE, Fluckey, JD, Crouse, SF, and Kreider, RB. Greater gains in strength and power with intraset rest intervals in hypertrophic training. *J Strength Cond Res* 27(11): 3116–3131, 2013

16 Zatsiorsky V, Kraemer J., *Science and Practice of Strength Training.* Champaign, Illinois: Human Kinetics; 2006.

16 Schoenfeld, BJ. The mechanisms of muscle hypertrophy and their application to resistance training. *J Strength Cond Res.* 2010;24(10): 2857–2872.

17 Campos GE, Luecke TJ, Wendeln HK, et al. Muscular adaptations in response to three different resistance-training regimens: specificity of repetition maximum training zones. *Eur J Appl Physiol.* 2002;88:50–60.

18 Pryor, RR, Sforzo, GA, and King, DL. Optimizing power output by varying repetition tempo. *J Strength Cond Res.* 2011, 25(11), 3029–3034.

19 McLester, JR, Jr, Bishop, P, Smith, J, Wyers, L, Dale, B, Kozusko, J, Richardson, M, Nevett, M, and Lomax, R. A Series of Studies-A Practical Protocol for Testing Muscular Endurance Recovery. *J Strength Cond Res.* 17: 259-273, 2003.

20 Zatsiorsky V, Kraemer J., *Science and Practice of Strength Training.* Champaign, Illinois: Human Kinetics; 2006.

21 Stone, MH. Literature review: Explosive exercises and training. *National Strength and Conditioning Assoc Journal* 15(3), 7-15, 1993.

22 Thomas, Michael H., and Steve P Burns, "Increasing Lean Mass and Strength: A Comparison of High Frequency Strength Training to Lower Frequency Strength Training." *International Journal of Exercise Science* 9.2 (2016): 159–167. Print.

23 Verkhoshansky, Y., *Special Strength Training: Manual for Coaches.* Verkhoshansky SSTM, 2011

24 http://www.verkhoshansky.com/Articles/EnglishArticles/tabid/92/Default.aspx

25 Verkhoshansky, Yuir. *Organization of the Training Process.* Translated from Italian

26 http://www.verkhoshansky.com/Portals/0/Articles/English/Organization%20Training%20Process.pdf, accessed 1/25/2018.

27 Selye, H. The general adaptation syndrome and the disease of adaptation. *Journal of Clinical Endocrinology,* 6, 117–231, 1945.

28 Rhea, MR, et al., "A Comparison of Linear and Daily Undulating Periodized Programs With Equated Volume And Intensity For Strength," *Journal of Strength and Conditioning Research,* 2002, 16(2), 250–255.

29 Gray Cook, *Movement: Functional Movement Systems,* pp 90–91, 191–201, 2010, On Target Publications, Aptos, CA

30 http://www.istvanjavorek.com/page2.html

31 Ortega, DR, et al. Analysis of the vertical ground reaction forces and temporal factors in the landing phase of a countermovement jump. *Journal of Sports Science and Medicine* (2010) 9, 282–287.

32 Todd T. Karl klein and the squat. Historical Opinion. *NSCA Journal.* June-July 1984: 26-67.

33 Bryanton MA, Kennedy MD, Carey JP, and Chiu LZF, "Effect of Squat Depth and Barbell Load on Relative Muscular Effort in Squatting," *Journal of Strength and Conditioning Research* 26(10): 2820-2828, 2012

34 Ciccone T, Davis K, Bagley J, Galpin A. Deep Squats and Knee Health: A Scientific Review. http://daily.barbellshrugged.com/wp-content/uploads/2015/04/DeepSquat-Review-Barbell-Daily-3-27-15.pdf. Accessed 03/20/2018.

35 Swinton, PA, Stewart, A, Agouris, I, Keogh, JWL, and Lloyd, R. A biomechanical analysis of straight and hexagonal barbell deadlifts using submaximal loads. *J Strength Cond Res* 25(7): 2000-2009, 2011.

36 Comfort, P., Allen, M., and P. Graham-Smith. (2011). Comparisons of peak ground reaction force and rate of force development during variations of the power clean. *Journal of Strength and Conditioning Research,* 25(5), 1235-1239.

37 Opar DA, Williams MD, Timmins RG, Hickey J, Duhig SJ, Shield AJ. Eccentric hamstring strength and hamstring injury risk in Australian footballers. *Med Sci Sports Exerc.* 2015 Apr;47(4):857-65.

38 Comfort, P., Allen, M., and P. Graham-Smith. (2011). Comparisons of peak ground reaction force and rate of force development during variations of the power clean. *Journal of Strength and Conditioning Research,* 25(5), 1235-1239.

39 https://www.strengthsensei.com/charles-r-poliquin/

40 Peterson, M.D., B.A. Alvar, and M.R. Rhea. The contribution of maximal force production to explosive movement among young collegiate athletes. *J. Strength Cond. Res.* 20(4): 867-873. 2006.

41 Palmer, T., Uhl, T. L., Howell, D., Hewett, T. E., Viele, K., & Mattacola, C. G. (2015). Sport-Specific Training Targeting the Proximal Segments and Throwing Velocity in Collegiate Throwing Athletes. *Journal of Athletic Training,* 50(6), 567–577.

42 Hoffman JR, Ratamess NA, Klatt M, Faigenbaum AD, Ross RE, Tranchina NM, McCurley RC, Kang J, Kraemer WJ. Comparison between different off-season resistance training programs in Division III American college football players. *J Strength Cond Res.* 2009 Jan;23(1):11-9.

43 Harries SK, Lubans DR, Callister R. Systematic review and meta-analysis of linear and undulating periodized resistance training programs on muscular strength. *J Strength Cond Res.* 2015 Apr;29(4):1113-25.

44 Colquhoun RJ, Gai CM, Aguilar D, Bove D, Dolan J, Vargas A, Couvillion K, Jenkins NDM, Campbell BI. Training Volume, Not Frequency, Indicative of Maximal Strength Adaptations to Resistance Training. *J Strength Cond Res.* 2018 Jan 5. doi: 10.1519/JSC.0000000000002414. [Epub ahead of print] PubMed PMID: 29324578.

45 Grgic J, Schoenfeld BJ, Davies TB, Lazinica B, Krieger JW, Pedisic Z. Effect of Resistance Training Frequency on Gains in Muscular Strength: A Systematic Review and Meta-Analysis. *Sports Med.* 2018 May;48(5):1207-1220. doi:10.1007/s40279-018-0872-x. Review. PubMed PMID: 29470825.

46 Gomes GK, Franco CM, Nunes PRP, Orsatti FL. High-frequency resistance training is not more effective than low-frequency resistance training in increasing muscle mass and strength in well-trained men. *J Strength Cond Res.* 2018 Feb 27. doi:10.1519/JSC.0000000000002559. [Epub ahead of print] PubMed PMID: 29489727.

[REFERENCES]

47 Jones, EJ, Bishop, P, Richardson, M, and Smith, J. Stability of a practical measure of recovery from resistance training. *J Strength Cond Res* 10: 756-759, 2006.

48 McLester, JR, Jr, Bishop, P, Smith, J, Wyers, L, Dale, B, Kozusko, J, Richardson, M, Nevett, M, and Lomax, R. A Series of Studies-A Practical Protocol for Testing Muscular Endurance Recovery. *J Strength Cond Res* 17: 259-273, 2003.

49 https://www.strongerbyscience.com/hypertrophy-range-fact-fiction/

50 https://www.strongerbyscience.com/hypertrophy-range-stats-adjustments/

51 A. S. Medvedyev, A System of Mult-Year Training in Weightlifting, trans. Andrew Jr. Charniga (Livonia, MI: Sportivny Press, 1989)

52 McCurdy, K, Langford, GA, Cline, AL, Doscher, M, and Hoff, R. The Reliability of 1- And 3rm Tests of Unilateral Strength in Trained and Untrained Men and Women. *Journal of Sports Science and Medicine* 2004, 3, 190-196.

53 Vingren, Jakob L., et al. "Testosterone Physiology in Resistance Exercise and Training." *Sports Medicine* 40.12 (2010): 1037-53. ProQuest. Web. 17 Apr. 2018.

54 https://www.charliefrancis.com/collections/ebooks

55 Jandačka, D., & Beremlijski, P. (2011). Determination of strength exercise intensities based on the load-power-velocity relationship. *Journal of Human Kinetics,* 28(1), 33-44.

56 Jidovtseff, B., Quièvre, J., Hanon, C., & Crielaard, J. M. (2009). Inertial muscular profiles allow a more accurate training loads definition. Les profils musculaires inertiels permettent une définition plus précise des charges d'entraînement, 24(2), 91-96.

57 https://www.charliefrancis.com/blogs/news/test

58 McBride, JM, Blow, D, Kirby, TJ, Haines, TL, Dayne AM, and Triplett, NT. Relationship between maximal squat strength and five, ten, and forty yard sprint times. *J Strength Cond Res* 23(6): 1633–1636, 2009

59 Paradisis, G.P., and C.B. Cooke. The effects of sprint running training on sloping surfaces. *Journal of Strength and Conditioning Research.* 20(4):767-777. 2006.

60 Chu, Donald A., and Gregory D. Myer. *Plyometrics: Dynamic Strength and Explosive Power.* U.S.A, Human Kinetics, 2013.

61 Athletic Performance Summit: The Legends. Professional Seminars. New York, 2017

62 *Plyometics, Dynamic Strengh and Explosive Power,* Donald A. Chu and Gregory D. Myer, Human Kinetics, 2013

63 Athletic Performance Summit: The Legends. Professional Seminars. New York, 2017

64 Menzies P, Menzies C, McIntyre L, Paterson P, Wilson J, Kemi OJ. Blood lactate clearance during active recovery after an intense running bout depends on the intensity of the active recovery. *J Sports Sci.* 2010 Jul;28(9):975-82.

65 McMaster, D.T., Gill, N., Cronin, J. et al. *Sports Med* (2013) 43: 367.

66 Hartmann H, Wirth K, Keiner M, Mickel C, Sander A, Szilvas E. Short-term Periodization Models: Effects on Strength and Speed-strength Performance. *Sports Med.* 2015, 45(10), 1373-1386.

INDEX

A

absolute speed
    maximal sprinting and jumping 205

absolute strength
    as it relates to starting strength 200

accessory work
    discussion of 129

adaptation
    to resistance training 45

advanced athlete
    football program, off-season 307
    football program, preseason 321
    football program, power emphasis 315–319
    football program, strength emphasis 307
    intensity zones 172
    monthly volume example 143
    off-season cycles 137–138
    profile of 352
    sample exercise selections 194
    sample program, off season 274

agility drills
    four corners drill 214
    lateral shuffle description 215
    zig-zag run diagram 215

A-run
    drill, description of 73

A-skip
    drill, description of 72

assessments
    1RM, estimating max lifts 163–164
    mobility and flexibility 61
    of athletes 59
    of squat pattern 61
    overhead squat 62

athlete
    biological age vs training age 37
    education of 22
    evaluation of 58
    injury progression 35
    medical history of 37
    sport skill vs training readiness 59
    training history of 37

athletic development, qualities of 26

B

back squat
    see also, squat
    discussion of 104
    progressions of 107

benchmarks
    following prep phase 94

bench press
    discussion of 109
    progressions of 111

block periodization
    description of 49

body control
    overhead squat, benefit of 63

Bompa, Tudor
    strength chart of 38

bounding
    jump drill description 213

box jumps
    drill, description of 82
    jump training progression 210
    key benefit of 82

break-in cycle
    for football 135
    novice or after layoff 133

build-ups
    sprint drill, description of 207

butt kick
    drill, description of 75

C

catch position
    progressions of 119

Charniga, Bud
    training manual translation 21

Chu, Don
    dedication 9
    impacts of plyometric exercise 216–217
    jump drills and return to play 213
    jump training limits 221

clean pull
- description of 114
- teaching progression 117

cleans
- catch position progression 119
- description of 118
- intensity, novice vs advanced 279
- programming example, intensity 180
- progressions of 119
- relative intensity, novice off-season 271

CNS stimulus
- lower volume for 158

complexes
- as a warmup or conditioning tool 70
- chart of exercises and reps 66
- Javorek Complex, description of 65
- long-term use for beginners 69
- purposes of 67

conditioning
- in-season considerations 252

continuum of recovery
- explanation of 35

Cook, Gray
- overhead squat assessment 62

corrective exercise
- consideration of 34

cycle examples
- off-season monthly 138
- weekly and monthly volume 146

D

deadlift
- use of Romainian style 112

depth jumps
- description of 211

dynamic effort
- description of 43
- fatigue and bar speed 43

E

elastic/reactive strength
- definition of 25
- jump training drills 78

elite athlete
- intensity zones 172
- monthly volume example 143
- profile of 353
- program design discussion 284

Emrich, Clyde
- as mentor 20

exercise intensity
- principles of 168

exercise repetitions
- minimal effective dose 152

exercise selection
- critical lifts for carryover to performance 140
- of local effect 130
- order of priority 100
- overview of 99
- principles 125
- programming, designing of 358
- progressions 125, 128
- relative importance in carryover to sport 100
- squat variations 103
- top choices 34
- exercise variation, considerations 127

explosive strength
- definition of 25

Eye of the Coach
- coaching overhead movements 110
- coaching the goblet squat 107
- cues for teaching pulls 116
- dead stops and jump drills 83
- developing speed with plyometrics 214
- exercise and rep distribution 161
- explanation of 30
- facilitating recovery 161
- finishing resisted running with sprints 205
- four corners drill challenge 215
- Hurry Go Get Em modification 85
- intensity-to-rep relationship 180
- limitations in a movement or transitions 67
- mastering movements 127
- over-reaching for a training effect 174
- overtraining: listen and observe 248
- positions of the clean 120

Eye of the Coach, *continued*
    programming agility work 216
    programming jumps, running, and lifting 228
    redistributing percentages if needed 145
    sprint training, moving backward 208
    standing triple long jump commentary 339
    sustaining gains over a season 253
    sweet spot of reps 236
    training arm motion in running 202
    using high-performance days 173
    volume of running and jumping 223
    what overtraining looks like to a coach 151
    what to look for in the wall march 76
    work capacity and body structure 167
    work capacity and speed 219

F

falling 20s
    sprint drill 341

female athlete training volume 37

football
    in-season training program 332
    off-season training program 285–319
    preseason training program 321
    program for novice 285
    program, strength emphasis 285
    variety of positions, training of 198

foot strike
    during running, coaching of 201

force
    absorbing, using the clean for 119

force-velocity curve
    description of 45

four corners drill
    agility drill, description of 214

Francis, Charlie
    speed training 198
    tempo run drill 201

frequency of training
    see training frequency

front squat
    discussion of 105
    progressions of 107

fundamental lifts
    see also, exercise selection
    top choices of 34

G

General Adaptation Syndrome
    description of 51

glute-ham
    progression of 113

goalpost touches
    drill, description of 81

goblet squat
    discussion of 107

Goldstein, Gregori
    dedication to 9
    eye of the coach 30
    mentor, The System 21
    movements and carryover to sports 100
    speed vs strength 176
    time necessary to create a training program 257

good morning exercise
    progression of 113

grip training
    sustained holds 130

H

hamstrings
    dedicated hamstring work 251
    see also, posterior chain

Hierarchy of Athletic Development
    see Vermeil, Al

high-intensity training
    recovery demands of 96

high pulls
    teaching progressions 117

high school athlete
    off-season volume chart 139
    weekly volumes 139

hopping
    single leg, double leg progression 81

hormonal release
    factors in training 188

hurry go get em
    drill, description of 84

hyperextension
    progression of 113

I

incline press
    progressions of 111

injury
    risks during in-season training 243
    stages of healing 35

ins and outs
    sprint drill, description of 206

in-season
    see also, program design
    conditioning considerations 252
    length of a training session 245
    program design principles 242
    vs off-season hamstring work 251
    weekly volume 244

intensity
    definition of 37
    effects of intensity ranges 166
    exercise intensity in an undulating range 161
    increasing vs decreasing volume 41
    narrow range, Soviet success 45
    over a training year, chart 183
    Prilepin's chart 40
    programming, planning of 357
    relative intensity 169, 175
    rep ranges of 38
    training, advance athlete, off-season 279

intensity zones 168–169

J

Javorek, Istvan
    complex, description of 65
    use as a warmup 192
    see also, complexes

jerk, exercise
    catch position progression 124
    description of 122
    not appropriate for novice lifters 124, 142
    progression of 124

John, Dan
    goblet squat 107

jump training
    as a technical skill 70
    bounding and hurdles 210, 213
    depth jumps description 211
    for heavier athletes 209
    for strength-speed and speed-strength 204

jump training, *continued*
    integrating into a training program 217
    jumps, standing, advanced, depth 210
    lateral box jumps 212
    monthly volume of, limitations 219, 221
    planes of motion 208
    planning the peak 226
    principles of 197
    program design 226
    progression of 78, 210, 226
    to emphasize speed 208
    vertical to linear 204
    work capacity weekly volumes 224

jump training drills 78
    box jumps 82
    goalpost touches 81
    hopping, single and two legs 81
    lateral box jumps 212
    rockets 82
    standing long jump 79

K

knee, the
    impact forces and jumping 78

Knoll, Chuck
    categorization of athletes 104
    coaching linemen 63

L

lateral shuffles
    agility drill description 215

linear periodization
    peaking during 183
    single event sports vs team sports 48
    standard, traditional model 29, 48

loading
    examples based on size 68
    progressions based on training age 68

M

mach running drills
    overview of 72

Main Adaptation Cycle Model
    Yuri Verkhoshansky periodization model 50

Matveyev, Leonid
    plyometric training 20

max effort
: description of 42

maximum repetition percentages
: description of 38

medical history
: consideration of 37

Medvedyev, A.S.
: narrow range of intensity 161
: training intensity analysis 39

Miller, Al
: closing thoughts 347
: Dan Reeves foreword 14
: dedication 9
: sample Friday workouts 247
: sample in-season program 335
: training with Coach Goldstein 21

minimum effective dose
: frequency, intensity, and volume 189

mobility
: restrictions in overhead squat 62
: *see also, assessments*

movement prep
: rep ranges 192

movement progression, example of 128

movement screen
: *see assessments*

muscular stimulus
: higher volume for 158

N

neck work
: rep ranges, planes of motion 130

nervous system
: elastic and reactive ability 71

nervous system output
: in sprinting and jumping 71

novice athlete
: example of cycles 144
: football program, off-season 285
: football program, power emphasis 297
: football program, strength emphasis 285
: intensity zones 171
: monthly volume example 143
: off-season cycles 136–138
: profile of 351

novice athlete, *continued*
: program example for football 259
: progression of training qualities 98
: sample week exercise selection 193
: session intensity comparison 228
: technical proficiency in a max lift 163
: three-day split, monthly and weekly 158
: training week including sprints and jumps 227

O

off-season
: monthly cycle example 138
: program design principles 233
: progressions, expectations of 236
: shortening of 239
: training progression during 137

Olympic lifts
: controversy in sports training 101–102

one-rep max
: range of intensity 36
: vs three-rep max 163

overhead press
: discussion of 108
: progressions of 111

overhead squat
: as assessment 62
: benchmarks of 62
: body control benefits 63

overtraining
: exercise volume principles 140
: volume and intensity levels 39

P

Panariello, Rob
: closing thoughts 347
: dedication 7

parachute training
: to improve foot speed 207

Parcells, Bill
: quote from 21

Pareto's Principle
: as it applies to exercise programming 34

Parker, Johnny
    closing thoughts 347
    Dan Reeves foreword 14
    dedication 11
    in-season programs 244
    strength of New York Giants players 188, 243

percentages
    determination of 163

periodization
    block model 29, 49
    critical errors 95
    linear model 29
    linear, novice vs advanced athletes 48
    linear, single event sports vs team sports 48
    preseason undulating volume chart 238
    primary and secondary training effects 29
    problems with linear or block models 95
    undulating model 51
    Yuri Verkhoshansky definition of 47

photos
    full listing of 363

physical potential
    progress of 60

Pittsburgh Steelers
    overhead squats and 63

plateau
    in training 131

plyometrics
    building a base for 209
    development of 20
    for heavier athletes 209
    impacts of 216
    lateral box jumps 212
    placement in a training program 70
    planning recovery after 214

Poliquin, Charles
    on exercise variation 127

posterior chain
    examples of 99
    overview of 111
    teaching progressions of 113

power
    definition of 25
    development of 102
    development, rep ranges for 38, 167
    development, volume vs speed 41
    output of during the snatch and clean 103
    output to velocity 44

power and speed movements
    rep chart for clean, snatch, jerk, pulls 155

power exercise volume
    principles of 152

power movements
    examples of 99
    pulls, clean pull, snatch pull overview 114

power snatch
    description of 121

prep phase
    base of strength, mobility, work capacity 60
    duration of 61
    focus of 60
    hardgainer 69
    introduction to 59
    purpose of 67
    running during 72
    sample four-week program 87
    successive cycles of 69
    timeframe of 68

preseason
    training cycle principles 237
    undulating volume chart 238

press
    examples of 99
    overhead, bench, incline, push press 108
    teaching progression of 111

Prilepin, A.S.
    intensity and volume 165
    Prilepin's chart, variations of 39–42
    principles, weightlifters vs sport players 42

program design
    adjusting during seasonal transitions 241
    advanced athlete, football, off-season 307–319
    advanced athlete, off-season 274–275
    advanced, sample week 194
    based on a sport season 229
    distribution of Zones of Intensity 177
    distributing and redistributing the reps 156
    elite athletes, discussion of 284
    example, three sessions per week 179
    exercise selection 358
    exercise volumes, principles of 154
    football, advanced, preseason 321–334
    football, in-season 332–337
    football, power emphasis 297
    football programming, off-season 285–319
    football, strength emphasis 285
    general progression of qualities 231
    goals, defining of 27, 48

program design, *continued*
    in-season training cycle principles 242
    in-season weekly volume 244
    intensity planning 357
    novice, off-season example 259–269
    novice, off-season, exercise reps per week 260
    novice, off-season, session volume per week 260
    novice, sample week 193
    off-season, integrating sprint and jumps 340–343
    off-season, preseason, in-season 231
    off-season training cycle 233
    percentage-based training 187
    predicted exercise volume, novice off-season 261
    preseason principles 237
    primary vs secondary emphasis chart 232
    principles of 177
    progression of in-season programs 248
    putting together a program 257
    relative intensity over three sessions 179
    sample four sessions per week 178
    sample three sessions per week 247
    sample training week 181
    sample two sessions per week 246
    single events vs team sports, Al Vermeil 230
    sprint and jump training sessions 226
    training template, four days 153
    undulation over the training week 177, 184
    unload, planned 177, 182
    volume 355

program examples
    see program design

progression
    advanced, off-season 283
    at the end of a cycle 272
    during off-season training 137
    of intensity and volume 95
    over periodization models 183
    planning intensity 183
    simple to complex 125
    sprinting and jumping 226
    training intensity in-season 240, 248

progressive overload
    goal of The System 97

pulls
    clean pull, snatch pull overview 114
    examples of 99
    starting positions of 115
    teaching progressions 117

pure sprinting
    sprint drills 207

push press
    discussion of 109

pyramid of development,
Al Vermeil, model of 23
    see also, Vermeil, Al

R

reactive strength
    training, taxing on the CNS 198

recovery
    what to look for in athletes 151

Reeves, Dan
    foreword 14

rehab exercises
    who prescribes 35

relative intensity
    determining training intensity 169
    of cleans, a chart 271

repetition method
    description of 43

rep schemes
    when to start counting reps 174

resisted running
    sprint drill discussion 203

reverse hyperextension
    progression of 113

Riecke, Louis
    as mentor 20

rockets
    drill, description of 82

Romanian deadlift (RDL)
    discussion of 112
    progression of 113

Roy, Alvin
    as mentor 20
    Dan Reeves foreword 13

running
    mechanics of 201
    sprinting as a technical skill 70
    weekly volume guidelines 223
    see also, running drills … speed … sprint training

running drills
    A-run 73
    A-skip 72
    butt kick 75
    tempo runs 76
    the hard way 201
    wall march 75
    warmups 72

S

sample four-week prep phase program option 87

sample training cycles 146

Seagrave, Loren
    speed training 198

set-and-rep schemes
    charts 155

single-leg squat
    as corrective exercise 64
    assessment of 64
    description of 64
    long-limbed or larger athletes 65
    progressions of 107

single-leg work
    drawbacks of 105

sled work
    resisted running sprint drills 204

snatch
    description of 120
    progressions of 122
    risk of 120

snatch pull
    description of 115
    teaching progressions 117

special physical preparation (SPP)
    Yuri Verkhoshansky, work capacity 50

Specific Adaptation to Imposed Demands (SAID)
    shifting curve of qualities 45

speed training
    acceleration 199
    adjusting the programming for rest 205
    building a base of work capacity 201
    definition of 26
    exercise volume, principles of 152
    foot strike, coaching of 201
    hierarchy, progression of 199

speed, *continued*
    improve the first 10 yards 200
    movement rep ranges 167
    teaching improvement 200
    top of the pyramid 205
    training to be fast 103
    using jumps for 208
    using the drills 200
    weekly volume comparison, Al Vermeil 225
    see also, sprint drills

speed-strength
    definition of 25
    description of 200
    jump training for 204
    training, taxing on the CNS 198
    weekly volumes for 225

speed-velocity curve
    description of 44

split squat
    discussion of 106

sport-specific training
    description of 33
    discussion of 129

sprint drills
    build-ups 207
    falling 20s 341
    hills and stairs 204
    hurry go get em 84
    ins and outs 206
    loaded vs unloaded 203
    overview of 83
    parachute training 207
    pure sprinting 207
    resisted running 203
    sled work 204
    sprints after strength-speed work 219
    starting positions 207
    20-yard dash 85
    see also, sprint training

sprint training
    integrating into a training program 217
    monthly volume of 219
    planning the peak 226
    princples of 197
    program design 226
    programming of 206
    progressions 226
    structuring the training days 218
    vs conditioning 206
    work capacity weekly volumes 224
    see also, sprint drills ... speed training ... running

squat
- assessing the pattern of 61
- back squat discussion 104
- comparison of work in foot-pounds 250
- examples of 99
- front squat discussion 105
- goblet squat discussion 107
- overhead assessment 62
- programming of 176
- progressions of variations 107
- pushing loads, is it worth it? 176
- single-leg, description of 64
- split squat, discussion of 106
- squat strength improves speed 203
- variations of 103
- volume over three months 186

stair running
- sprint drills 204

standing long jump (SLJ)
- distance goals for 79
- drill, description of 79

strength
- definition of 25
- hypertrophy vs strength, intensity ranges 38
- purpose of 33
- rep chart for squat, press, posterior chain 155
- reps per exercise 166
- strength continuum, acceleration 203
- strength exercise volume, principles of 152

strength-speed
- definition of 25
- description of 200
- jump training for 204
- sprints after to re-establish good mechanics 219

stretch-shortening cycle (SSC)
- and power 71
- description of 71

super-compensation
- adaptation model 51

System, The
- core principles 57
- key points in closing 346
- origin of 19
- progressions of the program 135

T

Tabachnik, Ben
- speed training 198

tables and graphics
- full listing of 359

tempo runs
- breakdown of expected 100-yard times 77
- coaching of 77
- description of 42
- drill, descrption of 76
- example 8-cycle 78
- Soviet models 42
- when to program with weight training 218

The Hard Way
- conditioning drill 201

training
- core principles 57
- determining goals first 27
- frequency of 46
- history consideration of 37
- injury prevention, performance vs max lifts 162
- intensity vs volume 165
- loads, selection of 171
- tempo 42
- variables , overview of 95
- volume, description of 36

training age
- biological vs training age 37
- providing a baseline 24

training cycle
- example of exercise percentages 191
- overview of principles 95
- volume considerations 37

training effect
- maximizing, minimizing risk of overtraining 188

training frequency
- affect on recovery 151
- based on monthly volume 187
- based on training goals 46
- frequency dictates volume 187
- schedule determined by sport season 46
- training age vs frequency 46

training session
- address all qualities 190
- designing of 189, 191
- factor in time of season 190
- *see also, program design*

trap bar deadlift
    example of 112
    progression of 113

U

undulating periodization
    adjusting to sport seasons 97
    allocating training time based on training age 97
    chart and use of in The System 95–96
    description of 51
    developing single quality 53
    four-week program example chart 97
    preseason volume 238
    training age 52
    variability 52

undulating progression
    graph of cycles 52
    sport seasons and 52
    volume, intensity, skill 52

unload, the
    discussion of 182

V

variation
    of exercises, overview 127

Verkhoshansky, Yuri
    block periodization model 49
    defining periodization 47
    Main Adaptation Cycle Model 50
    plyometric training 20
    undulating periodization 51

Vermeil, Al
    athletic quality development 27
    base of the pyramid 85
    building a foundation 50
    Chicago Bulls, coach of 23
    components of performance 48
    dedication 7, 9
    developing athletes 253
    Hierarchy of Athletic Development 23
    programming single events vs team sports 230
    running and jumping volume guidelines 222
    sequential order of training qualities 257
    shifting volumes per quality 221
    sprinting or jumping volume ranges 220
    top of the pyramid 197
    training on game day 248
    training volumes per session 223
    work capacity volumes for sprinting or jumping 224–225

volume
    advanced athlete, off-season 275
    affect on recovery 151
    comparing lifting, running, jumping volumes 225
    critical training variable 131
    definition of 36
    difference in density, three days vs four 151
    distributions of movements, monthly 140
    example based on training age 132
    exercise volume principles 140
    for power and speed 152
    for strength 152
    guidelines per week, Al Vermeil 222
    increasing intensity vs decreasing volume 41
    in-season programming 244
    lower vs higher, stimulus of 158
    minimal effective dose 152
    mistakes in percentage distribution 141
    monthly exercise distributions, percentages 141
    monthly total, examples per training age 143
    normal training over the seasons 239
    novice, advanced or elite monthly reps 145
    of sprint and jump training 219
    over monthly cycles 132
    place in training cycle 37
    Prilepin's chart, optimal reps 40
    programming, planning of 355
    reduced over longer season 240
    rep ranges in cycles 132
    rules for planning cycles 138
    running and jumping training guidelines 223
    strength, power, speed rep charts 154
    three-day weekly example 146
    undulation over seasons 239
    weekly and monthly charts 136
    weekly breakdown, weight training 144
    within-week volume 149

W

wall march
    drill, description of 75

warmup
    for prep phase workouts 87
    for running 72
    when to start counting reps 174

work capacity
    developing with complexes 70
    for speed 201
    special physical preparation (SPP) 50
    the foundational component 24
    volumes for sprint and jump training 224

workout classifications
    great, big, moderate and light 148

work-to-rest ratio
    optimal for Complexes 67

Z

zig-zag run
    cone setup diagram 215

zone of intensity
    determining the weights 173

Zones of Intensity
    overview 168
    using the Zones 169

JOHNNY PARKER

At the forefront of modern strength coaching for athletes, Johnny Parker began his coaching career in 1969 at Indianola Academy in Mississippi. Well before weight training was common in sports, he spent 10 years coaching at the collegiate level, where at Indiana University he became the first strength and conditioning coach in the Big 10.

From 1984 until his retirement in 2008, he spent 21 years as an NFL strength coach, beginning with nine years in the New York Giants organization. Under Coach Bill Parcells, he helped them win Super Bowls in 1986 and 1990. Playing against the Buffalo Bills in Super Bowl XXV, the Giants set an all-time Super Bowl record for ball-control possession at 40 minutes and 33 seconds. Parker's role as a strength and conditioning coach certainly contributed to the Giants' tradition of excellence.

He then went on to spend seven seasons with the New England Patriots, followed by helping the Tampa Bay Buccaneers win the first Super Bowl in team history in 2003. In 2005, Johnny went to the San Francisco 49ers before retiring in 2008. All told, his coaching practices, many of which are outlined in this book, helped to establish winning records with nine teams, including four Super Bowl appearances.

Twice during the 1980s, he went to the Soviet Union to study under Russian gold-medal winning Olympic weightlifting coaches. He took what he learned from these masters and applied it to his football players. Fundamental to Parker's training protocol were the inclusion of explosive movements derived from the Olympic lifts and a more scientific approach to program design. Strength, speed, and health became Parker's emphasis as he produced strong and durable athletes, significantly cutting the injury rates of his players.

Aside from his Super Bowl triumphs, in 1994 he received the President's Award from the Professional Football Strength and Conditioning Coaches Society, presented annually to the NFL's top strength and conditioning coach, and in 2003 was named to the USA Strength and Conditioning Hall of Fame's inaugural class, along with his co-authors Al Miller and Rob Panariello and mentors Alvin Roy, Clyde Emrich, and Lou Riecke.

The System is Johnny's second book, following *Ultimate Weight Training Program,* published in 1988. Coach Parker lives in Trinity, Florida, and continues to coach and mentor high school athletes and strength coaches.

AL MILLER

Al Miller is one of the most decorated strength and conditioning coaches in NFL history with a career that spanned more than four decades and left a lasting impact at every level of the profession. His contributions and vision advanced the field of strength and conditioning and positively impacted the development of thousands of young athletes.

After four years as a starting wide receiver at Northeast Louisiana State College, he began his coaching career at Lee Junior High School in Monroe, LA in 1970. For 15 years he steadily worked his way through the coaching ranks, moving to the collegiate level at Northwestern State University, Mississippi State, Northeast Louisiana State, and ultimately the University of Alabama under legendary head coach Paul "Bear" Bryant.

In 1985 he made the jump to the NFL coaching ranks under Head Coach Dan Reeves with the Denver Broncos. For the next 19 years, the two men worked side by side in Denver, New York, and Atlanta developing athletes such as John Elway, Phil Simms, and Michael Vick and would ultimately appear in five Conference Championships, and four Super Bowls. His Atlanta Falcons team would make one more appearance in the NFC Championship in 2004 under Head Coach Jim Mora.

After a brief retirement in 2006, he returned in 2012 with the Oakland Raiders before finishing his NFL coaching career in 2014. In addition to his multiple championship appearances over a 25 year NFL career, he also coached two Pro Bowl teams and received numerous awards, including the NFL President's Award (1993), the NFL Strength Coaches Emrich-Riecke-Jones Award (1998), the NFL Strength Coach of the Year Award (2004), and the NFL Strength Coaches Lifetime Achievement Award (2015).

Throughout his remarkable history, his accomplishments and contributions were also honored with his inclusion into the USA Strength and Conditioning Coaches Hall of Fame with his friend Johnny Parker, and being honored as a "Legend in the Field" by the Collegiate Strength and Conditioning Association.

ROB PANARIELLO

Robert Panariello MS, PT, ATC, CSCS, is a Founding Partner and Co-Chief Executive Officer at Professional Physical Therapy, presently with 180 facilities in five states, as well as the 20,000 square foot state-of-the-art Professional Athletic Performance Center located in Garden City, New York.

He has 38 years of experience in the related fields of sports physical therapy, athletic training, and the performance enhancement training of athletes. His experience includes the study of the science and art of coaching with National team weightlifters and various National sport team athletes in Bulgaria, the former Soviet Union, and the former East Germany.

Rob previously held the positions as the Head Strength and Conditioning Coach at St. John's University of New York, the World League of American Football NY/NJ Knights, and the WUSA NY POWER Women's Professional Soccer League. He has more than 60 peer-reviewed orthopedic and sports medicine research, sports physical therapy research, and strength and conditioning journal, book chapter, and book publications.

He received the 2016 National Strength and Conditioning Association (NSCA) Sports Medicine/Rehabilitation Specialist of the Year Award, the 2015 American Physical Therapy Association (APTA) Sports Physical Therapy Section Lynn Wallace Clinical Educator Award, was elected as one of the initial inductees to the 2003 USA Strength and Conditioning Coaches Hall of Fame, and received the prestigious National Strength and Conditioning Association's Presidents Award in 1998.

Rob lectures both nationally and internationally on the topics of sports rehabilitation and the performance enhancement training of athletes.

JEREMY HALL

Jeremy Hall, DPT, CSCS, USAW, is a physiotherapist, strength and conditioning coach, writer, and founder of Total Performance Science and Mind of the Coach.

He has worked as a strength and conditioning coach in the Philadelphia Phillies' minor league system and with countless amateur and professional athletes in private practice for both rehabilitation and performance enhancement. He has also taught at the graduate level at Nova Southeastern University, lecturing on the integration of performance training techniques into physical rehabilitation.

He is a true believer that success leaves clues, and he is constantly exploring the intersection of high performance and injury prevention, physical and mental conditioning, and the paths of the greatest coaches, athletes, and high-achievers. By pure luck and effort, he was able to befriend Coach Johnny Parker, which led to the opportunity to collaborate in the creation of this book.

A native Floridian, he currently resides in Jersey City, NJ with his wife, Deirdre.

Printed in Great Britain
by Amazon